ARISTOTLE
AND THE ARABS

NEW YORK UNIVERSITY
STUDIES IN NEAR EASTERN CIVILIZATION
NUMBER 1.

GENERAL EDITORS

R. Bayly Winder

Richard Ettinghausen

DESIGNED BY

J. Paul Kirouac

ARISTOTLE AND THE ARABS:

THE ARISTOTELIAN TRADITION IN ISLAM

F. E. PETERS

NEW YORK / NEW YORK UNIVERSITY PRESS
LONDON / UNIVERSITY OF LONDON PRESS LTD.
1968

Library of Congress Catalog Card Number 68-29431

Manufactured in the United States of America

NEW YORK UNIVERSITY STUDIES IN NEAR EASTERN CIVILIZATION

The participation of the New York University Press in the University's new commitment to Near Eastern Studies—building on a tradition of well over a century—will provide Americans and others with new opportunities for understanding the Near East. Concerned with those various peoples of the Near East who, throughout the centuries, have dramatically shaped many of mankind's most fundamental concepts and who have always had high importance in practical affairs, this series, New York University Studies in Near Eastern Civilization, seeks to publish important works in this vital area. The purview will be broad, open to varied approaches and historical periods. It will, however, be particularly receptive to work in two areas that reflect the University and that may have received insufficient attention elsewhere. These are literature and art. Furthermore, taking a stand that may be more utilitarian than that of other publications, the series will welcome both translations of important Near Eastern literature of imagination, and of significant scholarly works written in Near Eastern languages. In this way, a larger audience, unacquainted with these languages, will be able to deepen its knowledge of the cultural achievements of Near Eastern peoples.

July, 1968

Richard Ettinghausen
R. Bayly Winder
General Editors

PREFACE

I have intended this work for three different groups. It is obviously designed for the orientalist, and since he is its ultimate judge, I have tried to make it both useful and technically satisfactory to him by his own scholarly standards. But I have also been concerned to place in the hands of the Western medievalist, and particularly the student of Latin Scholasticism, an introduction to a tradition which is of great importance to him, but before which he stands technically and linguistically helpless. Wherever possible I have cited translations in Western languages so that he might turn to the texts themselves, and at the same time, I have attempted to give him some guide lines into the scholarship of Islamic Studies. Finally, I myself now read these lines as a classicist, and I hope they will be of some interest and use to my colleagues.

Islamic Studies, and especially the study of Islamic philosophy, are still in their infancy, and that fact is reflected in the present book. It has been my design to make it as complete as possible within its limits, but there are further levels of understanding and further degrees of nicety which wait upon the scarcely begun work of the editor and the philologist. The student of Aristotle has before him a whole series of critically edited and annotated texts and all the auxiliaries that classical scholarship has been able to devise. The Islamicist still awaits his Ross, his Bonitz, and, indeed, his Liddell-Scott-Jones. It is obvious that under such circumstances, when a large part of the important material is still in manuscript form, some of it even uncataloged, what follows here is in the nature of an interim report.

Since Arabic was used as a philosophical and theological *lingua franca* by all the peoples living in the Islamic empires during the Middle Ages, I have used the standardized Arabic forms and Arabic transliterations for all the Eastern names that appear on the following pages, no matter what their ethnic or religious provenance. The only exceptions are instances where an Anglicized form has become so familiar that to resort to anything else would serve merely to distract.

I have had to be somewhat arbitrary in other respects. There runs parallel to Islamic philosophy and theology a Jewish version of the same tradition which shares the same language, Arabic, and an almost identical methodology and problematic. Although I have averted in various places to some of the figures in this Jewish tradition, I have, in general, excluded the Jewish version of *falsafah* and *kalām* from my overall treatment.

A work such as this is obviously cumulative. It rests on the labors of others, and I have signaled my debt to these scholars in the footnotes and bibliographies in the text. But it has less easily acknowledgeable supports as well. Most of the research and writing of the book were sustained by generous grants from the Ford and Rockefeller Foundations, and some of the typing costs were borne by New York University. I am particularly indebted to the Ford Foundation which first enabled me to embark upon Islamic Studies, and then to travel to the Near East when this book was only an outline.

CONTENTS

LIST OF ABBREVIATIONS

I. Primary Sources

(Further material on these historical sources will be found in the Appendix, pp. 239-293 below.)

Al-Ash'ari, *Maqālāt*: al-Ash'ari. *Maqālāt al-islāmīyīn*, ed. H. Ritter. 2 vols. Istanbul, 1929.

Al-Baghdādi, *Farq*: al-Baghdādi. *Kitāb al-farq bayn al-firaq*, ed. Cairo, 1910. Trans. Part I: K. Seelye. N.Y., 1920; trans. Part II: A. Halkin. Tel Aviv, 1936.

Barhebraeus, *Ta'rīkh*: Barhebraeus, *Ta'rīkh mukhtaṣar al-duwal*, ed. A. Salhani. Beyrouth, 1890.

Al-Bayhaqi, *Tatimmat*: al-Bayhaqi, *Tatimmat ṣiwān al-ḥikmah*, ed. M. Kurd 'Ali under the title *Ta'rīkh ḥukamā' al-islām*. Cairo, 1946.

Fihrist: al-Nadīm, *Kitāb al-fihrist*, ed. G. Flügel, J. Rodiger, and A. Müller. 2 vols. Leipzig, 1871–1872.

Ḥājji Khalīfah: Ḥājji Khalīfah, *Kashf al-ẓunūn*, ed. and trans. Flügel. 7 vols. Leipzig, 1835–1858.

Ḥunayn, *Risālah*: Bergstrasser, G. *Ḥunayn ibn Isḥāq über die syrischen und arabischen Galen-übersetzungen*. Leipzig, 1925.

Ibn Juljul, *Ṭabaqāt*: Ibn Juljul, *Ṭabaqāt al-aṭibbā' wa al-ḥukamā'*, ed. F. Sayyid. Cairo, 1955.

Ibn Khallikān: Ibn Khallikān, *Kitāb wafāyāt al-a'yān wa anbā' abnā' al-zamān*, ed. F. Wüstenfeld. 2 vols. Göttingen, 1835–1843. Trans. M. de Slane. 4 vols. Paris, 1843–1871.

Al-Mas'ūdi, *Murūj*: al-Mas'ūdi, *Murūj al-dhahab*, ed. and trans. C. Barbier de Maynard and A. Pavet de Couteille. 9 vols. Paris, 1861–1877.

Al-Mas'ūdi, *Tanbīh*: al-Mas'ūdi, *Kitāb al-tanbīh wa al-ishrāf*, ed. M. de Goeje. Leyden, 1894. Trans. Carra de Vaux. Paris, 1897.

Al-Qifṭi: al-Qifṭi, *Ta'rīkh al-ḥukamā'*, ed. J. Lippert. Leipzig, 1903.

Ṣā'id, *Ṭabaqāt*: Ṣā'id al-Andalusi, *Kitāb ṭabaqāt al-umam*, ed. L. Cheikho. Beyrouth, 1912. Trans. R. Blachère. Paris, 1935.

Al-Shahrastāni, *Milal*: al-Shahrastāni, *Kitāb al-milal wa al-niḥal*, ed. W. Cureton. London, 1846. Trans. T. Haarbrucker. 2 vols. Halle, 1850–1851.

Tashköprüzādah, *Shaqā'iq*: Tashköprüzādah, *al-Shaqā'iq al-nu'manīyah fi 'ulamā al-dawlah al-'uthmānīyah*, ed. Bulaq, 1881. Trans. O. Rescher. Constantinople-Galata, 1927.

Uṣ.: Ibn abī Uṣaybi'ah, *'Uyūn al-anbā' fī ṭabaqāt al-aṭṭibbā'*, ed. A. Müller. 2 vols., Cairo, 1882.

Us. (ed. Jahier and Noureddine): Jahier, H. and Noureddine, A. *Sources d'Information sur les Classes des Medicins*; XIIIe *Chapitre*: *Médicins de l'Occident Musulman*. Algiers, 1958.

Yāqūt, *Irshād*: Yāqūt, *Irshād al-arīb ilā ma' rifat al-adīb*, ed. D. S. Margoliouth. 7 vols., Leyden-London, 1907–1926.

II. Periodicals and Serials

AGP	*Archiv für Geschichte der Philosophie*
AHDL	*Archives d'histoire doctrinale et litteraire du moyen âge*
Beiträge	*Beiträge zur Geschichte der Philosophie des Mittelalters*
BIFEO	Institut Francais de Damas, *Bulletin*
BSOAS	*Bulletin of the School of Oriental and African Studies*, University of London
BZ	*Byzantinische Zeitschrift*
CAG	*Commentaria in Aristotelem Graeca*, edita consilio et auctoritate Academiae Litterarum Regiae Borussicae
CSCO	*Corpus Scriptorum Christianorum Orientalium*
GGA	*Göttingische Gelehrte Anzeigen*
JA	*Journal Asiatique*
JHS	*Journal of Hellenic Studies*
JOAS	*Journal of the American Oriental Society*
JQR	*Jewish Quarterly Review*
JRAS	*Journal of the Royal Asiatic Society*
Memorie Lincei	*Atti della R. Accademia Nazionale dei Lincei*. Classe di Scienze Morali, Storiche e Filologiche
MFO	*Mélanges de la Faculté Orientale de l'Université Saint-Joseph*, Beyrouth
MIDEO	Institut Dominicain d'Études Orientales du Caire. *Mélanges*
OLZ	*Orientalische Literaturzeitung*
PAAJR	*Proceedings of the American Academy for Jewish Research*
PO	*Patrologia Orientalis*
RAAD	*La Revue de l'Academie Arab de Damas* (*Majallat al-majma' al-'ilmi al-'arabi*)
REG	*Revue des Études Grecques*
REJ	*Revue des Études Juives*
Rendiconti Lincei	*Rendiconti della R. Academia Nazionale dei Lincei* Classe di Scienze Morali, Storiche e Filologiche
RIMA	*Revue de l'Institut des Manuscrits Arabes* (*Majallat ma'hadi al-makhṭūṭāt al-'arabīyah*)
RFN	*Rivista di filosofia neoscolastica*

RNSP	*Revue Neo-Scholastique de Philosophie* (from XLIV (1946) *Revue Philosophique de Louvain*)
RSO	*Rivista di Studi Orientali*
RTAM	*Recherches de théologie ancienne et médiévale*
SbAW	*Sitzungsberichte der Akademie der Wissenschaften*: the German scientific academies will be cited by city and not by state; e.g., SbAWBerlin: *Sitzungsberichte der preußischen Akademie der Wissenschaften*, Berlin
WZKM	*Wiener Zeitschrift für die Kunde des Morgenlandes*
ZA	*Zeitschrift für Assyriologie und verwandte Gebiete*
ZDMG	*Zeitschrift der Deutschen Morgenländischen Gesellschaft*

III. Books and Articles

DTC	*Dictionnaire de Théologie catholique*
EI	*Encyclopedia of Islam.* 4 vols. Leyden-London, 1913–1937. *EI* Suppl.: *Encyclopedia of Islam.* Supplement Number I. Leyden-London, 1934. *Shorter EI*: *Shorter Encyclopedia of Islam.* Leyden, 1953. *EI²*: *Encyclopedia of Islam.* New Edition: I. Leyden-London, 1954–1960 (in course of publication).
GAL	Brockelmann, C. *Geschichte der arabischen Literatur.* I². Leyden, 1943. Suppl. I, Leyden, 1937. II², Leyden, 1949. Suppl. II, Leyden, 1938. III, Leyden, 1942.
GBL	Krumbacher, K. *Geschichte der byzantinischen Literatur²* (*Handbuch der Klassischen-Altertums Wissenschaft* IX, 1.) Munich, 1897.
GCAL	Graf, G. *Geschichte der christlichen arabischen Literatur* ("Studi e Testi," 118, 133, 146, 147, 172.) 5 vols. Vatican City, 1944–1953.
GGL	Von Christ, W., Stahlin, O. and Schmid, W. *Geschichte der griechischen Literatur* (*Handbuch der Klassischen Altertums Wissenschaft* VII.) Sechste Auflage. Zweiter Teil: "Die nachklassische Periode der griechischen Literatur." 2 vols. Munich, 1920–1924.
GSL	Baumstark, A. *Geschichte der syrischen Literatur.* Bonn, 1922.
RAC	*Reallexikon für Antike und Christentum.*
R–E	*Paulys Realenzyklopädie des klassischen Altertumswissenschaft*, Neue Bearbeitung von G. Wissowa, W. Kroll, K. Mittelhaus, K. Ziegler, 1894ff.

Ahlwardt, *Arabischen Handschriften Berlin*: Ahlwardt, W. *Verzeichniss der arabischen Handschriften zu Berlin.* 10 vols. Berlin. 1887–1899.

Alonso, *Teologia*: Alonso, M. *Teologia de Averroes* (*Estudios y Documentos*). Madrid-Granada, 1947.

Anawati, *Mu'allafāt*: Anawati, G. *Mu'allafāt ibn Sina.* Cairo, 1950.

Aristoteles Latinus: Lacombe G., *et al. Aristoteles Latinus*: I, Rome, 1939; II, Cambridge, 1955.

Badawi, "Makhṭūṭāt Arisṭū": Badawi, A. "Makhṭūṭāt Arisṭū fī al-ʿarabīyah," *RIMA*, I (1955), 215–231; II (1956), 46–62.

Badawi, *Manṭiq Arisṭū*: Badawi, A. *Manṭiq Arisṭū*. 3 vols. Cairo, 1948–1952.

Baumstark, *Aristoteles bei den Syrern*: Baumstark, A. *Aristoteles bei den Syrern vom V-VIII Jahrhundert*, Leipzig, 1900.

Beck, *Theologische Literatur*: Beck, H. G. *Kirche und Theologische Literatur im Byzantinischen Reich* (*Handbuch der Altertums-Wissenschaft*, XII, 2, 1). Munich, 1959.

Bouyges, *Notice*: Bouyges, M. *Averroes. Tafsīr Ma Baʿd Al-Ṭabiʿat. Notice.* Beyrouth, 1952.

Browne, *Literary History*: Browne, E. G. *A Literary History of Persia*. 4 vols. Cambridge, 1928.

Chwolsohn, *Ssabier*: D. Chwolsohn, *Die ssabier und der Ssabismus*. 2 vols. St. Petersburg, 1856.

Cruz Hernandez, *Filosofia Musulmana*: Hernandez, M. Cruz. *Historia de la Filosofia Española*: *Filosofia Hispano-Musulmana*. 2 vols. Madrid, 1957.

Diels, *Doxographi*: Diels, H. *Doxographi Graeci*. Berlin, 1958. (Photographic reprint of the third [1879] edition.)

Düring, *Biographical Tradition*: Düring, I. *Aristotle in the Ancient Biographical Tradition*. Goteborg, 1957.

Gardet, *Mélanges Gilson*: Gardet, L. "Le probleme de la philosophie musulmane," *Mélanges offerts à Etienne Gilson* (Toronto-Paris, 1959), pp. 261–84.

Gardet-Anawati, *Théologie musulmane*: Gardet L., and Anawati, G. *Introduction à la Théologie musulmane*. Paris, 1948.

Gerhardsson, *Memory:* Gerhardsson, B. *Memory and Manuscript. Oral Tradition and Written Transmission in Rabbinic Judaism and Early Christianity*. Uppsala, 1961.

Georr, *Catégories*: Georr, K. *Les Catégories d'Aristote dans leurs versions syro-arabes*. Beyrouth, 1948.

Grabmann, "Aristoteles im 12. Jahrhundert": Grabmann M., "Aristoteles im 12 Jahrhundert," *Mittelalterliches Geistesleben*, III (Munich, 1956), 64–124.

Grabmann, *Aristotelesübers. des XIII. Jahrhundert*: Grabmann, M. "Forschungen über die lateinischen Aristotelesübersetzungen des XIII Jahrhundert" (*Beiträge* XVII, 5–6 [Münster, 1916]).

Grabmann, "Methoden und Hilfsmittel": Grabmann, M. "Methoden und Hilfsmittel des Aristotelesstudiums im Mittelalter," *SbAWMunich* (1939), Heft 5.

Ivanow, *Guide*: Ivanow, W. *A Guide to Ismaili Literature*. London, 1933.

Jugie, *Theologia*: Jugie, M. *Theologia dogmatica christianorum orientalium ab ecclesia catholica dissidentium: De theologia dogmatica Nestorianorum et Monophysitarum* Vol. V. Paris, 1935.

Kraus, *Jābir*: Kraus, P. *Jābir ibn Ḥayyān. Contribution à l'histoire des idées scientifiques dans l'Islam.* 2 vols. Cairo, 1941–1942.

Kraus, "Zu ibn al-Muqqafa'": Kraus, P. "Zu ibn al-Muqqafa'," *RSO*, XIV (1933), 1–20.

Meyerhof, "Alexandrien nach Baghdad": M. Meyerhof, "Von Alexandrien nach Baghdad. Ein Beitrag zur Geschichte des philosophischen und medizinischen Unterrichts bei den Arabern," *SbAW Berlin*, XXIII (1930), 389–429.

Meyerhof, "Ḥunayn and his Period": Meyerhof, M. "New Light on Ḥunayn Ibn Isḥāq and his Period," *Isis*, VIII (1926), 685–724.

Moraux, *Listes Anciennes*: Moraux, P. *Les Listes Anciennes des Ouvrages d'Aristote.* Louvain, 1951.

Pines, *Atomenlehre*: Pines, S. *Beiträge zur islamischen Atomenlehre.* Berlin, 1936.

Plessner, *Bryson*: Plessner, M. *Der* σικονομικός *des Neupythagoreers Bryson und sein Einfluß auf die islamische Wissenschaft.* Heidelberg, 1928.

Pons-Boigues, *Historiadores*: Pons-Boigues, F. *Ensayo bio-bibliográfico sobre los historiadores y geografos arabigo-españoles.* Madrid, 1898.

Ritter, "Häresiographen": Ritter, H. "Philologika III: Muhammedanische Häresiographen," *Der Islam*, XVIII (1929), 34–59.

Ritter-Walzer, "Stambuler Bibliotheken": Ritter H., and Walzer, R. "Arabische Übersetzungen griechischer Ärzte in Stambuler Bibliotheken," *SbAW-Berlin*, XXVI (1934), 34–59.

Rosenthal, *Historiography*: Rosenthal, F. *A History of Muslim* Historio-*graphy*, Leyden, 1952.

Rosenthal, *Technique*: Rosenthal, F. *The Technique and Approach of Muslim Scholarship.* (*Analecta Orientalia* 24.) Rome, 1947.

Ruska, "Al-Bīrūni als Quelle": Ruska, J. "Al-Bīrūni als Quelle für das Leben und die Schriften al-Rāzis," *Isis*, V (1923).

Sarton, *Introduction*: Sarton, G. *Introduction to the History of Science.* 3 vols. of 5. Baltimore, 1927–1948.

Sayyid, *Makhṭūṭāt* I: Sayyid, F. *Jami'at al-duwal al-'arabīyah. Fihris al-makhṭūṭāt al-musawarrah* I. Cairo, 1954.

Steinschneider, *Al-Farabi*: Steinschneider, M. *Al-Farabi* (*Alpharabius*), *des arabischen Philosophen Leben und Schriften* (*Memoires de l'Academie Imperiale des Sciences de Saint-Pétersbourg*, ser. 7 vols. XIII, 4). St. Petersburg, 1869.

Steinschneider, *Arab. Übers.*: Steinschneider, M. *Die arabischen Übersetzungen aus dem Griechischen.* Graz, 1960. Reprint of four articles appearing in *Beihefte zum Centralblatt für Bibliothekswesen* V (1889) and XII (1893),

ZDMG, L (1896), and *Archiv für pathologische Anatomie und Physiologie* ser. 12, IV (1891). All citations of this work are according to the consecutive pagination of the Graz reprint.

Steinschneider, *Europ. Übers.*: Steinschneider, M. *Die europäischen Übersetzungen aus dem Arabischen bis Mitte des 17. Jahrhunderts.* Graz, 1956. Reprint, of articles appearing in *SbAW Wien.* CXLIX (1904) Heft 4, and CLI (1905) Heft I.

Steinschneider, *Hebr. Übers.*: Steinschneider, M. *Die hebraeischen Übersetzungen des Mittelalters und die Juden als Dolmetscher.* Berlin. 1893. Reprint, Graz, 1956.

Thorndike, *Magic and Experimental Science* II: Thorndike, L. *A History of Magic and Experimental Science during the First Thirteen Centuries of Our Era* II. New York, 1923.

Tkatsch, *Poetik*: Tkatsch, J. *Die arabische Übersetzung des Poetik des Aristoteles.* 2 vols. Vienna-Leipzig, 1928–1932.

Überweg-Geyer: *Friedrich Überwegs Grundriß der Geschichte der Philosophie* II *Die Patristische und Scholastische Philosophie.* Herausgegeben von Dr. Bernhard Geyer. Basel-Stuttgart, 1956. Reprint of the thirteenth edition.

Überweg-Praechter: *Friedrich Überwegs Grundriß der Geschichte der Philosophie* I *Die Philosophie des Altertums.* Heraŭsgegeben von Karl Praechter. Basel-Stuttgart, 1957. Reprint of the twelfth edition.

Vadja, *Pensée juive*: Vadja, G. *Introduction à la pensée juive du moyen-âge.* Paris, 1947.

Walzer, "Arisṭuṭālīs": Walzer, R. art. "Arisṭuṭālīs," *EI*², I, 630–33.

Walzer, "New Light": Walzer, R. "New Light on the Arabic Translations of Aristotle," *Oriens*, VI (1953), 91–142.

Watt, *Islamic Philosophy*: Watt, W. Montgomery *Islamic Philosophy and Theology.* University of Edinburgh Press, 1962.

Wüstenfeld, *Geschichtschreiber*: Wüstenfeld, F. *Die Geschichtschreiber der Araber und ihre Werke.* Göttingen, 1882.

INTRODUCTION

One of the more striking aspects of the Hellenic cultural achievement was the ability of the Greeks to make viable the artistic iterary, and intellectual concepts which they had evolved in their own particular milieu. Despite the Hellenes' notorious condescension toward the barbarians, their own peculiar vision of beauty and truth went abroad among these alien peoples and captured a man, Alexander, and an Empire, Rome. Through the latter it captured us as well, and we pay the Romans their exorbitant fee by speaking of the "Greek and Latin Classics" as if they were somehow the same thing.

But for someone who chooses rather to follow Alexander, a "Department of Greek and Arabic Classics" is an equally interesting prospect. The Western Hellenic trunk line whose way stations read: Ennius, Vergil, Horace, Quintillian, Cassiodorus, Alcuin, John of Salisbury, Dante, Petrarch, Scaliger, Bentley, Jowett, and Jebb has an Eastern counterpart, a shorter line to be sure, and bearing less traffic, but not without its interesting stops: Clement, Origen, Basil, Nemesius, John Philoponus, Sergius of Rishʿayna, Ibn al-Biṭrīq, al-Kindi, Ḥunayn ibn Isḥāq, al-Fārābi, Ibn Sīnā, Ibn Rushd.

Behind the obvious exoticisms of language the two lists are quite different. The Western series is composed of humanists; the Eastern knows only philosophers and theologians. Names could be added to either, Augustine, for example, or Ibn Khaldūn, to change its texture slightly, but the truth of each series remains. Western Hellenism is a variegated inheritance: philosophy, law, science, with a heavy insistence upon the humanities; *humanitas,* indeed, is a Roman word. Eastern Hellenism is constructed upon a much narrower base; its pillars are mathematics, geography, medicine, and philosophy; supporting them are Euclid, Ptolemy, Galen, and Aristotle. But for all this the East knows no Homer or Sophocles, and its Thucydides is a graceless Arab chronicler whose felicity is to collect endless chains of shaykish transmitters.

Eastern Hellenism, then, is only a torso. It is deficient in what the Westerner considers the essence of Hellenism: the exaltation of the human individual through his confrontation with Greek literary and political ideals. It is difficult to determine how much of this deficiency was deliberate. If faced with an exclusive choice we, who are more attuned to the universal values of poetry and the relativism of philosophical systems, would probably choose to have Homer rather than Aristotle. But there is really not a great deal of evidence that the Arabs had such a choice; it is not unlikely that they were given Aristotle and not given Homer.

"Given" is a somewhat inexact word to describe the transmission of Hellenic philosophy to the Arabs. They quite literally "took" philosophy from the all-but-vanished Greek philosophical tradition of the seventh century A.D., took it from the only sources available to them. The Arabs assiduously sought out Aristotelian manuscripts in the newly conquered cities of Damascus and Antioch and even over the frontier in Byzantine territory. They learned from scholars who, through a chain of events and motives only dimly understood by us now, had somehow preserved the school tradition of Alexandria and arrived in Baghdad about A.D. 900. They called to their aid intellectual Levantines, the Syriac-speaking Christians whose Christianity related them back to Hellenism through the Greek Fathers and whose Syriac language and Semitic culture made them ideal translators and instructors for their Arab cousins.

We know how the Arabs acquired their Aristotle, Plato, Plotinus, Galen, Euclid, and Ptolemy, but why these people, lately bedouins of the desert or half-urbanized stragglers of the sown, should be attracted in the first place to a thinker as complicated and as alien as Aristotle is more difficult to understand. Or *was* more difficult to understand, since contemporary history has treated us to another example of the same phenomenon. African nations have literally emerged from the jungle in less than a generation and are forcing themselves through an educational process which Europe experienced in a more leisurely evolution. The key to statehood and stature is the West's technology, no matter how forbidding an intellectual challenge that technology may present.

The problems of an emergent Islam in the first century and a half after the Prophet's death in A.D. 632 were similar. Islam was born into a family of advanced cultures, Byzantine, Sassanian, Indian, and by reason of its conquests, encompassed within itself sophisticated and belligerent minorities, Jews, Coptic and Syriac Christians, Iranian Zoroastrians. The reaction was swift and intelligent: the Arab masters of Allah's theocratic state reared Byzantine cupolas over Sassanian columns and built the magnificent, eclectic structure that is Islam. And set firmly as the keystone of the arch, at least as far as Islamic intellectual life is concerned, was Aristotelianism.

It is a notorious fact of religious history that heresy generates dogma; and polemic, theology. Islam, for all its lack of a hierarchy and a church, was not exempt from the truism. The *Qur'ān* is a descendent of *Deuteronomy* and not of the *Summa Theologica*, and the early religious literature of the Islamic community was casuisitic, gnomic, aphorisitic. When polemical pressures began to be exerted from within and without that community, the Muslim divine, like the statesman and the architect, seized the weapons from the hands of his opponents and began organizing the Prophetic heritage into a viable and defensible system. The *spoliatio Graecorum*, an activity pursued with profit by both Judaism and Christianity, had begun anew.

Contemporary demands that philosophy eschew systems and be somehow "existential," that it provide paradigms and martyrs instead of professors, may obscure the mechanics of this early, Islamic building process. Much of post-Aristotelian philosophy *was* "existential"; the final decades of Greco-Roman antiquity were marked by an attempt on the part of philosophy to step into the religious vacuum created by the decline of the city-state. Neoplatonism, particularly, not only concerned itself with ethical behavior, as the Cynics and Stoics had already done, but in the person of Iamblichus and his school took on a distinctly religious, ritualistic, and mystical tone. The triumph of

Christianity, which could make use of philosophy but insisted on supplying its own saints, aborted this movement. Where philosophy survived the advent of Christianity, it survived as a purely technical and metaphysical discipline with its chief base of operations in the lecture halls of Alexandria.

This was the type of Greek philosophy inherited by the Arabs: pedagogic in orientation, scholastic in method, logical and metaphysical in its interests, and purged of its "existential" tendencies by Christianity. It suited the Muslim situation. Islam, like Christianity, could provide its own *ethos* and its own saints; what it could not provide it adopted by following the example of Philo and Origen and Basil.

By the seventh century, on the eve of its passage from a Byzantine milieu to an Islamic one, Aristotelianism was a fully articulated system which provided a more or less consistent world view and a highly refined methodology developed over the course of the preceding centuries. At the core of the system stood the Aristotelian treatises themselves, arranged in a logical order and with the systematic gaps filled in here and there with pseudepigraphs. Attached to this central core was a growing body of professorial comment which both elucidated and fleshed out the system. Original and commentary alike shared in the authority of the system, a fusion that would have made—had anyone been interested in the project—any attempt at separating Aristotle from his secondary accretions extremely difficult.

Between A.D. 750 and A.D. 1050 this entire conglomerate, the Aristotelian works proper (all except the *Politica*; Arab interest in this area, which tended to be theoretical rather than practical, was satisfied by compendia of Plato's *Republic* and *Laws*), the pseudepigraphs, the commentaries, introductions, anthologies, epitomes, and glosses, were translated into Arabic. This considerable achievement was largely the work of one of Islam's fruitful minorities, the polyglot Syrian Christians who were uniquely able to control the Greek original, their native Syriac, and the Arabic of their Muslim patrons at the caliphal court in Baghdad.

The effects of the introduction of Aristotle into Islam were manifold. The first effect—and it is difficult to assess the full extent of this—was that the Aristotelian writings supplied a great deal of *knowledge* about the world and its workings to the early Muslim. They rendered him an intellectual cosmopolitan. Muḥammad had created Islam with links leading back into the past, but only through a theological affiliation of considerably narrower dimensions than those of the Christian *praeparatio evangelica*. Aristotelianism provided Islam with a view of intellectual history and a sense of direct connection with Hellenic antiquity. It introduced the Muslim to wholly new disciplines such as logic, biology, and mathematical geography. The bedouin cosmos disappeared.

Like all such intellectual experiences, the confrontation with Aristotelianism upset the equilibrium of the Islamic community. Pre-Aristotelian "theology" in Islam was, as has already been mentioned, casuistic in its approach. It handled its problems, which, like the *Qur'ān* itself, tended to be pragmatic rather than theoretical, by resort to a precedent derived, by authoritative transmission, from the Prophet. The collision with Christian polemic (the exuberance of the Christian debater who had a centuries-old acquaintance with at least the ground rules of this particular game can be well imagined) undoubtedly turned the discussion to more theoretical considerations. Aristotelianism would and did provide the Muslim with theoretical foundations for such discourse and, beginning about A.D. 800, and most visibly after A.D. 900, an Islamic adaptation of a Hellenic-type theology emerges.

Kalām, as the Muslim called his version of natural theology, was not a universally acclaimed panacea. It had within it certain disquieting epistemological premises which from time to time provoked the forces of reaction. But the final triumph of *kalām* over the fundamentalists was assured; despite the occasional protest of an Islamic Peter Damian before and since, between the eleventh and thirteenth centuries *kalām* became the orthodox Muslim position and remains so today: a natural theology erected on a scholastic, Aristotelian methodology and organized along the lines of a distinctly Hellenic-Patristic problematic.

The origins of Islamic *falsafah*, philosophy, are as transparent as its Greek etymology. From the very beginnings of the translation movement a number of Muslim intellectuals studied the new Greek material for its own importance rather than from religious or polemical motives. These earliest students of Aristotelianism were not philosophers in the mold of either their Greek predecessors or their Islamic successors. The translations they had to work with were halting and faulty and so the pioneers showed little of the technical philosophical skill that was to come later. Truly professional virtuosity and the ability to distinguish between the genuine problematic and the flash of novelty, in short, the resumption of the philosophical dialogue within Aristotelianism, began with the circulation of the new Ḥunayn versions of the *corpus* and with the first attempts at formal philosophical instruction. The latter began in Baghdad *ca.* A.D. 900 and thereafter can be traced the lineaments of a loosely organized group of scholars picking up the threads of a tradition left off some three hundred years earlier.

The Baghdad circle included Muslim and Christian alike and, like the Syriac Christian intellectual community there, it had close ties with the Greek medical tradition. Its period of vitality covers a scant century and a half, but in that time it produced two or three generations of philosophers and scholars not unworthy of the material they had before them. Some, like al-Fārābi, were philosophers in the classical post-Aristotelian mold, adding to the literature of Aristotelian commentary and through this rather forbidding scholastic work expanding, modifying, and developing the system in its Islamic milieu. Others, like Yaḥyā ibn ʿAdi, were accomplished textual critics who revised the translations of Ḥunayn and his school, collating not only the Greek originals and various Syriac and Arabic versions, but the *lemmata* in the commentators as well. A figure like Abū Sulaymān divided his time between formal philosophy and the wider Baghdad world of viziers, poets, philologists, and lawyers, long familiar from the pages of the *Thousand and One Nights*. A student of his has left a literary portrait of Abū Sulaymān moving through the Baghdad salons endlessly discussing philosophy, religion, poetry, and linguistics in the brilliant company produced by Islam at its height.

Converts were made in the provinces as well. On the eastern fringes of the empire, *falsafah* won Ibn Sīnā, an extraordinary combination of Prime Minister, physician, philosopher, and poet whose massive Aristotelian encyclopedia *al-Shifā'*, known in its Latin translation as *Liber Sufficientiae,* provided Islam with its definitive Hellenic synthesis. Ibn Sīnā was definitive in another sense; with him the golden age of Eastern *falsafah* comes to an end. This is something more than a nebulous playing out of creativity. The forces of reaction were building up within the orthodox community and, whatever the difficulties experienced by *kalām,* they were multiplied tenfold for *falsafah,* which had little inclination to dissemble its own role in the uneasy debate between faith and reason.

Aristotelianism as a purely philosophical discipline—and the Arabs were, despite unknowing contaminations of Neoplatonism, chiefly Aristotelians—was an exotic growth in Islam. Rejected by the religious establishment, and hence by the state, it formed part of no official curriculum and was taught in no school. It was taught privately and died privately, lingering on in Western Islam, in Spain, long enough to propagate a secondary strain that reached its culmination in Ibn Rushd, an Aristotelian commentator of penetration and learning who towers even in the company of Alexander of Aphrodisias and Simplicius.

Falsafah had no direct offspring in Islam, only the stepsisters of science and *kalām* borne by the same mother. Its own progeny were to be found in the medieval West where the Latin translations of the great *falāsifah,* now metamorphized into Alkindius, Alpharabius, Avicenna, and Averroes, helped produce thirteenth-century Scholasticism.

We are no longer surprised at the longevity and vitality of the Greek tradition. The twentieth-century Westerner modestly accepts the fact that he is a Hellene at root and that his intellectual pedigree runs back, via Irish monk and Florentine humanist, to Homer, Sophocles, and Aristotle. He can stand upon the Acropolis and feel at home. But he has no more than to descend from the Acropolis into the Byzantine byways that surround it, and he is confronted with the evidences of another Hellenism in which he has no part. This new phenomenon is not the Hellenism of the East, the familiar remains of Greco-Roman art found at every turn of the eastern Mediterranean, at Ephesus, Pergamum, Antioch, and Baalbek. It is rather Eastern Hellenism, the blend of the vaguely familiar and the unexplainably alien that characterizes the Romano-Semitic figures of the Palmyrene crypts and the Apollo-Buddha heads of Gandhara.

The Hellenism of the East is in ruins, and some modern Gibbon might well reflect, as he watches sheep grazing in the streets of what were once the cities of the Decapolis, that the Muslims, who had come to destroy a Byzantine state, had destroyed Hellenism as well. Islam did, in fact, destroy much in the lands snatched from the Eastern Roman Empire. In the final analysis, both Hellenism and Christianity were among its victims. But in the intervening period, for perhaps eight centuries, Islam created a synthesis that bears more eloquent testimony to the vitality of Hellenism (and the creativity of Islam) than the moldering heaps of Pergamum or Baalbek. The great edifice of Eastern Hellenism is primarily the work of Islam, and part of this synthesis, surely its most dazzling part, was the Arabs' reception, adaptation, and assimilation of Aristotelianism. To trace if only in outline, the dimensions of that achievement is the purpose of the present study.

ARISTOTLE AND THE ARABS

I

THE MAKING OF THE ARISTOTELIAN TRADITION

The philosophical tradition inherited by the Arab conquerors of the old preserves of Hellenism was precisely that, a tradition, and not something of their own creation. This fact is basic to almost everything that follows, and serves to explain much, in terms of both form and content, of what happens in Islamic philosophy. The history of *falsafah* properly commences not with the events of A.D. 750, but at the beginnings of the tradition.

To say that Aristotle and Aristotelianism are two different things is to state the obvious. And yet the implications of that bald fact for the history of philosophy are so immense that to gloss it over with a passing reference is to distort the very premises of *falsafah*. Aristotelianism, the tradition, is, of course, based on the writings of Aristotle and, insofar as they reflect his thinking, on the philosopher himself. Today we can identify the evolutionary trend in those writings with some assurance, and the *Metaphysica* has become a kind of casebook in which to read Aristotle's changing positions. That he himself was aware of what was happening is clear enough from that same work with its transitional passages inserted to bind together not entirely cohesive essays.

Why Aristotle did this is no great mystery. Almost every passage in the *corpus* reveals that he thought systematically, and so it is reasonable to expect that he would attempt to reintegrate passages in his work which the course of time had disoriented. But there is another reason. The *Metaphysica* also testifies to the fact that

Aristotle was a teacher, and the constant effort at systematization is the reflection of a man who attempted to teach as logically and as orderly as he thought. But since it is a living process, with the thinker as lecturer, the teaching will never be perfectly tidy and, by definition, never complete. That part of the process, the final arrangement and completion of what the master had left at hand, was the work of the epigones, the man or men who took the oral teaching and literary output of this singular thinker and, by a process of compressing and expanding, adding and subtracting, in short, of editing, quite consciously and deliberately molded what Aristotle thought into an even more coherent and well-defined system.

The editing and shaping process, now largely lost to sight,[1] was assuredly a distortion. But neither the magnitude nor the wisdom of this distortion, the legitimate concern of the student of what-Aristotle-thought, need trouble us here. Let it be admitted that Andronicus of Rhodes was nearly as much the father of Aristotelianism as was Aristotle himself, and proceed to make of it what we can. It was, after all, Aristotelianism and not what-Aristotle-thought which shaped the thinking of the philosophers and theologians of Islam. Once Andronicus had put his hand to the task, a real knowledge of the historical Aristotle passed almost entirely beyond the reach of the philosopher and historian alike until the first gropings of nineteenth-century research succeeded in ever so slightly raising the veil.[2]

Nor was Aristotle responsible for the exegesis of the system. It, like the systematization itself, was the work of later and lesser men who constructed around the *corpus* imposing outworks of gloss and comment which attained, vis-à-vis the *corpus*, the same stature that the exegetical works of al-Ṭabari and al-Bayḍāwi hold with regard to

1. For some attempts at a reconstruction see Moraux, *Listes Anciennes*, and L. Grayeff, "The Problem of the Genesis of Aristotle's Text," *Phronesis*, I (1955–1956), 105–22.

2. There is no need to retell here the well-known tale of the salvaging of the *Aristotele perduto* beginning with the appearance in 1863 of Bernay's *Die Dialoge des Aristoteles in ihrem Verhältnis zu seinen übrigen Werken*, and Valentine Rose's *Aristoteles Pseudepigraphicus*, down to Jaeger's *Entstehungsgeschichte der Metaphysik* (1912), and the triumphant *Aristoteles. Grundlegung einer Geschichte seiner Entwicklung.*

the *Qur'ān*. Each stage in the tradition added its own commentators who influenced the next, but it was undoubtedly the scholars of late classical times who held pride of place in the hierarchy of exegetes. Alexander of Aphrodisias, for example, is a consistent force from his own day to the Renaissance.

It is clear enough where the tradition begins. Though the exegesis of Aristotle's teaching—and thus the first stages in the transformation of what-Aristotle-thought into Aristotelianism—undoubtedly took place in the philosopher's own lifetime, the crucial collecting and editing of the *corpus* can be dated with some accuracy to the last century of the pre-Christian era and specifically to the work of one man, Andronicus of Rhodes (*fl.* 30 B.C.).[3]

Where to end is far more arbitrary. The purely philosophical elements of the system are still alive today, notably in the Thomistic synthesis formulated in the last half of the thirteenth century and which continues to serve as the philosophical basis of Catholic theology, as an element in the *dogmatica* of John of Damascus (d. *ca.* A.D. 750), still a fundamental part of Eastern Orthodox thinking, and in the traditional *kalām* of the Muslim, which in the course of the three centuries between al-Ash'ari (d. A.D. 935) and Fakhr al-Dīn al-Rāzi (d. A.D. 1209)[4] became heavily impregnated with a distinctly Aristotelian type of philosophy.[5]

There were many revisions of the system from within during the course of its long and mottled existence; the logic, physics, metaphysics, psychology, politics, and ethics all underwent modification at the hands of eager exegetes bent on showing that Aristotle was in complete agreement with some other system currently vying for favor

3. See p. 14 below.

4. On this interval see pp. 147–156 and pp. 169 below.

5. Catholicism has always admitted its debt to Aristotle via the Thomistic synthesis, the latter strongly reaffirmed in the encyclical *Aeterni Patris*, while Eastern Christianity is, for a variety of reasons, not the least of which was the association of fifteenth-century Aristotelians like John Cardinal Bessarion (d. A.D. 1472) with the unionist Council of Florence and the strong anti-Scholastic attitude propagated in Russia by Theophanes Prokopovich (d. A.D. 1736), considerably more reticent. Most disingenuous of all is the Muslim theologian who if he does not consider all of *kalām* a disaster, distinguishes rather sharply between *falsafah* and *kalām* and tends to limit, incorrectly, Aristotelian influence to the former.

or misled by the luxuriant growth of *pseudepigraphica*.[6] But the main assault on the tradition from without, dates from the late Middle Ages and the early Renaissance.

The strength of the "outsiders" was drawn from a variety of sources. First, and certainly best known, was the attack on Aristotelian science launched from the development of new techniques of observation and measurement. When, for instance, Tycho Brahe could observe the appearance of a new star in A.D. 1572 and conclusively prove that it was "beyond the sphere of the moon," a serious and effective blow had been struck against the Aristotelian thesis of the immutability of the superlunary world. And, when this development in the physical sciences is coupled with the growing strength of two other "outside" traditions, Renaissance Platonism and the Protestant rejection of the Christian-Aristotelian synthesis, the days of the tradition are clearly numbered. No hard-and-fast date can be set for the last shot heard in this battle. Perhaps it is enough to say that by the end of the sixteenth century the transformation of "The System" into "the systems" was an accomplished fact and that the medieval phase of Aristotelianism was over.

From Aristotle to A.D. 1600 stretches a period of nearly two thousand years. For a span of five of these twenty centuries the philosophical tradition connected with his name was in the hands of the Arabs, Persians, and Turks within the bosom of Islam, and almost solely in their hands. Aristotelianism was only part of the general heritage received by the Muslim from the Greek and later handed on to the medieval European; but no other part was better known, more assiduously studied and preserved, or more far-reaching in its effects.

6. Some of these revisions were apparently the product of further research and reflection, *e.g.*, the addition of the fourth figure of the categorical syllogism to the logic and the work done in physical theory by John Philoponus and Yaḥyā ibn ʿAdi (see S. Pines, "Un précurseur Bagdadien de la théorie de l'impetus," *Isis*, XLIV [1953], 247–51; the scholars who followed these leads in the fourteenth and fifteenth centuries in the West were generally outside the tradition), but in most other instances the changes came from a desire to "adjust" the tradition in the light of the current theology; al-Fārābi's theory of prophecy falls into this class, as well as the great struggles over the eternity of the universe and the immortality of the intellectual soul.

ARISTOTELIANISM IN LATE ANTIQUITY

The Arab version of the arrival of the Aristotelian *corpus* in the Islamic world has to do with the discovery of manuscripts in a deserted house.[7] Even if true, the story omits two very important details which may be supplied from the sequel: first, the manuscripts were certainly not written in Arabic; second, the Arabs discovered not only Aristotle but a whole series of commentators as well. In these two facts are the basic premises of Islamic Aristotelianism: the writings of Aristotle entered this new cultural ground via the translation route, and were to some degree colored by the interpretations attached to them in their earlier career.

The translation movement will be spoken of in due course, but first some attempt must be made to put the Islamic "moment" of Aristotelianism in its true context as a "successor state." The Arabs received this tradition after five hunderd years of shaping in the later Greek schools and another two hundred years at the hands of the Syrian Christians: between the *corpus* proper and the *falāsifah* stand the massive efforts incorporated into the Berlin Academy's *Commentaria in Aristotelem Graeca*. And, it would be difficult to overestimate the influence of these unfortunately little-studied savants on their Arabic-speaking successors.[8]

Whatever may be said of the interval between Alexander of Aphrodisias (*fl. ca.* A.D. 200) and Stephan of Alexandria (*fl. ca.* A.D. 616), it was certainly not "la periode finale de la philosophie grecque" as one scholar chose to call it; "en grecque," perhaps, for all that follows in Islam is, except for the language, cast in the image and likeness of Alexandrian Hellenism. Individual problems might be singled out and shown to persist from one phase to the next, but we shall here limit our attention to two of the more general charac-

7. *Fihrist*, p. 243

8. The best introduction to this period from the point of view pursued in the following pages is still a series of articles by K. Praechter: "Richtungen und Schulen im Neu-Platonismum," *Genethliakon C. Robert* (Berlin, 1910), pp. 105–156; "Christlich-neoplatonische Beziehungen," *BZ*, XXI (1912), 1–27; "Nikostratos der Platoniker," *Hermes*, LXII (1922), 481–517.

itself to textual matters and exegesis; thus, in the sixth century, Christians like John Philoponus, David, and Elias were in attendance there without prejudice to their faith. The result was that Alexandria became more and more associated with the technical questions of Aristotelian philosophy while still remaining at base Neoplatonic in its outlook.

The next step was purely historical. The Arabs, by reason of their conquests to the west and their being stopped at the line of the Taurus, fell heir to the traditions of Alexandria: technical Aristotelianism with a deep base of Neoplatonic metaphysics.

It is not known exactly when or where the spurious *Theologia* was introduced into the *corpus*. Its earliest extant version is in Arabic, but this anonymous abridgement of parts of the *Enneades*, which accords perfectly well with the spirit of either Greek Alexandria or Syrian Antioch, typifies the mixed nature of the Arab inheritance; an entire philosophical culture that was Plotinian to its roots knew its benefactor only under the name of Aristotle, or as "the Greek Sage."

THE ORGANIZATION OF THE TRADITION*

The effects of the syncretizing spirit of later antiquity are by no means simple to detect; the gradual shifts in emphasis by reason of polemical pressures or changes in interest, the slowly evolving technical vocabulary, the loss of part of the *viva voce* tradition, all demand a careful reading of the extant texts of comment. More obvious, though doubtless of less importance for the essence of philosophical thought, is the stamp of scholasticism impressed upon Arabic philosophical expression by the pedagogical orientation of the later Hellenistic schoolmen.

"Scholasticism" is a much abused word. It has become a potent term of abuse, accompanied, as often as not, by its proper and inevi-

* See Bibliographical Note I, p. 28 below.

table qualifier, "sterile." The abuse stems in part from a confusion between "scholasticism" as a methodology and "Scholasticism" as a philosophical and theological school which did, indeed, use the "scholastic" method, but which may be further identified by its principles and problems.[15] This later Scholasticism, a purely Christian phenomenon represented at its height by Thomas Aquinas, enters only incidentally here. The "scholastic" method, conceived of simply as method without reference to particular theses or points of view, is both older and broader in its application; before the full development of the method in the medieval West there were Greek, Roman, Muslim, and Jewish scholastics patiently plying their methodical trades in grammar, rhetoric, philosophy, theology, and law.

Not all the critics of scholasticism have been misled by the confusion between method and content. The method, too, has been found wanting. It has been judged dreary, repetitive, and destructive of creative thought. Perhaps there is, even here, a confusion. The same critics would not make similar stylistic and aesthetic demands for an article published in a journal of mathematics or an advanced text in geology or linguistics. The analogy is apt: scholasticism is an orderly method of progression developed to deal with deductive problems in the nonphysical disciplines like philosophy and theology. It has nothing to do with considerations of aesthetics; it is the language and procedure of the researcher. Treatises on rhetoric are notoriously unrhetorical; they are not designed to persuade. So too, the technical theological treatise is not designed to edify or otherwise effect a change in moral behavior; it is to be severely distinguished from the sermon.

Like its analogues in the physical sciences, scholasticism is essentially a method of measurement and classification, not, however, of something as relatively tractable as matter, but of such Protean entities as terms and concepts. Its yardstick is the definition; its laboratory, the syllogism; its master, Aristotle.

15. The differing viewpoints can be clearly seen in the definitions offered respectively by M. de Wulf, *Introduction à la philosophie néoscholastique* (Louvain-Paris, 1904), pp. 32–46, and M. Grabmann, *Die Geschichte der scholastischen Methode*, I (Freiburg, 1909), 28–37.

From beginning to end the scholastic method has been characterized by a strongly professorial tone. What finally emerged as a methodology for specialists and technicians was born not in a laboratory but in the classroom of strictly pedagogical necessities. Nor was it at the outset designed for philosophy or theology, the two disciplines most closely associated with it at a later date, but for rhetoric.

It is the definition, as has been said, that takes the measure of the elemental concept, and thus provides the keystone for the entire scholastic method. There is little point in seeking out the origins of definition among the fragments of pre-Socratic literature, but what does emerge from the somewhat later material points to a *technical* and *pedegogical* use of the definition in the period immediately preceding Socrates. The preserved tracts of Gorgias, though mostly showpieces and not textbooks, show clearly enough that the Sophists had developed a fairly well-articulated, technical terminology and an advanced formal procedure which they applied to rhetoric. From *Phaedrus* 266C–267D it is likewise clear that both the terminology and the procedure, including the technique of definition, had been reduced to manual form.

Handbooks have a reputation for longevity, but the only surviving testimonial to the Sophist pioneers of scholasticism is the *Rhetorica ad Alexandrum*, once attributed to Aristotle but actually the work of the Sophist Anaximenes of Lampsacus (380–320 B.C.). It is a scholastic work in the classical mold, but, more interestingly, it shows the infiltration of purely philosophical terminology into rhetorical preserves as surely as Plato's philosophical, but essentially nontechnical and hence nonscholastic, work betrays the movement in the other direction, i.e., techniques designed in the first instance for the *teaching* of rhetoric adapted to the *development* of philosophical ideas.

The embryonic scholastic techniques as devised by the Sophists and illustrated by Anaximenes may be compared to the now-classic evaluation of Babylonian and Egyptian science. The peoples of the Near East developed techniques; what differentiates them from the Greeks is that the latter theorized, and thus converted technology into a science. The Sophists were essentially technicians, and in this instance the touch of Greek genius was added by Aristotle; the *Analytica* converted scholasticism into a scientific procedure. Henceforward, the process of definition and analysis could be made to yield solid deductive results and thus come to be as congenial to the philosopher as it was to the professor.

The pedagogic cast of scholastic methods has already been remarked. It was so in its origins, and in its post-Aristotelian development it became markedly more so. It is part of the sad and inscrutable nature of things that the professors will always outnumber the philosophers, and at no time is the principle more cogently illustrated than in the Hellenistic Age. The preserved philosophical literature is admittedly scant, and to a certain degree the conclusions rest on material from Roman times; but, for all that, there is little doubt that the "Age of the Textbook" witnessed a steady succession of philosophical manuals, the earliest representatives of a type later in use from Baghdad to Oxford, and most closely associated with the Aristotelian tradition.

Aristotle began his own philosophical career in the Platonic fashion casting his earliest philosophical ideas in dialogue form. However, in his maturity he adopted a more informal method. The bulk of the preserved *corpus* is in the form of *hypomnemata*, not precisely "lectures"—the term applies to a pedegogical procedure which became prevalent only at a later date—but rather *aides-mémoires* designed perhaps for public discussions but based largely on a formula of query-response that provides a kind of transcript of the philosophical mind at work.[16]

The bulk of *Aristotelica* inherited by the Syrians and Arabs was far different from this collection of sketchy and loosely arranged treatises. In the interval, the *corpus* had been edited, systematically arranged, extensively commented, and parceled out into the familiar reading lists, textbooks, doxographies, and *morceaux choisis*.

16. For the nature of the Aristotelian "lectures" and their "publication" see Überweg-Praechter, pp. 363–64, and W. Jaeger, *Studien zur Entstehungsgeschichte der Metaphysik des Aristoteles* (Berlin, 1912), pp. 145–47.

According to the traditional account based on a passage in Strabo,[17] the "second birth" of Aristotle was effected by Andronicus of Rhodes (*fl. ca* 30 B.C.) who rescued the Aristotelian texts from obscurity and, with the aid of manuscript material from a recently discovered library at Skepsis, edited or reedited them for publication.[18] The mechanics of the process are unfortunately not known, but it is safe enough to conclude that the by then sophisticated techniques of critical scholarship evolved at Alexandria and elsewhere were employed.

Scholars have long dismissed the notion that the works of Aristotle were either lost or unknown until the time of Andronicus. But with Andronicus' recension, Aristotle was rediscovered in another real sense in that the works were introduced, in this new standardized edition, into the quickening Roman philosophical circles on the eve of the great syncretistic movements of the Empire. What is most notably different about the Aristotelian tradition when it finally enters Arab hands is that the system bears all the signs of having been *taught,* and with a thoroughness and ritual that immediately suggests "syllabus" and "curriculum."

Much of the responsibility for this transformation of philosophical notes into a pedagogically viable system again belongs to Porphyry. Not only did he hasten the syncretistic tendencies of the time by making the *Organon* an integral part of the Neoplatonic *cursus,* but by the same stroke he vitalized what had been until then a languishing tradition by connecting it with one of the most vital and flourishing of the later schools.[19]

It was Neoplatonism that finally emerged victorious in the philosophical skirmishing of the final days of pagan antiquity; but not before it had absorbed into itself many of the elements of Aristotelianism. It is only the ultimate of many ironies that it was these

17. Pp. 608–609, thence Plutarch, *Sulla,* XXVI, 1–3.

18. On this incident see H. Erbse in *Geschichte der Textüberlieferung,* I (Zürich, 1961), 231–32.

19. Porphyry has still another connection with the Peripatetic tradition. He used the Aristonican edition of Aristotle as the model for his own edition of the works of Plotinus; *Vita Plotini,* XXIV.

latter that were being taught and studied at the time and in the places where the Syrians and Arabs took up the study of philosophy and that Plotinus passed into *falsafah* under the name of Aristotle, while Porphyry was known primarily as the author of the *Eisagoge* and as an Aristotelian commentator.

The pedagogical tools fashioned by Porphyry to implement the use of the *Organon* in the *cursus*, the *Eisagoge*, and his catechetical commentary on the *Categoriae*, were not, of course, the first attempts at commenting the *corpus*; the work of Alexander of Aphrodisias antedates them by about a hundred years. However, they are important in the evolution of the tradition because they were the earliest preserved "school" commentaries, and both they and all subsequent comment had available to them the manifold scholarly techniques developed by the philologists, grammarians, and rhetoricians of the Hellenistic schools and particularly of Alexandria. The highly stylized sequel can be traced through the pages of the Berlin Academy's *Commentaria* and in the *vitae* of the Scholarchs, especially Marinus' *Life of Proclus*.

In both the Alexandrian and Athenian schools of philosophy there were two types of instruction: formal lectures and a species of graduate seminar. It was the custom of Proclus at Athens to hold formal lectures in the morning, possibly in the same type of auditorium (*theatron*) arrangement set up somewhat later in Constantinople. The lectures were essentially exegetical, that is, they had to do with explicating a text, and most of the extant Aristotelian commentaries are, in fact, the products of just such lectures. An analysis of these commentaries, especially those produced in the school of Alexandria, illustrates the stereotyped format followed in the lecture.

Before the exegesis proper (*praxeis exegeisthai*) began, the professor gave several preliminary lectures of a more general nature (*katholou logous prattein*) dealing with historical matters connected with the text at hand and setting the general exegetical direction (*skopos*). In the format developed by Olympiodorus at Alexandria, these preliminary lectures were complex, highly articulated affairs that gave rise to the wide range of prolegomena literature and whose general traits can be marked in almost every piece of Arabic philosophical prose.

The question of the *skopos* was of less importance in the context of Arab scholasticism. Both Porphyry and Iamblichus had used it to advantage in impressing their own philosophical point of view onto the text to be commented, and, in the case of the Platonic dialogues, it was a decisive influence on the direction taken in the later schools. But, among the Alexandrians, whose methods had a greater impact on the Arabs, the tendency was to concentrate on Aristotle and, even here to concentrate more closely on textual and technical matters.

After the more general lectures, the work of commenting the text (*eis biblia legein*) began. The text was separated into small section (*praxeis*) and treated section by section. First, the lecturer went over the general meaning of the section (*theoria*), and then recovered the same ground in more detail (*lexeis*), explaining the more difficult lines and phrases. The entire work was traversed in this fashion from beginning to end.

The preserved commentary is quite frequently a *reportatio* of a professor's lecture made by one of the students present, and is so designated in the manuscripts. This is clearly the case, for example, in the transmission of Ammonius' lectures on the *Metaphysica*: *scholia hypo Asklepiou apo phones Ammoniou* where the *reportatio* was made by Asclepius. In such a system it is not always clear how much the student has contributed to the process; the reports were certainly not stenographic.

The *apo phones* procedure was not the only one followed. Proclus, for instance, devoted the time between his morning lecture and the afternoon seminar to composition. Simplicius worked under different circumstances. His commentaries probably date from after the closing of the Athenian school by Justinian and so have no connection with actual lecture courses.

The afternoon sessions were in the form of seminars (*agraphoi synousiai*), and the method of procedure was more informal. No text was commented; the professor and his students gave themselves over to a discussion of philosophical problems and their solution (*aporiai kai lyseis*) in the fashion of some of the preserved writings of Alexander of Aphrodisias and, indeed, of Aristotle himself.

For all its seeming vitality, for all its technical virtuosity and organization, the days of Hellenic philosophy were numbered; there was no place for such atavistic pagan fortresses like the philosophical schools in the new Christian Roman Empire of the East. The school at Athens perished by imperial decree; the Syrian group went under with Julian the Apostate. Alexandria the prudent, the longest lived of all, disappears in characteristic fashion. The two youngest students of Olympiodorus, David and Elias, were Christians; they produced no scholarly progeny. John Philoponus had already turned his attention, with startling results, to the more fertile field of theology.[20] And the final figure in the history of the school, not quite the last of the ancients and not quite the first of the Byzantines, Stephan of Alexandria, was summoned by the Emperor Heraclius on the very eve of the Muslim invasion to take the chair of philosophy at the Patriarchal School in Constantinople.

But the patient was not quite dead. From Arab sources we are given a curious postscript.[21] The school survived the fall of Alexandria to the Arabs and was still operating there, in straitened circumstances, surely, until *ca.* A.D. 720 (already a century has elapsed since Stephan!) when it moved to Antioch, thence to Harran, until, *ca.* A.D. 900, three of the philosophy professors migrated to the Abbasid capital of Baghdad. The first two were products of the School of Alexandria, Baghdad branch: Abū Bishr Mattā and Abū Naṣr Muḥammad ibn Muḥammad ibn Trakhān al-Fārābi!

20. See H. D. Saffrey, "Le Chrétien Jean Philopon et le survivance de l'école d'Alexandrie du VIe siècle," *REG*, LXVII (1954), 396–410.

21. The story of the final days of the school of Alexandria as it is found in the Arab tradition has been narrated by Meyerhof, "Alexandrien nach Baghdad," and *idem*, "La fin de l'école d'Alexandrie d'aprè quelques auteurs arabes," *Bulletin de l'Institute d'Egypte*, XV (1933), 109–23. The book of E. A. Parsons, *The Alexandrian Library* (Amsterdam, 1952), is worthless for the Arab period.

ARISTOTLE AND THE FATHERS

The introduction of Aristotle into Islam was not simply a matter of absorbing the philosophical tradition of late antiquity. From as early as the middle of the fifth century, Aristotelian texts were being translated into the Syriac vernacular by scholars at Edessa and elsewhere in the only partially Hellenized hinterland of Syria, and it was these same Syrians who later served the Arabs as translators and guides.[22] Syriac literature shows little interest in philosophy as such; indeed, it is interested in little else but the ecclesiastical: hymnography, hagiography, church history, exegesis, theology. Where philosophy was pursued, it was pursued for utilitarian not speculative ends. And it was theology that defined these ends: philosophy was to serve as an instrument for the understanding of the Greek Fathers and as a weapon in the struggle against heresy.

The Syrian need was a real one and reflected a problem that confronted Christianity almost from its beginnings. Already from the time of the Apologists, Aristotle had begun to appear in Christian theological literature. In these earliest appearances the context is usually a pejorative one, linking the *Aristotelous kakotechnia,* for instance, with radical Arian apologetes like Aetius and Eunomius. Attacks on the heretics and their "dialectic" fill the pages not only of historians like Socrates, Sozomen, Theodoret, and Epiphanius, but also the more reflective refutations of Basil and the two Gregories.

As might be imagined, the attitude of the latter, trained in the methods of the Greek sophistic, betrays a certain degree of ambiguity. They may fulminate against Eunomius' use of a slippery Aristotelianism, but at the same time they show themselves masters of turning the same dialectic weapon against their adversary. The history of Greek learning in the church, much like the later events in Judaism and Islam, is, in fact, the story of this ambiguity, the inability of the Hellenistic intellectuals to throw off something that was a part of themselves.

22. See pp. 58–59 below.

The Cappadocians illustrate another, quieter aspect of the infiltration of Aristotelianism into Christian circles. The purely scientific material in the Aristotelian *corpus*, particularly the zoology and the meteorology, found an easy and natural home in the hexaemeron literature, notably in Basil's *Homily on the Hexaemeron* and Gregory of Nyssa's *De opificio hominis*. The supposed Arabic version of this latter, reputedly the work of Isḥāq ibn Ḥunayn, was actually a translation of the *De natura hominis* of Nemesius of Emessa.

The anthropological treatise of Nemesius represents an important inroad of Hellenistic philosophy into Patristic thinking. Though compounded of a rich selection of Middle Platonic material deriving ultimately from Poseidonius and incorporated into the hexaemeron works of Origen and Basil, the *De natura hominis* stands firmly within the Christian tradition and, as such, was a legitimate source for the later Fathers, particularly John of Damascus who appropriated long sections of it for the *De fide orthodoxa*.

Nemesius' work was translated into Syriac at an unknown date, but it was already being used by Moses bar Kepha (d. A.D. 903), possibly as early as Job of Edessa's *Book of Treasures* (A.D. 814). The Arabic version dates, as we have seen, from the time of Isḥāq (d. A.D. 910). The *De fide orthodoxa* was available in an Arabic translation in the latter part of the ninth century.

Another of Nemesius' sources, Galen's *De demonstratione*, though now no longer extant, was translated into Syriac by Job of Edessa and later, from a better copy, by Ḥunayn, and then into Arabic by ʿĪsā ibn Yaḥyā and Isḥāq. The Arabic version was still being used, though possibly not firsthand, as late as Ibn Rushd (d. A.D. 1198).

Despite the Cappadocians' use of dialectical arguments against their Arian opponents, the organization of Christian theology and theological literature along clearly scholastic lines did not begin until the opening years of the sixth century. From that date, the *floruit* of Oecumenius and John the Grammarian, theological literature comes to resemble more clearly the externals of Hellenistic philosophy.

In the wake of the Monophysite controversy, not only is the *Organon* used as a dialectical weapon, as previously, but the *Categoriae* begin to make their appearance as an *exegetical instrument* in the complicated terminological debates against the Severians. As the tendency grows ever stronger, chapters of logical and philosophical definitions are incorporated into purely theological works[23] or, in the case of John of Damascus and the *De sectis*, full-blown logical introductions appear, the so-called *capita dialectica*, much in the style of the earlier prolegomena literature and the introductory chapters in the later works of Muslim theology.

In addition to the use of the technical terms of the Aristotelian logic, there are other indications of philosophy shaping theology to its own image, just as rhetoric had once left its imprint on philosophy.

The *De fide orthodoxa*, the third part of John of Damascus' *Fons scientiae*, has frequently been cited as the first theological *summa* or the first work of systematic theology. But, as has been almost as frequently pointed out, the tradition goes at least as far back as the *De principiis* of Origen. Leaving aside the designation of "first," the *De fide orthodoxa* does show many of the characteristics present in the later *systema*-works, and exhibits them in a more advanced degree than in the earlier theologians.

1. Theological "classicism," i.e., the narrowing of the bases of the *traditio* to a few "acceptable" theologians: the Cappadocians and Cyril for dogma, Chrysostom for exegesis, Basil for asceticsm, and pseudo-Dionysius and Maximus the Confessor for mysticism, to which should be added, in the case of John, Nemesius for the more profane aspects of philosophy.

   A corollary of the formation of such a canon is that John's knowledge of profane literature, and specifically of philosophy, is no wider than that of his *auctoritates*.

2. The use of citation *Hilfsmitteln*. The most recent student of John's theological work, Father Basilius Studer, judges that the only original texts actually consulted by John were those of Gregory Nazianzum, pseudo-Dionysius, Maximus, and possibly Nemesius. The rest of the many Father-citations comes from the

23. Anastasius of Sinai, *Viae dux*; the *Doctrina patrum*, and Chaps. XXVII ff. of the *De fide orthodoxa*.

wide variety of dogmatic and exegetical *florilegia* available since the fifth century. The entire *De fide orthodoxa* is a compilation (the famous phrase of the prologue, *ero de emou ouden*, is literally true) of dogmatic theses (*kephalia*) taken out of their original polemical context and grouped systematically, after the fashion of Origen and Theodoret.

3. Philosophical technical terminology. As has already been mentioned, logic served the Fathers not only as a dialectical weapon but also as an exegetical tool in the controversies surrounding such terms as *physis, hypostasis, prosopon*. The same twofold use is reflected in John.

4. Substance of Greek philosophy, chiefly through Nemesius.

5. Methodology and terminology of the schools. The *Schulwissenschaften*, long ago noticed in the *De sectis* of Theodore (of Raithu?), is found in almost all the Greek Fathers. The closest parallels between the Patristic practice and the techniques developed in Alexandria are in the area of exegesis where the presence of the text of Scripture naturally evoked the methods of exegesis (*hypomnemata, scholia*) already perfected by the philologists. The more pedagogical methods of procedure are likewise in evidence. The technique of *aporiai* (*quaestiones*) and *lyseis* (*solutiones*) is applied to theological matters, and there is evidence that at least some Patristic works were transmitted by *reportatio*, though by the time of John of Damascus the expression *apo phones* is already shading off into its later meaning of "composed by."

One final development of Aristotelianism within a purely theological context should be noted. John of Damascus' use of the logic was, as has been remarked, chiefly in the area of the Christological controversies, a usage that was neither new nor peculiar to him. When faced with a problem proper to his own time, that of Iconoclasm, the weapon of logic borrowed from the Cappadocians is not used. The next generation of anti-Iconoclasts were, however, more imaginative and once again the exegetical technique was applied in the *Antirrhetici* of Theodore of Studion (d. A.D. 826) and the *Apologeticus atque antirrhetici* of the Patriarch Nicephorus (d. A.D. 828).

It was from these two main sources, the scholarly tradition adumbrated in the declining schools of late antiquity and a Christian theology which had taken eagerly and aptly to Greek thought, that the Arabs became Hellenes and learned philosophy. The Arabs did not "discover" Aristotle; from the philosophical texts placed in their hands emerged a figure who had already, as early as A.D. 500, taken on much of the aura of *il maestro di color che sanno*; his eager readers in Baghdad could only concur.

THE BYZANTINE PHILOSOPHICAL TRADITION

The debt of the Arabs to Alexandria was explicit and often acknowledged by the Arabs themselves. There was, however, another point of direct contact with Greek philosophy and science. The scholarly relations between Arab and Byzantine are ill-defined at best and complicated by a political and religious hostility now blowing hot, now cold. But for all the skirmishing through the Taurus and Armenia, for all the tracts and pamphlets, the lines between Constantinople and Baghdad remained open, at least until the arrival of the Franks and the Turks.

The comparisons between Harūn al-Rashīd or al-Ma'mūn and the court of Charlemagne "dabbling in the art of writing their names" are not lacking in piquancy, but neither are they entirely apposite. The dealings of Harūn with Charlemagne were a ploy against a troublesome vassal in the distant West. Of far more immediate concern than Aachen to the Caliphs was the immense presence of the Byzantine Empire. Theophilus, Autocrator of the Romans was certainly no Charlemagne, and this was not only the century of Ḥunayn ibn Isḥāq but of Photius as well, just as the eleventh century saw not only Ibn Sīnā in Islam but also Mauropus, Xiphilinus, Psellus, and John Italus in Byzantium. This latter was the culture that could still produce, three hundred years after Ibn Rushd, George Gemistus Plethon and Cardinal Bessarion.

The school tradition at Constantinople—and it is at the capital that, except for the philosophy school of John Vatatzes (A.D. 1225-1254) at Nicaea, higher education is centralized—is a somewhat uneven thing. From the time of the reorganization of the State University by Theodosius II in A.D. 425 (the faculty included one chair of philosophy) interest now waxes, now wanes. One of the important projects of Heraclius (A.D. 610–641) was the strengthening of the Patriarchal School, and we have already seen how Stephan of Alexandria was summoned to Constantinople during this period to fill the role of Ecumenical Professor. Although there was a revival of this Patriarchal School under John II Comneus (A.D. 1118–1143) when Michael Italicus and Theodore Prodromus were professors, it was the State University to which the academic fortunes of philosophy were tied for as long as the Empire survived.

During the period that Hellenic philosophy was seriously being cultivated in the Abbasid capital, *ca.* A.D. 800–1050 (the earliest translations go back to *ca.* A.D. 780, Ibn Sīnā died in the provinces A.D. 1037), the State University at Constantinople enjoyed three striking periods of prosperity: *ca.* A.D. 830–860 under Michael III's Caesar, Bardas; under Constantine VII Porphyrogenitus (A.D. 913–959); and under Constantine IX Monomachus (A.D. 1042–1055).

In the first period it is the figure of Photius (d. *ca.*A.D. 891) who dominates. Before his ecclesiastical career began, he held the chair of philosophy at the University and was responsible for forming a whole generation of scholars including Leo the Mathematician, whom al-Ma'mūn wished to bring to Baghdad. After serving as Metropolitan of Thessalonika, Leo was appointed, in A.D. 863, professor of philosophy and Rector of the University. Photius himself, according to the well-known passage in the dedicatory epistle to the *Bibliotheca*, traveled on an embassy *ep 'Assyrious* (Samarra?) and used the opportunity to gather manuscript material for his anthology.[24]

24. On this episode see B. Hemmerdinger, "Les notices et extraits des bibliothèques grecques de Baghdad par Photius," *REG*, LXIX (1956), 101–103, and H. G. Beck in *Geschichte der Textüberlieferung* I (Zürich, 1961), 429.

Another of the students of Photius was Arethas (d. after A.D. 932), theologian, scholar, editor of Plato, and one of the central figures of the Renaissance associated with the name of Constantine VII.

Despite the obvious learning of these men, the tenth century was not a particularly notable time for Aristotelian studies. The logic had by this time become part of the liberal arts *trivium*, and in this area and in that of dialect, Photius showed his chief interest, both in the fragmentary minor treatises and in the *Amphilochianae*.

From the death of Constantine VII to the accession of Constantine IX, higher education in Constantinople languished. It was a period of political vitality, as witness the great counterstrokes against the Arabs, and even of poetical activity; but philosophy, bound so closely to university life, was in eclipse.

Michael Psellus (*ca.* A.D. 1018–1079), the focal point of the eleventh-century philosophical Renaissance, was not educated at the now-defunct University, but privately by two eminent scholars, Nicetas and John Mauropus. But, with the restoration of the University in A.D. 1045, higher studies in philosophy were restored to a formal basis, Psellus himself holding the chair.

In the *Chronographica*, Psellus sets forth his views on the philosophical cycle:

> *There were some who belittled the simplicity of the Greeks but I sought to learn more, and I met some of the experts in the art. I was instructed by them how to pursue my studies in a methodical way. One passed me on to another for tuition, the lesser light to the greater, and he again recommended me to a third, and he to Aristotle and Plato ....*
> *Starting from these authors I completed a cycle, so to speak, by coming down to Plotinus, Porphyry, and Iamblichus. Then, continuing my voyage, I put in at the mighty harbor of the admirable Proclus, eagerly picking up there his doctrine of perception, both in its broad principles and in its exact interpretation.*[25]

25. VI, 37–38; trans. E. Sauter.

The passage is a fair summary of the emphases apparent in Psellus' own philosophy, which is at Platonic base, but at the same time deeply indebted to the scholars of Neoplatonism: Plotinus, Iamblichus, Proclus. But, as the passage also indicates, there is a place for Aristotle in this scheme. Psellus commented at least two Aristotelian works: the *De interpretatione* and the *Physica*. Contrary to the implication of this latter commentary, it is for Aristotle the logician that Psellus reserves his praise; in more metaphysical speculation Plato is *philosophoteros*.

The presence close to the throne of a man of Psellus' intellectual vigor had its repercussions. Psellus stands at the beginning of a genuine philosophical revival which was to move, against the prevailing current of Christian theology, in the direction of Aristotle rather than that of Plato. The friend of Psellus, John Xiphilinus, had been an Aristotelian, but his chief activity—his philosophical works are lost—was in the field of law. It was not until John Italus succeeded Psellus as *hypatos ton philosophon* at the University that the stronger Aristotelian accent began to be felt.

The new Aristotelianism nearly perished at its birth. A change in political fortunes brought a new intellectual climate. Aristotelian and Platonic studies were banned by a Patriarchal Synod; the works of Psellus were burned and John Italus was tried, at least once, perhaps twice, for heresy and on precisely philosophical grounds. But the Comnenian orthodoxy did not completely stifle philosophical activity. Michael of Ephesus and Eustratius of Nicaea, probably contemporaries of Italus, commented Aristotle, and Theodore of Smyrna, the successor of Italus at the University, continued the Aristotelian tradition.

The eleventh century, richer in philosophical interest than the earlier flowering in the circle of Photius, gives less evidence of maintaining open lines to the Arab centers. Psellus mentions in one of his letters the presence of Arabs in his school, but the whole passage has an unmistakable rhetorical cast to it, which opens the literal interpretation to some doubt. More important, a new force had intruded itself between Arab and Byzantine in the person of the Seljuk Turks. In A. D. 1071, during the lifetime of Psellus, they had delivered a stunning blow to Byzantine fortunes along the eastern frontier by crushing an imperial army and capturing the reigning emperor, Romanus IV Diogenes, in the field. From this date on, the increasing pressure of the Turks and the crumbling power of the Abbasid caliphate effectively blocks cultural interchange between Constantinople and Baghdad.

In Constantinople, philosophy was, as it had been in Alexandria, a university discipline and, as such, supported by the state. Because the subject was taught formally, philosophical production among the Byzantines bears the same unmistakable pedagogical cast as the work turned out in the pagan schools: the chief forms are the commentary (Michael of Ephesus, Eustratius), the paraphrase (Theodore Prodromus and, particularly, Sophronius) and the *aporiai* (Psellus' *De omnifaria doctrina* is in this form); it is a continuation of the age of the *Handbuch* (Nicephorus Blemmydes and George Pachymeres).

But in one very important respect the Byzantine philosophers differed from their Alexandrian forebears: they had to come to terms with Christian theology. Like John Philoponus and al-Ghazāli, they had to know where to draw the line. Surprisingly enough, most of them were successful; John Italus was the first of the philosophers to fail in this equilibrium. Surprisingly, too, in a state where theology dominated literature, the philosophical curriculum in the University, as distinguished, apparently, from the course in the Patriarchal School, was completely independent of theology; though, in the larger scheme of things, philosophy was undoubtedly the *ancilla theologiae*, this view was not reflected in the curriculum.

When cast in the scales of Hellenism, the Byzantines had, of course, heavily weighted factors in their favor. No document in Arabic Persian, or Turkish, no matter how "Hellenizing" the author, reveals the same wealth of material available to a Photius, for instance, or a Suda, or a Theodore Metochites; the Muslim had, in reality, relatively few texts at his disposal. In a few fields, like medicine and mathematics, he was quite well off; in some others, like history, drama, and poetry in general, he had nothing. Further, the Byzantine scholar had the advantage of working with the original text; the Muslim labored over a secondhand translation. The Byzantine was heir to a long scholarly tradition; the Muslim had to create his own, almost *ex nihilo*.

Why, then, does Islamic *falsafah* show the unmistakable signs of vitality while Byzantine philosophy, despite its occasional flashes of brilliance, appears to be an afterthought? At least part of the answer lies in the historical circumstances surrounding the entrance of philosophy into Islam. Indeed, "Entrance" is decidedly the wrong word; philosophy was only part of a larger Greek "explosion" that in the course of three or four generations whirled the ninth-century Muslim through all the painful intellectual experiences that the Greeks had undergone in the time between Homer and Paul of Aegina. Both the novelty and the vigor of this unparalleled assault on the intellectual life of Islam attracted some of its greatest talents. It was the kind of moment that the Byzantine Empire could never, from the very nature of things, hope to experience; the heirs presumptive of great fortunes have never been much moved by stories of buried doubloons.

The classic struggle between faith and reason has almost no echo in the Byzantine tradition; the battle had been fought by the Fathers, and Italus was only a very late and quite extraordinary casualty. In Islam, as in the medieval West, it was quite otherwise. The primitive state of Muslim theology before the advent of philosophy gave the *falāsifah* the precious century between al-Fārābi and Ibn Sīnā in which to put down firm roots.

The subsequent battle between *kalām* and *falsafah* will be described in a later section; it is enough to note here that it is the excursions and alarums of that struggle that make vivid the career of medieval Arabic philosophy. The *falsafah* of Islam was vital because it was new and challenging and dangerous; it perished only when the entire culture ceased being these things.

BIBLIOGRAPHICAL NOTES

1. LATER HELLENISTIC SCHOLASTICISM

H. I. Marrou, *Histoire de l'education dans l'antiquité*[4] (Paris, 1958), an overall view of the Hellenistic school tradition.

R. Beutler, art. "Olympiodorus," *R-E*[2], XXXV Halbband (1939), cols. 221–27 (on *Theoria* and *Lexis*).

K. Praechter, "Richtungen und Schulen im Neuplatonismus," *Genethliakon C. Robert* (Berlin, 1910), pp. 103–56 (espec. pp. 122–50 on the exegetical method).

Idem, "Die griechischen Aristoteleskommentare," *BZ*, XVIII (1909), 516–30. (A review of the Berlin Academy's edition of the Aristotelian commentators; the review, like the original publication, has become a landmark in the study of the Aristotelian tradition.

M. Richard, "ἀπὸ Φωνῆς," *Byzantion*, XX (1950), 191–222.

O. Schissel, "Der Stundenplan des Neuplatonikers Proklos," *BZ*, XXVI (1926), 265–72.

R. Vanvourt, *Les derniers commentateurs alexandrins d'Aristote* (Lille, 1941), espec. pp. 7–16: "La forme de l'enseignement philosophique dans l'école d'Alexandrie."

2. ARISTOTLE AND THE EARLY FATHERS

A. J. Festugière, *L'Idéal religieux des Grecs et l'évangile* (Paris, 1932), Excursus C: "Aristole dans la litterature chrétienne jusqu'au Theodoret."

J. de Ghellinck, "Quelques appréciations de la dialectique et d'Aristote durant les conflits trinitaires du IVe siècle," *Revue d'histoire ecclésiastique*, XXXVI (1930), 5–46. *Idem, Patristique et Moyen-Age*, III (Brussels-Paris, 1948), pp. 245–310: "Un aspect de l'opposition entre Hellenisme et Christianisme. L'attitude vis-à-vis de la dialectique dans les débats trinitaires."

J. Waszink and W. Heffening, art., "Aristoteles," *RAC*, I, cols. 657–67.

3. HEXAEMERON AND ALLIED LITERATURE

On the hexaemeron literature in general see: K. Gronau, *Poseidonius und die jüdisch-christliche Genesisexegesis* (Leipzig, 1914).

Basil: Y. Courtonne, *Saint-Basile et l'hellénisme* (Paris, 1934), and J. F. Callahan, "Greek Philosophy and Cappadocian Cosmology," *Dumbarton Oaks Papers*, XII (1958), 29–57.

Gregory of Nyssa: E. Corsini, "Nouvelles perspectives sur le problème des sources des l'Hexaemeron de Gregoire de Nysse," *Studia Patristica* I (*Text und Untersuchungen*, LXIII [Berlin, 1957]), 94–103 and G. B. Ladner, "The

Philosophical Anthropology of Saint Gregory of Nyssa," *Dumbarton Oaks Papers*, XII (1958), 59–94.

Nemesius: There is a résumé of the recent work on Nemesius by E. Skard, art., "Nemesius," *R-E*², VII, Supplementband (1950), cols. 562–66. For Nemesius in the Syriac and Arabic tradition see: O. Braun, *Moses bar Kepha und sein Buch von der Seele* (Freiburg, 1891); Kraus, *Jabir*, II, 278–80; *GCAL*, II, 136 where the MSS of Isḥāq's version are listed.

John of Damascus: for his use of Nemesius see: K. Burkhard, "Johannes von Damaskus' Auszüge aus Nemesios," *Wiener Eranos. Zur fünfzigsten Versammlung Deutscher Philologen* (Vienna, 1908), pp. 89–101; B. Studer, *Die theologische Arbeitsweise des Johannes von Damaskus* (Ettal, 1956), p. 110; on the Arabic translation of the *De fide orthodoxa* by Antonius, monk of the convent of St. Simeon near Antioch: *GCAL*, II, 41.

Galen: The text has been partially reconstructed from the available Greek, Latin and Arabic testimonia of the *De demonstratione* by I. von Müller, "Über Galens Werk vom wissenschaftlichen Beweis," *AbMun*, XX (1897), 405–78. The translation history is narrated in Ḥunayn, *Risālah*, 115.

4. PATRISTIC SCHOLASTICISM

Beck, *Theologische Literatur*, pp. 371–449 (the period from the Council of Chalcedon to the end of the Monergism controversy).

M. Grabmann, *Die Geschichte der scholastischen Methode* I, (Freiburg, 1909), 92–116 (the *De sectis*, however, is no longer attributed to Leontius of Byzantium; see Beck, *op.cit.*, pp. 373–74.

C. Moeller, "Le chalcédonisme et le néo-chalcédonisme en Orient de 451 à la fin du VIe siècle" in *Das Konzil von Chalcedon*, I (Würzburg, 1951), 637–720.

John of Damascus: Beck, *Theologische Literatur*, pp. 476–86.

B. Studer, *Die theologische Arbeitsweise des Johannes von Damaskus* (Ettal, 1956), esp. pp. 102–25: "Die Philosophie in der theologischen Arbeit des Johannes von Damaskus."

For the Islamic milieu see P. Nasrallah, *Saint Jean de Damas* (Harissa, 1950).

The important question of the influence of John on the Muslim scholastics is still very much *sub judice*. There are some very modest tentatives in Gardet-Anawati, *Théologie musulmane*, pp. 200–207; it may well be that the Christian polemics directed against Islam made a deeper impression than the purely systematic treatises; see C. H. Becker, *Islamstudien*, I (Leipzig, 1924), 432–49, the extensive literature noted in Beck, *op.cit.*, p. 338, nn. 1 and 2, and P. Khoury, "Jean Damascene et l'Islam," *Proche-Orient Chrétien*, VII (1957), 44–63, VIII (1958), 313–39.

On the use of logic in the Iconoclastic controversy: P. J. Alexander, *The Patriarch Nicephorus of Constantinople* (Oxford, 1958), pp. 189–213.

5. THE BYZANTINE TRADITION

A complete bibliography of the political relations between the Byzantines on the one hand and the Arabs, Seljuks, and Mamluks on the other is given in G. Moravcsik, *Byzantinoturcica*, I² (Berlin, 1958), 28–29, 98–100, and 101–102.

Two aspects of the cultural interchange have been explored by K. Weitzmann "The Greek Sources of Islamic Scientific Illustrations," in *Archaeologica Orientalia in Memoriam Ernst Herzfeld* (New York, 1952), pp. 244–66, and for the movement of religious information in the opposite direction, W. Eichner, "Die Nachrichten über den Islam bei den Byzantinern," *Der Islam*, XXIII (1936), 133–62, 197–244.

Byzantine philosophy is a neglected field. There are brief sketches in Überweg-Geyer, pp. 218–87, and *GBL*, pp. 428–49, but the first and only attempt to treat it as an independent discipline is B. Tatakis, *La Philosophie Byzantine* (Paris, 1949), who has only succeeded in pointing up the chief obstacle to a really penetrating understanding of the subject: the lack of critical texts — in many cases of any text at all — and of individual monographs. Eustratius, Michael of Ephesus, and Sophronius are the only Aristotelian commentators who appear in the *CAG*. Most of the other edited texts go back to Migne and beyond. Psellus is the only one of the philosophers about whom the semblance of a *corpus* is being collected. L. Westerink's edition of the *De omnifaria doctrina* (Nijmegen, 1948), together with the *Epistulae*, *Orationes*, and the *Chronographia*, provide a solid footing for the investigation of his philosophical career. Though Psellus' commentary on the *Physica* is still unpublished, it has recently been the subject of a methodological study: L. Benakis, *AGP*, XLIII (1961), 215–38. It should be noted, however, that the treatise *Synopsis ton pente phonon kai ton deka kategorion* once attributed, with reservations, to Psellus, has now been identified as a later Greek translation of most of Peter of Spain's *Summulae logicales*, vitiating the long discussion of Byzantine logic in Prantl's *Geschichte der Logic im Abendland;* see *BZ*, LII (1959), 412.

John Italus is still somewhat of an enigma, but the recent monographs of P. Stephanou, *Jean Italos, Philosophe et Humaniste* (Rome, 1949), and P. Joannou, *Christliche Metaphysik in Byzanz*, I: *Die Illuminationslehre des Michael Psellos und Joannes Italos* (Ettal, 1956), together with Joannou's edition of the *aporiai kai lyseis* (Ettal, 1956), have made him better known than most of his less complicated contemporaries.

A systematic study has been made of the history and organization of higher learning at Constantinople: F. Fuchs, *Die höheren Schulen von Konstantinopel im Mittelalter* (Berlin, 1926), to be completed by the two briefer studies by L. Brehier, "Notes sur l'histoire de l'enseignement supérieure à Constantinople," *Byzantion*, III (1926), 73–94; IV (1927–1928) 13–28, and F. Dvornik,

"Photius et la réorganisation de l'Academie patriarcale," *Mélanges Peeters*, II (Brussels, 1950), 108–25. The findings of Fuchs have been integrated into the general literary and historical background of the eleventh century in J. Hussey, *Church and Learning in the Byzantine Empire* (London, 1937).

On the transmission of the Byzantine learning to the West, see the excellent study by K. Setton, "The Byzantine Background to the Italian Renaissance," *Proceedings of the American Philosophical Society* C (1956), 1–76, and R. Klibansky, *The Continuity of the Platonic Tradition during the Middle Ages* (London, 1939), pp. 19–21.

II

THE GROUND PREPARED: THE HELLENIC AND IRANIAN NEAR EAST

Islam began under rather unpromising circumstances; the community of the Prophet was born in a wedgelike crevice between two millennial cultures, the Greek and the Iranian, and two apparently flourishing religions which, like the Muslim's own, issued a universal call, Christianity and Zoroastrianism. Its own cultural equipment for this type of forbidding apostolate was meager: certain bedouin techniques like folk medicine and folk astronomy and a penchant for genealogies, an oral tradition in poetry which, whatever its charms, was extremely parochial in tone, a religion that had certain thin, intellectual roots back into Christianity and Judaism, and The Book, the *Qur'ān*.

The *Qur'ān,* and the pre-Islamic poetry to a somewhat lesser extent, provide the keys to the Arabs' success: Islam had at its disposal an intellectual and cultural weapon of the first order in the Arabic language. Blessed with the power and directness that make it an ideal idiom for the speech of God to the hearts of men, it possesses as well the nuance and flexibility proper to the exegesis of the Word. Muḥammad spoke to the heart, but there remained for his successors the thankless task of becoming theologians and wrestling with their minds. The older religions, Christianity, Judaism, and Zoroastrianism, had the choice of field; theology was their science and they had long since become adept in it. But the Arabs, because of the dynamics of the conquest, had the choice of linguistic weapons, and the four-cornered dialogue was conducted in Arabic.

The linguistic Arabization of the Near East is a curious event, given the small number of Arabic speakers who came into the area; one reckoning places them at 200,000—the figure seems very high—out of a total population of about four million in Syria-Palestine *ca.* A.D. 750. But against this must be balanced the fact that this Arab minority, and it was they who held the political power and patronage, congregated in new urban centers of their own making where they were, in fact, a majority. Again, the Islamic client system hastened the incorporation of new converts into the Arab tribal structure, and hence into the Arabic linguistic milieu.[1] Finally, and more importantly from our point of view, Islam, as a religion and apart from all the parallel commercial and political considerations, was not so much a State with an Established Religion as a Religion with an Established Language. The *Qur'ān* was in Arabic, and the prime miracle persuasive of the fact that it was indeed the Word of God was the perfection of its language. And Arabic held fast; there was no Septuagint in Islam. Even after the intrusion of Persian and Turkish into this linguistic unity, the language of the fundamentally Islamic sciences continued to be Arabic.

Arabic, then, a Semitic tongue, became the language of theology, a Greek science, and it was ideally suited for this task. Greek and Arabic share a lexicographical richness, particularly in their ability to express the abstract, defining concepts which are part of the systematic of scholasticism. Arabic is not a perfect vehicle for the translation of all types of Greek literature; it is weak in hypotaxis, for instance, and Plato, to cite only one apposite example, would come off very poorly. But it translated the abstract, conceptualized, technical Aristotelian treatises very well indeed.

The Muslim, however, had first to rise to the level of interest and sophistication where he could both want and be able to cope with this forbidding tradition of Hellenism. This was the function of Islam's religious minorities. The wide-spread net of the Arab conquest had gathered up a mixed catch of Christians, Zoroastrians, and Jews,

1. See N. Polliak, "L'Arabisation de l'Orient sémitique," *REI* (1938), 35–63.

and it was particularly through the first of these, the Syriac-speaking Christians, whose Christianity related them back to Hellenism through the Greek Fathers and whose Syriac language and Semitic orientation made them ideal translators and instructors for their Arab cousins, that Aristotle came to Islam.

THE SYRIAN MILIEU

Except for an ephemeral and unimportant period as tiny client states to the Roman Empire, the Syriac-speaking community never had a national existence of its own. Its political history is that of the Roman, Byzantine, Sassanian, and Islamic Empires, first as part of the ecumenical Christian community, then as a religious minority.

The existence and physiognomy of this community is due to the uneven nature of Hellenism in the East. In the days after Alexander, Greek culture and letters took their deepest root in the dense urban centers of the Mediterranean littoral. The indigenous Semitic population of these cities was not, of course, completely submerged; but the prevailing cultural tone was Hellenic. Farther inland the Hellenic veneer became progressively thinner. Christianity followed the same traces and fell into the same general patterns. The Christianity of the coastal areas was Hellenized; it used the Greek Scripture and a Greek version of the liturgy. In the hinterland the Scripture was read and the divine worship was performed in the vernacular.

The vernacular in this instance was Syriac, an Aramaic dialect from the region of Edessa, one of the primitive seats of Christianity in this area and later the chief Syriac cultural center as well. Thus by the time of the death of Constantine, the missionary activity of the Church had propagated groups of Syriac-speaking Christians from the Lebanon as far as the Iranian highlands, developing, it should be noted, along slightly divergent lines from the Hellenized version, that looked to Antioch, Alexandria, and Constantinople. From the very first, Syriac Christianity tended to be more ascetic in its general practices, more idiocentric in its monasticism, and, in general, more prone to Iranian influence.

The great landmark in the history of this community was not the Arab conquest, but Jovian's cession, in A.D. 363, of the trans-Tigrine provinces of the Roman Empire to the Sassanians. At a stroke the religious ecumene was shattered and there occured, for the first time in the history of the new religion, the phenomenon of a Christian community living outside the borders of the Empire. The effect was not fatal. These Syriac-speaking Christians survived as a linguistic and religious minority inside Persia,[2] dependent, it is true, on the fluctuating goodwill of the successive Shahs, and increasingly independent of ecclesiastical control, whether it emanated from Antioch or Constantinople.

As was to happen later in Islam, it was chiefly in their piety and ritualistic practices that these churches of the East preserved a distinctly Semitic cast; their theology was Greek, and hence scholastic. They drew their *auctoritates* from the great Greek Fathers of the third and fourth centuries, then available to them in translation, and followed the same general pedagogical techniques practiced in theological circles in Antioch and Alexandria.

The second critical event, or rather, series of events, in the life of Syriac Christianity were the series of schismatic movements in the fifth century, climaxing in the Councils of Ephesus (A.D. 431) and Chalcedon (A.D. 451), which in effect detached the Syrian Churches from the Imperial (Melkite) Church. The official grounds for this separation were, as always, dogmatic, but it is undeniably true that other less intellectualized forces were at work: nationalism, the progressive breakdown of Byzantine administration and consequent disenchantment with the central authority, the previous separation of the church in Persia from imperial control, and the assiduous

2. Perhaps not even a numerical minority, at least in the western sections of the Sassanian realm. One authority has suggested that on the eve of the Arab invasion Zoroastrianism was here represented only by the military, some civil officials, and the Magian clergy; see E. Sachau, *Mitteilungen des Seminars für Orientalische Sprache*, X (1907), 72.

efforts of "Persianizing" elements inside that church to make it more acceptable to the Zoroastrian majority.

Dogmatically, the differences between the orthodox and the dissidents center on the positions of two Constantinopolitan churchmen, Nestroius and Eutyches. Put in its simplest terms, the two men represented two different emphases in contemplating the person of Christ: Nestorius, following the prevalent trend of Antiochene theology, chose to emphasize the humanity of Christ; while Eutyches, in the Alexandrian tradition, placed his emphasis on the divinity.[3]

Nestorius was condemned at Ephesus and in the following years the partisans of Eutyches, the Monophysites, drove the Nestorian teachers from the Syrian schools. There was just such a purge at Edessa in A.D. 457 when the Nestorian theologians, led by the redoubtable Barsauma, fled across the Persian frontier and began teaching at Nisibis. Another wave followed in A.D. 489 when the Emperor Zeno closed the Edessan school for good. The result was the propagation of Nestorian ideas among the Syrian congregations in Persia, a move that was, on the counsel of Barsauma, supported by the Shah as a counterweight to Byzantine influence.

At Chalcedon, the Monophysite position was in turn condemned, and henceforward there were two Syrian Christian Churches: the Nestorian Church of Persia, now doctrinally beyond the pale and administratively beyond the reach of the Emperor,[4] and the so-called

3. The most complete systematic treatment of Syrian theology, embracing both the Eutychian and Nestorian positions, is M. Jugie, *Theologia Dogmatica Christianorum Orientalium ab Ecclesia Catholica Dissidentium*, V, *De Theologia Dogmatica Nestorianumum et Monophysitarum* (Paris, 1935). The struggles of the fifth century are studied in both their theological and historical contexts in A. Grillmeier and H. Bacht, *Das Konzil von Chalkedon. Geschichte und Gegenwart*, I and II (Würzburg, 1951 and 1953); particularly important is the monograph of Msgr. Lebon, "La Christologie du monophysisme syrien," *op.cit.*, I, 425–580, which, together with his classic *Le monophysisme sévérien* (Louvain, 1909), forms the single most important treatment of this complex subject.

4. There are two collections of primary material on the Nestorians in J.-B. Chabot, *Syndicon Orientale* (Paris, 1902), the canonical documents of the Nestorian Church, and F. Nau, "Documents pour servir à l'histoire de l'église nestorienne," *PO*, XIII (1919), fasc. 2; see G. Badger, *The Nestorians and their Rituals*, (2 vols.; London, 1852), (the pertinent material is in Vol. II); L. Delaporte, "Dignitaires de l'Eglise nestorienne," *ZA*, XXIII (1909), 378–90; J. Labourt, *Le Christianisme dans l'Empire perse sous la dynastie Sassanide* (A.D. 224–632) (Paris, 1904); I. Ortiz de Urbina, "Storia e cause dello scisma della Chiesa di Persia," *Orientalia Christiania Periodica*, III (1937), 456–85; E. Tisserant, art. "Nestorienne (Eglise)," *DTC*, XI, 157–323.

Jacobite Church of the Monophysites, subject to constant persecutions from the Byzantine State, yet vital enough to propagate itself even in Nestorian preserves in Persia.[5]

More than one student of the subject has noted the unhappy fact that the substance of the Christological debates of the fifth century, and particularly those between the orthodox adherents of Chalcedon and the Monophysite theologians, arose from a series of semantic misunderstandings. It is not difficult to understand why this should be so; fifth-century Christology was a war of terms and of definitions and carried with it all the Aristotelian paraphernalia developed for just such warfare. It is the beginning of the high noon of Patristic scholasticism. The definition and syllogistic techniques of the *Organon* enter the scene, and there is the expected reflex in the organization of the theological curricula.

There was an analogous developement among the Syriac communities. Their theology took on the same scholastic tinge, and Aristotle found a restricted but firm place in the school at Edessa as a propaedeutic to the study of theology.[6] It was this type of situation that gave rise to the beginnings of the Aristotelian translation movement in Syriac, and the composition of the earliest commentaries on the beginning of the *Organon*, from *ca.* A.D. 450 to well past the Arab conquest.

5. In addition to the usual historical sources, there is important primary material in E. W. Brooks, "John of Ephesus' *Lives of the Eastern Saints*," *PO*, XVII (1923), 1–307; *idem*, *Vitae virorum apud Monophysitas celeberrimorum* (CSCO, *Scriptores syri*, Ser. 2, Vol. IV [Paris, 1907]); J.-B. Chabot, *Documenta ad origines Monophysitarum illustrandas* (*ibid.*, Vol. XXXVII [Louvain, 1933); see also E. Honigmann, *Évèques et Évèchés Monophysites d'Asié antérieure au VIe siècle* (Louvain, 1951); *idem*, *Le Couvent de Barsauma et le Patriarchat d'Antioch et de Syrie* (Louvain, 1954); P. Kawerau, *Die jakobitische Kirche in der syrischen Renaissance: Idee und Wirklichkeit* (Berlin, 1955); A. van Roey, "Les débuts de l'église jacobite" in *Das Konzil von Chalkedon*, II (Würzburg, 1953), 339–60; B. Spuler, "Die westsyrische (monophysitische) Kirche unter dem Islam," *Saeculum*, IX (1958), 322–44.

6. The bulk of the source material pertains to the Nestorian school at Nisibis, but there is little reason to think that the Jacobite schools were organized differently. Two important documents are Barhadbashabba, *Cause de la Fondation des Écoles*, ed. and trans. A. Scher, *PO*, IV (1907), 319–404, and Thomas of Marga, *The Book of Governors*, ed. and trans. E. A. W. Budge, (2 vols.; London, 1893). On the school of Nisibis see *GSL*, pp. 113–14; T. Hermann, "Die Schule von Nisibis vom V. bis VII. Jahrhundert," *Zeitschrift für neutest. Wissenschaft*, XXV (1926), 89–122; J.-B. Chabot, "L'École de Nisibe, son histoire et ses status," *JA* Sér. 9, Vol. VIII, 43–93. On Edessa see E. R. Hayes, *L'École d'Edesse* (Paris, 1930).

It is difficult to group the resultant literature under the heading of "Syrian Philosophy." Strictly speaking, there never was, until considerably later, when *falsafah* influences came into play, such a thing as a "Syrian philosopher," any more than there ever existed a "Scholastic philosopher" in the medieval West. The Aristotelian translations and studies in the Syriac-speaking community always had very strong theological overtones, and the great figures involved in this activity were, without exception, churchmen. The study of their intellectual activity is uniquely the study of their theology.

The fact remains that the theology of these Syrian thinkers was scholastic and therefore Aristotle-oriented, and thus the Arabs came into contact with a Semitic culture akin to their own which had an interest and familiarity with technical Aristotelianism. This tradition of Syriac Peripateticism had an independent existence for no more than three centuries,[7] yet its technical equipment was sufficiently advanced and its enthusiasm was such that Arab Peripateticism could be erected on solid and lasting foundation.

Philosophy, even in her position as *ancilla theologiae,* has a few of her own profane handmaidens, and among the Syrians the art of grammar maintained its prerogatives more firmly than in the Arts Faculties of the West.[8] Even in a thirteenth-century figure like Yuḥanna bar Zoʿbi,[9] grammar and logic are still in balance. This early Syrian interest in grammar, a grammar founded directly on Greek models, it should be noted, had as a natural concomitant activity in the field of lexicography. An early Syriac lexicographer was the monk ʿEnanishuʿ (*fl. ca.* A.D. 650) who, in addition to his purely grammatical lexicon of the *aequaelitterae* (consonantally identical words), composed a glossary on the more difficult terms in the

7. Roughly from the period of Probha (*ca.* A.D. 450) to the death of George, Bishop of the Arabs in A.D. 724. Most of these Syrian scholastics were Monophysites working in Syria. After A.D. 750, the point where the Arabs begin entering the tradition, the center of gravity shifts, together with the center of political power, from Syria to Iraq; these later Syrians are chiefly Nestorian and it can no longer be said that there is an independent Syriac tradition. Henceforward there are reciprocal influences between Christians and Muslim *falāsifah.*

8. See A. Merx, *Historia artis grammaticae apud Syros* (Leipzig, 1887), and J. B. Segal, *The Diacritical Point and the Accents in Syriac* (Oxford, 1953).

9. *GSL,* pp. 310–11; Jugie, *Theologia,* V, 37; Tkatsch, *Poetik,* I, 85 b.

pire, and who had served their Iranian masters much in the same fashion as they now served the Caliphs.

The lines between Baghdad and Constantinople were not closed between A.D. 800 and 1050, the apogee of Aristotelianism in Islam. There are references to scholarly expeditions into Byzantine territory in search of manuscripts, to embassies back and forth between the capitals.

But the record is, for all that, a disappointing one. The procession of Hellenizing scholars and apprentices came to Baghdad from quite another direction, from towns in the Iranian highlands and the border of the eastern steppe, an area which, until the sixth century, had been as little known to the Byzantines as it had to Herodotus.

Clearly the flowering of Greek studies in Islam was something more complex than the mere encounter of the Arabs, newly thrusting from the desert, with the Byzantine guardians of the Hellenic legacy. Nor is the question "How did Greek learning pass into Islam?" to be answered simply by "Through the Nestorians." On all sides there is evidence of an Iranian cultural synthesis which was, in the final analysis, to provide the soil from which the "Greek sciences" were to bloom.

The age of the Abbasids was not the first time that Hellene and Iranian had met on these grounds. Strewn across Iran were the cities founded by Alexander, ephemeral creations for the most part that left no roots, even in the promising soil of the philhellene Parthian Empire. But as the Seleucid successor state was slowly rolled back to Syria by the advancing Parthians, it left isolated at the other end of the Iranian homeland Alexander's most durable legacy to Central Asia, the Indo-Bactrian kingdoms.

Before the last Greek princeling of Bactria capitulated before the oncoming Kushan nomads in 135 B.C., these kingdoms had been in existence in central Asia for about two hundred years. Did they have any lasting effect on the culture of the region? There is, of course, the art of Gandhara whose Apolline Buddhas can be traced in a clear flow to the East into Chinese art and, less obviously, into the iconography of Sassanian art. But, for all that, Bactria is the "silent kingdom" among the successor states. Of the broader aspects of its cultural life we know nothing. It produced no literature that has been preserved, and the tracing of its history is primarily an exercise in numismatics.

In the west the Romans replaced the Seleucids, and in A.D. 226 the Sassanians occupied the disintegrating Parthian kingdom. From then until the Arab eruption in the seventh century, the Iranian frontiers were, with some important exceptions, stabilized. On the west, the frontier with the Romans was in fact the Arabian desert and the Syrian steppe, extended north of the Euphrates and into Armenia through a series of hotly contested fortresses. In the east the Sassanians held the line Merv-Herat against the Hephthalites, though the nomads once managed to get as far as Rayy. But *ca.* A.D. 560, Khusraw Anosharvan settled affairs with the Byzantines and could give his complete attention to the Hephthalites. Working in concert with the western Turks (Tü-kueh), who had appeared behind the Hephtalites, Khusraw broke the Hephthalites; the Sassanians moved into Balkh and the land south of the Oxus, while the Turks occupied Transoxania. Thus the Sassanians were never in political control of Transoxania, and in some parts of Khorasan their hegemony was established for no more than a hundred and fifty years. Conversely, the lands north of the Oxus knew no other master but the nomads, first Iranian, then Turkish, for many centuries until the arrival of the Arabs. Beyond lay the Khanates of the Tü-kueh, and beyond them, China's expanding protectorate.[18]

Within this area, from the Tigris on the west to the Tarim River Basin on the east, occurs the confrontation of four major religious

18. The years between A.D. 550–750 were marked by the thrust and counterthrust of the Chinese and Tü-kueh. Between A.D. 552–565, the Tü-kueh unified their empire between the Sassanians and the Great Wall of China. At about the same time the Chinese were putting their house in order, and by the first decade of the seventh century began to restore their sovereignty over eastern Turkestan. In A.D. 630 the eastern Khanates of the Tü-kueh became vassals of the Chinese, and in A.D. 642 the western Khanates were also reduced, Chinese domination extending to the western edge of the Tarim Basin. The years A.D. 665–715 marked a reversal of Chinese influence with all branches of the Tü-kueh in full revolt. The final counterthrust of the Chinese carried them into Ferghana, and from A.D. 718 to 750, they had established protectorates over Bukhara, Samarqand, Balkh, Kashmir, and Kabul. In A.D. 751 the Arabs and western Tü-kueh halted the Chinese on the River Talas, a date that marks the end of Chinese hegemony in Central Asia.

groups, three of which were active carriers of at least part of the Hellenic heritage: at the heels of the advancing Arab forces.[22] But in at least some cases the missionaries were in advance of the soldiery: the famous Nestorian inscription of Ch'ang-an commemorates a church built there in A.D. 638.

It is somewhat risky to draw cultural conclusions from the mere existence of these communities. The Jesuit Reduções of South America hardly produced Thomistic scholars among the Indians. If one such were to appear, however, on the faculty of the University of Coimbra, the evidence would be somewhat more persuasive. This is, indeed, more or less what happened in Iran. The presence of so many "easterners" studying *falsafah* at Baghdad and elsewhere suggests a type of preparatory milieu to which the Nestorians may have contributed their share.

There is, as has been remarked, a Patristic heritage of Aristotelianism in Nestorian theology; the logical works of Aristotle were studies in preparation for approaching the writings of the "Great Exegete," Theodore of Mopsuestia (d. A.D. 428).[23] More than this, the subject was of some concern in official circles, as is testified to by the letters of the Nestorian Catholicos Timotheus I (d. A.D. 823),[24] who was not only engaged in Aristotelian translation himself, but was also in correspondence on various philosophical problems with the Caliph's personal physician, member of the Nestorian Bakhtīshū' family.[25]

The Bakhtīshū' family[26] provides firmer evidence for Nestorian philhellenism. It was they who provided the leadership at the medical school at Jundishapur and, after Jūrgīs ibn Jibrīl ibn Bakhtīshū' was summoned to Baghdad in A.D. 765, were court physicians to the Caliph.

Jundishapur itself had long been a Nestorian center, and, from its origins, an Hellenic preserve. It had been founded sometime after

22. See A. Mingana, "The Early Spread of Christianity in Central Asia and the Far East. A New Document," *Bulletin of the John Rylands Library*, IX (1925), 297–371.

23. Translated into Syriac *ca.* A.D. 440 by a certain Ma'na, a Persian: see Tkatsch, *Poetik*, I, 63a.

24. R. J. Bidawid, *Les Lettres du Patriarch Nestorien Timothée I* (*Studi e Testi* 187 [Vatican City, 1956]).

25. See R. J. Bidawid, *op.cit.*, p. 19.

26. Biographies in Uṣ., I, 123–48.

A.D. 260 by Shapur I as a camp for his Roman captives.[27] The Sassanian custom of transplanting large groups of captured peoples probably kept Jundishapur well supplied with Hellenes. At any rate, there is an unbroken series of Nestorian metropolitans for Jundishapur (*syriace* Bayt Laphat) from A.D. 410 to A.D. 585, then a break until *ca.* A.D. 754 when the list resumes once again. It was the hospital at Jundishapur that provided both Aristotelian translators and a model for similar establishments in Baghdad itself.[28]

The Zorostrian tradition presents more difficulty, particularly due to the unfortunate textual state of the Pahlevi Scriptures which, though they were either first written down or compiled in Islamic times, report, in their unsure fashion, traditions going back to the beginnings of the Sassanian dynasty.[29]

According to the *Denkart*,[30] Zoroastrianism was in a lamentable state at the accession of Ardashir I (A.D. 226), and it was his high priest Tansar who put its scriptural canon into some order. Whatever the historicity of this event, Tansar himself is of some interest since he occurs in other, more philosophical contexts. He is called a "Platonist" by al-Masʿūdi,[31] and his interest in philosophy is confirmed by a letter that has been preserved under his name. It was originally translated from Pahlevi into Arabic by Ibn al-Muqaffaʿ, who has a known connection with the Aristotelian translation movement; the Arabic has been lost, but a subsequent Persian version by Ibn Isfandiyār is preserved.[32] The first part of this letter—its authenticity

27. Al-Tha ʿālibi, *Ghurar akhbār muluk al-fars*, ed. H. Zotenberg (Paris, 1900), pp. 494, 503–504; cf. pp. 612–13; see T. Nöldeke, *Geschichte der Perser und Araber zur Zeit der Sasaniden* (Leyden, 1897), pp. 32–33. The Roman Emperor Valerian, who was captured in Shapur's campaign of A.D. 260, may have died in Jundishapur; Mani certainly did; he was flayed and his skin hung on one of the city gates.

28. See D. M. Dunlop, art. "Bimaristan," *EI*², I, 1222–24.

29. On these see M. Molé, "Deux aspects de la formation de l'orthodoxie zoroastrienne," *Mélanges H. Gregoire*, IV (Brussels, 1953), 289–324; J. Tavadia, *Die Mittelpersische Sprache und Literatur der Zarathustrier* (Leipzig, 1956), pp. 55–61; H. W. Bailey, *Zoroastrian Problems in the Ninth Century Books* (Oxford, 1943), pp. 81–92; R. C. Zaehner, *Zurvan, A Zoroastrian Dilemma* (Oxford, 1955), pp. 8 ff.

30. Maden (ed.), p. 412, ll. 17 ff.; see Zaehner, *op. cit.*, pp. 8–9.

31. *Murūj*, II, 161.

32. J. Darmesteter (ed.), *JA*, Sér. 9, Vol. III (1894), 185–250, 502–55, and later, from older MSS by M. Minovi (Teheran, 1932); see A. Christensen, "Abarsam et Tansar," *Acta Orientalia*, X (1931), 43–55.

is difficult to establish—contains a note from Alexander to Aristotle and Aristotle's response, a typical format in the pseudepigraphical epistles.

For the reign of Ardashir's successor, Shapur I (A.D. 241–272), the *Denkart* takes specific notice of the penetration, or rather, of the deliberate incorporation of Greek ideas into the Iranian heritage:

> *The King of Kings, Shapuhr, son of Artaxsathr, further collected those writings from the Religions which were dispersed throughout India, the Byzantine Empire, and other lands, and which treated of medicine, astronomy, movement, time, space, substance, creation, becoming, passing away, change in quality, growth (?), and other processes and organs. These he added to the Avesta and commanded that a fair copy of all of them be deposited in the Royal Treasury.*[33]

The testimony, then, for the introduction of Hellenic concepts into Zoroastrianism under Shapur is quite clear; what is more, some of the terminology of this passage seems unmistakably Aristotelian. Were there Aristotelian works extant in Pahlevi in the third century? There seems no good reason to doubt the *Denkart*, even though the expected Syriac intermediaries of such would antedate the earliest known Syriac translation by two to three centuries. Perhaps the reason for such a move is to be sought in Shapur's concern with the growth of Manichaeism, with which he himself conducted a brief flirtation.[34] Unlike the Zoroastrianism of this period, both Manichaeism and Christianity claimed a universality for its message, a universality buttressed by the profane learning of the time, and it may be that Shapur's intent was to revise the image and appeal of Zoroastrianism by a similar incorporation of learned material from outside the Iranian tradition.

A number of sources suggest that there was a xenophobic reaction under the successors of Shapur, and the *Denkart* is silent on this period. With Khusraw I Anosharvan (A.D. 531–687), however, the

33. R. C. Zaehner (trans.), *Zurvan*, p. 8.
34. See H.-C. Puech, *Le Manichéisme. Son Fondateur. Sa Doctrine* (Paris, 1949), nn. 188, 189.

Denkart resumes its theme.[35] Here Khusraw appears the fierce pursuer of heretics (Mazdakites?), but there is quite divergent testimony elsewhere. One of his own edicts proclaims: "Those who say that it is possible to understand Being through the revelation of Religion and also by analogy, are to be deemed Researchers (after truth),"[36] Here we see raised the question of reason and revelation, a question that was to plague Islam during all of its dealings with the *falāsifah*, and Khusraw's settlement of it by admitting analogy, the Greeks' *syllogistike*, and the Arabs' *qiyās*, as a source of religious truth.

This is quite in keeping with the Khusraw of the Greek historians. Procopius describes him as a kind of philosopher-king investigating the heavenly phenomena and concerned with theological problems.[37] Agathias is even more specific.[38] He states that Khusraw had works of Greek philosophy translated for himself and became skilled in Aristotle and Plato, so that "not even the *Timaeus* escaped him"; a considerable feat indeed!

There is reason to believe that the Sassanian Shah had skilled instructors to guide him in his Hellenic interests. In A.D. 529 Justinian had closed the philosophical school at Athens,[39] and as a result sometime after Khusraw's accession in A.D. 531 members of the faculty took up residence in Persia, the best known being Damascus, the eminent Aristotelian commentator Simplicius, and Priscian.[40] We do not know the duration of this curious sojourn—it was probably not very long—but it points to an intellectual freedom which belies the *Denkart's* portrait of Khusraw as a witch burner.

There are still other documents dating from his reign that confirm the philosophical and philhellenic interests of Khusraw.[41] A

35. Madan (ed.), *Denkart*, p. 413. 11.9ff.
36. Zaehner, (trans.), *Zurvan*, p. 48.
37. *Anecdota*, XVIII, par. 29. It was a thriving time for imperial intellectuals, though Procopius had some reservations on the theology emanating from the palace in Constantinople.
38. Agathias, II, par. 2.
39. Malalas, XVIII, 451.
40. Agathias, II, par. 30.
41. Of the Greek philosophers only Priscian left a direct memorial of his stay in Persia. His *Solutiones eorum de quibus dubitavit Chosroes Persarum rex*, preserved only in Latin, has been edited by I. Bywater in *Supplementum Aristotelicum*, I, 2 (Berlin, 1886). All of Simplicius' commentaries on Aristotle probably date from after his return.

contemporary was the philosopher and theologian Paul the Persian or Paul of Nisibis (d. A.D. 571). At an earlier stage in his career he was in Constantinople engaged in theological debates with the Manichaeans,[42] but later when he moved his field of operations back to his native soil, he aspired, according to Barhebraeus,[43] to be Catholicos, and when he was disappointed in this hope he apostatized to Zoroastrianism. Paul is the author of an exegetical work in the style of Theodore of Mopsuestia, but what concerns us here are his philosophical treatises. While in Persia, he composed (originally in Persian?) an introduction to logic, now preserved in Syriac[44] and a commentary on the *De interpretatione* later translated from Pahlevi into Syriac by Severus Sebokht (d. A.D. 667).[45]

At the same time, interest in India increased. According to a later Arab account, Burzoe, a physician of the time of Khusraw, hearing of a herb that revivified the dead, traveled to India in search of it, only to discover that the herb was of the *genus allegoricum*: the restorer of the "dead" was the collection of fables known in Sanscrit as the *Pañčatantra*, and in Arabic as *Kalīlah wa Dimnah*.[46] The *Kalīlah* has had an interesting history, passing from Burzoe's Pahlevi *Vorlage* into a Syriac[47] and an Arabic version,[48] the latter by Ibn al-Muqaffaʿ, but it is the autobiographical preface that Burzoe attached to his translation that is eloquent of the kind of intellectualistic humanism that prevailed at the court, and which provided the necessary seedbed for Hellenism in an alien culture, whether it be under the Zoroastrian Shah Khusraw or the Muslim Caliph al-Maʾmūn.[49]

42. See Beck, *Theologische Literatur*, p. 386.
43. *Chronicon Ecclesiasticum*, II, 97.
44. J. P. Land (ed.), *Anecdota Syriaca*, IV (Leyden, 1875).
45. MSS in Georr, *Catégories*, pp. 25–26.
46. So Thaʿālibi, *Ghurar*, ed. Zotenberg, pp. 629–33.
47. Done by a certain "Bud" in pre-Islamic times, and J. Bickell (ed.), *Der Buch von Kalilag und Damnag* (Leipzig, 1876); see F. Schultess, *Kalila und Damna* (Berlin, 1911); *GSL*, pp. 124–25.
48. L. Cheiko (ed.), (Beyrouth, 1908); see M. Minovi, "The Abridged Version of *Kalila wa Dimna* by al-Maʾmūn the Caliph," *Akten des Vierundzwanzigsten Internationalen Orientalen-Kongresses München* (Wiesbaden, 1959), pp. 316–18.
49. For an evaluation of the intellectual atmosphere under Shapur in terms of Burzoe's preface see T. Nöldeke, *Burzoes Einleitung zu dem Buche Kalila Dimna übersetzt und erläutert* (Straßburg, 1912); A. Christensen, "La legende du sage Buzurjmihr," *Acta Orientalia*, VIII (1929), 81–128, espec. pp. 104 ff.; P. Kraus, *RSO*, XIV (1933–1934), 14–20.

One may cite in evidence both the Pahlevi *Denkart*[50] and the *Bundahishn*,[51] both of which contain material that antedates their early Islamic recension and is at the same time derived from other than purely Iranian sources.

The final act in the Hellenic drama is played out under Khusraw II Parvez (A.D. 590–628), "that flashy and deplorable monarch," as Zaehner characterizes him,[52] astrologer, brother-in-law, and erstwhile protégé of the Byzantine Emperor Maurice, perhaps even a Christian himself, but at least a devotee of Saint Sergius and his shrine of Rusafah (Sergiopolis).[53]

There is little or no evidence for assessing the intellectual results of this intensely personal eclecticism on the part of Khusraw Parvez. In A.D. 604 hostilities broke out once again between the Byzantines and Sassanians, and one must conclude that the Hellenophile period in Persia was ended for once and for all. Its fluctuations cannot be traced in detail, but for two intervals, the reigns of Shapur I and Khusraw I, there is good reason to think that Iran was open to the most diverse kinds of influences: Indian, Greek, Christian,[54] and, almost fatally for Zoroastrianism, the teachings of Mani.

50. See J. Tavadia, *Die Mittelpersische Sprache*, pp. 45–73, and J.-P. De Menasce, *Une encyclopédie mazdéene. Le Denkart* (Paris, 1958); on the author's knowledge of Greek philosophy, H. W. Bailey, *Zoroastrian Problems*, pp. 81–92.

51. See Tavadia, *op. cit.*, pp. 74–82, espec. pp. 77–78 where it is a question of some of the profane material in the *Bundahishn* being used by the Muslim Iranophile Ḥamzah al-Isfahāni (d. *ca.* A.D. 961). Ḥamzah is an interesting example of the catholicity of early Islamic scholarship. In addition to being able to dip into the *Bundahishn*, he had his own private Greek sources. For a translation of his historical material on the Byzantine Emperors he turned to the household of the Caliphal Prefect in Isfahan where one of the servants could read and write Greek. Ḥamzah's informant knew but little Arabic, however, and so his bilingual son served as a second intermediary. The father read from the Greek historians, the son translated orally into Arabic, and Ḥamzah noted down the pertinent material; see Ḥamzah, *Ta'r kh* (ed. Gottwaldt), p. 70.

52. See *Zurvan*, p. 51.

53. See Theophylact, *Historiae*, IV, 14; V, 1, 13, 15; T. Nöldeke, *Geschichte der Perser und Araber zur Zeit der Sasaniden* (Leyden, 1879), pp. 287, n. 2, and 304; for the connection with St. Sergius: Evagrius, *Hist. Eccles.*, VI, 21, and P. Peeters, "Les ex-voto de Khosrau Aparwez a Sergiopolis," *Analecta Bollandiana*, LXV (1947), 5–56, Rusafah was more than a retreat for a Sassanian religious eclectic; it was also the shrine and center where the semi-nomadic Arab auxiliaries of the Byzantines, the Ghassanids, pursued their Christian devotions, and, as such one of the possible areas through which Christian doctrine and ritual, filtered down into the Hejaz and into the awareness of the Prophet; see J. Sauvaget, "Les Ghassanides et Sergiopolis," *Byzantion*, XIV (1939), 115–30.

54. It was almost certainly under Khusraw Anosharvan that the Nestorian community had

Whatever Mani's (A.D. 216–276) own plans were for the conversion of the Shah[55] and the usurpation of Zoroastrianism's place as the state religion, Manichaeism had its greatest success not in Mesopotamia, but as a missionary religion in the West[56] and as a rival with Nestorianism in Central and East Asia. It is this latter developement that is important here since Manicheism is essentially eclectic in nature and thus, like Nestorianism and Zoroastrianism, was one of the factors in the philosophical and theological acculturation of the East before Islam.

The doctrines of Mani are gnostic at root[57] and hence represent a systematized body of knowledge in which consists the *gnosis* that saves. This, in its soteriological, and particularly its cosmological and philosophical aspects, is taken in part from orthodox Christianity and its gnostic outgrowths, both of which had already supplied themselves with an intellectual understructure derived from Greek philosophy. To this same extent, then, Manichaeism was a potential carrier of certain philosophical positions—Neoplatonic, to be sure, rather than Aristotelian—into the Iranian hinterland.

These positions were embodied in the writings of Mani,[58] "the Apostle of Jesus Christ," and "the Seal of the Prophets." Manichaeism, as later Islam was to do, prided itself on being a Religion of the Book because its Prophet had committed his teachings to writing and not allowed them to suffer the corruption that is inherent in an oral tradition. The writings of Mani, all but one originally composed in

the Psalms translated into Pahlevi, probably for missionary activity in areas where Christianity had outdistanced the Syriac language sphere. Fragments of this version have been found in Turkestan; see F. C. Andreas and K. Barr, "Bruchstücke einer Pahlevi-Übersetzung der Psalmen," *SbAWBerlin* (1933), pp. 91–152.

55. The one work he wrote in Persian, the *Shahpuhragan*, was dedicated to Shapur I with whom Mani had a colloquium sometime after he began his ministry in A.D. 242; see H.-C. Puech, *Manichéisme* (Paris, 1949), p. 45.

56. After its spread and inital check by Christianity in the sixth century—Augustine was part of this early harvest—it reappeared in a mitigated form as Paulicianism in the seventh century, in the tenth century as Bogomilism in the Balkans, and in the south of France as Albigensianism up to the fifteenth century.

57. On the system see H. J. Polotsky, art. "Manichäismus," *R-E*, Suppl. VI (1935), 240–71; H.-C. Puech, *op. cit.*; H. H. Schaeder, "Urform und Fortbildungen des manichäischen Systems," *Vorträge der Bibliothek Warburg*, IV (1924–1925), 65–157.

58. Syncretism is a continuing process and much of it went on after Mani; see Puech, *op. cit.*, p. 70, and Schaeder, *art. cit.*, p. 155.

Syriac, are but fragmentally preserved, and this not entirely in the language of their original composition. Manichaeism's adulation of the Book differed from the Arabs' in that it did not extend to the language. Mani's apostle to the east, Mar Ammo, made Parthian the language of the church, and as the tide rolled on, this was replaced, probably in the second half of the sixth century, by still another Iranian dialect, Sogdian.[59]

Manichaeism found fertile soil in eastern Iran and beyond.[60] Mar Ammo had preached in Merv, thence the church, which saw its mission as a universal one, crossed the Oxus into Sogdian linguistic territories: Bukhara and Samarqand. When the Chinese Buddhist pilgrim Hüen-tsang visited the regions south and east of the Oxus *ca.* A.D. 630, he found that Manichaeism was the chief religion of the area.[61] By the end of the century it had reached China.[62] In A.D. 763 the Khan of the Uighurs, a Turkish people of Mongolia, was converted, and his tribes with him. This probably marks the apogee of Manichaeism in central Asia. In A.D. 840 the Uighurs were destroyed by the Chinese, and in the west of Iran the church was being submerged by Islam. But in the interval the Sogdians, the commercial middlemen of central Asia,[63] had spread Manichaeism over a wide area. Their memorials are the extensive finds of Manichaean manuscripts, chiefly written in Sogdian, that have come to light in Chinese Turkestan.[64] Their aggressive proselytizing instinct was re-

59. See W. B. Henning, *BSCAS*, XXI (1947), 49; *idem*, *Sogdica* (London, 1940), pp. 12–13

60. See H. H. Schaeder, "der Manichäismus und sein Weg nach Osten," *Festschrift Friedrich Gogarten* (Gießen, 1948), pp. 236–54.

61. The important account of his travels has been translated by S. Julien, *Voyages des Pélerins Bouddhistes* (3 vols.; Paris, 1853–1858), preceded, in Vol. I, by a biography of Hüen-tsang by Hui-Li.

62. See E. Chavannes and P. Pelliot, "Un traité manichéen retrouvé en Chine," *JA*, Sér. 10, Vol. XVIII (1911), 499–617; Sér. 11, Vol. I (1913), 99–199, 261–394, espec. pp. 376–77. Another mission from Sogdia arrived in A.D. 719, this one, it should be noted, headed by an astronomer. The Manichaeans had anticipated the same scientific approach to the Chinese later developed by Matthew Ricci and other Jesuit missionaries of the sixteenth and seventeenth centuries; see Chavannes and Pelliot, *op. cit.*, pp. 152–53.

63. See Ṭabari, II, 1186; according to Ibn al-Athīr, V, 54ff. the Sogdians became Muslims for economic reasons. General material on Sogdian history, language, and literature has been collected in R. Frye, *JAOS*, LXIII (1943), 14–16; M. J. Dresden, *Ex Oriente Lux* (1942), pp. 729–34; *idem*, *Bibliotheca Orientalis*, VI (1949), 28–31.

64. The work on these documents is surveyed by W. Lentz, *ZDMG*, CVI (1957), 3*–22*.

pressed with the coming of Islam and the first years of purely Arab domination. But later, with the accession of the Iranian Samanid dynasty (A.D. 864–1005), the Sogdians once again pursued their missionary ways, now on behalf of Islam, and the result was the conversion, in A.D. 960, of the Qarakhanids, the first Turkish people to become Muslims.[65]

Finally, some mention should be made of the ebbing influence of Buddhism during this period. Mahayana Buddhists had penetrated the area during the Kushan period (135 B.C.–A.D. 425), and its influence had crested under the aggressive Kushan ruler Kanishka (*fl. ca.* A.D. 120–162) when it became the dominant religion of the Kushans, and spread north across the Oxus into Sogdia and Kashgaria as well.[66] The way to China now lay open, and in the course of the sixth century, Buddhists followed the classical transit through Turkish tribes of the Tarim Basin into Chinese territory.[67]

These new roots were put down at an opportune time since, in the following century, the central-Asian Buddhist communities were being pressed by the Zoroastrian and Manichaean competition, particularly in Sogdia where the Chinese pilgrim Hüen-tsang found the situation in Samarqand *ca.* A.D. 630 serious in the extreme. Things were better south of the Oxus, and Buddhist strength in Balkh and Kabul persisted until the Arab conquest and beyond.[68] There were Buddhist temples and monasteries on these sites, and the buildings were sometimes turned into mosques at the arrival of the Muslims.[69]

65. See W. Barthold, *Histoire des Turcs d'Asie Centrale*, trans. M. Donskis (Paris, 1945), pp. 48–49; *idem*, *ZA*, XXVI (1911), 252, 262; the intellectual life under the Samanids is touched upon on p. 54 below.

66. See the excellent survey by A. von Gabain, "Der Buddhismus in Zentralasien," in *Handbuch der Orientalistik*, VIII, 2 (Leyden, 1961), 496–514.

67. See Liu Mau Tsai, *Die chinesischen Nachrichten zur Geschichte der Ost-Türken*, I (Wiesbaden, 1956), 461–62.

68. See W. Fuchs, *SbAWBerlin* (1938), pp. 426–69, espec. pp. 448–51 (an account of another Buddhist pilgrim, Huei-ch'ao, who visited the area in A.D. 726); W. Barthold, "Der iranische Buddhismus und sein Verhältnis zum Islam," *Oriental Studies in honour of C.E. Pavry* (London, 1933), pp. 29–32; B. Spuler, *Iran in frühislamischer Zeit* (Wiesbaden, 1952), pp. 217–20.

69. B. Spuler, *loc. cit.*

Even more importantly, the Buddhist *Vihara* or school may have provided the original pattern for the later Muslim *madrasah*.[70]

Eastern Iran, then, was not a waste, nor were the caravan cities, which skirted the southern edge of the steppe, completely lacking in culture before Islam. Four sophisticated religions were in competition there, each possessing a body of Scripture, i.e., a literary tradition, with appropriate methods of exegesis, and incorporating a considerable body of profane learning: cosmology, astronomy, philosophy, and medicine, some of it Iranian, some Indian, and a good deal of it Greek. Very little of this Greek inheritance was in its natural textual state; there is no evidence, for instance, that any of the texts of Aristotle were circulating in translation, save, perhaps, within the narrow confines of intellectual circles in the Sassanian capital. What there was of Hellenic thought had been assimilated into the various religious systems as organic parts; if it sacrificed something in purity, it undoubtedly gained in longevity.

None of this completely disappeared when the Arabs came in the seventh and ninth centuries. The sudden appearance of men of culture and learning in these very same lands under Islam must in some sense be a historical illusion fostered by a deficiency of historical and biographical records before the ninth century. The list of these Eastern savants,[71] and they, together with the Nestorian community of Jundishapur-Baghdad comprise most of the scholars working in the Hellenic sciences, is ample enough testimony to the presence of some kind of fructifying tradition in the East.

It is also noteworthy that the Caliph under whom the great flowering of Greek studies took place in Baghdad, al-Ma'mūn, had lived for a considerable period in Khorasan and had close ties to the Iranian tradition.[72] Most of the early patrons of these same sciences were likewise from the East. Theodore abū Qurrah dedicated his

70. W. Barthold, *Four Studies on the History of Central Asia*, trans. V. and T. Minorsky, I (Leyden, 1956), 4–5; see pp.53–54 below.
71. For a general sampling see G. Wiet, *Soieries persanes* (Cairo, 1947), pp. 147–63.
72. See Spuler, *op. cit.*, pp. 56–57. His court astrologer was a Persian Zoroastrian: *Fihrist*, p. 143; al-Bayhaqi, *Tatimmat*, # 15.

translation of the pseudo-Aristotelian *De virtutibus* to the governor of Khorasan, Tāhir ibn al-Ḥusayn, and particularly under the native Iranian dynasty of the Samanids a whole series of works were patronized: Muḥammad ibn Zakarīyā al-Rāzi's *Kitāb al-Manṣūr* and *Kitāb al-asrār*, al-Khawarizmi's *Mafātīh al-ʿulūm*, and the Persian *Ajāʾib al-buldān* by Abū al-Muʿayyad al-Balkhi, to cite but a few. It was in the library of the Samanid Nūḥ II (A.D. 976–997) that the young Ibn Sīnā received his first revelation of the riches of the intellectual life. The passage occurs in his autobiography:

> *Now the Sultan of Bukhara at that time was Nūḥ ibn Manṣūr. . . . One day I asked his leave to enter their library, to examine the contents and read the books on medicine; he granted my request, and I entered a mansion with many chambers, each chamber having chests of books piled one upon another. In one apartment were books on language and poetry, in another law, and so on; each apartment has set aside for books on a single science. I glanced through the catalogue of the works of the ancient Greeks, and asked for those which I required; and I saw books whose very names are as yet unknown to many—works which I had never seen before and have not seen since. I read these books taking notes of their contents; I came to realize the place each man occupied in his particular science.*[73]

It is difficult ot believe that this is a completely new tradition. Ruska and others[74] are right in turning the attention of students of the intellectual life of early Islam away from the Aramaic areas to those farther east. But just as in the Aramaic regions, the ground in the East had been prepared over the course of six centuries by a variety of ingredients, among which was Hellenism. The striking intellectual vitality of the newly appeared Islam was due partly to this long-range preparation of the perennially fertile cultural ground of the Near East, but also to the sudden "second birth" of Hellenism which followed upon the new translations of Aristotle in Baghdad.

73. Uṣ., II, 4; A. J. Arberry (trans.), *Avicenna on Theology*, pp. 12–13.
74. *Tabula Smarigdana* (Heidelberg, 1926), pp. 167–76.

BIBLIOGRAPHICAL NOTE

SYRIAC SCHOLASTICISM

The first to address himself to a study of the Peripatetic tradition in Syriac was E. Renan, *De philosophia peripatetica apud Syros* (Paris, 1852), the chief source for two subsequent survey articles:

C. Sauter, "Die peripatetische Philosophie bei den Syrern und Arabern," *AGP*, n.f. X (1904), 516–33.

G. Klinge, "Die Bedeutung der syriachen Theologen als Vermittler der griechischen Philosophie an den Islam," *Zeitschrift für Kirchengeschichte*, LVIII (1939), 346–86.

Since the time of Renan the bulk of the original work has been done by two men:

A. Baumstark, *Aristoteles bei den Syrern vom V–VIII Jahrhundert* (Leipzig, 1900).

Idem, "Griechische Philosophen und ihre Lehren in syrischer Überlieferung," *Oriens Christianus*, V (1905), 1–25.

G. Furlani, "Meine Arbeiten über die Philosophie bei den Syrern," *AGP*, XXXVII (1925), 2–25.

Idem, "I miei lavori dal 1925 al 1940 sulla filosofia greca presso i Syri," *Rivista di Filologia e d'Instruzione classica*, LXIX (1941), 121–49.

III

THE EASTERN TRANSLATION MOVEMENT

The course of Peripateticism in the East shows a remarkable series of parallels with its counterpart in the medieval West. And the most striking and, indeed, the most fundamental parallelism is the fact that in both instances the Aristotelian tradition is represented by an important translation movement extending over rather long periods of time. In the West it began about AD. 355 with the Latin translations of the *Categoriae* by Marius Victorinus, continued through the career of Boethius, who began his planned translation of the entire *Organon* in A.D. 507, experienced a fresh impetus in the middle of the twelfth century, and again in the thirteenth century on this occasion in the person of the Flemish Dominican William of Moerbeke, and did not end until well into the Renaissance.[1]

The Eastern translation of Aristotle began about A.D. 450, not, however, into Arabic, but into Syriac. It was about this time that a certain Probha, "chief physician and archdeacon of Antioch," translated the *De interpretatione* and the *Analytica priora* into Syriac.[2] For the later philosophical movement in Islam the significance of the earliest versions' being Syriac rather than Arabic is rather minimal since, in any event, the shading off from Syriac speaker to Arabic speaker

1. The translation history of the individual works in the Aristotelian *corpus* has generated an imposing bibliography of its own; see F. E. Peters, *Aristoteles Orientalis* (Leyden, 1968). Further details on the Western translation movement will be found in the Epilogue below.
2. The translation are not easily identified. The Probha problem is reviewed in Tkatsch, *Poetik*, I, 58a–62a.

after the Muslim conquest was quite gradual. Not only were the later Arabic translations done from intermediary Syriac versions, but during the *Hochscholastik* in Islam most of the best men working in philosophy were effectively and actively bilingual.

The position held by Boethius in the West is roughly that of Sergius of Rish ʿayna (d. A.D. 536)[3] and the translators trained in the school of Qennesre in Syria by Severus Sebokht: Athanasius of Balad (d. A.D. 696), James of Edessa (d. A.D. 708), and George, Bishop of the Arabs (d. A.D. 724), all translators of the Logic. Neither the Syrian philosopher-theologians nor the early Western scholastics knew the entire *Organon*. The *logica vetus* in use in the West from Boethius to *ca.* A.D. 1130 covered only the *Eisagoge*, *Categoriae*, and the *De interpretatione*.[4] The Syrians went a little further, including *Analytica priora*, I, 1–7.[5] The reason they stopped here, al-Fārābi explains,[6] was that they felt that to read the rest of the work would be prejudical to their faith. Another explanation is even more probable: the Syrians, whose primary interest in this area was scriptural exegesis and not philosophy, were following the academic techniques used since Hellenistic times to explicate the merely *verbal* difficulties of a given text. The *De interpretatione* is the preserve of the philologist: beginning with the *Analytica*, the analysis becomes more philosophical, and hence of less interest to the exegete, whether of Alexandria or Qennesre.

The beginnings of the Aristotelian translation movement in Islam are exceedingly obscure. There is no evidence that Aristotle was translated during the period when the Umayyads ruled in Damas-

3. Sergius, the most prolific and versatile of the Syriac translators of Aristotle, also produced versions of Dionysius Thrax, Porphyry, Ptolemy, Isocrates, Themistius, Plutarch, the *Geoponica*, and various collections of *Sententiae*. Two full-length studies have been devoted to Sergius: A. Baumstark, *Lucubrationes Syro-Graecae* (*Suppl. Jahrb. für klass. Philol.*, XXI (1894), 353–524), and V. Ryssel, *Über die textkritischen Werth der syrischen Übersetzungen griechischen*, Klassiker, I–II (Leipzig, 1880–1881). Further bio-bibliographical material in *GSL*, pp. 167–69, and Tkatsch, *Poetik*, I, 66a–74a.

4. The earliest recorded use of the entire *Organon* occurs in the *Heptateuchon* of Thierry of Chartres, written *ca.* A.D. 1135–1141.

5. An exception to this self-imposed restriction is Sergius' translation of the *De mundo*.

6. Uṣ., II, 135.

cus,[7] but as soon as the center of the empire was moved to Baghdad under the Abbasids, a paradoxical shift away from the Hellenized littoral of Syria and into the Iranian hinterland, the Arabic versions of Aristotle begin appearing. The two facts are connected. The translation movement was not, in the first instance, dependent upon contact with the older Hellenic centers like Alexandria and Antioch, but rather with the Hellenized Syro-Christian communities in Iraq. Under the Caliph al-Manṣūr (A.D. 754–775) the Syriac Christian Jūrjīs ibn Bakhtīshūʿ, head of the hospital at Jundishapur, was summoned to be court physician at Baghdad.[8] The date was A.D. 765 and it is probably the single most important one in the translation movement. The Baghdad-Jundishapur relationship was to be a lasting one: other members of his illustrious family succeeded Jūrjīs at court and, with the exception of the dubious case of Ibn al-Muqaffaʿ, most of the following translators were Syriac-speaking Christians or neo-Muslims trained in Jundishapur medical circles.

The Baghdad translation movement had three distinct phases. The first, beginning with Ibn al-Muqaffaʿ[9] or his son under al-Manṣūr, included Ibn Nāʿimah[10] and Eustathius,[11] both of whom translated for al-Kindi, the student of John of Damascus and Bishop of Harran, Theodore abū Qurrah, [12] the Sabian mathematician Thābit ibn

7. There was translation activity under the Umayyads, but it did not concern Aristotle. Under the Caliph ʿUmar ibn ʿAbd al-Azīz (A.D. 701–720) the Jewish physician Masarjawayh translated from Greek into Arabic the *Pandects* of Ahron of Alexandria; see Ibn Juljul, *Ṭabaqāt*, p. 61; Ritter-Walzer, "Stambuler Bibliotheken," p. 831; *GSL*, p. 189, and B. Hemmerdinger, *BZ*, LV (1962), 66. In al-Jāḥiz, *Kitāb al-ḥayawān* (ed., Cairo, A.H. 1323), I, 38, there is a list of translators in which a "Khālid" is mentioned as a translator of Plato. That this is, as has sometimes been maintained, the Umayyad prince Khālid ibn Yazīd is unlikely; see P. Kraus, *RSO*, XIV (1933), 3, n. 6.

8. Biography of Jūrjīs in Uṣ., I, 123–25.

9. *GAL*, I², 158, Suppl. I, pp. 233–37; D. Sourdel, "La Biographie d'Ibn al-Muqaffaʿ d'après les sources anciennes," *Arabica*, I (1954), 307–23. Ibn al-Muqaffaʿ, from a Zoroastrian family of Fars, is the most enigmatic figure connected with the translation movement. His obvious and presuasive connection with *Iranica* rather than *Hellenica* has cast doubt on the ascription to him of Aristotelian translations from the Greek, but his interest in Greek philosophy is confirmed from other sources.

10. *Fihrist*, pp. 249, 250; Uṣ., I, 204; *GAL*, I², 222, Suppl. I, pp. 364–65; *GCAL*, II, 228–29.

11. *Fihrist*, p. 251; *GAL*, Suppl. I, pp. 363–64; *GCAL*, II, 256–57; Bouyges, *Notice*, pp. cxviii–cxxi.

12. *GCAL*, II 7–21; Beck, *Theologische Literatur*, pp. 488–89; D. M. Dunlop, *JRAS* (1959), p. 145, n. 3; I. Dick, *Proche-Orient Chrétien*, XII (1962), 209–23.

Qurrah,[13] and Ibn al-Biṭrīq,[14] a member of the circle of the Caliph al-Ma'mūn. The reign of the liberal, Muʿtazilite-leaning Ma'mūn (A.D. 813–833) who founded a research center in Baghdad[15] marks the watershed between the older, more literal type translations,[16] the Islamic *veteres*, and the more polished versions done in the school of Ḥunayn ibn Isḥāq (d. A.D. 876)[17] which was directly connected with the study and practice of medicine in Baghdad and environs, and whose translation activity embraced Galen and the Greek physicians, as well as Aristotle.

The third phase of translations, the *recentiores*, were more frequently revisons and school editions of the older versions at the hands of members of the Baghdad philosophical circle *ca.* A.D. 900–1020: Abū Bishr Mattā (d. A.D. 940),[18] al-Fārābi (d. A.D. 950),[19] Yaḥyā ibn ʿAdi (d. A.D. 974),[20] Abū Sulaymān al-Sijistāni (d. *ca.* A.D. 985),[21] Ibn Zurʿah (d. A.D. 1008),[22] Ibn Suwār (d. A.D. 1017),[23] and Abū al-Faraj

13. Ḥunayn, *Risālah*, # 113; Ibn Juljul, *Ṭabaqāt*, p. 75; Bayhaqi, *Tatimmat*, # 4; Barhebraeus, *Chronicon Syriacum* (trans. Budge), pp. 152–53; *Fihrist*, p. 272; Qifṭi, pp. 115–22; Uṣ., I, 215–18; *GAL*, I², 241–44, Suppl. I, pp. 384–86; Chwolsohn, *Ssabier*, pp. 546–67; Meyerhof, *Isis*, VIII (1926), 705; Ritter-Walzer, "Stambuler Bibliotheken," pp. 831–32.

14. Ibn Juljul, *Ṭabaqāt*, pp. 67–68; Ḥunayn, *Risālah*, # 83; Qifṭi, p. 379; Uṣ., I, 205; *GAL*, Suppl. I, pp. 364, 955; *GCAL*, II, 32, 113; Meyerhof, *Isis*, VIII (1926), 705; Ritter-Walzer, "Stambuler Bibliotheken," p. 827; D. M. Dunlop, "The Translations of al-Biṭrīq and Yaḥyā (Yuḥannā) b. al-Biṭrīq," *JRAS* (1959), pp. 140–50.

15. Muʿtazilite activity under Ma'mūn is described by Musʿudi, *Murūj*, VIII, 301.

16. There is a list of these early translators, many of them mere names, in *Fihrist*, p. 244.

17. The bibliographical material on this truly remarkable scholar, physician, and translator has been collected by G. Gabrieli, "Ḥunayn ibn Isḥāq," *Isis*, IV (1924), 282–92, by Lutfi Sadi, "A Bio-bibliographical study of Ḥunayn ibn Isḥāq al-Ibadi," *Bulletin of the History of Medicine*, II (1934), 409–46, and in Meyerhof's notes to al-Bayḥaqi's *Tatimmat* in *Osiris*, VIII (1948), 122–217. His translation group, including his son Isḥāq ibn Ḥunayn, is treated in Meyerhof, "Ḥunayn and his Period."

18. *Fihrist*, pp. 263–64; al-Bayḥaqi, *Tatimmat*, # 14; al-Qifṭi, p. 323; Uṣ, I, 235; Barhebraeus, *Ta'rīkh*, pp. 285, 296; al-Tawḥīdi, *Imtāʿ*, I, 111–112; GAL, I², 228, Suppl. I², p. 370; Tkatsch, *Poetik*, I, 126a–128a, 148a–149b; *GCAL*, II, 153–54.

19. See p. 161, n. 120 below.

20. *Fihrist*, p. 264; al-Masʿūdi, *Tanbīh* (trans. de Vaux), p. 171; al-Bayḥaqi, *Tatimmat*, # 48; al-Tawḥīdi, *Imtāʿ*, I, 37; al-Qifṭi, pp. 361–64; Uṣ., I, 235; *GAL*, I², 228, Suppl. I², pp. 370, 956; Meyerhof, Alexandrien nach Baghdad," pp. 417–18; *GCAL*, II, 233–49; Jugie, *Theologia*, V, 468–69.

21. See pp. 162–163, 176 below.

22. *Fihrist*, p. 264; al-Bayḥaqi, *Tatimmat*, #30; al-Qifṭi, pp. 245–46; Uṣ., I, 235; al-Tawhīdi, *Imtā*, I, 33; Barhebraeus, Ta'rīkh, pp. 315–16; Yāqūt, *Irshād*, V, 494–506; *GAL*, I², 229, Suppl. I, p. 371; *GCAL*, II, 252–56; Jugie, *Theologica*, V, 470; S. Pines, "La loi naturelle et la société: La doctrine politico-théologique d'Ibn Zurʿa, philosophe chrétien de Baghdad," *Studies in Islamic History and Civilization* (Jerusalem, 1961).

23. *Fihrist*, pp. 245, 265; al-Qifṭi, p. 164; Uṣ., I, 323, al-Tawḥīdi, *Imtāʿ*, I, 33–34; *GAL*, I²,

ibn al-Ṭayyib (d. A.D. 1043).[24] These later versions bear witness not only to the heightened technical mastery of the apparatus of textual criticism,[25] but also to more purely philosophical and pedagogical interest than had their ninth-century predecessors, an interest directly connected with the beginning of more formal philosophical studies in Baghdad *ca.* A.D. 900.

By the middle of the eleventh century the translation movement was over; during its three-hundred-year duration it carried into Arabic every extant Aristotelian treatise except the *Politica,* and a great mass of *pseudepigraphica* besides.

Two important sources testify to the really careful work that went into the preparation of a textual base for these translations. Little is known of the textual preliminaries for the *veteres,* but Ḥunayn has left a detailed document in which he describes some of the techniques used in putting together a text.[26] How these worked out in practice can be seen in the critical and textual notes appended to the various extant translations, notably the *Organon* collection in Paris BN 2346, put together by scholars of the Peripatetic school of Baghdad.

The first stage was the search for the manuscripts. Undoubtedly many of the translations were done from whatever manuscripts chanced to be at hand, but there was also a realization that the quality of the translation depended on the number and quality of the manuscripts upon which it was based. The older Greek cultural center

236, Suppl. I, p. 378; Meyerhof, "Alexandrien nach Baghdad," p. 421; Walzer, *Oriens,* VI (1953), 97, n. 1; B. Lewin, "L'idéal antique du philosophe dans la philosophie arabe. Un traité d'ethique du philosphe Baghdadien Ibn Suwār," *Lychnos* (1954–1955), pp. 267–84; *idem,* "La notion de *muhdath* dans la *kalām et* dans la philosophie," in *Donum Natalicum H. S. Nyberg Oblatum* (Uppsala, 1954), pp. 84–93.

24. *Tatimmat* # 23; al-Qifṭi, p. 223; Uṣ., I, 239–41; Barhebraeus, *Ta'rīkh,* pp. 330–31; *GAL,* I², 635, Suppl. I, p. 884; *GCAL,* II, 160–177; Meyerhof, "Alexandrien nach Baghdad," p. 425; S. Pines, *AHDL,* XXIX (1952), 16–21, 35–37.

25. The best appreciation of the work done in this school of translators, editors, and exegetes is that of R. Walzer, "New Light on the Arabic Translation of Aristotle," *Oriens,* VI (1953), 91–142, reprinted, with additions, in *Greek into Arabic* (Cambridge, Mass.: 1962), pp. 60–113.

26. His *Risālah* was intended to give a survey of his translation efforts on the Galenic *corpus,* but it is filled with textual information of a more general nature; it has been edited and translated by G. Bergsträsser, *Hunain ibn Ishaq über die syrischen und arabischen Galen-Übersetzungen* (Leipzig, 1925).

now in Muslim hands were searched,[27] and there were even expeditions into Byzantine territory.[28]

Whatever could be found was collated (*qābala*). Ḥunayn's technique was to employ an oral collation; an assistant read one manuscript and he checked the readings in his own copy.[29] The collation process included not only the Greek manuscripts but also the *lemmata* in the Greek commentators and whatever Syriac versions were available.[30]

The result was an eclectic base that was essentially the Aristotelian text as studied in the Greek schools, and the value of the Arabic *testimonia* for a reconstruction of the Greek text lies precisely in this *quality* of the manuscript tradition. Whatever the age of the Arabic manuscript, it represents an "arrested" tradition uncorrupted by any Greek recension later than the sixth century.[31] Nor were the variants discarded; the margins of the Paris *Organon* are filled with the variant readings from the older versions.[32] Later, Ibn Rushd, looking at the text as an exegete rather than an editor, would cite the variants where they had a bearing on the interpretation. In his *Great Commentary* on the *De anima*, for example, he uses an unidentified translation as the basis for his comment, and cites the variants from Isḥāq's version in the body of the *lectio*.[33]

27. Ḥunayn, *Risālah*, # 115 mentions Mesopotamia, Syria, Palestine, and Egypt "as far as Alexandria"; he finally found the elusive manuscript in Damascus.

28. *Fihrist*, p. 243, a foray now connected with a collection of MSS in Constantinople under Leo the Armenian in A.D. 814; see B. Hemmerdinger, *BZ*, LV (1962), 66–67. Compare the analogous expedition of Photius to Ṡamarra noted on p. 23 above.

29. Ḥunayn, *Risālah*, # 20. It should be recalled that in antiquity the normal method of reading was aloud, a practice that prevailed into Islamic times; see Gerhardsson, *Memory*, p. 163 and the literature cited there.

30. See, for example, *Fihrist*, p. 249, ll. 17–21, the colophon of the Paris MS of the *Topica* in Badawi, *Manṭiq Arisṭū*, II, 531–32, and that of the *Physica* from Leyden Warner 583 studied by S. M. Stern in *JRAS* (1956), pp. 31–41.

31. The best studies of this neglected side of the translation literature are connected with the *Metaphysica*: M. Bouyges, "La critique textuelle de la *Métaphysique* d'Aristote et les anciennes versions arabes," *MFO*, XXVII (1947–1948), 147–152, and R. Walzer, "On the Arabic Versions of Book A,α and Λ of Aristotle's *Metaphysics*," *Harward Studies in Classical Philology*, LXIII (1958), 217–31. The purely linguistic difficulties of a comparison of the Greek and oriental versions is touched upon on pp. 66–67 below.

32. The variants from the Syriac versions were translated into Arabic.

33. On another level Ibn Rushd shows an extremely eclectic approach to the choice of a text to be commented. The *Metaphysica* text to the *Great Commentary* on that work is sewn together from a whole series of versions, some from among the *veteres*, some from the school of Ḥunayn, some from the Peripatetic *recentioers*.

Finally the base text was translated into Arabic, usually through a Syriac intermediary. These Syriac versions produced in the school of Ḥunayn for translation into Arabic by a coworker frequently give the impression of being purely vestigial in nature, calculated to make up for the scarcity of scholars who could operate directly from the Greek.[34] In the school of Ḥunayn the process was normally handled by two men, Ḥunayn typically doing the Syriac *Vorlage*, which his son Isḥāq then turned into Arabic. Again, one of the older Syriac versions, by Athanasius of Balad, for example, might be chosen as the base for the Arabic version. In any event, if the base was felt to be unsatisfactory, Ḥunayn, for one, did not hesitate to redo the translation when better material turned up.[35] If the Baghdad Aristotelians then chose one of these Ḥunayn texts for their school edition, the version was subjected to another collation and to another painstaking revision.

Medieval students of the translation literature were well aware of the pitfalls awaiting the prospective translator. In addition to the well-worn theme of *traduttore-tradittore*[36] and a feeling of inadequacy for the demanding work,[37] there was the question of the best approach to the text. The problem is summed up by the fourteenth-century Muslim biographer al-Ṣafadi:

> *There are two methods of translations used by the translators. One is the method of Yuḥannā ibn Biṭrīq, Ibn an-Nāʿima al-Himsi, and others. According to this method the translator renders each Greek word by a single Arabic word of an exactly corresponding meaning, thus establishing the translation of one word after the other, until the whole has been translated. This method is bad on two counts. (1) There are*

34. Abūʿ Uthmān al-Dimashqi's version of the *Topica* is one of the rare translations done directly from the Greek; see the colophon to the Paris MS BN 2346 printed in Badawi, *Manṭiq Arisṭū*, II, 531–32.

35. Ḥunayn, *Risālah*, # 3.

36. See the complaint of al-Sīrāfi that the translation medium is essentially corruptive, preserved in al-Tawḥīdi's *Imtāʿ* I, 111–12.

37. The difficulties are rehearsed by Ibn Suwār in a note to the *Sophistici Elenchi* (in Georr. *Catégories*, pp. 198–99) and by Maimonides' translator Samuel ben Tibbon; see Steinschneider, *Hebr. Übers.*, p. 419.

no corresponding Arabic words for all Greek words; therefore, in this kind of translation many Greek expressions remain as they are. (2) Syntactic peculiarties and constructions are not the same in one language as in the other. Mistakes are also caused by the use of metaphors which are frequently used in all languages.
The other method of translating into Arabic is that of Ḥunayn ibn Ishāq, al-Jawhari, and others. According to this method the translator grasps in his mind the meaning of the whole sentence and then renders it by a corresponding sentence in Arabic, regardless of the congruence or lack of congruence of the individual words. This method is the better. Therefore Ḥunyn's books need no revision, except in the field of mathematics which he did not completely master.[38]

Al-Ṣafadi is somewhat conservative in his division; the extant Arabic versions of Aristotle range from the unintelligibly literal to the abusively free. But as he correctly noted, the earliest translators into Arabic, the pre-Ḥunayn *veteres* of Ibn Nā'imah, Ibn al-Biṭrīq, *et al.*, are of the literal type favored by the Syriac translators. Syriac, unlike the soul of Aristophanes, has never been a proposed site for a shrine of the Graces. It developed under the stylistic and lexicographical shadow of the Christian literature in Greek, and bears particularly strong evidence of its concern with preserving the inspired words of God, words that came to the Syrians in an alien tongue.

The concept of Scripture, both in its narrower and its wider sense plays an important role in the translation literature. The Syrians were conscious that they were dealing with a sacred text, and the translation history of the Syriac New Testament from the *da Mephareshe* to the Harclean version shows an increasingly slavish adherence to the very words of the Greek original.[39] The Harclean has as its ideal the first type of translation mentioned by al-Ṣafadi, a

38. Quoted by F. Rosenthal, *Isis*, XXXVI (1945–1946), 253. Similar divisions into the "literal" and the "free" translation can be found in Maimonides' injunction to his translator; see Steinschneider, *Hebr. Übers.*, p. 417.
39. See G. Zuntz, *The Ancestry of the Harclean New Testament* (Oxford, 1945), pp. 10–12.

word-for-word version of the original, even though it involves considerable violence to Syriac syntax and the general Semitic preference for parataxis. The Syriac Aristotle is cast in the same mold; the versions are rather straightforward, literal reproductions of the Greek text, stylistically deplorable, but otherwise excellent *testimonia* to the Greek original.

The Arabs began translating in the same fashion, usually with far less happy results since they were dealing with Syriac texts that made sense only when confronted with the Greek original. Completely lacking in a technical philosophical vocabulary of their own, the early Arabs adopted the technique described by al-Ṣafadi; they kept the transcribed Greek words or the Syriac makeshifts. The *veteres* have, for example, *qaṭighūriyās* = *kategoriai*, where a later, more sophisticated translator would use *maqūlāt*; or, again, *kiyān* = syr. *keyōnō* = *physis* instead of the later *ṭabīʿah*.[40]

From the time of Ḥunayn the versions move away from a literal adherence to the text as the emphasis shifts from a reproduction of Aristotle to an understanding of him. Aristotle was never a sacred text in Islam, nor, indeed, did the text itself become a matter of polemical importance and lead, as it did in the West, away from al-Ṣafadi's second, *ad sensum* type of translation and back to a more stringent literalism.[41] The versions produced in Baghdad *ca.* A.D. 900–1020 are faithful without being slavish; their defisiencies are not those of the translators, but stem from the radical irreducibility of the two languages in question and from the poverty of the Arabs' general background in Greek culture.

While these versions were generally faithful to the concept of a *text* to be *translated*, the Arabs very soon began cultivating another genre midway between textual reproduction and the literature of comment. Side by side with the versions were produced *summulae*,[42]

40. For the use of these lexicographical changes in dating translations see P. Kraus, *RSO*, XIV (1934), 7–10.

41. As, for example, in the movement from the freedom, in itself not staggering, of Jacobus Venticus to the closer literalness of William of Moerbeke; see L. Minio-Paluello in *Autour d'Aristote* (Louvain, 1955), p. 226, and the same author's more general assessment of translation styles in *Traditio*, VIII (1962), 288–89.

42. Called in Arabic, without an apparent difference in meaning, *mukhtaṣar* and *jawāmiʿ*.

abridged paraphrases of the text, frequently with elucidations or additions by the paraphrast. The type is rare in Syriac, Sergius' treatment of Plutarch's *De ira cohibenda* being one example,[43] but is well represented in Arabic. Ibrāhīm ibn ʿAbdullāh's version of Bk. VIII of the *Topica* approaches the paraphrase because of the translators' careful insistence on filling out Aristotle's ellipses of thought and expression. The paraphrase pure and simple is the text of the *De anima* preserved in Esc. 649[44] where the paraphrast—the manuscript identifies him as Isḥāq—begins by giving a résumé of the entire work followed by his own digression on the nobility of the science of medicine.

It is obviously difficult to render a general judgment on the value of these translations for Greek textual criticism. The standard Syriac translations—the paraphrase type apart—are excellent for purposes of textual criticism, not because the Syrians had higher standards than their Arabic-speaking opposite numbers, but simply by reason of the genius of the Syriac language which, to express it in Aristotelian terms, becomes the form of the other. The Syriac of the translators is perfectly capable of taking on an entirely Greek cast down to the smallest details. Mention has already been made of the Harclean New Testament; its translator went to the prodigious length of reproducing the Greek article in a language that is innocent of the article, a shameful accomplishment, perhaps, from the point of piew of Syriac stylistic, but a considerable boon to the editor of the New Testament text.

Arabic, however, shows little of these chameleon-like qualities. There is in the Arabic translations a greater insistence on purely Semitic or Arabic idiom. Witness, for instance, the relatively few Greek philosophical terms domesticated in Arabic as compared to what has gone on in Syriac. Syntactically, too, the Greek text is recast into a Semitic mold. The temporal system of the Greek verb disappears into the Semitic aspect system; substantivization goes far be-

43. See V. Ryssel, *op. cit.*, I, 4; II, 8, 55.
44. A. Ahwani (ed.), *Ibn Rushd talkhīṣ kitāb al-nafs* (Cairo, 1950), pp. 128–75.

yond what occurs in the Syriac; hypotaxis is almost completely superseded by parataxis.

The use, then, of Arabic translation material for purposes of Greek textual criticism presents formidable difficulties.[45] Its validity depends, it would seem, on a far more detailed study of the Arabic translation techniques than has hitherto been attempted. The use of any given Arabic expression for a certain Greek expression must be reduced to its closest probabilities. Parallel with this is the publication of critical editions of the Arabic translations based on the fullest range of manuscripts possible, together with the manuscript notes. The publication, for instance, of the editors' notes in Paris BN 2346 has opened prospects previously seen only darkly through the lines of Ḥunayn's *Risālāh.*

45. Even more formidable are the difficulties of emending a Greek text on the basis of a modern translation of a Syriac or Arabic version. Ryssel had early studied the Greek text of the *De mundo* in terms of its Syriac version. His generally sound results were incorporated into Lorimer's Greek edition of the *De mundo* (Paris, 1933), but since Ryssel had studied only Chaps. 1–4, Lorimer then turned to an improbably bad German translation of the rest of the Syriac, and on the basis of this, produced emendations to the Greek that can only be described as surrealistic.

IV

THE TRANSMISSION OF THE NEW LEARNING

The Arabic translations of Aristotle were a remarkable achievement. But it is likely that they would have remained as no more than an isolated tour de force had there not begun, side by side with the translation movement, the equally formidable task of integrating them into the pattern of the Islamic intellectual life. Just as the translations had exploited the latent possibilities of the Arabic language, so the work of philosophical integration demanded nothing less than a recasting of the conceptual structure of Islam. The instruments of pedagogy and propagation were implicit in the scholastic nature of the texts and commentaries that had been translated; what remained was to adapt them to the alien circumstances of a Semitic thought-world still in its primitive stage.

PHILOSOPHY AND THE TRADITIONAL SCIENCES

Muslim historians of their own culture have always been aware of the cleavage between the traditional approach to learning and the methods and techniques of scholarship which they inherited from the Greeks. The encyclopedists were merely following an established tradition when they divided the sciences into Arab and non-Arab or, more instructively, into "rational" and "traditional."[1] An inspection

1. See p. 247, n. 23 below.

of the latter shows them to be, essentially, the techniques of writing and the disciplines connected with the *Qur'ān*, tradition (*ḥadīth*), jurisprudence (*fiqh*), and poetry;[2] in short, the "sciences" pursued by the Arabs since the very beginnings of Islam and markedly similar to the practices current in Judaism since the time of Ezra.[3]

The "Arab sciences" par excellence, *ḥadīth*, *fiqh*, *Qur'ān*, are fundamentally compilatory: *ḥadīth* is anecdotal; *fiqh* is casuistic,' and Quranic revelations were, except for occasional abrogations, unrelated, The result is that the subject matter of these disciplines can be transmitted piecemeal, collected and, the discrete pieces assembled like a mosaic. The goal to be striven for was completeness, or rather—since no one could pretend that he had collected all the pieces—multiplicity.

The foundation stones upon which all these collections rested were utterances: in the first instance revelatory utterances of the Prophet, and then, in ever-widening circles, utterances about the Prophet. Although this oral tradition gradually shaded off into a written one, the oral element continued to influence the pedagogical methodology of the medieval Muslim. The clearest indication of this is the fact that parallel with the more-or-less formalized education in the *madrasah* there runs a firm tradition of private instruction which has as its premise the transmission of material from individual to individual. And the nearest equivalent to a degree that a medieval scholar could possess, the *ijāzah*, was nothing more than a notarized attestation that a student had *heard* or had *recited* in the presence of an accredited scholar specific traditions which he was then licensed to transmit himself.[4]

2. Theology (*kalām*) is likewise classified as an "Arab science," while another heading, *al-'ilm al-ilāhi*, corresponds, on the non-Arab side of the ledger, to the position held by the *Metaphysica* in the school *corpus*. The distinction is valid as far as the subject matter is concerned, but methodologically speaking the two disciplines are identical and belong among the "rational" sciences.

3. See B. Gerhardsson, *Memory and Manuscript* (Uppsala, 1961), and G. Widengren, "Oral Tradition and Written Literature among the Hebrews in the Light of the Arabic Evidence," *Acta Orientalia* (Copenhagen), XXIII (1959), 232–62.

4. See S. Munajjid, "Ijāzāt al-samā'i fi al-makhṭūṭāt," *RIMA*, I (1955), 232–51, and G. Vadja, *Les Certificates de Lecture et de Transmission dans les Manuscrites Arabes de la Bibliothèque Nationale* (Paris, 1957), and pp. 251–252 below.

Behind all this is the notion of authority. It was of the utmost importance that the text (the anecdote, ruling, paradigm, etc.) be based in an unquestionable fashion on an unquestionable authority. The first element gave rise to the elaborate apparatus of criticism (*al-jarh wa al-ta' dīl*), while the search for authoritative transmitters produced the extensive *ṭabaqāt* literature. In neither case was it the internal textual criticism that chiefly interested the Muslim, but the text tradition (*isnād*). The great monument to this critical bent of the Arabs, the commentary on the *Qur'ān* of the historian al-Ṭabari (d. A.D. 923), cites no less than 24,502 of these chains of transmitters, of which 11,364 are unique.[5]

Philosophical scholarship was, from the outset, quite different. Its first appearance is in the guise of translation, and hence of a written text that produced a series of editors instead of transmitters. The concern of the editor was not usually with the date or provenance of manuscript texts as the *ḥadīth* scholar might make enquiries into the chronology and travels of a certain transmitter, but had to do almost exclusively with internal criteria; nowhere is the *isnād* principle in evidence. As a result, the object of philosophical education was comprehension and not transmission. The student of a great traditionalist *shaykh* might be content to hear his mentor repeat various traditions in his presence; but while Ibn Sīnā read the *Metaphysica* over and over again, certainly in itself a scholarly credential in an Arab science, he never really understood it until he read al-Fārābi's commentary.

Closely connected with these differing views is the notion of the coherence of philosophy. At first glance the doxographical collections available to the Arabs might appear to provide perfect analogies to the piecemeal transmission of *ḥadīth*. But it should be recalled that the doxographies were exegetical and polemical instruments and were

5. See H. Horst, "Zur Überlieferung im Korancommentar aṭ-Ṭabaris," *ZDMG*, CIII (1953), 290–307. Later critics, e.g., fifteenth-century commentators on the *ḥadīth* collectinos of al-Bukhāri (d. A.D. 870), developed a considerably greater respect for criticism of the text itself; see J. Fück, "Beiträge zur Überlieferungsgeschichte von Bukharis Traditionssammlung," *ZDMG*, XCII (1938), 60–87, espec. p. 85.

used *selectively* and not *collectively*. In the transmission of the *doxai* the Arabs followed their Greek models; the opinion of Thales, for example, was accepted on the authority of the last transmitter, Plutarch, and just as there is no connective *isnād* stretching form Thales to Plutarch in the Greek sources, so, too, there is none in the Arab sources between Plutarch and Ibn Sīnā; *Thales dixit* sufficed, a tempting invitation, of course, to the fabrication of *pseudepigraphica*.

How, then, was philosophical learning transmitted? Ḥunayn tells us that medicine was taught to the Arabs of his day in the same manner as it was "in the *schole* of our Christian friends."[6] That a similar situation existed in philosophy is doubtful; we know that philosophical studies in the Syrian schools—Nisibis provides the best example—were restricted, just as they were in the days of the *logica vetus* in the West, to the opening books of the *Organon* and used strictly as a propaedeutic to the study of exegesis and theology. The Syrians provided no models of philosophical curricula for the Arabs.

Nor does the traditional *madrasah* suggest itself as an alternative.[7] Whatever its absolute origins,[8] the *madrasah* has long been considered a center of reaction against the so-called *bāṭinīyah* movement which had, as part of its theological equipment, a syncretistic, gnostic-like system that owed a marked debt to both Greek philosophy

6. Ḥunayn, *Risālah*, # 20.

7. For a general survey of higher education in Islam see J. Pederson, art. "Madrasa," *Shorter EI* pp. 300–10, with notices on the older treatments. Some of the universities have been treated separately:

al-Azhar: Maqrīzi, *Khiṭāṭ*, IV, 49–56; J. Jomier, art. "al-Azhar," *EI*², pp. 813–21; M. Khafaji, *Al-Azhar fi alf am*, (3 vols.; Cairo, 1955).

Niẓamiyah: A. Talas, *La Madrasa Niẓamiyya et son histoire* (Paris, 1939).

Mustanṣiriyah: N. Marouf, *Ta'rīkh 'ulamā'mustanṣiriyah* (Baghdad,. 1939).

Spanish higher education: J. Ribera y Tarrago, "La ensenanza entre los musulmanes espanoles," *Disertaciones y Opusculos*, I (Madrid, 1928), 229–360.

Ottoman higher education: H. A. R. Gibb and H. Bowen, *Islamic Society and The West*, I, 2 (Oxford, 1957), pp. 143–16; J. Heyworth-Dunne, *Introduction to the History of Education inModern Egypt* (London, 1939).

and natural science. It was to combat this movement, politically linked to the rival Fatimid Caliphate in Egypt, that in the sixties of the eleventh century the Seljuk vizier Niẓām al-Mulk (d. A.D. 1092) founded schools in Baghdad, Nisapur, Balkh, Mosul, and Herat as centers of orthodoxy and of Ashʿarite theology.

This picture of the spread of the *madrasah* system has recently undergone serious revision.[9] What has emerged is, from the point of view of philosophical education, an even more reactionary institution. There were no chairs of *kalām* at the various foundations of the Niẓām al-Mulk;[10] they were primarily law schools, and the teaching was in strict accordance with traditional practice. Students were set to copying the lexture notes (*taʿlīqah*) of a professor under his personal supervision. Needless to point out, neither the material nor the approach of *falsafah* had any place here.

There is another Muslim institution known under a variety of titles (*bayt al-ḥikmah, dār al-ḥikmah, dār al-ʿilm*) where the connection with Greek learning is more promising. Al-Ma'mūn founded a *bayt al-ḥikmah* in Baghdad, and there was a *dār al-ʿilm* in the same city under the Buwayhid vizier Sabūr ibn Ardishīr (d. A.D. 1025). The Hamdanids founded similar institutions in Mosul, Aleppo, and Tripoli. Finally, in A.D. 1005 the Fatimid caliph al-Ḥākim instituted a *dār al-ḥikmah* in Cairo.[11]

Not much is known about the Buwayhid and Hamdanid foundations, but in the case of the institutions of al-Ma'mūn[12] there is little reason to think that they were schools in the ordinary sense of the word. It would be nearer to the truth to call them "research centers" rather than "academies." They were primarily libraries with permanent (resident?) staffs (*aṣḥāb*), and the *bayt al-ḥikmah* of Ma'mūn was, in addition, the place where the translations from the Greek were

8. Indian? So W. Barthold, *Four Studies on the History of Central Asia*, I (Leyden, 1956), 4–5.

9. See G. Makdisi, "Muslim institutions of learning in eleventh-century Baghdad," *BSOAS*, XXIV (1961), 1–56.

10. For the implication of this in the history of Islamic *kalām*, see p. 155 below.

11. Al-Maqrīzi, *Khiṭāṭ*, IV, 55–63.

12. The brief notices on the *bayt al-ḥikmah* in the *Fihrist* (pp. 243, 267) and al-Qifṭi (p. 98) have been analyzed by D. Sourdel in *EI²*, I, 1140.

done and had an observatory attached to it. Their libraries differed from similar collections in the *madrasahs* in having materials on the "ancient" as well as the Islamic sciences.[13]

From the ninth century to the fourteenth century, that is, during its most vigorous period, *falsafah* had no representation on any of the curricula of higher education in Islam, with serious consequences for philosophy. There was no Muslim Isocrates to mediate between philosophy and the "traditional sciences," no Cassiodorus or Augustine to lead the secular heritage of Greece into the domain of theology. The result was that not only did *falsafah* stand convicted of heresy in some of its basic theses, but lacking a humanistic bridge into the general educational philosophy of Islam, it was left completely cut off from the schools and, hence, from the means of its own propagation.

The essentially private nature of philosophical instruction is confirmed by an investigation of the literary sources. Nothing is known of al-Kindi's teachers; Ḥunayn attended the sessions (*majālis*) of the Christian Yūḥannā ibn Masawayh,[14] but once again it is in the context of medical education. The educational ground becomes somewhat firmer *ca.* A.D. 900 with the arrival from Harran of the remnants of what was a continuation of the philosophical faculty at Alexandria. According to Ibn abī Uṣaybiʿah's quotes from the lost "Appearance of Philosophy" of al-Fārābi,[15] Quwayri, one of the Harran masters, came to Baghdad and "began to teach" (*akhadha ... fī taʿlīm*); Abū Bishr, another member of the group, "was taught by" al-Marwazi

13. Extensive materials on the Islamic library have been collected by K. Holter, "Der Islam," in *Handbuch der Bibliothekswissenschaft*, III, 1 (Wiesbaden, 1953), pp. 188–242. Among the older studies see A. Mez, *Die Renaissance des Islams* (Heidelberg, 1922), pp. 162–80; M. Meyerhof, "Über einige Privatbibliotheken im fatimidischen Ägypten," *RSO*, XII (1929–1930), 286–90; O. Pinto, "Le biblioteche degli Arabi nell' Eta degli Abbasidi," *Bibliofilia*, XXX (1928), S. K. Padover, "Muslim Libraries" in J. W. Thomson, *The Medieval Library*, (Chicago, 1939), pp. 347–72; J. Ribera y Tarrago "Bibliofilos y Bibliotecas en la Espana musulmana," *Disertaciones y Opusculos*, I (Madrid, 1928) 181–228; and K. Adwad, "Khazāʾ in kutub al-ʿiraq al-ammah," *Summer* (1946), pp. 218–23. Recently there has been a brief study of Ibn Sīnā's use of the princely libraries in the eastern provinces: M. Weisweiler, "Avicenna und die iranischen Fürstenbibliotheken seiner Zeit," *Avicenna Commemoration Volume* (Calcutta, 1956), pp. 47–63.

14. Uṣ., I, 185.

15. Uṣ., II, 135.

(*taʿallama min* . . .). As for al-Fārābi himself, he "studied the *De demonstratione* to its end with Yūḥannā ibn Ḥaylān" (*taʿallama min Yūḥann . . . ilā akhīrah kitāb al-burhān*) or, as he puts it a few lines later, "He read to the end of the *De demonstratione*" (*qarāʾ ilā akhīrah kitāb al-burhān*). This latter expression," to read (something) in the presence of someone" (*qarāʾʿalā fulān*), to study (something) with somebody, apparently borrowed from the transmission of *ḥadīth,* is the most common method of expressing the teaching relationship in the discipline of philosophy and is clearly analogous to the *miqra* of Rabbinical Judaism and the *legere* and *lectio* of the Latin West.

Before entering upon a discussion of philosophical education proper, some distinctions must be made in the Arabs' general approach to philosophy. The study of *falsafah* was never very homogenous. With the absence of public instruction, individuals tended to seek out others from whom they might learn. The great figures stand in a kind of isolated splendor, linked at best by names that are no more than just names. Even in the closest thing to a "school" ever produced in Islam, the Peripatetic group in Baghdad,[16] where *falsafah* was cultivated intensely for a century and a half, two very distinct approaches to philosophy may be discerned. There was, first of all, a strong current of textual criticism exemplified by scholars like Abū Bishr, Yaḥyā ibn ʿAdi, Ibn al-Samḥ, Ibn Suwār, and Ibn Zurʿah. In the textual aspect of their work there is an obvious connection with the translation work done in the atelier of Ḥunayn.

Connected with the textual criticism was the work of commenting. Commentaries on the Aristotelian *corpus* are credited to Abū Bishr, Yaḥyā, and others, but the preserved fragments are all in a textual context, e.g., the marginal notes to the Organon, and give the appearance of being in the form of philological *glossae.* While still connected with this tradition, the works of al-Fārābi and Ibn al-Ṭayyib, two other members of the "school," are more representative of the purely philosophical commentary.

16. See pp. 171–173 below.

After the death of Yaḥyā ibn ʿAdi in A.D. 974 and the apparent assumption of leadership of the Baghdad circle by Abū Sulaymām al-Sijistāni, *falsafah* begins turning into broader, more humanistic channels, typified by such men as al-Tawḥīdi, Ibn Hindū, Miskawayh, and ʿĪsā ibn ʿAli, the philosopher son of the famous vizier. The emphasis on text and commentary declines and is superseded by an attempt to blend philosophy into the general fabric of belles-lettres and ethics.

These different approaches had a formative influence on the pedagogy of philosophy. First, the preparation of editions was not essentially a pedagogic process, though the editions themselves undoubtedly served educational ends. They were prepared privately through the series of collations and emendations already described. The finished product, the *kitāb*, was then used in instruction, providing a text that was read with the master, just as al-Fārābi read the *Analytica posteriora* with Yūḥannā ibn Ḥaylān. Students, it seems, often made their own transcriptions of the text.[17] In addition to the text, commentaries by both Greek and contemporary philosophers were employed. The student read the text, and if a written commentary of the professor were not being used, the latter would dictate his remarks.[18] On a more advanced level the comment would be reciprocal, both the student and the teacher exchanging views in a cooperative investigation.[19] In at least one instance an *ijāzah* was given for a reading course in the *Analytica posteriora*.[20] Much of the study was of a private nature. Abū al-Faraj ibn al-Ṭayyib spent twenty years

17. A. Badawi, *Manṭiq Aristū*, I, 24. In the days of al-Fanāri (d. A.D. 1431) in Brussa, the students spent their two free days a week making copies of their textbook, a work by al-Taftazāni; this process took so much time that al-Fanāri gave them another "free day" to work on their copying; see Tashköprüzādah, *Shaqā'iq* (trans. Rescher), p. 15.

18. Al-Tawḥīdi, *Muqābasāt*, #61, #82. The use of dictation is quite normal in all forms of Islamic instruction; see M. Weisweiler." Das Amt des Mustamli in der arabischen Wissenschaft, *Oriens*, IV (1951), 27–57. A well-known example in the theological sciences is the *ʿAqīdah niẓāmīyah* dictated by al-Ghazāli to Abū Bakr ibn al-ʿArabi and specifically described as a *reportatio* of a lecture by al-Ghazāli's teacher al-Juwayni.

19. For an example from the career of Ibn Sīnā see p. 90 below.

20. Al-Qifṭi, pp. 314–15; an extant *ijāzah* given by Ibn al-Ṭayyib to Ibn Buṭlān.

in meditating the *Metaphysica* and nearly died of the effort.[21] Al-Fārābi read the *De anima* two hundred times and the *Physica* forty times.[22] Both Ibn Sīnā and Abū al-Barakāt were largely self-educated in philosophy. There is the well-known story of the young Ibn Sīnā outstripping his teacher al-Nātili, and of his excitement at the sight of the library of one of his patrons.[23] But the going was not easy. He plowed through the *Metaphysica* many times without understanding it,[24] and Abū al-Barakāt had similar difficulties.[25]

However, when we turn to the *Muqābasāt* of al-Tawḥīdi and its sketches of the circle of Abū Sulaymān we are introduced to the less formal classes in which philosophical texts were studied, and al-Tawḥīdi himself attended these.[26] But there were also more catholic gatherings (*majājis*) of scholars from various fields where more general problems were discussed and the conversation went whither it would.[27]

Al-Tawḥīdi may have attended another type *majlis* current in Baghdad at the time. He knew not only the writings, but also the names of the authors of the *Rasā'il* of the Sincere Brethren,[28] and it is not impossible that he attended one of the meetings described in another of their works as taking place once every twelve days in a secluded location.[29] By happy chance a miniature describing just such a gathering has been preserved in an Istanbul manuscript of the *Rasā'il* completed in Baghdad in A.D. 1287.[30]

21. On the testimony of his student, Ibn Buṭlān, quoted in Schacht-Meyerhof, *Medico-Philosophical Controversy*, pp. 87–88.
22. Ibn Khallikān (trans. de Slane), III, pp. 307–308.
23. See M. Weisweiler, "Avicenna und die iranischen Fürstenbibliotheken seiner Zeit," *Avicenna Commemoration Volume* (Calcutta, 1956), pp. 47–63.
24. Al-Qifṭi, pp. 414–42; the scales fell from his eyes when he read al-Fārābi's commentary.
25. *Kitāb al-mu'tabar*, p. 3.
26. *Muqābasāt*, # 61, # 77, # 78, etc.
27. *Ibid.*, # 2; compare al-Mas'udi, *Murūj*, VII 172ff.
28. *Imtā'*, II, 4.
29. *Al-Risālah al-jami'ah* (ed. Damascus, 1949), II, 395–96.
30. MS Sulaymaniyah, Esat effendi 3638; the miniature, together with interesting parallels from the *Maqāmāt* of al-Harīri, has been reproduced in *Mélanges Massignon*, II (Damascus, 1957), pl. II, III, IVb, and Vb.

In the end, neither the philological nor the humanistic school survived. The final stages of Arab philosophy had as its rallying point neither Plato nor Aristotle, but a long-dead Ibn Sīnā caught in controversy between Fakhr al-Dīn Rāzi and al-Ṭūsi.[31] Manuscripts of the Aristotelian translations are rare; the earliest purely philosophical text to proliferate in manuscript is the *Ishārāt* of Ibn Sīnā. In general, the most common philosophical manuscripts are those of texts which, like the *Ishārāt*, were used in the *madāris* when philosophy finally made its entrance into the curriculum of the upper schools, probably sometime in the fourteenth century.

Al-Jabarti (d. A.D. 1822), the historian of Ottoman Egypt, has preserved a list of textbooks used at al-Azhar at the end of the eighteenth century.[32] Their textual history, the general conservatism of the institution, and a comparison of what was being read in philosophy by a Turkish scholar of the sixteenth century,[33] all indicate that al-Jabarti's list probably goes back far beyond the date of the historian's visit. It is enlightening to read what were being used for texts in the higher courses in philosophy and to reflect that here at base was the legacy of *falsafah* to Islam. In logic the primary text was the *Īsaghūji* of al-Abhari (d. A.D. 1264) with its various commentaries including the *Sullam al-marawnaq*, a metrical paraphrase by al-Akhdari (d. A.D. 1546). Also in use were the *Risālah shamsīyah* of al-Kātibi (d. A.D. 1276), the *Maṭāliʿ al-anwār* of al-Urmawi (d. A.D. 1283), and the *Mukhtaṣar fī al-manṭiq* of al-Sanusi (d. A.D. 1490). In philosophy proper, all the texts, with the exception of the *Ishārāt*, were encyclopedic: al-Abhari's *Hidāyat al-ḥikmah*, al-Kātibi's *Ḥikmat al-ʿayn*, and the *Tahdhīb al-manṭiq wa al-kalām* of al-Taftazāni (d. A.D. 1389). In what is even today one of the few overall treatments of Arab philosophy, De Boer devotes two lines to al-Abhari; the rest are not even mentioned.

31. See p. 195 below.
32. Reproduced in J. Heyworth-Dunne, *An Introduction to the History of Education in Modern Egypt* (London, 1939), pp. 45–65.
33. See the autobiography of Tasköprüzādah included in his own *Shaqā'iq*.

ISLAMIC SCHOLASTICISM

THE *EISAGOGE* COMPLEX

Of all the purely methodological techniques appropriated by the Arabs from their Greek masters, the *eisagoge* complex was both the most elaborate and the richest in effects. As an element in the scholastic method, the *eisagoge* is purely and simply a pedagogic device, an introduction to the study of an author and his work through the development of a series of standard *topoi*. Like the general scholastic handbook, its origins are probably to be sought in rhetorical circles, and it had a wide vogue for solely literary ends.[34]

The philosophical *eisagoge*, cultivated at least from the time of Chrysippus and Poseidonius,[35] assumes its characteristic ten-point form with Proclus,[36] and thenceforward becomes a standard part of the Aristotelian literature of comment.

As a pedagogical tool, the *eisagoge* complex was designed to introduce the philosophical neophyte to the reading and lectures of the Aristotelian *corpus* proper which were to form the bulk of his curriculum. As a type of proseminar it began with the treatment of more generic problems raised by the study of philosophy and continued, through a series of standardized and well-defined steps, to a consideration of more specifically Aristotelian problems. In its most complete form the *Introductio in Aristotelem* may be schematized as follows:[37]

34. See E. Norden, "Die Composition und Literaturgattung der horazischen Epistula ad Pisones," *Hermes*, XL (1905), 508–28; H. Rabe, "Aus Rhetoren Handschriften 10 Einleitungen," *Rh. Mus.*, LXIV (1907), 539–78; A. J. Festugière, *La Révélation de Hermès Trismégiste*, II (Paris, 1949), 345–49.

35. Norden, *art. cit.*, pp. 524–25; thence, by way of Varro, into Latin literature under the title *Institutiones* and, later, *Introductio*, to develop, finally, into the elaborate medieval *accessus ad auctores*; see E. Quain "The Medieval *Accessus ad Auctores*," *Traditio*, III (1945), 215–64, and R. B. C. Huygens, *Accessus ad Auctores*," *Latomus*, XII (1953), 296–311, 460–84.

36. So Elias, *In Cat.* (*CAG*, XVIII, 1), p. 107; compare H. Rabe, *art. cit.*, p. 542.

37. The form is somewhat idealized in that not all the points are treated by all the authors who use the technique, and there is a certain interchangeability of parts. For reconstructions of the Aristotelian *eisagoge* see Düring, *Biographical Tradition*, pp. 444–57, and L. Baur, *Gundisallinis de Divisione philosophiae* (*Beiträge*, IV, 2–3 [Münster, 1903]).

I. On philosophy in general. A discussion of the definitions and divisions of philosophy.

II. Prolegomena to Porphyry's *Eisagoge*
   a. The aim of the work
   b. Its usefulness
   c. Its authenticity
   d. Its order
   e. Its division into chapters (*kephalaia*)
   f. To which branch of philosophy it belongs

III–IV. Reading and commenting of Porphyry's *Eisagoge*

V. On the philosophy of Aristotle
   a. On the names of the various philosophical schools (*haireseis*)
   b. On the division of the *corpus*
   c. On the point of departure
   d. On the end
   e. On the natural progression of parts which lead to the end, e.g., Logic, Ethics, Physics, Mathematics, Theology
   f. On Aristotle's style
   g. On the reasons for obscurities
   h. On the qualities desirable in the student
   i. On the qualities desirable in the lecturer
   j. On what must be considered by way of prolegomena to the individual works. A transition into VI.

VI. Prolegomena to the *Categoriae*. Same *topoi* as II *supra*

VII–VIII. Reading and commenting of Aristotle's *Categoriae*

It was this propaedeutic *schema*, beginning as a lecturer's outline and then progressing, via the *reportatio* route, into the preserved

Aristotelian commentaries, which became an important part of the philosophical equipment of *falsafah*.[38]

The opening point of this *schema*, "On philosophy in general," has been particularly fruitful in Islam. As found in Ammonius, Elias, and David,[39] the theme is developed in two directions: the definition of philosophy and its division. Under the definition of philosophy, the procedure is both logical and historical. The existence of philosophy, its object, and its methods are all discussed and various objections are refuted. Definitions are proferred from several Greek philosophical schools (the Pythagorean etymological derivation from *philos-sophia* is everywhere in evidence) and a contrast drawn between the Platonic theological definition and the Aristotelian definition from philosophy's relationship with the other arts.

These *topoi* find frequent parallels in the oriental tradition. Bazud's *Book of Definitions* opens with a series of definitions of philosophy, the first four of which are designated as "Socratic, Aristotelian, Stoic, Platonic."[40] The encyclopedia of the later Syriac Christian Severus bar Shakko (d. A.D. 1241) includes similar passages.[41]

A logical epitome in Arabic is preserved in Beyrouth MS St. Joseph 338. In this work, possibly the oldest preserved translation of Aristotle into Arabic, preceding the abridged compendium of Porphyry's *Eisagoge* (fols. 12–21), some few pages (fols. 2–11) are devoted to a series of definitions similar to those found in the Greek *eisagoge* literature.[42] The Greek antecedents are even clearer in a work like the *Mafātīḥ al-ʿulūm* of al-Khawārizmi (*fl. ca.* A.D. 975–

38. Since the introductory material pertained to the very beginnings of the *corpus*, it has also left its mark on the Syriac milieu where the theologians made particularly insistent use of Porphyry. *Vat. syr.* 158 contains fragments of an *eisagoge* complex; see Baumstark, *Aristoteles bei den Syrern*, pp. 157–66.

39. Ammonius, *CAG*, IV, 3, pp. 1–20; *Elias*: *ibid.*, XVIII, 1, pp. 1–34; David: *ibid.*, XVIII, 2, pp. 1–79. Compare Philoponus *ibid.*, XIII, 1 p. 1 where he refers to a work of his in this mold. Since Philoponus had a far wider reading in Islam than the other three, the loss of his *eisagoge* work is particularly regrettable.

40. *Memorie Lincei*, Ser. 6, Vol. II 20–25, and Baumstark, *Aristoteles bei den Syrern*, p. 213. On this author and his work see p. 102, n. 12 below; his contact with the *eisagoge* complex probably goes back to Philoponus.

41. See Baumstark, *op. cit.*, pp. 192–210 and pp.107–108 below.

42. See P. Kraus, *RSO*, XIV (1934), 6.

987) who begins his treatise on the "foreign sciences" with the now-familiar etymology:

> *On the division of philosophy.* Falsafah *is derived from a Greek word, namely* filasufiyah, *which means "lover of widsom." When it is translated into Arabic it becomes* faylasūf, *and then* falsafah *is derived from that. The meaning of philosophy is the science of the truth of things and the science of that which is better.*[43]

By the time of Abū al-Faraj ibn al-Ṭayyib (d. A.D. 1043), the definition *topoi* had become thoroughly domesticated in the Baghdad Peripatetic circle. Ibn al-Ṭayyib's commentary on Porphyry's *Eisagoge*[44] opens with passages that are an almost exact replica of pages from David and Elias, right down to a reproduction of the six standard definitions of philosophy from its subject matter (two, both Pythagorean), from its name (Pythagorean), from its end (two, both from Plato), and from its relationship with the other arts (Aristotle).

The definitions did no more than become standardized, but the second major consideration, the division of philosophy, gave birth to an entire sub-genus of literature in Arabic. It is difficult, and perhaps unimportant, to separate Arabic classificatory works of the type of Ibn Sīnā's "On the Division of the Sciences" from philosophical encyclopedias like the same author's *Kitāb al-shifā'*,[45] and both of these in turn from the division of philosophy found here in Part I of the *eisagoge* complex and the classificatory *pinax* associated with Part VII, but some fundamental precisions may be made. The division of philosophy discussed by Ammonius, David, and Elias is that of subject matter, e.g., the basic division into theoretical and practical philosophy and the subdivision of the former into physics, mathematics, theology, and of the latter into ethics, economics, politics, with, finally, some attention to the question of whether logic is a part

43. *Mafātīḥ* (ed. Van Vloten), p. 131; see pp. 109–110 below.

44. E. M. Dunlop, *Iraq*, XIII (1951), 76–94. On the author of this work preserved in MS Bodl. Marsh 28 and formerly attributed to al-Fārābi, see S. M. Stern, "Ibn al-Ṭayyib's Commentary on the Isagoge," *BSOAS*, XIX (1957), 419–25.

45. See pp. 105–106 below.

of philosophy or a propaedeutic instrument (*organon*) to its study. This type of purely theoretical division is represented in Arabic by passages from al-Shahrastāni's (d. A.D. 1153) *Milal wa niḥal*,[46] which, though somewhat more successfully integrated into the Islamic tradition than parallel passages from the *falāsifah*, still betray their Greek origins.

The *pinax* in Part VII of the complex begins as a simple listing of Aristotle's works, organized, it is true, along lines of division suggested by the theoretical discussions on the nature of philosophy.[47] But within the Islamic tradition, the lines separating I and VII of the complex blur and the simple *pinax* turns into a *catalogue raisonée* (al-Ya'qūbi and al-Kindi) and then, into a brief philosophical encyclopedia (al-Fārābi, Ibn Sīnā), thence, with the introduction of non-philosophical material, into the "mixed" encyclopedia.[48]

The bibliographies of al-Kindi note two works which may well be of the classificatory type: "The Essence of Science and Its Division" and "The Division of Human Science,"[49] but the preserved "On the Number of Books of Aristotle," like the parallel passages in al-Ya'qūbi's *Ta'rīkh*.[50] takes as its point of departure a division *schema* into which a number of Aristotle's works have been integrated.[51] Of the two authors, al-Ya'qūbi's information is somewhat fuller, as, for instance, on the *De coelo*:

> *And the second book* (*of the* Libri Naturales) *is called the* Book of Heaven and the Universe *and his purpose in it is an explanation of spherical things which are not subject to corruption. And these are of two types. One type is of a circular nature and one whose motion is circular, and this is the sphere which surrounds things and is the fifth*

46. Cureton (ed.), pp. 251–53; trans. Haarbrucker, II, pp. 77–80; on the nature of this work see pp. 285–6 below.
47. See Düring, *Biographical Tradition*, p. 447.
48. See p. 156 below.
49. *Fihrist*, p. 256; Uṣ., I, 209.
50. See pp. 290–91 below; it is curious that both al-Ya'qūbi al-Kindi erect a separate category for the *psychologica*, while most other authors in this genre group them under the *physica*.
51. M. Guidi and R. Walzer (ed. and trans.), *Studi sul al-Kindi*, I (Rome, 1938).

> *element which is not subject to generation and corruption. The second type is that which is spherical and circular in its generation even though not circular in its motion. These are the four elements: fire, air, earth, and water which, while they are not circular in their motion, move in a straight line and are circular in generation. Circularity of generation is that which is generated, one from another, by conversion, like something which goes in a circle and is converted into something else. It is like the case of fire which goes in a circular fashion and is converted into something else. For it is generated from air, and air from water, and water from earth. And each one of these elements is circular in generation, one into the other: fire and air upwards, water and earth downwards.*[52]

Al-Kindi on the same subject has considerably less:

> *And his intention in his second book, the one called the* Book of Heavens *is the appearance of the whole and the separation of the first five bodies, and what is the body of the whole, and what are the natural states which happen to bodies, those, I mean, which are proper to their natures and common to most of them, and the causes and moving forces.*[53]

Closest of all to the classificatory *pinakes* of the Greek commentators is the speculative division of the works offered by Ṣāʿid al-Andalūsi,[54] and similar Greek classifications lie behind the breakdowns of the *corpus* in al-Nadīm, al-Qifṭi, and Ibn abī Uṣaybiʿah.

The classic *falsafah* works on the classification of the sciences,[55] al-Fārābi's *Iḥsāʾ al-ʿulūm,*[56] and Ibn Sīnā's *Fī aqsām al-ʿulūm,*[57] belong

52. *Taʾrīkh* (ed. Houtsma), p. 148.

53. Guidi and Walzer, (ed.), p. 402.

54. See pp. 283–284 below. The division is found on pp. 24–26 of Cheikho's edition of the *Ṭabaqāt* and pp. 63–66 of Blachère's translation.

55. On the classification of the sciences among the Jewish *falāsifah* see H. Wolfson, *Hebrew Union College Jubilee Volume* (Cincinnati, 1925), pp. 263–315.

56. Gonzalez Palencia (ed.), *Alfarabi: Catalogo de las Ciences* (Madrid, 1932), together with the medieval Latin version known as the *De scientiis* and probably done by Gerard of Cremona, though it is attributed to Gundisalvo by Alonso, *al-Andalus,* XII (1947), 298–308. The medieval Latin version is not to be confused with either the *De divisione philosophiae,* an original work by Gundisalvo, or the *De ortu scientiarum,* a Latin translation

to the next generation of descendants from the classificatory *pinakes*; there is less of a formal tie to the actual works of Aristotle. The two authors differ on a number of points; al-Fārābi, for instance, departs from the common tradition of the commentators and accepts logic as a separate subdivision of philosophy, while Ibn Sīnā puts it in its more customary position as an *organon*. But more important for the future is both authors' fleshing out of the outline in directions unforeseen by the commentators and dictated by the exigencies of life in Islam. In al-Fārābi the first of the sciences is the "Science of Language," some parts of which seem to echo discussions in the *De interpretatione* but which also includes more purely Islamic considerations like the science of orthography, of correct reading, and of prosody. Ibn Sīnā's interpolations go off in other directions. At the end of the *Iḥsā'*, al-Fārābi had allowed a modest new place for *fiqh* and *kalām*,[58] but Ibn Sīnā has considerably broadened the category of *metaphysica* to bring it more in line with the realities—and the ever-increasing polemic—of Islamic natural theology.

The prolegomena type works (II and VI) may be illustrated briefly. Al-Kindi's "On the Intention of Aristotle in the *Categoriae*" is known only by title,[59] and, on the basis of al-Kindi's periphrastic approach to philosophy, may be supposed to be a résumé of the *Categoriae*. More firmly in the *eisagoge* tradition are a series of works produced by the Baghdad Peripaticians: al-Fārābi's prolegomena to the *Categoriae*,[60] which follows his work on Porphyry's *Eisagoge*[61] and precedes the series of paraphrases and commentaries on the *Organon*. Similar is the brief but very scholastic introduction of Ibn Suwār to

whose Arabic original, attributed to al-Fārābi, has not come to light. The *Iḥsā'* and its version have been studied by Gardet-Anawati, *Théologie musulmane*, pp. 102–106; M. Bouyges, *MFO*, IX (1923–1924), 49–70; H. Bédoret, *RNSP*, XLI (1938), 83–88; pp. 88–93 of Bédoret's article discussed the *De ortu scientiarum*.

57. Ed. in *Tis' rasā'il* (Cairo, 1908).

58. See the remarks in Gardet-Anawati, *Théologie musulmane*, pp. 104–105.

59. Uṣ., I, 209.

60. D. M. Dunlop (ed. and trans.), "Al.Fārābi's Introductory *Risālah* on Logic," *Islamic Quarterly*, III (1956), 224–235; compare the same author's opening statement on logic in the *Iḥsā'* (ed. Palencia), p. 128.

61. Dunlop (ed.), *ibid.*, pp. 117–138.

his edition of the *Categoriae*.[62] His fellow Peripatetic Ibn Zurʿah's "On the Intentions of Aristotle's Logical Works" appears to belong to the same genre.[63]

The final element in the *Introductio in Aristotelem*, the ten-point treatment "On the Philosophy of Aristotle" (V) was likewise adopted into the Islamic tradition. A form of these ten points is found in Ibn abī Uṣaybiʿah,[64] taken over from Ḥunayn ibn Isḥāq. Al-Fārābi's "What Must Precede the Study of Philosophy" belongs in the same category.[65] All the points are given in résumé by al-Masʿūdi in his *Tanbīh*.[66]

It was probably the first of these ten points, "On the names of the various philosophical schools," that supplied the *falāsifah* with some of their admittedly rudimentary knowledge of the history of Greek philosophy, but the knowledge remained rather firmly tied to the scaffolding of the *eisagoge* complex. However, some of the later encyclopedists and historians have fairly elaborate treatments of the Greek philosophical schools: al-Qifṭi,[67] Ibn Ṣāʿid,[68] and Severus bar Shakko[69] all deal with the subject, and, in at least the first two instances, the original Islamic sources for this type of information were al-Fārābi's lost "The Appearance of Philosophy," and Ḥunayn ibn Isḥāq's philosophical gnomonology *Nawādir al-falāsifah*.[70]

The influence of the *eisagoge* complex in Islam was not limited to the presence of these various *topoi* in the works of the *falāsifah*. It has long been recognized[71] that the student in the Hellenistic schools had in his hands not only an edition of the text of Aristotle but also a biography and bibliography, and that the latter particularly was discussed within the context of these introductory lectures (cf. VII).

62. Georr (ed.), *Catégories*, pp. 361–64. Many of the following notes by Ibn Suwār use the same scholastic *topoi*.
63. *Fihrist*, p. 264, l. 23.
64. I, 54–69 (on Aristotle); see Düring, *Biographical Tradition*, p. 220.
65. Dieterici (ed.), pp. 49–55; trans. *idem*, pp. 82–91.
66. Carra de Vaux (trans.), p. 169.
67. P. 25.
68. Blachère (trans.), pp. 74–75.
69. *Book of Dialogues*, II, 8; text and trans. by Ruska in *ZA*, XII (1897), 149–51.
70. See p. 125 below; on the "philosophical sects" passage in Ḥunayn see K. Merkle, *Die Sittensprüche der Philosophen* (Leipzig, 1921), pp. 36–40.
71. See K. Praechter, *BZ*, XVIII (1909) 528–29.

Both the biography and the *pinax* of Aristotelian works have left considerable traces in Islam.[72] The book list is of substantial interest to the student of ancient philosophy in that it provides *testimonia* for an independent Greek source on the writings of Aristotle. But unlike the more classificatory bibliographies mentioned above, it is a bare list of titles, many as garbled and unintelligible to the Arab transmitter of the Middle Ages as they are today. The students of things Aristotelian in Islam were antiquarians enough to preserve, like some Mycenaean catalog of ships, this ungainly list of strange titles. But they both understood and used the scholastic *topoi* of the *eisagoge* complex, not only in the philosophical contexts for which they were designed, but in broad areas of Islamic encyclopedic literature as well.

THE LITERATURE OF COMMENT

The Arab is an indefatigable bibliographer; his concept of tradition and scholarly authority, coupled with an almost rabbinic love of "the word," has led to the compilation of lists of books read, seen, or heard in the sacred, profane, and occult sciences. The lists show an extensive literature devoted to *falsafah* and allied disciplines, but just how extensive is difficult to determine without a much closer scrutiny of the mere fraction of these bibliographies represented by extant manuscripts. Apart from the Arab love of the metaphorical title—not every "key" opens "the sciences," and not every "garden" encloses "wisdom," as the authors would have us believe; the effect is undeniably musical but not always illuminating—the descriptive terminology of philosophical titles is somewhat haphazard.

The generic name used for a philosophical treatise is *kitāb* (*liber*, frequently combined as in *kitāb risālah*, *kitāb sharḥ*, etc.) and, for

72. Considerable research has been done in both these areas; see Moraux, *Listes Anciennes*, and Düring, *Biographical Tradition*.

shorter treatments, *dhikr* (*commemoratio*; the derivatives *mudhākirah* and *tadhkīr* are less comon) and *qawl* (*sermo*). Equally common is the expression *risālah* (*epistula*), and, in one of the rare historical asides in this area, we are told in an abridgement of Abū Sulaymān's *Ṣiwān al-ḥikmah* that al-Kindi was the first to use it as a philosophical vehicle;[73] indeed, in some of al-Kindi's works it still has the primitive form of a letter addressed to an individual, frequently to answer objections or questions proposed by the addressee. Later it loses all its epistolary associations and becomes a short philosophical essay.

Falsafah literature in Arabic falls into two general types: that which takes as its point of departure a text and develops in terms of that text, i.e., the literature of comment *qua tale,* and in the second instance, that which develops independently of a text. In both types there is a clear affiliation to Greek norms of substance and form; the organization and problematic of the Hellenistic schools is everywhere apparent, but particularly so in the first category, the literature of comment, where there is a greater emphasis on technique.

Most of the Greek textual comment developed out of the *eisagoge* complex, and something has already been seen of this and of the procedures in the later philosophical schools. From the time of Alexander of Aphrodisias, the Aristotelian commentary was primarily exegetical, in the form known to the medieval Latins as *per modum commenti*: the text was divided into paragraphs and treated by the professor paragraph by paragraph. His remarks were preserved in the notes taken down by students present at the lecture.[74]

Not all the commentaries were of the *reportatio* type, however; some, those of Alexander and Simplicius, for example, were of purely literary origin, done by the professor independently of his lecture commitments and hence more polished and more profound than a mere *apo phones* performance.

Though dictation was an important element in Islamic pedagogy, the preserved Arabic commentaries are not notably reportorial

73. BM *or.* 9033 fol. 60a.

74. See the example cited on p. 16 above and the lecture notes of Damascius on the *Philebus* copied by one of his students and edited by L. G. Westerink (Amsterdam, 1959).

in nature. One reason for this is the difference between the Hellenic and Islamic school traditions. As has been pointed out, philosophy never managed to penetrate the school tradition in Islam; there were no public lectures on *falsafah*; instruction was invariably private.

The Arabic commentaries on Aristotle are, then, primarily literary in nature. There are, unfortunately, but few indications of the actual procedures in composing these works. We are told that al-Fārābi wrote most of his work on loose leaves and in a brief form, which explains the somewhat fragmentary nature of his preserved work.[75] But for a more detailed explanation we have two biographical fragments which are filled with interesting items.

The first, concerning Abū al-Barakāt (d. A.D. 1165), is from his own hand and serves as an introduction to his philosophical encyclopedia, the *Kitāb al-mū'tabar*.[76] When Abū al-Barakāt began his study of philosophy, he worked through the various Hellenic texts and the commentaries written on them. He consigned in writing to various bits of paper (*awrāq*) his notes and comments on his own reading. These came to the attention of Faramarz ibn 'Ali 'Alā' al-Dawlah, Seljuk vassal-prince and philosopher,[77] who expressed a desire to see them put together in a more polished and complete form. Abū al-Barakāt refused on the grounds that they might fall into the hands of people incapable of understanding. Meanwhile, the notes kept growing until the philospher finally surrendered to his public. He dictated the work, presumably from his notes, to his chief disciple, who not only checked the finished work but also made suggestions in the course of the dictation.

The second notice pertains to Ibn Sīnā (d. A.D. 1037). Al-Jawzajāni, his student and the continuator of his autobiography, had asked him to compose a commentary (*sharḥ*) on Aristotle.[78] Ibn Sīnā pleads

75. Ibn Khallikān (trans. De Slane), III 307–10.

76. Pp. 2–4; see S. Pines, *Nouvelles Études sur Abū al-Barakāt* (Paris, 1955), pp. 9–13. On Abū al-Barakāt's philosophical activity see pp. 172–174 below.

77. See Meyerhof, *Osiris*, VIII (1948), 169–72 for the analysis of the notice of 'Alā' al-Dawlah in al-Bayhaqi's *Tatimmat*. The founder of the same dynasty, Abū Ja'far 'Alā' al-Dawlah, had no less than Ibn Sīnā as his vizier.

78. Uṣ., II, 5.

that he has not the time for such an undertaking, then continues: "... but if you will be satisfied with a work in which I set down my own scientific convictions and do not take issue with the opinions of other scholars I shall compose such a work." The outcome of this modest proposal was nothing less than the *Kitāb al-shifā'*, and thanks to the assiduity of al-Jawzajāni, we have a vivid description of just how this massive piece of learning took shape. Ibn Sīnā had once begun it, but political events had interrupted the work. Al-Jawzajāni continues the narrative:

I requested him to complete the Shifā', and he summoned Abū Ghālib and asked for paper and ink; these having been brought the master wrote in about twenty parts (each having eight folios) in his own hand the main topics to be discussed; in two days he had drafted all the topics, without having any book at hand or source to consult, accomplishing the work entirely from memory. Then he placed these parts before him, took paper and began to examine each topic and wrote his comments on it. Each day he wrote fifty leaves, until he had completed the natural sciences and metaphysics save for the books of zoology and botany. He commenced work on the logic and wrote one part of this ...

The work was interrupted when Ibn Sīnā was thrown into jail. During the confinement he managed to finish three more books. But his fortunes changed; he was released and appointed vizier at the court of 'Alā' al-Dawlah at Isfahan.

At Isfahan he set about completing the Shifā'; he finishe thed logic and the Almagest and had already epitomized Euclid, the arithmetic, and the music. In each book of the mathematics he introduced supplementary materials as the thought necessary; in the Almagest he brought up ten new figures on various points of speculation, and in the astronomical section at the end of the work he added things which had never been discovered before. In the same way he introduced some new examples into Euclid, enlarging the arithmetic with a number of excellent refinements, and discussed problems of music which the ancient Greeks had wholly neglected. So he finished the Shifā', all but the botany and zoology which he composed in the year when 'Alā' al-Dawlah marched to Sabur-Khwast; these parts he wrote en route, as well as the Kitāb al-najāt.[79]

Earlier, Ibn Sīnā had mentioned his inability to "take issue with the opinions of other scholars." He did finally find the time, and Arabic *Aporienliteratur* was enriched with the *Kitāb al-mabaḥithāt,* unorganized answers to questions posed to him by his students.[80] The scene is vividly described in the *Chahār maqālah.*[81] Ibn Sīnā, then at the court of 'Alā' al-Dawlah, would rise long before dawn, certainly an act of heroic intellectual virtue in a man of Ibn Sīnā's nocturnal habits, and work on the *Shifā'*. As dawn began breaking his pupils, Bahmanyār, Ibn Zaylah, and others, would join him and the discussions preserved in the *Mabahithḥāt* took place. Later in the morning, Ibn Sīnā went off to the goverment offices to fulfill his duties as vizier.

Whatever the mechanical procedures involved, the direction taken by the literature of comment is more radically determined by other considerations. Something has already been said of the paraphrases favored by al-Kindi that stood midway between translation and exegesis. There are many reasons why an author might prefer to employ this technique, but one that suggests itself somewhat more forcibly at this particular historical point is the absence of a reliable text and the still developing philological skills of the exegetes. There is an obvious parallel between the state of textual matters in Islam *ca.* A.D. 850 and that at the University of Paris before A.D. 1250 when Roger Bacon was commenting the *Physica* on the Arts Faculty there *per modum quaestionis.*

But we need not anticipate; there are equally illuminating analogies in the Greek literature of comment. In the Hellenic tradition the first "commentaries" on Aristotle after Andronicus' edition were in the form of paraphrases. Most of these are known only by title, but the most significant for the later Arabs were those done by

79. Al-Qifṭi, pp. 420–22 trans. A. J. Arberry, *Avicenna on Theology* (London, 1951), pp. 17–19
80. See S. Pines, *AHDL*, XXIX (1954) 43–55.
81. Chap. XXXVIII; trans. Browne, p. 92.

Nicolaus of Damascus (d. A.D. 25), which were translated into Arabic and which appear and reappear at different points in the oriental *corpus* as *testimonia*, e.g., for the *Metaphysica*, *Historia animalium*, and the *De plantis*.[82] The truly exegetical, *per modum commenti* type first appears with Alexander of Aphrodisias (*fl. ca.* A.D. 200), and the subsequent commentaries done in Athens, and particularly at Alexandria, generally followed this prototype.

TEXTUAL COMMENT: *TAFSĪR, TA'LĪQ*

With the coming of age of the Baghdad school, the exegetical/gloss commentary takes its place at the side of the paraphrase. With al-Fārābi the distinction of "small", "middle," and "large" commentary is first seen,[83] a pedagogical device which has its counterpart in the Greek tradition. Porphyry's work on the *Categoriae*, for example, included not only the extant *Eisagoge*, but also the "Great Commentary" in seven books which formed the basis of Simplicius' commentary and is known only from later authors,[84] and a smaller one, *Kata peusin kai apokrisin*.[85]

Ibn Sīnā, who preferred the expanded paraphrase to the exegetical commentary, introduced the same distinction of types into his encyclopedias,[86] but the Islamic *locus classicus* for the division into a "small," "middle," and "great" commentary is undoubtedly to be found in the work of Ibn Rushd.

Ibn Rushd's commentaries on Aristotle are usually labeled *jawāmi'ah*, *talkhīṣ*, and *tafsīr*; since the first two fall more properly under the heading of paraphrases, we are here concerned with the

82. See H. J. Drossaart Lulofs, *JHS*, LXXVII (1957), 75–80.
83. Al-Qifṭi, p. 279.
84. Simplicius, *In. Cat.* (Ed. Kalbfleisch), p. 2, ll. 5 ff., p. 3, ll. 13 ff.
85. Busse (ed.), *CAG*, IV, 1, pp. 55 ff.
86. See p. 104–105 below.

third type alone. The Averroan *tafsīr*,[87] the "Great Commentary," is the crown of the Arabic literature of comment on Aristotle. Formally derived from the great Greek commentaries of the third-through-sixth centuries of the Christian era,[88] the Averroan *tafsīrs* are, nonetheless, monuments to Islamic learning and to the man who composed them. The Great Commentary on the *De anima* was written *ca.* A.D. 1190, near the end of Ibn Rushd's career, and, like his other works of the same dimension, it is put together *per modum commenti*, i.e., the text, reproduced here from the version of an as yet unidentified translator, is commented paragraph by paragraph.[89] In it is exhibited the wide range of learning amassed by the Arabs across the many centuries of their devotion to Aristotle. Ibn Rushd ranges widely through the *corpus*: the *Analytica posteriora, Topica, Physica, De generatione, De coelo, Meteorologica, De sensu, De somno, Historia animalium, De motu animalium, Metaphysica*, and the *De anhelitu* ("I have not seen this work") are all drawn upon in the course of this single commentary. Nor are the commenters neglected. The Greeks: Alexander, Nicolaus of Damascus, Galen, Themistius, and Theophrastus, are all there, as are the Arabs: al-Fārābi, Abū al-Faraj ibn al-Ṭayyib, Ibn Sīnā, and Ibn Bajjah.

As Aristotelians, this is as far as the Arabs ever went. Nor does the formal Averroan *tafsīr* represent any more than a fraction of the comment activity in Islam. There was a marked preference for either the gloss commentary or the paraphrase.

87. *Sharḥ*, the more generic Arabic expression for commentary on a text, is roughly synonymous with *tafsīr* used nontechnically. The narrower meaning of *tafsīr* as a paragraph-by-paragraph commentary has been consecrated by the Averroan usage.

88. A glance at the text histories of Aristotle will illustrate the extent of the Arabs' knowledge of the Greek commentators. One explicit quotation must suffice: Yaḥyā ibn ʿAdi is speaking of his work on the *Topica*: "For this work I found no other commentaries but those of Alexander . . . and Ammonius. And I relied according to my intention in this commentary, on what I learned from Alexander and Ammonius." *Fihrist*, p. 249.

89. The text is normally introduced by *qālā Arisṭū*, and the comment again reproduces the text line by line as *lemmata*. There are other ways of distinguishing text and comment. Jamāl al-Dī Ḥilli, commenting the *Ḥikmat al-ʿayn* of al-Ṭūsi, prefixes the former with *qālā* (Ṭūsi) and the latter with *aqulu* (Ḥilli). An equally common distinction is that found in Berlin MS 5096, the text of Ṣadr al-Sharīʿah's *Taʿdīl al-ʿūlum* with the author's own commentary. The text begins with ما (*matn*), the comment with ش (*sharḥ*).

The gloss, *ta'līq 'alā hashīyah* or simply *al-hashīyah*,[90] was, as the name implies, a marginal notation which in the Aristotelian context varies from the preponderantly philological glosses prepared in the Baghdad Peripatetic school to the philosophical *marginalia* of Ibn Sīnā.

The Baghdad glosses on the *Organon* are cumulative, written by succeeding scholars on the margins of the school texts in use there and finally incorporated in the edition prepared by Ibn Suwār (d. A.D. 1017). Ibn Suwār approaches the text of Aristotle as both a commentator and editor. He suggests emendations,[91] comments on the linguistic difference between Arabic and Greek,[92] cites the evidence of the Greek manuscripts, *lemmata* from the commentators,[93] the autograph of Isḥāq's translation,[94] the Syriac versions,[95] and the Greek and Arab commentators.[96] The paraphernalia of scholarship is impressive, but it is being brought to bear almost exclusively on textual problems.

To turn from these glosses to those of Ibn Sīnā is to leave the world of philology for that of philosophy. On two notable occasions Ibn Sīnā turned to the gloss method, once to comment the Aristotelian *corpus* and again to gloss his own Aristotelian encyclopedia, the *Kitāb al-shifā'*. The former resulted in the *Kitāb al-inṣāf*, an attempt systematically to annotate the entire Aristotelian *corpus*.[97] It was destroyed once, then redone, and is today represented only by

90. For a definition of the two terms see Hajji Khalifah, III, # 4366. The compound term is used in the title of Ibn Sīnā's glosses on the *De anima*. The expression *ta'līq/ta'līqah*, when used alone, apparently had a somewhat wider extension even in a philosophical context. Al-Fārābi called his treatment of the *Eisagoge Kitāb ta'līq*, and while it is impossible to know what this looked like in its original form, the reworking in Istanbul Hamidiye 812 published by D. M. Dunlop (*Islamic Quarterly*, III [1956], 117–38) is clearly a paraphrase type. More illustrative is Ibn Suwār's *prolegomena* to the *Categoriae* which he calls "somewhat in the manner of notes"; see Georr, *Catégories*, p. 364.
91. Georr, *Catégories*, p. 179, # 112.
92. *Ibid.*, p. 181, # 130.
93. *Ibid.*, p. 162, # 21.
94. *Ibid.*, p. 176, # 67.
95. *Ibid.*, p. 174, # 50.
96. *Ibid.*, p. 160, # 4; p. 173, # 49.
97. On the complicated question of the purpose of this work see H. Pines, *AHDL*, XXIX (1952), 5–37.

sections from the *Metaphysica*, *De anima*, and *Theologia*.[98] The glosses themselves are severely philosophical in tone, and their general texture is no different from what a reader might find in opening a random page of one of Ibn Rushd's *Great Commentaries*.

The other occassion for Ibn Sīnā's use of the gloss is described in his preface to the *Eisagoge* section of his own *Shifā'*.[99] According to his own account his major works on philosophy are three: the *Shifā'*, an encyclopedic exposé of Peripatetic philosophy, and done, as been seen, somewhat hastily. The *Shifā'* will be supplemented by his own continuing glosses on it, the *Kitāb al-lawāḥiq*. Finally there is the *Ḥikmat al-mashriqīyah*, a self-standing work that represents strictly his own point of view.

The subsequent history of the *Lawāḥiq* illustrates the hazards which frequently awaited an oriental text of this nature.[100] The collection of glosses was edited after the master's death by his student Bahmanyār (d. A.D. 1066),[101] who changed the announced title to the synonymous *Ta'līqāt*. His edition, represented in MS Cairo 6 *ḥikmah*, keeps the somewhat haphazard arrangement of the original, an unsatisfactory situation once the originally glossed text was removed. The defect was remedied by Bahmanyār's student, al-Lawkari (d. *ca.* A.D. 1109), who prepared another recension (Aya Sofia 2390) in which the notes were inventoried and numbered. While the orderly tendencies of late Islamic scholasticism continue through a whole series of Iranian manuscript which further systematizes the original glosses, syncretistic forces are also at work; in the list of Ibn Sīnā's works appears a collection of aphorisms, the *Fuṣūl fī al-ḥikmah*,[102] which now represents excerpts from the *Lawāḥiq* mixed in with material from al-Fārābi.

98. See A. Badawi, *Arisṭū 'ind al-'arab* (Cairo, 1947), pp. 119–22.

99. Ed. Cairo, 1952, p. 10; this important preface has been studied by A. Birkenmajer, *RNSP*, XXXVI (1934), pp. 308–20, and more appositely for the present subject by M. El-Khodeiri, "Autour de deux opuscules d'Avicenne traduits en Latin," *MIDEO*, II (1955), 341–50.

100. The fate of the *Lawāḥiq* has been traced by El-Khodeiri, *op. cit.*

101. See p. 192 below.

102. Anawati, *Mu'allafāt*, # 188.

EPITOMES: *JAWĀMIʿAH, MUKHTAṢAR, TALKHĪṢ*

The epitome/paraphrase was a venerable pedagogical device in the Hellenic tradition long before the Arabs learned to profit from that tradition.[103] We also know that the ancient school tradition, particularly that in medicine, was unbroken in its transit from Greek to Syrian to Arab.[104] It is natural, then, to find the Arabs using the convenient and clear paraphrase form in dealing with the "classical" authors. Just such a synopsis of sixteen books of Galen in use in Alexandria *ca.* A.D. 600 was still current in the schools of Baghdad three centuries later.[105] Indeed, what is apparently the oldest version of *Aristotelica* in Arabic is a similar epitome of a commentary on the beginning of the *Organon*,[106] and the presence of Nicolaus of Damascus epitomes in Arabic has already been noted.

The free use of paraphrases and the consequent loss of a sense of verbal citation led inevitably to syncretizing. Al-Kindi, whose philosophical activity was based on the pre-Ḥunayn *veteres* and who favored the periphrastic approach, provides three notable examples. In his work entitled "An Essay on Opinions concerning the Soul Epitomized (*mukhtaṣar*) from the Books of Aristotle and Plato,"[107] he, or his Greek prototype, has included not only verbal citations and paraphrases from the *De anima* but also what is apparently a section, unidentified to be sure, from the lost dialogue, *Eudemus*. A second work on astronomy contains extensive reworked passages from Ptolemy's *Syntaxis astronomica*,[108] while a third ethical treatise is a slightly disguised paraphrase of Themistius.[109]

103. See I. Opelt, art. "Epitome," *RAC*, V, cols. 944–72; E. Von Ivanka, κεφαλεια, eine Byzantinische Literaturform und ihre antike Wurzeln," *BZ*, XLVII (1954), 285–91.
104. Ḥunayn, *Risālah*, # 20.
105. Meyerhof, "Alexandrien nach Baghdad," pp. 395–96.
106. Beyrouth MS St. Joseph Univ. 338; see P. Kraus, *RSO*, XIV (1933), 5–6.
107. Abu Rida (ed.), *Rasāʾil al-Kindi*, I (Cairo, 1950), 272–80.
108. See F. Rosenthal, "Al-Kindi and Ptolemy," *Studi Orientalistici in onore Giorgio Levi della Vida*, II (Rome, 1956), 436–56, espec. pp. 439–40, and p. 448, n. 4.
109. See H. Ritter and R. Walzer, *Studi sul al-Kindi*, II *Memorie Lincei* Ser. 6, Vol. VIII, 1 (Rome, 1938).

The nomenclature of the Arabic epitome literature is not very well defined. Passing over the less frequent *mujiz,*[110] and, *gharāḍ*[111] the usage becomes more stabilized at *mukhtaṣar, jawāmi'ah,* and *talkhīṣ,* the latter two used for the "small" and "middle" commentaries—better paraphrases—of Ibn Rushd. It is notable that even in Ibn Rushd, where the terms are used to designate two separate approaches to the same Aristotelian work, the difference is one of scale and not of kind, and even within the individual types the scale is so varied that at least one student of Ibn Rushd has denied the distinction between the Averroan *jawāmi'ah* and *talkhīṣ.*[112]

The mechanical procedure varies somewhat from work to work, but some general remarks may be offered on the Islamic philosophical paraphrase. The initial sections usually contain an introductory and/or an *intentio auctoris* familiar from the prolegomena in the *eisagoge* complex. Almost always there is a summary of the contents, frequently quite detailed.[113] Rarely are there verbal reproductions of the original author; the texts are paraphrased and hence are usually of little value for restoration or emendation of the original.[114] There is a certain amount of editorializing. Isḥāq has fleshed out some of the argumentation in his treatment of the *De anima,*[115] and Ibn Rushd, when dealing with something as difficult as the *Poetica,* has not hesitated to omit obscurities and irrelevancies in Abū Bishr's translation, going so far as to substitute Arabic literary and linguistic examples for the original Greek ones.[116]

110. Ibn Sīnā: Anawati, *Mu'allafāt,* # 43, # 45.

111. *Gharad,* "intention," is probably the *skopos* of the Neoplatonic commentators; see p. 16 above. Us., II, 139 mentions a treatise of al-Fārābi entitled "on the Intentions of Aristotle in Each of His Works." Given the normal fluctuations in nomenclature this would seem to be Fārābi's epitome of Aristotle; see p. 101, n. 5 below.

112. A. Ahwani, *Ibn Rushd talkhīṣ kitāb al-nafs* (Cairo, 1950), pp. 9–18; compare E. Renan, *Averroes et l'averroisme* (Paris, 1862), pp. 58–61.

113. The range can be seen in comparing the brief opening of Ibn Rushd's *talkhīṣ* of the *Categoriae* with the same author's elaborate introductory note in his paraphrase of the *De anima* or with Isḥāq's *divisio* preceding his epitome of the *De anima.*

114. See the remarks of Bouyges, *Notice,* p. lii, and the more general observations in his edition of the *tqalkhīṣ* of the *Categoriae* (Beyrouth, 1932), p. xl.

115. See espec. p. 132 of Ahwani's edition.

116. See Tkatsch, *Poetik,* pp. 132 b–134 a; the same procedure is not uncommon in the translations themselves.

It is difficult to give an adequate idea of the range and ubiquity of the Arabic philosophical *mukhtaṣar/talkhīṣ* since the genre embraces the entire spectrum between al-Kindi's rapid résumé of the Aristotelian *corpus* and Ibn Sīnā's monumental Aristotelian encylopedia, the *Kitab al-shifā'*. The preceding remarks deal only with the vast middle ground, neither summary nor encyclopedic, which provided the Arab intellectual with hundreds of approaches, second hand but by no means undemanding, to either an individual Aristotelian work or to some higher complex like the *Organon*.

V

THE DIFFUSION OF ARISTOTELIANISM

Thus far the effects of the reception of Aristotelianism in Islam have been considered within the narrow limits of the formation of a professional, philosophical elite, and the further consequences of this will be seen again in Chapter VI when the various philosophical schools born of the translation movement are discussed. But first some effort must be made to take the measure of the extraordinary impact of this philosopher on the intellectual life of Islam in its wider aspects. It would be difficult, and perhaps even meaningless, to separate Aristotle from the even broader confrontation with Hellenic learning as a whole,[1] and so what follows will attempt to focus on the Aristotelian elements within the Muslim's Hellenic legacy rather than delimit them in any rigorous fashion.

The uses of Aristotle in Islam are very nearly those of the medieval West. At one end of the scale is the Aristotelian *auctoritas*, the species of scholarly name-dropping where Aristotle, and to an even greater extent the pseudo-Aristotle, becomes all things to all men: alchemist, musician, mineralogist, political sage. At the other end is the textual citation by chapter and verse, a technique as rare among the Arabs as it is among their Latin and Byzantine contemporaries. Between the two stretches the whole range of influence that a thinker

1. C. H. Becker, *Islamstudien* (Leipzig, 1924), pp. 24–39; *idem*, *Das Erbe der Antike im Orient und Okzident* (Leipzig, 1931); H. Schaeder, "Der Orient und das griechische Erbe," *Die Antike*, IV (1928), 226–65; G. von Grunebaum, "Islamkunde und Kulturwissenschaft," *ZDMG*, CIII (1953), 2–16; B. Spuler, "Hellenistisches Denken im Islam," *Saeculum*, V (1954), 179–93; A. Badawi, "L'humanisme dans la pensée arabe," *Studia Islamica*, VI (1956), 67–100; A. A. Toynbee, *A Study of History*, XII (London, 1961), 446–54.

may exert on an alien culture, and the diverse manifestations of that influence: reminiscences, epitomes, loose paraphrases, and, with the passage of time and the growth of philosophical sophistication, Aristotelian concepts used without identification or hesitation, the *lingua franca* of culture.

The more formal *vestigia* of Aristotelianism are not too difficult to trace in their philosophical and para-philosophical contexts. Their Hellenistic teachers had given the Arabs various forms of philosphical expression to which they generally remained faithful. As is manifest in their preservation of the *eisagoge* complex and in their general approach to the literature of comment, the purely formalistic side of Aristotelianism in Islam was extremely conservative, as normally occurs in a scholastic tradition. Almost all the devices fashioned in the Hellenistic schools were in use among the *falāsifah*, even though philosophy itself was no longer a part of any formal curriculum. What had begun as pedagogy was now part of the method of philosophy itself.

EPITOME AND DEFINITION LITERATURE

The epitome most frequently concerns itself with a single Aristotelian work and, as such, belongs to the translation history of the individual works of the *corpus*. But here a word must be said about two derivative epitome types: the epitome of Aristotelian philosophy and the "Book of Definitions."

A summary of the Aristotelian system, at least in its barest outlines, is inherent in the classificatory lists of the *eisagoge* complex and in their derivative encyclopedias. The continuation of another branch of the Hellenistic tradition can be seen in the Arabs' reception of the work of Nicolaus of Damascus, historian and philosopher at the court of Herod the Great. His "On the Philosophy of Aristotle" was translated into Syriac by Ḥunayn (d. A.D. 876),[2] sub-

2. The authority for Ḥunayn as the translator is Barhebraeus, *Ta'rikh*, p. 140.

sequently translated into Arabic by Ibn Zur'ah (d. A.D. 1008). It later turns up at various points in the translation history of the *corpus*,[3] and in Ibn Rushd's (d. A.D. 1198) *Great Commentary* on the *Metaphysica*.[4]

Seemingly from native hands, but most likely as an adaptation of a Greek work like Nicolaus', is the epitome of Aristotle's philosophy attributed to al-Fārābi (d. A.D. 950), a parallel to the already published epitome of Plato's philosophy.[5] An epitome of Aristotelian ethics preserved in Greek in Stobaeus' *Eclogae*[6] was also available in the Arab tradition via the ethical compendium of Miskawayh (d. A.D. 1030), *Tahdhīb al-akhlāq*,[7] and in more complete recension than that in Stobaeus.[8]

An obstacle to a more exact understanding of Islamic Aristotelianism is our very sketchy knowledge in precisely this area of the epitome literature of antiquity. A representative selection of the exegetical type commentary initiated by Alexander of Aphrodisias has been preserved; but the epitome approach, common from the time of Andronicus' editing of the *corpus* until the beginning of the third century A.D., is poorly represented, at least in a form that can be identified, among the extant philosophical texts. Until such a time as this lacuna can be filled, and it may well be that it will be filled from the Arabic material, judgements on either the originality or the philosophical presuppositions of the *falāsifah* must of necessity remain provisional.

The original connection of a collection of definitions with the *eisagoge* complex can be seen from Ibn Suwār's introduction to the

3. The Syriac version of this important text is extant in Cambridge MS Gg 2.14 and has been published, with translation and commentary, by H. J. Drossaart Lulofs, *Nicolaus Damascenus on the Philosophy of Aristotle* (Leyden, 1965).

4. See Bouyges, *Notice*, p. cxxxiii, and R. Walzer, *Orientalia*, XX (1951), 338.

5. Preserved in Aya Sofia MS 4833 fols. 19^v–59^r. In one of its forms the epitome included résumés of both Plato and Aristotle. The sections on Plato were edited and translated by F. Rosenthal and R. Walzer, *Alfarabius de Platonis Philosophia* (Plato Arabus, II [London, 1943]), and the entire work was edited by M. Mahdi, *Falsafat Aristūtālis* (Beyrouth, 1961), and translated *idem*, *Alfarabi's Philosophy of Plato and Aristotle* (Glencoe, 1962).

6. Meineke (ed.), II, 81, l. 26–p. 82, l. 15.

7. Ed. Cairo, 1911, pp. 63–65; on this work see pp. 125–126 below.

8. See S. Pines, *AHDL*, XXVI (1956), 6–7.

Categoriae.[9] After an exact reproduction of an Hellenistic "Prolegomena to the *Categoriae,*" Ibn Suwār has put together a kind of glossary of technical terms (*kategoriai, homonoma,* etc.) culled from the Greek commentators, much as al-Fārābi compiled a list of etymologies of the names of Greek philosophers.[10]

A slightly different orientation is evidenced in the Syriac *Book of Definitions* by an obscure Bazud (*aliter* Abzud, Michael) where a series of definitions follows upon a "On Philosophy in General."[11] The type, then, is a species of *Hilfmittel* to the study of Aristotelian logic, and it has an extensive history among both the Syrians and the Arabs.

Its earliest traces among the Syrians is in the *Book of Definitions on all the Subjects of Logic* by the Nestorian Ahoudemmah (d. A.D. 575), who is known only by citation, and in the preserved but unpublished *Definitions and Distinctions* by the monk ʿEnanishūʿ (*fl. ca.* A.D. 650).[12] The Arabic series opens with al-Kindi's (d. *ca.* A.D. 870) *On the Definitions and Descriptions of Things,*[13] and continues down through Ishāq al-Isrāʾīli's (d. *ca.* A.D. 932) *Book of Definitions,*[14] Jābir,[15] Ibn Sīnā (d. A.D. 1037),[16] ʿUbaydallāh ibn Bakhtīshūʿ (d.

9. Georr, *Catégories*, pp. 361–71.
10. F. Rosenthal (ed.), *JAOS*, LXII (1943), 73–74.
11. See p. 81 above.
12. On Syriac definition literature see Baumstark, *Aristoteles bei den Syrern*, pp. 213–19, where the collection of Bazud is derived from ʿEnanīshū; a brief study by G. Furlani, "Enanisho, Ahudemmah e il Libro delle Definizione di Michele l'Interprete," *Rendiconti Lincei*, Ser 5, Vol. XXXI (1922), 143–48, traces Bazud back to Ahoudemmah rather than to ʿEnanīshūʿ. The text to Bazud according to Berlin MS Peterman 9 is published in Baumstark, *op. cit.*, and the entire range of MSS is used in Furlani's edition in *Memorie Lincei*, Ser. 6, Vol. II (1926), 1–194.
13. Published from Aya Sofia 4832, by Abu Ridah, *Rasāʾil al-Kindi*, I, 165–80; MS BM add. 7473 has been correlated with this by J. M. Stern, "Notes on al-Kindi's Treatise on Definitions," *JRAS* (1959), pp. 32–43; as Stern points out, al-Kindi's definitinos were used as a source in Chap. XCI of al-Tawḥīdi's *Muqābasāt*.
14. The Arabic text has not been found, but parts of the Hebrew version were edited by H. Hirschfeld in *Festschrift Steinschneider* (Leipzig, 1896), pp. 131–41, 233–34; the complete Latin translation by Gerard of Cremona was edited by J. T. Muckle, *AHDL*, XI (1938) 300–25, and an abridgement, *ibid.*, pp. 328–40, this latter attributed, on stylistic grounds, to Dominic Gundisalvo; see M. Alonso, *al-Andalus*, XII (1947), 325–28.
15. Kraus, *Jābir*, I, # 2745.
16. *Risālah fi al-ḥudūd* ed. in *Tisʿrasāʾil* (Cairo, 1908), pp. 72–102; French translation and annotations by A. M. Goichon, *Introduction à Avicenne; son Epitre des Definitions* (Paris, 1933).

A.D. 1058),[17] Sa'īd ibn Hibatallāh (d. A.D. 1101),[18] al-Īlāqi (d. A.D. 1141),[19] and Fakhr al-Dīn al-Rāzi (d. A.D. 1209).[20]

The use of philosophical concepts with theology necessitated a further adaptation of the definition method. In the Christian tradition the problem is largely confined to the technical terms used in Christological treatises, and collections of such are extant in Syriac from the pen of James of Edessa (d. A.D. 708),[21] and from Yūḥannā bar Zo'bi (*fl.* thirteenth century),[22] the former giving the Monophysite exegesis the latter the Nestorian. The same genre is represented in Arabic by the unedited treatise on theological definitions by the Baghdad Peripatetic Ibn Zur'ah (d. A.D. 1008).[23] Among the Muslims it was more than the explanation of a few extremely technical terms, but rather with the introduction of the entire structure of Aristotelian logic and physics into orthodox theology, so that from the time of al-Maqdisi (*fl. ca.* A.D. 960) down to that of al-Bayḍāwi (d. A.D. 1286), al-Ījī (d. A.D. 1355) and beyond, treatises of *kalām* are in part devoted to an explanation of philosophical concepts like substance and accident which had by then supplied the theoretical and conceptual foundation for discussions of the divine attributes.[24]

17. *Al-Rawdat al-ṭibbīyah*, ed. P. Sbath (Cairo, 1927), and analyzed by M. Meyerhof, "An Arabic Compendium of Medical-Philosophical Definitions," *Isis*, X (1928), 340–49; see p. 128 below.
18. *GAL*, I², 640.
19. *GAL*, Suppl. I, p. 887.
20. *GAL*, Suppl. I, p. 923.
21. Text with Italian translation published from BM add. 12154, by G. Furlani, "L' εγχειριςιον di Giacomo d'Edessa nel testo siriaco," *Rendigconti Lincei*, Ser. 6, Vol. IV (1928), 223–49, and *idem*, "D'alcune passi della *Metafisica* di Aristotele presso Giacomo d'Edessa," *Rendiconti Lincei*, Ser. 6, Vol. XXX (1928), 268–73.
22. Ed. with Italian translation by G. Furlani, "Yohanna bar Zo'bi sulla differenza tra natura, persona, e faccia," *RSO*, XII (1930), 272–85.
23. Paris BN *ar.* 173, fols. 75–76; Vat. *ar.* 113, fols. 97–98.
24. On the Muslim works of *kalām* and the sections devoted to philosophical terminology see Gardet-Anawati, *Théologie musulmane*, pp. 164–69, who do not, however, consider the treatise of al-Māqdisi (Chaps. I–IV of the *Bad' al-khalq*) where the method of development is by definition followed by objections and their solution.

ENCYCLOPEDIAS

Encyclopedism, and particularly Arab encyclopedism, is frequently cited as a hallmark of cultural decadence. But such a symptom is at best relative. No one will fail to hear the death rattle in the glosses-upon-glosses that bloom in such profusion in the second volume of Brockelmann's *Geschichte der arabischen Literatur*; what, however, is to be said of a discipline that is all but born in encyclopedism? Surely a distinction is in order.

The encyclopedias with which we are here concerned have their roots in two distinct traditions, one of which is clearly a cultural borrowing from Alexandrian Hellenism, while the other is composite in nature.[25]

The first of these traditions is that of the classificatory lists connected with the *eisagoge* complex and treated in Chapter V above. In addition to a simple listing of Aristotelian titles, represented in Islam by the so-called Ptolemy *pinax*,[26] there was the far more speculative breakdown of the *corpus* under the section entitled "On Philosophy in General." And within the larger divisions of the *schema*, the distribution of the *akroamatica* into *theoretika and pratika* represents a division, according to its subject and its method, of the entire field of systematized knowledge itself (*episteme*, the Arabic *ʿilm*). The other category, the *poietika*, was largely ignored in the schools, and logic was assigned its traditional role as an *organon*. The student, then, was presented with a *schema* that was not only an instrument for subdividing a bibliography, but also a classification of all the "sciences" and that, as such, had its encyclopedic implications.

Something has already been said of the first generation descendants of this *schema*, the "division-of-the-sciences" type works.[27]

25. There is no study of the encyclopedia as a genre. The most detailed coverage is to be found in M. Plessner, *Der OIKONOMIKOS des Neupythagoreers* "Bryson" (Heidelberg, 1928), which is not, however, interested in the material *qua* encyclopedia; there is a rapid survey by H. A. R. Gibb, art. "Arabiyya," *EI²*, I, 594–95. For the encyclopedia as a cultural symptom see C. Pellat, "Les Etapes de la Décadence Culturelle dans les Pays Arabes d'Orient," in *Classicisme et Déclin Culturel dans l'Histoire de l'Islam* (Paris, 1957), p. 89.

26. See p. 83 above.

27. See pp. 84–85 above.

The next direct descendant is the philosophical encyclopedia, a literary sub-genus cultivated by both the Syriac- and Arabic-speaking communities in Islam and whose finest, and earliest, example is the *Kitab al-shifā'* of Ibn Sīnā (d. A.D. 1037).

The *Shifā'*, though the most elaborate and complete, is but one of a series of encyclopedic treatments that Ibn Sīnā devoted to Aristotelianism. They proceed from the extremely brief *al-Ḥikmah al-'arūdīyah*, done at the beginning of his career and covering only the first part of the Aristoelitan *corpus*,[28] to the monumental *Kitāb al-shifā*,[29] the *Liber sufficientiae* of the medieval West,[30] which anticipates the same periphrastic, expository method (*per modum expositionis*) made familiar to the Latin Scholastics by the *Summa de creaturis* of Albert the Great (A.D. 1206–1280).[31]

IBN SĪNĀ, *KITĀB AL-SHIFĀ'*

I. *Logica*

(Part 1: *Eisagoge* to Part 9: *Poetica*, following the structure of the *Organon*)

28. Anawati, *Mu'allafāt*, # 10; see M. Anawati, "La *Hikma arudiyya* d'Ibn Sina," *Proceedings of the XXII International Congress of Orientalists* (Leyden, 1957), pp. 171–76.

29. A critical edition is underway. The first volume covering the *Eisagoge* appeared in Cairo, 1950. The section dealing with the *Analytica posteriora* was published independently by A. Badawi (Cairo, 1954).

30. The Latin versions of the *Shifā'* have been dealt with by M. T. d'Alverny, "Notes sur les traductions médiévales d'Avicenne," *AHDL*, XXVII (1952), 337–58, and by M. Alonso, "Traducciones del Arabe al Latin por Juan Hispano (Ibn Dāwūd)," *al-Andalus*, XVII (1952), 142–47, 149–51; *idem*, "Traducciones del Arcadiano Domingo Gundisalvo," *al-Andalus*, XII (1944), 333–36. For the spurious *De coelo* inserted in the Latin versions of the *Shifā*, see M. Alonso, *al-Andalus*, XVI (1951), 37–47.

31. Albert's manifesto at the beginning of *Physica* I, *tract.* 1, *cap.* 1 of the same work might serve equally well to illustrate the *intentio Avicennae:*

> *Erit autem modus noster in hoc opere Aristotelis ordinem et sententiam sequi et dicere ad explanationem ejus quaecumquae necessaria esse videbantur; ita tamen quod textus ejus nulla fiat mentio. Et praeter hoc digressiones faciemus declarantes dubia subeuntia, et supplentes quaecumque minus dicta in sententia philosophi obscuritatem quibusdam attulerunt.*

II. *Naturalia*
  A. *Auscultatio physica*
  B. *De coelo et mundo*
  C. On Natures
  D. Agents and Patients
  E. Inanimate Beings
  F. *De anima*
  G. *De plantis*
  H. *De animalibus*

III. *Mathematica*
  A. Geometry
  B. Arithmetic
  C. Music
  D. Astronomy (the *Almagest*)

IV. *Theologia*
  A. (Parts 1 to 7 on various metaphysical concepts: substance, accidents, quantity, quality, cause, etc.)
  B. (On the First Principle)
    8. On a Knowledge of the First Principle
    9. On the Procession of Things from the First Principle
  C. (Part 10 is a catch-all division including Prophetology and Politics)

The *Shifā'* is not all Aristotle, to be sure. The sections on the *Logica* and the *Naturalia* adhere to the Aristotelian framework, but Part III, the *Mathematica*, has been freely compiled from Euclid and Ptolemy, while the final section on theology profits from the Aristotelian *pseudepigraphica*, as well as the abundant Neoplatonic strains in Ibn Sīnā's own thought. By his own admission he has felt free to go beyond his model.[32]

32. See p. 90 above.

Some note has already been made of the method of composition behind the *Shifā'*. It was done hastily and apparently without direct access to the Aristotelian texts themselves. But it was not Ibn Sīnā's final word on the subject. In addition to his own glosses on the *Shifā'*,[33] he epitomized his own encyclopedia on two later occasions. The *Kitab al-najāt* was done immediately after the *Shifā'*,[34] followed, *ca.* A.D. 1021–1037, by a similar epitome in Persian, the *Danesh-nāme.*[35]

The *Shifā'* served to usher in the line of philosophical encyclopedias of the thirteenth century and beyond: two directly called forth by the work of Ibn Sīnā, the *Al-Mu'tabar fī al-ḥikmah of* Abū al-Barakāt (d. A.D. 1165)[36] and the *Al-Mabāḥith al-mashriqīyah* of Fakhr al-Dīn al-Rāzi (d. A.D. 1209),[37] as well as the *al-Shajarah al-ilāhīyah* of al-Sharazūri (*fl.* thirteenth century),[38] the *Hidāyat al-ḥikmah* of al-Abhari (d. A.D. 1264),[39] and the encyclopedias of al-Kātibi (d. A.D. 1276).[40]

Syriac encyclopedism flourished at a time when the earlier debt incurred by the Arabs toward their Syriac translators and professors was being repaid by influences generated in the other direction, chiefly from Ibn Sīnā and al-Ghazāli to the key figures of the thirteenth century "Syriac Renaissance." Severus bar Shakko (d. A.D. 1241), for instance, had as a professor of philosophy Kamāl al-Dīn Ibn Yūnus,[41] a renowned interpreter of Fakhr al-Dīn al-Rāzi (d. A.D. 1209) and the mentor of al-Ṭūsi (d. A.D. 1274), two Muslim

33. The *Kitāb al-lawāḥiq*; see p. 95 above.
34. Ed. Cairo, 1939; the section on the metaphysics has been translated into Latin by N. Carame, *Avicennae Metaphysices Compendium* (Rome, 1926), and the section on psychology by F. Rahman, *Avicenna's Psychology*, (Oxford, 1952).
35. Ed. Meshkat and Mo'in (Teheran, 1953); partial translation by M. Achena and H. Massé, *Le Livre de Science* (2 vols.; Paris, 1955).
36. *GAL*, Suppl. I, p. 831; see above and p. 89 below.
37. Two vols.; ed. Hayderabad, 1924–1925; on Rāzi see pp. 194–196 below.
38. *GAL*, I², 617, Suppl. I, p. 851; Ahlwardt, *Arabischen Handschriften* (*Berlin*), # 5063; additional material in M. Plessner, *Islamica*, IV (1931), 529–31, and *idem*, *Bryson*, pp. 262–73; see pp. 127–128 below.
39. *GAL*, I², 608–609, Suppl. I, pp. 839–41.
40. *Ḥikmat al-'ayn* (*Physica* and *Metaphysica* only; *Logica* treated separately): *GAL*, I², 613–14; *Jami' al-daqā'iq*: *GAL*, I², 614.
41. See Ibn Khallikān, ed. Wüstenfeld, IX, 122.

encyclopedists of the same period. Severus' own philosphical encyclopedia, *Book of the Dialogue*,[42] was intended, ideally of course, as a kind of curriculum of higher studies in the Jacobite Church and betrays a close contact with the *eisagoge* material of later Hellenism.

In Gregorius Abū al-Faraj Barhebraeus (d. A.D. 1286), the Syriac tradition of secular learning, begun so uncertainly with "Hibha, Kumi and Probha," reaches its climax and, indeed, its end. A true polymath, Barhebraeus composed works in both Syriac and Arabic on science, history, philosophy, canon law, and dogmatic, ascetic, and mystical theology which found their readership in both Christian and Muslim circles.[43]

In accordance with the practice begun by Ibn Sīnā, Barhebraeus wrote three distinct types of philosophical encyclopedias: a full statement of Aristotelianism, the *Cream of Wisdom*, according to the traditional division into *Logica*, *Physica*, *Metaphysica*, and *Practica*; a "middle" encyclopedia covering the same ground, the *Treatise of the Treatises*; and, finally, a summary exposition, the *Conversation of Wisdom*.[44]

The deficiencies of the Aristotelian *schema* for Arab purposes are clear. It takes account of neither the arts and crafts nor the areas

42. See *GSL*, pp. 311–12; J. Ruska, "Studien zu Severus bar Shakku's Buch der Dialogue," *ZA*, XII (1897), 8–41, 145–60, with an excellent survey of Syrian higher studies of the period. The mathematical sections have been edited and translated by Ruska in his *Das Quadrivium aus Severus bar Shakku's Buch der Dialogue* (Leipzig, 1896).

43. See *GSL*, pp. 312–20; Jugie, *Theologia*, V, 474–78, and Index *s.v.*

44. On the three types of encyclopedias see H. Janssens, *L'Entretien de la Sagesse* (Liege, 1937), pp. 7–12; only bits and pieces of the encyclopedias have been edited, but an idea of the comparative treatment may be gained from the psychological passages edited by G. Furlani, "La psicologia di Bar Hebreo secondo il libro La Crema della Sapienza," *RSO*, XIII (1931), 24–52; *idem*, "Di tre scritti in lingua siriaca di Bar Hebreo sull'anima," *RSO*, XIV (1933), 299–305 (*Treatise*), and pp. 305–307 (*Conversation*), to which can be added the psychological material from the more theological *Candelabrum*, ed. J. Bakoš, *Psychologie de Gregoire Aboulfaradj dit Bar Hebraeus* (Leyden, 1948), and the self-standing treatise in Arabic edited by Malouf, Eddé, and Cheikho, in *Traités inédites d'anciens philosophes arabes musulmans et chrétiens* (Beyrouth, 1911), pp. 76–102.

The dependence of Barhebraeus for much of his Hellenic learning on his Muslim contemporaries and predecessors has been thoroughly investigated: G. Furlani, *RSO*, XIII (1931), 6, and H. Janssens, *Muséon* (1932), p. 372 (Ibn Sīnā); H. Koffler, *Die Lehre des Barhebraeus von der Auferstehung der Leiber* (Rome, 1932), p. 30 (al-Ṭūsi); A. Wensinck, *Bar Hebraeus' Book of the Dove* (Leyden, 1919 [al-Ghazāli]).

thought by the Muslims to qualify as "science" and to be traditionally Arab. To deal with these omissions, encyclopedists either expanded the existing framework or added a completely new master division, i.e., the "Arab Sciences."

The expanded list is already apparent in the *Iḥsāʾ al-ʿulūm* of al-Fārābi where the base has been widened, in the first instance on a Greek or Syriac model, to include Linguistic Science, or, better, Diction.[45] More striking is the expansion of the final category in Fārābi's scheme to include not only Politics, as we should expect, but the more properly Islamic sciences, Jurisprudence (*fiqh*) and Theology (*kalām*), as well. The anomaly in this is that there is another "Theology" earlier in the *Iḥsāʾ* which corresponds in position, if not in content, with the Aristotelian *Metaphysica*, and which is called "The Divine Science" (*al-ʿilm al-ilāhi*). The two theologies exist in uneasy juxtaposition thereafter, even in professed works of synthesis like the *Muḥaṣṣal* of Fakh al-Dīn al-Rāzi.[46]

The division of the sciences into "Arab" and "non-Arab" or "foreign" (or, from a slightly different standpoint, into "rational" and "traditional") is the most common Islamic method of putting the Aristotelian classification into a proper historical perspective. "Mixed" encyclopedias based on this new *schema* appear quite early in the Arab world: it is the system used by Ibn Farighūn (*fl. ca.* A.D. 950)[47] and al-Khawārizmi (*fl. ca.* A.D. 975–987).[48]

45. On the *Iḥsāʾ* see pp. 84–85 above.

46. The *Muḥaṣṣal*, and its commentary by al-Ṭūsi, has been the subject of two long studies by M. Horten, *Die philosophischen Ansichten von Razi und Tusi* (Bonn, 1910), and *Die spekulative und positive Theologie im Islam nach Razi und Tusi* (Leipzig, 1912), and more briefly in Gardet-Anawati, *Théologie musulmane*, pp. 162–64.

47. In *GAL*, Suppl. I, p. 435 as "Ibn Paraiʿin"; for his *Jawāmiʿ al-ʿulūm* see D. M. Dunlop in *Zeki Veledi Togana Armagan* (Istanbul, 1955), pp. 348–55, an analysis of MS Esc. 950; a Turkish MS of the *Jawāmiʿ* is described by H. Ritter, *Oriens*, III (1950), 83–84. A still earlier division work, *Aqsām al-maʿlūm*, is credited in *Fihrist*, p. 138, to Ibn Farighūn's teacher, Abū Zayd al-Balkhi (d. A.D. 934), himself a student of al-Kindi.

48. *Mafātīh alʿulūm*, ed. G. van Vloten (Leyden, 1895); see M. Plessner, *Islamica*, IV (1931), 529.

IBN FARIGHŪN, *JAWĀMIʿ AL-ʿULŪM*

- I. A. The Arabic Language
  - B. Writing
  - C. Reckoning
  - D. Religion (*al-dīn*, i.e., *cultus*)
- II. A. Politics
  - B. Ethics
  - C. *Scientia* (*al-ʿilm*)
    - 1. *kalām*
    - 2. Philosophy
      - a. Theology
      - b. Mathematics
      - c. Logic (lit. "propaedeutic", *riyāḍi*)
      - d. Physics
  - D. The Occult Sciences

AL-KHAWĀRIZMI, *MAFĀTĪH AL-ʿULŪM*

- I. The Arab Sciences
  - A. Jurisprudence
  - B. *kalām*
    - 1. On expressions used in *kalām*
    - 2. On Islamic sects (*madhāhib*)
    - 3. On the types of Christians and their expressions
    - 4. On the types of Jews and their expressions
    - 5. On various religious groups
    - 6. On idolaters among the Arabs and the names of their idols
    - 7. On the topics debated by the *Mutakallimūn*
  - C. Grammar
  - D. Writing
  - E. Prose and Poetry
  - F. History

1. On the Kings of Persia
2. On the Kings and Caliphs of Islam
3. On the Kings of the Yemen: Part I
4. On the Kings of the Yemen: Part II
5. On the Kings of *Rūm* (from Alexander, with gaps, to Constantine)
6. Terms frequently used in Persian history
7. Terms frequently used in Arab historical literature
8. Terms frequently used in ancient Arab history
9. Terms frequently used in *Rūmi* (here obviously Byzantine) history

II. The Foreign Sciences
   A. Philosophy
      1. On the division of philosophy
      2. On the divine science (definitions)
      3. On expressions frequently used in philosophy
   B. Logic
      (Part i to Part ix: the *Organon*)
   C. Medicine
   D. Arithmetic
   E. Geometry
   F. Astronomy
   G. Music
   H. Mechanics
   I. Chemistry

It appears in the Ibn Sīnā-inspired list of al-Ṭūsi (d. A.D. 1274)[49] and the exhaustive breakdown of the sciences in Ibn Khaldūn's (d. A.D. 1406) *Prolegomena*.[50]

49. The division of the sciences appears in the Persian *Akhlāqi Naṣīri* (*GAL*, Suppl. I, p. 928, n. 1) and has been analyzed by J. Stephenson, "The Classification of the Sciences according to Nasiruddin Tusi," *Isis*, V (1923), 364–99. Stephenson has misread or misunderstood the section dealing with the *Auscultatio physica* (Stephenson: "The Dervish Dance of Physical Science") and the *De coelo et mundo* (Stephenson: "The Dance and the World").

50. *Muqaddimah*, ed. M. Quatremère (3 vols.; Paris, 1958); most recent translation by F. Rosenthal (3 vols.; New York, 1958); see E. I. J. Rosenthal, "Ibn Jaldun's Attitude toward the Falasifah," *al-Andalus*, XX (1955), 75–85, and Gardet-Anawati, *Théologie musulmane*, pp. 123–24.

IBN KHALDUN, *MUQADDIMAH*[51]

I. Traditional Sciences
   A. *Qur'ān*
   B. *Ḥadīth*
   C. *Kalām*
   D. Sufism
   E. Interpretation of Dreams

II. Intellectual Sciences
   A. Logic
   B. Mathematics
      1. Arithmetic, and its derivatives: reckoning and business arithmetic
      2. Geometry
      3. Astronomy, and its derivatives: tabular computation (*zij*) and astrology
      4. Music
   C. Physics
      "the elemental substance perceivable by the senses, namely the minerals, the plants, and the animals which are created from the elementary substances, the heavenly bodies, natural motions, and the soul from which the motions originate, and other things"
   D. Metaphysics

The encyclopedia was not always expository; it could and did serve educational purposes, often with a strong element of special pleading. Pedagogical works of this type by Ibn Ḥazm (d. A.D. 1064)[52] and al-Ghazāli (d. A.D. 1111)[53] are not really encyclopedias at

51. Ed. Quatremère, II, 386, III 209, trans. Rosenthal, II, 437, III, 246; Ibn Khaldūn gives two breakdowns of the sciences; the one outlined here represents his *schema* when actually discussing the sciences; the other, reproduced in Gardet-Anawati, *Théologie musulmane*, p. 123, is a summary analysis.

52. *Marātib al-ʿulūm*; this work has been analyzed, on the basis of an Istanbul MS (Fatih 2704), by M. Asin Palacios, "Un codice inexplorado del cordobés Ibn Ḥazm," *al-Andalus*, II (1934), 46–56.

53. *Fātihat al-ʿulūm*: *GAL*, Suppl. I, p. 755; see M. Asin Palacios, *Compendio musulmano de pedagogia, el libro de la introduccion a las ciencias de Al-Ghazzali* (Saragossa, 1924).

all but represent curriculum sketches. Devoted to considerably stranger ends are a series of works which can only be described as "gnostic" encyclopedias: the tenth-century *Rasāʾil* of the "Sincere Brethren," the *Repose of the Intellect* by the Ismāʿīli al-Kirmāni (*fl. ca.* A.D. 1020),[54] and the *Treasure of the Sciences* of Ibn Tūmart (*fl.* thirteenth century).[55]

The *Rasāʾil* are at first glance a traditional "mixed" encyclopedia of the Arab science-foreign science type.[56] But the texture of the work is quite different from its mere outline. There are frequent statements made directly to the reader detailing the ends to be pursued and the fruits to be gained, not from a mere perusal of the work, but from a penetration into its principle. And its principles, at least in the core sections on the psychological and rational sciences (Part III) and on the Divine Law (Part IV), are hardly Aristotelian at all, but are redolent of the hermetic Neoplatonism practiced by Iamblichus and the Syrian School.

IKHWĀN AL-ṢAFĀʾ, *RASĀʾIL*[57]

I. Mathematical Sciences
   A. Number
   B. Geometry
   C. Astronomy
   D. Geography
   E. Music
   F. On arithmetical and geometrical relations

54. *Rāhat al-ʿaql*, ed. M. Hussein and M. Hilmy (Leyden, 1953). On this author see p. 175 below.
55. Not the Almohad Mahdi, as in *GAL*, I², 274 and Suppl. I, p. 424.
56. *Rasāʾil* (ed. Cairo, 1928). The considerable (secondary!) material on the "Sincere Brethren" (*Ikhwān al-ṣafāʾ*; for the name see I. Goldziher, *Islam*, I [1910], 22–26) is historically reviewed by A. Awa, *L'Esprit critique des Frères de la Pureté* (Beyrouth, 1948), and A. Tibawi, "Ikhwān al-ṣafāʾ and their *Rasāʾil*. A Critical Review of a Century and a Half of Research," *Islamic Quarterly*, II (1955), 28–46.
57. The following *schema* is the actual order of the treatises. In the seventh treatise of Part I another summary *schema* is given; this is reproduced in Gardet-Anawati, *Théologie musulmane*, p. 109.

G. The theoretical studies and their object
H. The practical studies and their object
I. On practices, the cause of their variety, and their types
J. *Eisagoge*
K. *Categoriae*
L. *De interpretatione*
M. *Analytica priora*
N. *Analytica posteriora*

II. Natural Sciences
A. Matter, form, movement, time, and space
B. *De coelo et mundo*
C. *De generatione et corruptione*
D. *Meteorologica*
E. *De mineralibus*
F. On the essence of nature
G. On the species of plants
H. Formation of animals and their species
I. Composition of the human body
J. Senses and their objects
K. Embryology
L. Man the Microcosm
M. Development of the human soul
N. Limits of human understanding
O. Extent of life and death
P. Properties of pleasure
Q. Languages and their transcription

III. Psychological and Rational Sciences
A. Rational Principles according to the Pythagoreans
B. Rational Principles according to the Brethren
C. Universe as Macrocosm
D. Intellect and Intelligible
E. Periods and Epochs
F. Essence of Passion
G. Resurrection
H. Species of Movements

I. Causes and Effects
J. Definitions and Descriptions

IV. *Nāmūs* and *Sharīʿah*
A. Doctrines and Religions
B. The ways to Allah
C. Beliefs of the Brethren
D. Method of the Brethren
E. Essence of Faith
F. Essence of the Divine *Nāmūs*: Prophethood
G. Manner of calling upon Allah
H. States of Spiritual Beings
I. Types of Polity
J. Hierarchy of the Universe
K. Magic, Talismans, etc.

The collection of Ibn Tūmart is quite another matter.[58] The physical sciences, except for their occult representatives, have been dropped from the *schema* and the emphasis has been redirected to the "spiritual" sciences; and within these the material is again Neopythagorean rather than representative of the Aristotelian tradition. That the *Treasure* represents a program is not immediately apparent; that it is a *gnosis* is undeniable.

IBN TŪMART, *KANZ AL-ʿULŪM* (OUTLINE AFTER VADJA)

I. Science of Law and Reality
(Species and sources of knowledge and reason; natural and supernatural science)

II. Principles of the science of created natures, from the beginning to the end (a "history" of the divine emanation)

58. *Kanz al-ʿulūm*: see G. Vadja, "Une synthèse peu connue de la révélation et de la philosophie," *Mélanges Massignon*, III (Damascus, 1957), 359–74.

III. On the human virtues and the knowledge of Creator and creatures
("Anthropologie philosophique" showing the relation of the human faculties to the supernatural)

IV. Exposition of the obscure sciences (Mélange of genuine and pseudo-science: alchemy, astrology, divination)

The second major type of Islamic encyclopedia, what might be called the "Book-of-Knowledge" type, is not primarily philosophical in origin, make-up, or content. But philosophy does find a place in these collections, especially the areas of the natural sciences that have always accounted for a large share of the labors and interests of Aristotelianism. The encyclopedias in question are extremely heterogeneous, and it is difficult to set down an inclusive definition of them. They may embrace many fields: history, geography, zoology, and botany are the most common, but there is also meteorology, mineralogy, anthropology, eschatology, and *kalām* to be found as well. What they most resemble, their historical content apart, is the *hexaemeron* literature of the Greek and Syriac Christian tradition. Indeed, the *Book of Treasures* of Job of Edessa (*fl. ca.* A.D. 817),[59] a Syriac representative of the "Book of Knowledge" encyclopedia, is almost indistinguishable, on the basis of content, from the *hexaemera* of Severus bar Shakko and Barhebraeus.

Two of the earliest examples of this type in the Islamic tradition are the *Tanbīh* of al-Mas'ūdi (d. A.D. 956),[60] and the *Bad' al-khalq* of al-Maqdisi (*fl. ca.* A.D. 960).[61]

59. Ayyūb al-Ruhāwi al-Abrash of the Arabic sources: *Fihrist*, p. 114, l. 14; al-Maqdisi, ed. Huart, p. 140; Uṣ., I, 170, 204; Ḥunayn, *Risālah, passim* Meyerhof, "Hunayn and his Period," pp. 703–704; his *Book of Treasures*, ed. A. Mingana (Cambridge, 1935); see Kraus, *Jābir*, II, 175, n. 1, and B. Lewin, "Job d'Edesse et son Livre des Trésors," *Orientalia Suecana*, VI (1957), 21–30.
60. See p. 130 below.
61. See p. 130 below.

AL-MASʿŪDI, *TANBĪH*[62]

I. Preface
II. Cosmography
  A. Celestial Spheres and the Stars
  B. Divisions of Time and Seasons
  C. The Winds (digression on the climate of Egypt)
  D. Shape and Size of the Earth
  E. The Climes
    1. Related to Heavenly Bodies
    2. Characteristics of the Fourth Clime
  F. The Seas
    1. Abyssinian Sea
    2. Sea of Rum
    3. Sea of Khazars
    4. Pontus
    5. Ocean
III. History
  A. Pre-Muslim History
    1. The Seven Nations of Antiquity:
      Persians, Chaldeans, Greeks and Romans, Libyans, Turks, Indians, Chinese
    2. The Kings of Persia
    3. Kings of Greece
    4. Roman Emperors
      a. Pagan Emperors
      b. Christian Emperors to Hijrah
      c. Christian Emperors after Hijrah
      d. Provinces of the Roman Empire.
        Note: Exchange of captives between Romans and Greeks
  B. Islamic History
    Introduction: The eras of various peoples and their division

62. For a detailed outline of III, A 3 see pp. 275–276 below.

1. The Prophet
2. The Orthodox Caliphs
3. Umayyad Caliphs
   Note: On the dispersion of the Umayyads and the Caliphate of Cordova
4. Abbasids to A.D. 976

AL-MAQDISI, *KITĀB BAD' AL-KHALQ WA AL-TA'RĪKH*

I. *Kalām*
   A. Science and ignorance; the establishment of proof and certitude
   B. Proofs for the existence of God
   C. Attributes and names of God
   D. Prophetship

II. Hexaemeron-type
   A. Creation, its beginning
   B. The divine paraphernalia, the Book, Throne, etc.
   C. Creation of the heavens and the earth
   D. Creation and nature of man

III. History
   A. History of the Prophets
   B. Kings of Persia
   C. Religions and peoples of the world
   D. The climes
   E. Genealogy of the Arabs
   F. The Prophet, his life and character
   G. The Companions
   H. The Orthodox Caliphs
   I. Umayyads
   J. Abbasids to A.D. 961

In the thirteenth century, the high-water mark of Arab encyclopedism, the genre, is represented by the *Marvels of Creation* of

Zakarīyā ibn Muḥammad al-Qazwīni (d. A.D. 1283),[63] a work which testifies to the degree of differentiation that has taken place in such encyclopedias during the intervening period. The elements of history and *kalām,* so prominent in Masʿūdi and Maqdisi, are no longer the preserve of the author of the "Book-of-Knowledge"; the *mirabilia* of al-Qazwīni are restricted almost entirely to the natural sciences.

Encyclopedias of all types proved fertile ground for the nourishing of the new Aristotelianism and, later, worthy instruments for its diffusion. But the encyclopedias are also instructive mirrors of the heterogeneous nature of Arabian Aristotelianism, and Ibn Sīnā's *Kitāb al-shifā'*, the most Aristotelian of the genre, is a perfect case in point. The *Shifā'* is unashamedly Aristotelian in its make-up and in its intent; yet, as has already been mentioned, some very un-Aristotelian elements have been introduced into the substance of the work. First, there are additions that serve to fill out the framework, e.g., the inclusion of a treatment of plants in the *Naturalia* and the expansion of the *Mathematica,* a division within which, on the testimony of the *pinakes,* Aristotle composed treatises, none of which, however, entered the Islamic tradition. Within the *Naturalia* the Arabs had a full complement of spurious works with which to plug the interstices; in the *Mathematica* they merely turned to other equally well-known sources like Ptolemy and Euclid.

The second development within the *Shifā'* is the substitution of non-Aristotelian for Aristotelian doctrine. An examination of Chapter VI of the *Naturalia* shows that the Aristotelian *De anima* has undergone a transformation at the hands of its commentators, as well as at the hands of Galen, Plotinus, and Ibn Sīnā himself.[64]

The phenomenon of substitution is common in Arabian Aristotelianism, progressing, with varying degrees of rapidity and thoroughness, from area to area. In metaphysics, for example, the Aristotelian theory of movers was quickly supplanted by a more congenial, or at

63. *ʿAjā'ib al-makhlūqāt*: *GAL,* I², 633–34, Suppl. I, pp. 882–83; ed, F. Wüstenfeld (Göttingen, 1848).

64. Instructive in this regard is the painstaking source-searching by Bakoš in his edition of this section of the *Shifā'*: *Psychologie d'Ibn Sina (Avicenne) d'après son oeuvre Aš-šifa* (2 vols.; Prague, 1956); another edition by F. Rahman, *Avicenna's De anima* (London, 1959).

least more persuasive, emanationism which moved, via the *Theologia* and the commentators, into the realm of psychology as well. In the *Naturalia* the ground was more strongly held, particularly in fields like zoology and biology. In politics, the Arabs never knew the genuine Aristotelian doctrine, and what usually passes as such is the spurious *Secreta secretorum* and the elaborate correspondence with Alexander. Finally, the *Logica* were the first to arrive on the scene and, as in the West, the last to depart, if depart they did; there are strong reasons for doubting the truth of Ibn Khaldun's account of how *kalām* took over the Aristotelian logic and transformed it;[65] perhaps "rearranged" is the better word.

DOXOGRAPHIES AND GNOMONOLOGIES

Doxographical collections were one of the most potent research, polemical, and mnemonic devices at the disposal of Greek scholasticism. At root the doxography is a literary device for the gathering and organization of the *doxai* of philosophers by subject matter rather than by author or any other historical or chronological principle. The technique appears in Aristotle, in *Metaphysica* A, 3–10, for example, or in Book I of the *De anima*, where the opinions of the philosophers's predecessors are marshaled and then subjected to a rigorous *aporialysis* treatment. With Theophrastus this methodological principle becomes the basis for the first complete doxographical collection of which we know, *On the Opinions of the Physical Philosophers*.

The problem of collecting, identifying, and sorting the doxographies of Greek antiquity is only somewhat less complicated than the parallel problem in Islam. We are in possession of only two fairly extended examples of what must have been a popular genre, the *Placita philosophorum*, falsely attributed to Plutarch, and the excerpts

65. *Muqaddimah* ed. Quatremère, III, 112–13, trans. Rosenthal, III, 141–43.

in Book I of Stobaeus' *Eclogae*;[66] both of these works apparently go back to a single source, as does similar material in Theodoret, Nemesius, etc.

Even as early as Aristotle, the polemical implications of the collection of *endoxa* are not entirely absent, but it was only with the mounting pressures of scepticism that the full value of the doxography as a weapon began to be realized, either as a method of refutation (the *auctoritas* principle was already at work) or to ring the changes on the now familiar theme of "the harmony of Plato and Aristotle."[67] The genre also had a wide vogue in Christian circles, generating the Patristic "garlands" and "chains" with which the Christian theologian snared his heretical prey.

The connection of doxographies with the syncretism of late antiquity was likewise a feature of the growing scholasticism. The scholastic method, in its pedagogic as contrasted to its commentating aspect, represents a movement away from original texts in the direction of anthologies and handbooks, of which the doxography is but one example. A scholastic author like Philo, for instance, or John of Damascus will derive a great deal of his citation material from collections arranged according to the doxographical principle rather than from a perusal of the integral original texts.[68]

The Arabs were no different from their Greek predecessors. The philosophical route from the end of antiquity into Islam is paved with doxographies that are equally difficult to identify on either side of the Christian-Islamic frontier. The list of the translated works of Aristotle described in al-Nadīm's *Fihrist* is indeed impressive, but it provides no indication of the research habits of the Arab philosopher. We know that there were textual specialists who worked over the integral *Aristotelica* with painful care, but how many of these texts were read by al-Kindi, for example? In the case of the pre-Aristote-

66. Both edited in Herman Diels, *Doxographi Graeci*[3] (Berlin, 1879).

67. On the polemical origins of philosophical doxographies see A.-J. Festugière, *Révélation d'Hermès Trismégiste*, II, 350–69.

68. For Philo see R. Arnaldez, *Les Oeuvres de Philon d'Alexandrie*, I (Paris, 1961), 116; on John of Damascus: B. Studer, *Die theologische Arbeitsweise des Johannes von Damaskus* (Ettal, 1956), pp. 80–81, 91–95.

lian philosophers, and particularly with the pre-Socratics, it is clear that the Arabs were working from doxographical sources.

Certain doxographical collections are attributed to the Arabs themselves. Such, for instance, is the *Treatise on the Soul Abridged from the Books of Aristotle and Plato* by al-Kindi (d. *ca.* A.D. 873),[69] the *Sources of Questions* of al-Fārābi (d. A.D. 950),[70] the *Book of the Opinions of the Natural Philosophers* of al-Rāzi (d. A.D. 923),[71] and the *Heavenly Bodies* (a doxographical collection on their essence) by Ibn Sīnā (d. A.D. 1037).[72] Such works lead, in many instances, back to the doxographical passages in Aristotle himself, or, and here the question of doxographical identification becomes critical, translations of Greek collections.

A number of these latter have come to light. Isḥāq ibn Ḥunayn's version of a doxographical collection attributed to Gregory of Nyssa is known,[73] and a collection of aphorisms on the soul circulating in Syriac under the name of Aristotle has also been correctly identified as Patristic.[74] In his investigations of the sources of the Jābir *corpus*, Kraus has found a textual correspondence between a doxographical psychology in "Balīnūs" (Apollonius of Tyana),[75] *Sirr al-khalīqah*, and a similar collection in the *Book of Treasures* of Job of Edes-

69. The work has been edited by M. Abu Ridah in his *Rasā'il al-Kindi*, I (Cairo, 1950), 272–80. It was in this treatise that the alleged fragments of the *Eudemus* were discovered.
70. The *'Uyūn al-masā'il* is a short collection of Aristotelian *sententiae* known in the Latin tradition as the *Flos* (or *Fons*) *alpharabii*. The *'Uyūn* has been edited in the *Kitāb al-majmū'āt* (Cairo, 1907) and reproduced from this edition together with the medieval Latin version in M. Cruz Hernandez, *AHDL*, XXV–XXVI (1950–1951), 316–17; see M. Alonso, *al-Andalus*, XXIV (1959), 251–73.
71. The work is known only from the bibliographical sources, e.g., *Fihrist*, p. 301, 1.22; see Pines, *Atomenlehre*, p. 93, # 28, and n. 2. The collection may, however, be alchemistic. Preserved in various British MSS is a collection containing the *Tabula smaragdina* together with a commentary by al-Rāzi cast in the form of a collection of *dicta* from the ancient alchemistic sources; see D. W. Singer, *Catalogue of the Latin and Vernacular Alchemical Manuscripts of Great Britain and Ireland*, I (Brussels, 1928), 20.
72. Anawati, *Mu'allafāt*, # 53; printed in *Tis' rasā'il* (Cairo, 1908), pp. 257–79.
73. Preserved in MS Sbath 1010; cf. *GAL*, Suppl. I, 369).
74. It is preserved as an anonymous treatise in a Sinai MS (A. S. Lewis, *Studia Sinaitica*, I, 19–26) and under the name of Sergius of Rīsh 'aynā (B.M. add. 14658; see E. Sachau, *Inedita Syriaca*, pp. 76–79); on its identification as Christian see G. Furlani, *JAOS* (1914), pp. 154–75 (Gregory Thaumaturgus), and B. Einarson, *Classical Philology*, XVIII (1933), 129–30 (Maximus Confessor).
75. On the Arabic versions of Apollonius see M. Plessner, art. "Balīnūs," *EI*², I, 994–95.

sa (*fl. ca.* A.D. 817) which derives ultimately from the *De natura hominis* of Nemesius of Emessa.[76]

More important than these are two doxographies going directly back to the Greek philosophical tradition. The first is of considerable interest. Preserved in an Istanbul manuscript[77] is a doxography as yet unidentified in any Greek source. Entitled *On the Opinions of the Philosophers,* it is attributed in the manuscript to Ammonius, presumably the professor of Olympiodorus and John Philoponus at Alexandria who was himself a student of Proclus (d. A.D. 485). The work was known in the Arab tradition before the discovery of the manuscript; it was cited by al-Bīrūni[78] and was used as the Empedocles source in Shahrastāni's *Milal.*[79]

Until the Istanbul manuscript of the Ammonius work has been studied, it is impossible to discern its affiliations with what is, to date, the premiere doxographical text in Islam, the Arabic version, done by Qusṭā ibn Lūqā (d. A.D. 923), of pseudo-Plutarch's *De placitis philosophorum,* the same collection that looms so large in the Greek tradition. Qusṭā's translation has been edited, on the basis of a single manuscript,[80] but additional material has since come to light.[81] The uses of the *De placitis* among the Arabs was considerable, though in many cases it is difficult to determine whether the doxographical passages in the Syriac and Arabic tradition go back to the *De placitis* or directly to Aristotle's own doxographies. The opening chapter of al-Yāqūt's *Muʿjam,* for instance, includes a doxographical section on the shape of the earth which reproduced both *De coelo* 393b and a section of the *De placitis.*[82] Likewise, the introduction to the Second Foundation of Barhebraeus' *Candelabrum* could stem from either the *De placitis* or the *Metaphysica,* or even from Al-Maqdisi's *Book of*

76. Kraus, *Jābir,* II, 278.

77. Aya Sofia 2450, 4 fols. 107–135; see Sayyid, *Makhṭūṭāt,* I, Part VII, # 301.

78. *India,* trans. Sachau, p. 85.

79. Pp. 230ff.

80. Damascus MS Zahiriyah 4871; A. Badawi (ed.), *Arisṭūṭālis fī al-nafs* (Cairo, 1954), pp. 89–188.

81. Princeton MS. Yahuda 308, 19 (see *MIDEO,* III [1956], 379) and Istanbul MS Koprülü 1623, fols. 79a–88b (see F. Rosenthal, *JOAS,* LXXXI [1961], 7–9). Rosenthal has done a partial collation of the Istanbul and Damascus MSS.

82. Diels, *Doxographi,* pp. 376–77.

Creation.[83] But the residue of borrowing still remains impressive, even though it is certain that we are dealing with but a fraction of its actual use.[84]

Related to the doxography in spirit, if not in form, is the ancient gnomonology where the material, usually brief *sententiae*, is chosen on the basis of the ethical rather than the strictly philosophical content.[85] Some of these collections could, with a little reworking, fit quite conveniently into Christian ethical theory and so found new readers in Christian circles. This seems to have been particularly true of the many Neopythagorean gnomonologies of late antiquity, and thus the collections of ethical *gnomai* attributed to "Secundus" and to "Sextus," to choose only two from a number of examples, passed under Christian auspices into Syriac Christian literature and ultimately into Arabic.[86]

Like the doxography, the Greek-derived gnomonology quickly passed from a translation stage into an "original" Arabic literary genre. The collection of proverbial wisdom or the utterances of sages is obviously not the preserve of a single people or culture. But it is equally true that the Arabic gnomonologies betray material and emphases which are not indigenous. If any purely literary influence is to be sought, it should probably be in the direction of the Middle Persian *handarz* literature with its collections of the moral maxims of princes;[87] the gnomonological work of Miskawayh (d. A.D. 1030)

83. Huart (ed.), I, text pp. 135–40.

84. For the manifold uses of the *De placitis* see P. Kraus, *Jābir*, II, 331–39 (for Jābir); *ibid.*, II, 337, n. 4 (for pseudo-Jāḥiẓ, *al-Dalāʾil*); *ibid.*, II, 338, n. 2 (for al-Maqdisi); P. Kraus, *Bulletin de l'Institut d'Egypte*, XIX (1937), 207, n. 4 (for Abū Ḥātim al-Rāzi and al-Shahrastāni); S. Pines, *Atomenlehre*, p. 93, n. 2 (for al-Rāzi and al-Nawbakhti); M. Meyerhof, *Isis*, X (1928), 340–49 (for ʿUbaydallāh ibn Bakhtīshūʿ); A. Baumstark, *Philologisch-Historische Beiträge Curt Wachsmuth ... überreicht* (Leipzig, 1897), pp. 152–54 (al-Shahrastāni).

85. On the ancient gnomonology see K. Horna and K. von Fritz, art. "Gnome," *R-E*, Suppl. VI (1935), cols. 74–90, and J. Barns, "Gnomic Anthologies: Their History and Use," *Classical Quarterly*, XLIV (1950), 132–37, XLV (1951), 1–19.

86. *GSL*, pp. 169–70; Steinschneider, *Arab. Übers.*, pp. 146–47; J. Gildmeister, "Pythagorassprüche in syrischen Überlieferung," *Hermes*, IV (1869), 81ff. The "Secundus" collection has been edited by E. Sachau, *Inedita Syriaca* (Vienna, 1870), pp. 84–88, and that of "Sextus" by V. Ryssel in *Zeitschrift für wiss. Theologie*, XXXVIII (1895), 617–30; XXXIX (1896), 568–624; XL (1897), 131–48; see H. Chadwick, *The Sentences of Sextus. A Contribution to the History of Early Christian Ethics* (Cambridge, 1959).

87. See J. Tavadia, *Die Mittelpersische Sprache und Literatur der Zarathustrier* (Leipzig, 1956), pp. 103–107.

certainly suggests the operation of this kind of influence. What is more properly Greek is the association of these ethical statements not with political leaders but with philosophers. The identification in later antiquity of the philosophical and ethical way of life is well known, as is its literary corollary, the identification of biography with the collection of moral anecdotes. Such is clearly the genesis of a gnomonology attributed to Ḥunayn ibn Isḥāq (d. A.D. 873) under the titles *Nawādir al-falāsifah* or *Adab al-falāsifah*,[88] a work that contains material on the life of Aristotle that served as a basis for both Ibn abi Uṣaybiʿah[89] and al-Qifṭi.[90]

Three similar works were produced by men who, while they were not at the center of the Baghdad Peripatetic school, had connections with this philosophical circle. The first is Ibn Hindū (d. A.D. 1029), a physician and the student of the Aristotelian editor Ibn Suwār.[91] In addition to writing an *Introduction to Philosophy*,[92] Ibn Hindū was the author of a gnomonological collection professedly derived from Greek sources and which includes various sayings attributed to Aristotle.[93] A better-known contemporary, Miskawayh (d. A.D. 1030), stands in a somewhat more clearly defined relationship to the Baghdad Aristotelians.[94] That he was a member of the circle is clear enough from the sketch devoted to him by al-Tawḥīdi, and more technical interests

88. The Arabic text, which is extant in a number of copies, has not as yet been edited. The most recently discovered MS is that in Koprülü 1608, 74–77 (= Sayyid, *Makhṭūṭāt*, Part VII, # 386), and indeed the collection, which is almost entirely gnomonological, seems to include two copies of Ḥunayn (cf. Sayyid, # 387). The *Nawādir* has been studied by both K. Merkle, *Die Sittensprüche der Philosophen* (Leipzig, 1921), and M. Plessner, "Analecta to Ḥunayn ibn Isḥāq's 'Apophthegems of the Philosophers' and its Hebrew translation," *Tarbiz*, XXIV (1954), 60–75.

89. Uṣ., I, 28, l. # 11; p. 47, l. # 17; p. 51, l. # 6; p. 57, l. # 18, etc.

90. Qifṭi, p. 25, where the material concerns the *topos* "How were the schools named?" and derived ultimately from the *eisagoge* complex. The connection indicates that a good deal of Ḥunayn's material, at least as far as Aristotle is concerned, came from a biography read in the philosophical schools.

91. Uṣ., I, 323–26; Yāqūt, *Irshād*, V, 168–73; GAL, I², 277, Suppl. I, pp. 425–26; Meyerhof, "Alexandrien nach Baghdad," p. 426.

92. Uṣ., I, 326; no MS of this work is known.

93. *Al-kalim al-rūḥānīyah fī al-ḥikam al-yūnānīyah*, ed. M. Qabbani (Cairo, 1900); on the apophthegms of Aristotle in Ibn Hindū see Merkle, *op. cit.*, pp. 25–27.

94. Tawḥīdī, *Imtā*, I, 35; Uṣ., I, 245; Qifṭi, p. 331; Yāqūt, *Irshād*, II, 88–96; *GAL*, I², 417–18, Suppl. I, pp. 582–84; Rosenthal, *Historiography*, pp. 122–23; Meyerhof, "Alexandrien nach Baghdad," p. 423.

are suggested by the fact that al-Tawḥīdi sent him a copy of Ibn al-ʿAbbād's commentary on the *Eisagoge* and the *Categoriae*.[95] But these are mere indirect testimonies. A scrutiny of the work of Miskawayh has shown the degree of his involvement in the Greek tradition. His chief ethical treatise, the *Tahdhīb al-akhlāq*, has recently been studied by Walzer, who has traced its affiliations not only to Aristotle but also to the Neoplatonic ethical tradition and particularly to Porphyry.[96] Similarly, in his more theological *al-Fawz al-asghār* Miskawayh has drawn upon the Platonic tradition.[97]

Like Ibn al-Muqaffaʿ, Miskawayh stands at the juncture of the Greek and Iranian tradition, and the blending of the two strains can be seen most clearly in his gnomonological collection, *Kitāb adab al-ʿarab wa al-fars*.[98]

Part V of this work is devoted to the Greeks and a large part is derived from the *Tabula Cebetis*. The sections pertaining to Aristotle seem to stem from the *pseudepigraphica* and consist of recommendations of Plato to Aristotle and of Aristotle to Alexander. Part I of the same work, the so-called *Jāwidhān khirad*, stems rather from Iranian sources,[99] but even here there has been contamination from the Greek tradition, in this case traces of the Neopythagorean "Golden Verses."[100]

The importance of the gnomonological work of al-Mubashshir ibn Fātik (*fl. ca.* A.D. 1048–1049) for the Aristotelian tradition has long been recognized. The author spent most of his life in Egypt, but his connection with the Baghdad School runs back through Ibn al-Āmidi, with whom he studied philosophy, to the Christian Peripatetic Ibn Zurʿah (d. A.D. 1008).[101] He was, as well, the student of two other

95. Yāqūt, *Irshād*, II, 89.

96. "Some Aspects of Miskawaih's *Tahdhīb al-Akhlāq*," *Studi Orientalistici in onore di Giorgio Levi della Vida*, II (Rome, 1956), 603–21.

97. See F. Rosenthal, *Islamic Culture*, XIV (1940), 398–401, and *ibid.*, p. 398, n. i, for the MSS of this work.

98. A. Badawi (ed.), (Cairo, 1952).

99. See W. Henning, "Eine arabische Version mittelpersischen Weisheitsschriften," *ZDMG*, CVI (1956), 73–77.

100. See F. Rosenthal, *Orientalia*, X (1941), 104–15.

101. Biographical and bibliographical material in Qifṭi, p. 269; Uṣ., II, 98–99; Yāqūt, *Irshād*, VI, 241; *GAL*, I², 600, Suppl. I, p. 829.

eminent contemporary Hellenists, Ibn al-Ḥaytham in astronomy and mathematics, and Ibn Riḍwān in medicine. His gnomonology, *Mukhtār al-ḥikam*, recently edited by Badawi,[102] was widely diffused in medieval Latin and vernacular translations but has attracted the attention of orientalists chiefly for its preservation of an elaborate biography of Aristotle derived from a source no longer extant in Greek.[103] And the Aristotle *vita* by no means exhausts the ancient material which is plentiful and interesting.[104] As in the case of Ḥunayn's *Nawādir* and the *Ṣiwān al-ḥikmah* of Abū Sulaymān al-Sijistani,[105] both of which the *Mukhtār* resembles, the evidence points to an at least partial use of Porphyry's *Philosophos historia*.[106]

The influence of al-Mubashshir as a gnomonologist historian in the Hellenic tradition can be seen chiefly in the work of Ibn abī Uṣaybiʿah (d. A.D. 1270)[107] and even more directly in the *Rawḍat al-afrāḥ* of the Persian savant al-Shahrazūri (*fl.* thirteenth century) who has already been noted as the author of a philosophical encyclopedia. The *Rawḍat* is cast in the form of a history of philosophers—or, better, of sages—from Adam to the Persian philosopher and mystic Suhrawārdi (d. A.D. 1191) for whose life it is the chief source.[108] For the pre-Islamic sages, Shahrazūri adheres fairly closely to al-Mubashshir,

102. Madrid, 1958; F. Rosenthal had also planned an edition; his valuable supplementary notes to Badawi have been puplished in *Oriens*, XIII–XIV (1960–1961), 132–58. Two important reviews of Badawi's edition have appeared: C. Kuentz in *Revista del Instituto de Estudios Islamicos en Madrid*, V (1957), 255–69, and S. A. Bonebakker, *Bibliotheca Orientalis*, XVII (1960), 212–14.

103. Most recently studied by Düring, *Biographical Tradition*, pp. 197–207, where the older literature is cited.

104. Some of this has been extracted by B. Meissner, "Mubashshirs *Akhbar al-Iskander*," *ZDMG*, XLIX (1895), 583–627, which is an edition of Alexander's biography, and by F. Rosenthal, "Arabische Nachrichten über Zenon den Eleaton," *Orientalia*, VI (1937), 21–67, who has gathered the material on Zeno, Pythagoras, and Solon.

105. See pp. 162, 255–256 below.

106. See F. Rosenthal, as well as F. Altheim and R. Stiehl, *Porphyrios und Empedocles* (Tübingen, 1954), pp. 19–22.

107. See pp. 262–263 below, and Rosenthal, *Oriens* XIII–XIV, (1960–1961), 145–47.

108. *GAL*, I², 617, Suppl. I, pp. 850–51; Storey, *Persian Literature*, I, 2, pp. 1107–1108. There is no biographical material on al-Sharazūri. The *Rawḍat al-afrāḥ* is still unedited, though the Persian version, *Kanz al-ḥikmah*, was printed in Teheran in 1938; there is an analysis of the Berlin MS of the *Rawḍat* in Ahlwardt, *Arabischen Handschriften Berlin*, # 10055. For the use of al-Mubashshir in the *Rawḍat* see Rosenthal, pp. 147–48. The relationship between Shahrazūri and Suhrawārdi is discussed in H. Corbin, *Oeuvres philosophiques et mystiques de Shihabaddin Yahya Sohrawardi* (Teheran-Paris, 1952), pp. 64–66.

though he omits some of the *gnomai* and transposes others. It is probably fruitless to expect to be able to derive direct affiliations back to the Greek sources of this material. Proverbial wisdom is notoriously promiscuous in its liaisons, and its transmission through generations of compilers with varying interests and an increasingly shadowy understanding of the historical person or historical circumstance behind the utterance makes true bloodlines singularly unlikely. Some of the material is clearly old; the biography of Aristotle, for instance, must go quite far back in the Peripatetic tradition. Again, some of the information has transparently come from Christian sources; the mere presence of the Cappadocian Fathers among these collections of sages is evidence enough. Neopythagoreanism strains run through the collections.[109] Finally, there is the persistent influence of the ancient medical tradition which is bound up with *falsafah* from beginning to end.[110]

One example of the latter may be cited here. An authority frequently cited by Ibn abī Uṣaybiʿah is the Christian zoologist-physician-philosopher ʿUbaydallāh ibn Jibrīl who had his residence near Amida in northern Iraq and who died sometime after A.D. 1058. ʿUbaydallāh was a member of the Bakhtīshūʿ family whose connection with the Hellenic tradition long antedated Islam and which supplied the first Baghdad caliphs with court physicians. And the works of ʿUbaydallāh reveal that the tradition was still alive in the eleventh century.[111] His *Manāqib al-aṭibbāʾ*, the source used by Uṣaybiʿah and probably a gnomonology, is not extant, but the blending of the strains Christianity-Islam and philosophy-medicine is equally well illustrated by another treatise of ʿUbaydallāh which has already been cited in another context.[112] *Al-Rawdah al-ṭibbīyah* is a typically amorphous compilation of medical and philosophical definitions from the rich variety of sources available to an eleventh-century savant.

109. See F. Rosenthal, "Some Pythagorean Documents Transmitted in Arabic," *Orientalia*, X (1941), 104ff., 383ff.

110. See pp. 163–165 below. The linkage of the two traditions was not, of course, peculiar to Islam; it goes back to Aristotle himself.

111. Uṣ., I, 148; *GAL*, I², 636–37, Suppl. I, pp. 885–86; *GCAL*, II, 111–12.

112. See p. 102 above.

ʿUbaydallāh can reach back, via the doxographies like the *Placita philosophorum,* from which he has derived his definitions of the soul, for example, to the pre-Socratics, thence forward through the continuous Greek-Roman-Syriac-Islamic tradition in both philosophy and medicine. The results are assuredly not profound, but they show a breadth of intellectual heritage that was, at this period and much later, the sole possession of Islam.

NONPHILOSOPHICAL TESTIMONIA

The influence of Aristotle and Hellenism on the nascent Islamic community was in no wise restricted to the technical areas of *falsafah* and *kalām.* The Aristotelian writings supplied a great deal of general knowledge about the world and its workings to the early Muslim, and some measure of the growth of this influence may be taken from the changing concepts behind the Arabic word *adab.*[113] In its earliest usage it is much like the Homeric *arete* in its expression of the sum of virtues, chiefly ethical material, which were prized in the society. Again, like its Greek counterpart, *adab* became increasingly spiritualized as Islam moved from the desert to the town, then, eventually, to the large urban areas of Syria and Iraq. *Adab* came to mean culture, i.e., familiarity with the developing Arab disciplines: poetry, rhetoric, grammar. In the ninth century, Hellenic influences had begun to appear and there was a corresponding change in the concept of the *adīb,* the man of culture.

The type of the new *adīb* is al-Jāḥiẓ (d. A.D. 872), the universal savant moving with grace and ease between Islam, Hellas, and Iran. We know something of his Hellenic formation; Jāḥiẓ studied the "new" theology, *kalām,* with al-Naẓẓām (d. A.D. 846), and he frequented the circle of that other great Muʿtazilite Abū al-Ḥudayl

113. See F. Gabrieli, art. "Adab," *EI²*, I, 175–76.

(d. A.D. 849),[114] and it was probably through these channels that he came in contact with Baghdad Aristotelianism.[115]

There was, of course, reaction, a reaction stemming from a sense of loss of cultural identity and, more importantly, of theological purpose. The struggle between Hellenism and Islam, between Greek and Arab, between Aristotle and Muḥammad can be traced in its most virulent form on the pages of theological treatises, but it appears, too, in the context of *adab* in the wide literature devoted to "the *adab* of the secretary" or "what the bureaucrat should know." It is, for example, the point behind Ibn Qutaybah's *Adab al-Kātib*, written *ca.* A.D. 847–861, that is, in the period of reaction against the Muʿtazilites, which rails against the "new learning."[116] The "new learning" is Aristotle's logic and physics which, to Ibn Qutaybah's way of thinking, were turning the heads of the cultured men of his day.

In *adab*, no less than in theology, it was a futile struggle. Within a century of Ibn Qutaybah's complaint, Aristotle was thoroughly domesticated in the encyclopedias of al-Masʿūdi (d. A.D. 956) and al-Maqdisi (*fl. ca.* A.D. 960). Masʿūdi's *Tanbīh* does not use the division-of-the-sciences principle employed in the more Hellenizing type of encyclopedia, but the author has drawn heavily upon Aristotle, particularly the *De coelo*, the *Meteorologica*, and, to a lesser extent, the *Physica*. Unlike the *Murūj*, which uses the *Zoologica* extensively, the *Tanbīh* cites them only once. Finally, there are textual citations from the *Politica* (*Secreta secretorum*?), the *Metaphysica*, together with Themistius' commentary on Lambda in the version of Isḥāq, and from a whole series of letters from Aristotle to Alexander. Al-Maqdisi's *Kitāb badʾ al-khalq wa al-taʾrīkh*[117] is really three works: a treatise on

114. For these two theologians and their work see pp. 136–146 below.

115. See C. Pellat, *Le Milieu Basrien et la Formation de Jahiz* (Paris, 1953), p. 69; for the influence of Aristotle's zoology on Jāḥiẓ see p. 133 below.

116. The passage in question occurs in the Introduction; see G. Lecomte, "L'Introduction du *Kitāb adab al-kātib*" in *Mélanges Massignon*, III (Damascus, 1957), 45–64, and *idem*, "Muhammad b. al-Jahm al-Barmaki, Gouverneur philosophe, jugé par Ibn Qutaybah," *Arabica*, V (1958), 262–71.

117. C. Huart (ed. and trans.), *Le Livre de la Création et de l'Histoire* (6 vols.; Paris, 1899–1919).

kalām (Chaps. I–IV), a *Hexaemeron* (Chaps. V–IX), and a universal history from the earliest prophets to A.D. 961 (Chaps. X–XXII), including chapters on cultural history (XII), geography (XIII), and heresiography (XIX), and permeated throughout with material from Greek authorities.

The broader, Jahizian type of *adab* is likewise illustrated in the career of al-Tawḥīdi (d. A.D. 1018).[118] Al-Tawḥīdi was not a professional philosopher, yet his two books of "conversations," which are formally purely literary creations, are filled with a kind of philosophical knowledgeability which suggests more than a dilettante's acquaintance with philosophers and things philosophical. Indeed, he had studied with the eminent Aristotelian Yaḥyā ibn ʿAdi in A.D. 971,[119] and ten years later we find him going through the *De anima*, this time under the tutelage of Yaḥyā's successor as the head of the Baghdad philosophical circle, Abū Sulaymān.[120] The *Muqābasāt*[121] and the *Imtāʿ*[122] are the records of public and private conversations which took place in Abū Sulaymān's circle on a great variety of subjects; they are, indeed, the Platonic dialogues of *falsafah* whose rich philosophical content has hardly been touched. Of special interest is the author's appraisal of contemporary philosophers,[123] and the celebrated debate between the translator-philosopher Abū Bishr Mattā (d. A.D. 940) and the grammarian al-Sirāfi (d. A.D. 979) on the merits of their respective disciplines.[124]

The Aristotelian *corpus* provided a broad spectrum of information and techniques for the learned of Islam, but it was probably Aristotle the natural scientist who had the broadest influence on Arab letters.

118. *GAL*, I², 283, Suppl. I, pp. 435–36; S. M. Stern, art. "Abū Ḥayyān al-Tawḥīdi," *EI*², I, 126–27; Meyerhof, "Alexandrien nach Baghdad," pp. 422–23; I. Keilani, *Abū Ḥayyān Al-Tauḥīdi . . . Introduction à son Oeuvre* (Beyrouth, 1950).

119. *Muqābasāt*, p. 156.

120. *Muqābasāt*, p. 246.

121. H. Sandubi (ed.) (Cairo, 1929).

122. A. Amin and A. Al-Zayn (ed.) (3 vols.; Cairo, 1939–1944).

123. *Imtāʿ*, I, 31–37.

124. *Imtāʿ*, I, 107–29; see D. S Margoliouth, "The Discussion between Abū Bishr Mattā and Abū Said al-Sirāfi on the Merits of Logic and Grammar," *JRAS* (1905), pp. 79–129, and K. Fariq, "Abū Ḥayyān al-Tawḥīdi and his *Kitābul-Muqābasāt*," *Islamic Culture*, XXVIII (1954), 372–88.

Generally free of sectarian controversy and not tied to any particular viewpoint, the fund of learning to be found in the physical treatises was broadcast from Spain to India by Arab cosmographers, geographers, zoologists, and physicians. Not all the material was pure Aristotle: witness the *De plantis*, the *De metallis*, and the *De lapidibus*; but it all bore the magic name and, ultimately, muddied the waters to a far lesser degree than the notorious *Theologia* or the *De causis*.

The transmission of this material to the Arabs was, as in the case of the philosophical works, chiefly through translations of the original or of a Syriac version of the original, doxographical collections, and the multitude of epitomes beloved by Alexandrian and Arab alike. But in addition to these, there were other channels peculiar to scientific material. There was, for instance, the Syrian *Physiologus* literature on the qualities, real or imaginary, of nonhuman creation,[125] and the collections of scientific and pseudo-scientific lore organized in the form of a commentary on *Genesis*, the *Hexaemeron* literature going back to Basil the Great and, by way of Origen, to Poseidonius' conjectured commentary on the *Timaeus*, and represented in the Syriac tradition by James of Edessa (d. A.D. 708),[126] Moses bar Kepha (d. A.D. 903),[127]

125. Among the older studies see M. Goldstaub, "Der Physiologus und seine Weiterbildung in der lateinischen und byzantinischen Literatur," *Philologus*, Suppl. VIII (1899–1901), 337–404; M. Wellmann, *Der Physiologus, eine religiongeschicht-naturwissenschaftliche Untersuchung* (Leipzig, 1930); *GBL*, pp. 876–77; more recently: A. van Landtschoot, "Fragments syriaques du *Physiologus*," *Muséon*, LXXII (1959), 37–51; J. Bakoš, *Archiv Orientální*, VI (1934), 267; *GSL*, pp. 170–71.

126. *GSL*, pp. 248–56; Jugie, *Theologia*, pp. 465–66, and Index *s.v.*; Tkatsch, *Poetik*, I 76–77; for his *hexaemeron* see Abbé Martin, "L'Hexaemeron de Jacques d'Edesse," *JA*, Ser. 8, Vol. XI (1888), 155–219, 401–90. The integral text has been published by J.-B. Chapot and A. Valschade (Paris, 1932). The work is divided as follows:

1. Creation of incorporeal and intellectual substances
2. Creation of heaven and earth and all they contain
3. Creation of dry land, seas, rivers, gulfs, mountains, etc.
4. Creation of the stars
5. Creation of birds, fish, reptiles
6. Creation of domesticated and wild animals
7. Creation of man

127. *GSL*, pp. 281–82; Jugie, *Theologia*, pp. 467–68, and Index *s.v.*; the zoological sections of his *hexaemeron* have been edited by J. Bakoš in *Archiv Orientální*, II (1930), 327–61, 460–91; *idem*, "Quellenanalysis aus dem Hexaemeron des Mose bar Kep(h)a," *Archiv Orientální*, VI (1934), 266–71.

Severus bar Shakko (d. A.D. 1241),[128] and Barhebraeus (d. A.D. 1286).[129]

After the material found its way into the Arab tradition, it began appearing in various genres: the already mentioned encyclopedias of al-Mas'ūdi and al-Maqdisi and the "conversations" of al-Tawḥīdi, in zoologies like the *Kitāb al-ḥayawān* of al-Jāḥiẓ (d. A.D. 872),[130] a work which al-Baghdādi found to be little more than a plagiarism of the *Liber animalium* of Aristotle,[131] thence into the natural history sections of Ibn Qutaybah's (d. A.D. 889) *'Uyūn al-akhbār*,[132] and the *Hayāt al-ḥayawān* of al-Damīri (d. A.D. 1405).[133] in popular encylopedic cosmologies like the *'Ajā'ib al-makhlūqāt* of al-Qazwīni (d. A.D. 1283), and in geographies like the *Mu'jam al-buldān* of Yāqūt (d. A.D. 1229).[134]

The point should be made that none of these are technical handbooks for the eyes of the expert alone. Jāḥiẓ, Qazwīni, and Damīri, particularly, were popular authors in Islam and the Hellenic information and attitudes incorporated into their work were shared with a wide circle of readers. Moreover, this was only the scientific side of the Aristotelian heritage. Scarcely a beginning has been made in

128. Part IV of his *Book of Treasures* is a *hexaemeron*; it has been analyzed by F. Nau "Notice sur le Livre des Trésors de Jacques de Bartela, Évêque de Tagrit," *JA*, Sér. 9, Vol. VII (1896), 286–331; there is abundant use of both his Syriac predecessors.

129. His *hexaemeron* constitutes the Second Foundation of the encyclopedic *Candelabrum*, edited by J. Bakoš, *PO*, XXII (1930), 542–621, and XXIV (1933), 299–428, with detailed indications of the relationship between Aristotle (and the pseudo-Aristotelian *De mundo*), the *De placitis*, Ptolemy, Basil, James, Severus, Moses, al-Qazwīni, and the author.

130. A preliminary confrontation of the parallel passages in the *Kitāb al-ḥayawān* and the Arabic version of the *Liber animalium* has been done by B. Lewin, *Lychnos* (1952), pp. 239–44.

131. *Farq*, p. 162; interestingly enough the same charge was leveled against Aristotle himself with regard to a certain Asclepiades of Pergamum.

132. See L. Kopf and F. S. Bodenheimer, *The Natural History Section from a Ninth Century Book of Knowledge. The 'Uyūn al-akhbār of Ibn Qutaybah* (Paris-Leyden, 1949), and the important corrections *à* propos of the Aristotle source by B. Lewin in his review in *Oriens*, V (1952), 355–57.

133. Sarton, *Introduction*, III, 2, pp. 1639–41; J. de Somogyi, "Al-Damīri's *Hayāt al-ḥayawān*. An Arabic Zoological Lexicon," *Osiris*, IX (1950), 33–43; *idem*, "Index des Sources de la *Hayāt al-ḥayawān*," *JA*, CCIII (1928), 5–128, espec. pp. 112–13 (Aristotle).

134. On Yāqūt see pp. 292–293 below. The sources of the opening chapter of the *Mu'jam* have now been traced in some detail by W. Jewaideh, *The Introductory Chapters of Yāqūt's Mu'jam al-buldān* (Leyden, 1959), espec. pp. 19–20 for the connection with the *De coelo*.

pursuing the course of the *Ethica* and the *Poetica*,[135] both of which had their influence outside philosophical circles. The legendary Aristotle also had his place as themes from the Alexander Romance became domesticated in the *adab* literature of the Arabs. But the most pressing need in this regard is surely in the domain of logic. It is clear from even the most cursory glance at the literature that Aristotle transformed the dialectic of Islam in the fields of law and theology; the syllogistic logic became the focus of an extensive literature of both explanation and polemic. Very few of these have been studied. Arab logic, *manṭiq*, like the translation literature itself, awaits a preliminary lexicographical study of the terminology.[136]

135. For a general orientation see Tkatsch, *Poetik*, and S. A. Bonebakker, *The Kitāb Naqd al-Shi'r of Qudāma b. Ja'far al-Kātib al-Baghdādi* (Leyden, 1956), pp. 36–44.

136. I have not seen the typescript thesis of Soheil Afnan, *La Connaissance du grec parmi les Philosphes islamiques. Lexique des termes de Logique en grec, anglais, francais, persan, pehlevi, et arabe*, described in *Revue des Etudes Islamiques* (1954), p. 131; see the same author's "Some Arabic and Persian Terms of Philosophy," *Oriens*, X (1957), 71–76.

VI

PHILOSOPHICAL MOVEMENTS IN ISLAM

Aristotle was a philosopher. He came to the Arabs as such and his primary influence in Islam was in the formation and growth of a philosophical tradition. Whatever his secondary effects in science and literature, he must be sought in the first instance in the philosophical schools and in the works of the philosophers. How well did the philosophers know Aristotle and what was their general impact on the intellectual life of the Islamic community?

The answer to the first part of the question is relatively simple. Both as textual technicians and as commentators the Arabs were capable of advanced work. Enough has been said of the translation movement and its techniques to indicate the careful and painstaking work that went into the preparation of an Aristotelian text.[1] And the best of the Aristotelian commentators in Islam, Ibn Rushd (d. A.D. 1198),[2] produced a body of comment that was in no way inferior to anything seen in either the ancient Greek tradition or in the Latin West.

The second part of the question deals with matters considerably more complex. Hellenism created philosophy in Islam; its origins are as patent as the Greek etymology of *falsafah,* the only word the Arabs had to describe this utterly new phenomenon. And *falsafah* in its turn created Muslim theology, insofar as theology is to be understood as a systematic discipline concerned with the study of God and

1. See pp. 61–67 above.
2. See pp. 217–220 below.

His manifestation in His creation. Before the introduction of the "new Aristotle" *ca* A. D. 1150, the West had a flourishing and highly sophisticated theological tradition born of Christianity's first contact with Greek learning. But there was no pre-Ḥunayn Augustine in Islam. There were, to be sure, certain theological positions emerging from the political crises of the early community and from exegetical *cruses* inherent in the *Qur'ān* and the *ḥadīth*; there were creeds but no theology. *Kalām*, natural theology, is the direct result of the working of the philosophical leaven in the body of Islamic thought. And it was *kalām* that guaranteed the survival of the philosophical tradition after the decease of *falsafah* itself.

Any attempt, then, to take the measure of Aristotle in Islam must deal with both these elements, *falsafah* and *kalām*. What follows is not, of course, intended to be a history of either. It ambitions nothing more elaborate than to lay out some of the textual and bibliographical material, and to give a sketch of the developing problematic. The material on *falsafah* proper is quite brief, and designedly so; because of their connection with medieval philosophy in the West the *falāsifah* have enjoyed considerable attention, and I have generally contented myself with referring the reader to the readily available material.[3] While the treatment of *kalām* is somewhat more extended, it is designed to emphasize only one aspect of the subject: the growth of philosophical elements within theology. Thus the emphasis, unjustified in the more general context of theology, on the epistemological and physical theses of the *mutakallimūn*.

THE MU'TAZILITE MOVEMENT

Even during the lifetime of the Prophet, the "nation" he had so laboriously assembled from disparate loyalties and beliefs began to disintegrate. Muslim authors are fond of tracing the somewhat later

3. See p. 156–157, "Bibliographical Note," below.

fissures to the old tribal rivalry of northern and southern Arab. Tribal differences there certainly were, soon to be further complicated by ethnic (Arab *vs.* Persian) and dynastic (Umayyad *vs.* 'Alid) rivalries. From such mundane stuff was born Islamic heterodoxy and, by the same inexorable process that brought the Council of Nicea on the heels of Arius, Islamic systematic theology.

The *Qur'ān* is no more a scholastic treatise than are the Gospels. Questions are raised in it but not answered definitively; other questions, obvious to the nonprophetic hindseer, are not touched upon at all. Before a clearly defined *magisterium* could be worked out it was inevitable that there should be differences of opinion on what had been revealed and individual attempts to answer the unasked or unanswered questions. The grinders of partisan axes were not slow to profit from the situation.

Early Islamic dogmatics are a disconcerting blend of politics and exegesis, and the most common interpretation is to underscore the politics. Thus, the Kharajites become disappointed supporters of 'Ali's hopes of retaining the Caliphate, and the Murji'ites, a species of political quietist, supported by the Umayyads. Whether these interpretations are true need not be settled here. Less easily disposed of are groups such as the Qadarites, the proponents, in the face of the ambiguous statements in the *Qur'ān,*[1] of man's free will. The ground appears firmly theological, or at least the political motives for holding such a position are so deeply buried in the multiple confusions of the seventh and early eight centuries that they are no longer visible. It has been suggested[2] that the origins of such predestinarian discussions are to be sought in contemporary Christian circles,[3] but, foreign inspired or not, the Qadarites had embarked on the course of pure speculation.

1. Many of these passages have been collected in W. Watt, *Free Will and Predestination in Early Islam* (London, 1948).

2. C. H. Becker, *Islamstudien*, I (Leipzig, 1924), 439–41.

3. Possibly *provoked* by Christian polemic but hardly inspired by similar Christian discussions. The eighth-century point at issue was Iconoclasm; Bañez, Molina, and the *Congregatio de auxiliis* were still very far in the future.

Heresiographers tended to identify the Muʿtazilites with the Qadarites, and, in fact, on the crucial question of the human will they held identical positions: man is free. But while the Qadarite theses cluster about the question of predestination, the Muʿtazilites, as they begin emerging into the light of history, are identified with a *series* of positions. Though there are, perhaps, too many gaps in the series to characterize it as a system, it is a body of dogma resting on definite rational principles. Further, it represents the first introduction of Greek philosophy into Islamic thought.

The *muʿtazilah* begins inconspicuously enough in the essentially Arab milieu of Basrah. Its early physiognomy resembles that of both the Kharijites and the Murjiʿites, and Nyberg is undoubtedly correct in tracing the theses of its founder, Wāṣil ibnʿAṭā' (d. A.D. 748/9), to the paratheological controversies surrounding ʿAlid claims to the Caliphate.[4] The real founder of the group as a theological movement was not a Muʿtazilite at all. Jahm ibn Safwān (d. A.D. 745/6),[5] by his intransigent position on predestination, involved Wāṣil in the speculative area already essayed by the Qadarites. Wāṣil rejected the determinism of Jahm (hence the later identification of the Muʿtazilites with the Qadarites), but followed him in denying attributes to Allah. It was a fateful decision in that it brought Wāṣil and his followers into collision with the hard core of Islamic orthodoxy, the traditionalists, who were, at least at that stage in their development, willing to adhere to the letter of the *Qur'ān*, even if it led to the most obvious kind of anthropomorphism (*tashbīh*).[6] Thus Jahm was to some degree responsible for two basic Muʿtazilite theses: the affirmation of free will in man and the denial of the attributes separate from God's essence, exactly the points which the Muʿtazilites used to characterize them-

4. *Shorter EI*, p. 422; see Watt, *Islamic Philosophy*, p. 61.

5. Jahm, like most of the earliest heretics, can be seen only through the eyes of the orthodox; see the full-scale reputation *Kitāb al-radd ʿalā al-jahmīyah* of al-Dārimi (d. A.D. 895), ed. and trans. by G. Vitestam (Lund and Leyden, 1960); al-Ashʿari, *Maqālāt*, pp. 279 ff.; al-Shahrastāni, *Milal*, p. 60; A. Subhan, "Al-Jahm ibn Safwan and his philosophy," *Islamic Culture*, XI (1937), 221–27.

6. Later rejected by the orthodox who, under the influence of the Muʿtazilites, allowed a measure of "interpretation" (*ta'wīl*) of the Sacred Text. In al-Sanusi, *Muqaddimāt* (ed. Luciani), pp. 134–35, the admission of *ta'wīl* is associated with the name of al-Juwayni.

selves.[7] Jahm, Wāṣil, and their contemporaries had to cope with both their Muslim and Manichaean[8] opponents as well as the pressure of Christian theological concepts; but it was not until the next generation that serious attention was given to a new element that was just then beginning to infiltrate Muslim intellectual circles: Greek philosophy.

In his *Munqidh*, al-Ghazāli divides the *falāsifah* into three groups:[9] the materialists (*dahriyūn*), the naturalists (*ṭabī'iyūn*), and the metaphysicians (*ilāhiyūn*); and it was this first group, the so-called *Dahrīyah*, that brought the new learning into Mu'tazilite circles by propagating a completely naturalistic world without creator and subject only to the laws of nature and the movement of the spheres.[10] The defense against this atheism was taken up by the Mu'tazilite Abū al-Ḥudhayl al-'Allāf.[11]

Though generally reckoned as a member of the "Basrah School" of Mu'tazilites, Abū al-Hudhayl and his disciple al-Naẓẓām (d. A.D. 845)[12] spent most of their professional careers in Baghdad at the

7. According to al-Mas'ūdi, *Murūj*, VI, 22, there were five propositions that characterized the Mu'tazilites; but the other three are paratheological, and the Mu'tazilites themselves seemed willing to be qualified by the first two: "partisans of divine unity and divine justice." The pre-Jahm origins of the complicated question of the divine attributes are obscure. Once the question had been introduced, however, Christian influence began to be felt; see H. Wolfson, "Philosophical Implications of the Problem of Divine Attributes in the Kalam," *JAOS*, LXXIX (1959), 76 à propos of al-Naẓẓām and al-Ḍirār.
8. Generally called "dualists" but frequently included in the more general designation of *zindīq*. In Mu'tazilite eyes the chief *zindīq* was Ibn al-Rawāndi (d. *ca.* A.D. 850–900) and it was his *The Dishonor of the Mu'tazilites* (no longer extant) that provoked the famous *Book of Triumph* of al-Khayyāt (d. A.D. 915), the sole original document for this period of the sect (*Kitāb al-intiṣār*, ed. H. Nyberg [Cairo, 1925], and reprinted, with a French translation, by A. Nader [Beyrouth, 1957]). On Ibn al-Rawāndi (*aliter* al-Rawāndi) see P. Kraus, "Beiträge zur islamischen Ketzergeschichte. Das *Kitab az-Zammurudh* des Ibn al-Rawāndi," *RSO*, XIV (1933–1934), 93–129, 335–79. For the larger question of Manichaean and *zindīq*: M. Guidi, *La Lotta tra l'Islam e il Manicheismo* (Rome, 1927), with the extended review by H. Nyberg in *OLZ* (1929), cols. 425–41, and G. Vadja, "Les Zindiqs en pays d'Islam au début de la période abbaside," *RSO*, XVII (1937–1938), 172–229; for the pre-Islamic Manichaean background see pp. 49–62 above.
9. Pp. 96–101
10. Al-Khawārizmi, *Mafātīh al-'ulūm*, p. 35.
11. The date of his death is variously given as A.D. 840 or A.D. 850; *GAL*, Suppl. I, p. 338; A. Nader, *Le Système . . . des Mu'tazila*, pp. 26–27; H. Nyberg, art. "Abū al-Hudhayl al-'Allāf," EI², pp. 127–29; R. M. Frank, *The Metaphysics of Created Being According to Abū l-Hudhayl al-'Allāf* (Istanbul, 1966).
12. *GAL*, Suppl. I, p. 339; A. Nader, *Le Système . . . des Mu'tazila*, pp. 29–32; M. Abu Ridah,

court of the Caliph al-Ma'mūn during the height of the translation activity under Ḥunayn ibn Isḥāq.[13] It was during this same period that the more politically minded of the Muʿtazilites caught the ear and the favor of the Caliph and, from *ca.* A.D. 833–848, Muʿtazilitism was the "established" theology of Islam.[14]

Abū al-Hudhayl has been called "the first speculative theologian of the *Muʿtazila*."[15] It was he, at any rate, who introduced many of the Greek metaphysical concepts that were to characterize subsequent Muʿtazilite *kalām*. Al-Shahrastāni singles him out as the founder of the Muʿtazilite methodology,[16] and there was little doubt in the minds of most of the heresiographers as to the origins of that methodology: the Muʿtazilites read the books of the Greek philosophers and then proceeded to mix this *yūnāni* godlessness with the traditional approach to theology.[17] Al-Naẓẓām falls under the same kind of criticism.[18]

Although it is customary to associate the Muʿtazilites with theses like the denial of divine attributes and the eternity of the *Qur'ān*, their clear and unmistakable debt to Greek philosophy is best traced in two different areas: their epistemology and their metaphysics of atoms and accidents.

The epistemological problem is not one first raised by the Muʿtazilites; its genuine origins are to be found in one of the sciences propaedeutic to the study of law, the *uṣūl al-fiqh*, the "sources of the law." There was general agreement that Islamic law was grounded

Ibrāhīm ibn Sayyār al-Naẓẓām (Cairo, 1946 [in Arabic]); R. Paret, "An Naẓẓām als Experimentor," *Der Islam*, XXV (1939), 228–33.

13. Al-Masʿūdi, *Murūj*, VIII, 301.

14. The events of those years are described in W. Patton, Ahmed ibn Hanbal and the Mihna (Leyden, 1897), and with further precisions on the Alid political questions that lie in the background, by W. Watt, JRAS (1963), 38–57, and D. Sourdel, REI, XXX (1962), 27–48. The touchstone of Muʿtazilite "orthodoxy" was the thesis that the *Qur'ān* had been created. The prime movers were Thumānā ibn al-Ashras (d. A.D. 825/6) and Ahmad ibn abī Duʿād (d. A.D. 854/5), the latter serving as chief magistrate under the Caliphs al-Wāthiq and al-Mutawakkil.

15. H. Nyberg, *EI*², I, 127.

16. *Milal*, p. 34.

17. Al-Sharastāni, *Milal*, p. 18; Ibn Khaldūn levels the same charge of mixing philosophy and theology against the post-Ghazāli theologians; see *Muqaddimah* (trans. Rosenthal), III, 52–54, 152–55, and p. 194 below.

18. Al-Shahrastāni, *Milal*, p. 37.

in the *Qur'ān* and the customary practice of the Prophet (*sunnah*). But very soon jurisprudents were passing judgments, based on their personal opinion (*ra'y*), where there was no clear directive in either revelation or the *sunnah*. The method generally applied in reaching such decisions was that of analogy (*qiyās*),[19] deriving conclusions *a maiori* and *a minori*. The process was somewhat haphazard but *qiyās* was to be a last resort and to be applied only when there was no explicit statement in the *Qur'ān* or *sunnah*.[20]

The Mu'tazilites, though not forming a separate legal school, took quite another view of *qiyās* in particular and the rational process (*naẓār*) in general. For them it was a distinct and autonomous source of truth, and where the conclusions of reason and tradition were in conflict they used reason to correct the latter,[21] a view which, strangely enough, the Mu'tazilites later abandoned in law, though they continued to support the philosophical position behind it.[22] In the theological counterpart of the *uṣūl* problem, the question of the "channels of knowledge" (*asbāb al-'ilm*), the Mu'tazilites did not desert their stand on the autonomy of rational knowledge. Indeed, they erected upon it a further thesis on natural religion (*fiṭrah*), whereby an individual might, by his unaided reason and independent of revelation, become a believer in the true God.[23]

The theses on the autonomy of reason, whether suggested by or borrowed from Greek philosophy, mark a major triumph for Mu'tazilitism and a no less meaningful incursion of a philosophical principle into the domain of the old orthodoxy. For although al-Ash'ari (d. A.D. 935), the "hammer of the Mu'tazilites," displays most of the

19. This is also the technical term for the Aristotelian syllogism, but in a legal context it never implied more than the loose logical method of analogy.

20. Al-Shāfi'i, *Risālah* (ed. Bulaq), p. 65.

21. Ibn Qutaybah, *Ta'wīl mukhtalif al-ḥadīth* (ed. Cairo, 1908), p. 76; al-Baghdādi, *Farq*, pp. 93–94; al-Shahrastāni, *Milal*, p. 36; A. Nader, *Le Système ... des Mu'tazila*, p. 250.

22. J. Schacht, *The Origins of Muslim Jurisprudence* (Oxford, 1950), p. 259.

23. A. J. Wensinck, *The Muslim Creed* (Cambridge, 1932), pp. 214–15. The Mu'tazilite *fiṭrah* was not, however, quite so rationalistic as it first appears. There are definite overtones of the Stoic *koinai ennoiai*: the Mu'tazilites may well have looked upon the *fiṭrah* as divinely implanted in the mind at birth and subsequently "discovered" by reflection, much as al-Ash'ari's contemporary Sa'adya ibn Yūsuf (d. A.D. 942) did; see I. Efros, *JQR*, XXXIII (1942–1943), 147–49 and pp. 151–154 below.

trappings of the traditional orthodox position in his *Elucidation of Islam's Foundation*,[24] in his other work, notably the *Vindication of the Science of Kalām*,[25] he is a defender of the new methodology, though still carefully linking it with the *Qur'ān* and the *sunnah*.[26]

The second Muʿtazilite thesis that betrays an unmistakable Greek influence is the division of creation into bodies (sing. *jism*) that are aggregates, and their component parts (sing. *juz'* or *jawhar*), which are indivisible.[27]

According to the Muʿtazilite view, the first entity perceptible by the senses is the body, which is, however, merely a composite of atoms. Atom was equated with substance.[28] Though the body obviously had qualities, the Muʿtazilites were divided on the question of whether or not the atoms themselves had properties (*ṣifāt*). The more common view was that the atoms had no qualities of their own save motion and rest. The occurrence of properties in bodies resulted from the inherence (*ḥulūl*)[29] of accidents (sing. *ʿaraḍ*) in the atom. Accidents, as well as the atom-substance, have their own existence. Finally, each accident persists for but a moment and must be continuously re-created by God.[30]

24. *Al-Ibānah ʿan uṣūl al-diyānah* (ed. Cairo, 1929); trans. W. Klein (New Haven, 1940).

25. *Istiḥṣān al-khawd fi ʿilm al-kalām* (ed. Hyderabad, 1925); trans. R. McCarthy, *The Theology of al-Ashʿari* (Beyrouth, 1953), pp. 119–34.

26. Typical is al-Ashʿari's defense of the principle of causality on the basis of an utterance of the Prophet: "On a certain occasion he (Muḥammad) said: 'There is no contagious disease and no bad omen.' And a Bedouin said: 'Then what is the matter with camels, flawless as gazelles, which mingle with scabby camels and become scabby?' And the Prophet said: 'And who infected the first?' And the Bedouin was silent because of what he had made him understand by that rational argument." *Istiḥṣān* (trans. McCarthy), p. 126.

This little parable finds its amusing parallel in an anecdote told by Niẓāmi in his *Haft Peikar*. A pious believer named Bishr was strolling one day with a philosopher. "Why are some clouds white and others black?" the philosopher asked. "Because," replied Bishr, "God made them that way." "Nonsense," returned the philospher. "The white ones are composed of humidity and the black of vapor." There was more of the same, but the attacks on the faith of the pious Bishr ceased when the philosopher fell, Thales-like, into a cistern and drowned. Bishr, savoring the Divine Providence to the full, married the philosopher's widow.

27. An important exception was al-Naẓẓām, who held that the atoms were infinitely divisible *a parte mentis*.

28. The term used for atom, *jawhar*, becomes, even in the nonatomic physics of the *falāsifah*, the standard term for substance; see Pines, *Atomenlehre*, pp. 3–4.

29. See Pines, *Atomenlehre*, p. 21, n. 1.

30. This was certainly the view of the later Ashʿarites, though there is some doubt as to its exact position in the Muʿtazilite system; see Pines, *Atomenlehre*, pp. 25–26.

These, then, were the basic positions of Muʿtazilite "physics."[31] Each of the theses led to a parallel theological position, but, as Pretzl has pointed out,[32] early Islamic atomism appears as a given of the system; like the atoms themselves, it had an existence independent of the theology to which it led. Where did it come from? The answers are divided between there main categories: Greek philosophy, Indian philosophy, and Christian and/or Gnostic influences, all present in this area long before the arrival of Islam.

The Arabs were themselves the chief proponents of the Greek philosophy theory and, though at first unable to distinguish the types of Greek atomism, were later well aware of the differences between what the Muʿtazilites had held and the position of Democritus.[33] Later students of the problem have attempted to be still more precise. The case for Stoic origins has been put forth by Horovitz,[34] and Pines has pointed out the parallels with the atomism of Epicurus.[35]

The chief advocate of an Indian origin has been Horten who, in his *Die philosophischen Systeme der spekulativen Theologen im Islam*, has collected analogous material from the *corpus* of Indian atomism.[36] Finally, Gnostic parallels have been signaled by Pretzl,[37] and a Muʿtazilite treatise recently attributed to al-Jāḥiẓ (d. A.D. 872) has shown that the movement used Patristic material among its sources.[38]

If Greek, the system is certainly not Aristotelian. There are those who found parallels,[39] but neither the Ashʿarites who adopted it nor the Muslim Peripatetics who opposed it ever confused the Muʿtazilite

31. Necessarily simplified; very few of these theses, for instance, were adopted by al-Naẓẓām, who had his own atomic theory and who was the object of most of the criticism directed against Muʿtazilite physical theory by the Ashʿarite atomists; see al-Baghdādi, *Farq* (trans. Halkin), p. 179; A. Nader, *Le Système ... des Muʿtazila*, pp. 155–58; Pines, *Atomenlehre*, pp. 10–16.
32. *Der Islam*, XIX (1931), 124–25.
33. First in Fakhr al-Dīn al Razi; see Pines, *Atomenlehre*, pp. 96–97.
34. *ZDMG*, LVII (1903), 177–96.
35. *Atomenlehre*, pp. 97–99.
36. Compare Pines, *Atomenlehre*, pp. 102–23.
37. *Der Islam*, XIX (1931), 127ff.
38. *Kitāb al-ʿibar wa al-iʿtibār*, studied by H. Gibb, "The Argument from Design. A Muʿtazilite Treatise attributed to al-Jāḥiẓ," *Ignace Goldziher Memorial Volume*, I (Budapest, 1948), 150–62.
39. A. Nader, *Le Système ... des Muʿtazila*, p. 152; M. Fakhry, *Islamic Occasionalism*, pp. 34–35.

atomism with the teaching of Aristotle. The *falāsifah* particularly—and they adhered, by and large, to the Aristotelian physics[40]—maintained an unbroken line of polemic against atomism in all its shapes and forms.[41]

There was, however, one important respect in which the Muʿtazilites departed from their atomism and it is here that their resemblance to Aristotelianism is most marked. The world of discrete atoms was of necessity an occasionalist one. The Ashʿarites, the defenders of the omnipotence of God, delighted in this aspect of atomism and embraced the doctrine of continuous re-creation (*khalq fī kull waqt*) whereby God sustained His original creation by continually renewing it. But the Muʿtazilites were committed to an affirmation of man's freedom as a correlative of God's justice. They were unanimous in holding that man had an inner freedom of choice (*ikhtiyār*). Was there, then, a causal relationship between this internal act of the will and the external action which followed hard upon it? At least one Muʿtazilite, Bishr ibn al-Muʿtamir (d. A.D. 825), thought so, maintaining that man generated (*tawallada*) this external action and was responsible for it.[42] His contemporary, Abū al-Hudhayl, hedged somewhat: man does indeed generate his own acts, but he is responsible for only those acts which he intends directly; for other possible results of his acts he is not responsible.[43]

Certainly the concept of *tawallud* is an abrogation of atomic occasionalism and an affirmation of secondary causality. There is another. Muʿammar ibnʿAbbād (*fl. ca.* A.D. 786–809) is credited with introducing the concept of nature (*ṭabʿ* = *physis*) into Muʿtazilite physics and the position was also adopted by al-Naẓẓām. According to Muʿammar, accidents act one upon the other either through natural necessity (*ṭabʿān*) or by an act of human volition (*ikhtiyārān*).[44] God creates substances; accidents are subject to secondary causality.

40. Except the time-place theories of the Platonic tradition; see pp. 170–172 below.
41. A list of representative philosophers has been compiled by Pines, *Atomenlehre*, p. 94, n. 4.
42. Al-Ashʿari, *Maqālāt*, p. 401; Al-Shahrastāni, *Milal*, p. 44.
43. *Ibid.*, p. 492.
44. Al-Shahrastāni, *op. cit.*, p. 46.

God is thereby freed of the troublesome responsibility of having created evil.[45]

Despite its inconsistencies and deficiencies, the Muʿtazilite "system" opened new areas of exploration for Islamic theology. For the celebrated dictum of the traditionalists: "I affirm this position on faith alone without asking *how* it may be true," it substituted a healthy dosage of intellectualism;[46] it provided an insight into the physical world, and it gave to the orthodox theologian a supply of metaphysical concepts with which further to elucidate the Faith. It also prepared the theologians for their true opponents; Abū al-Hudhayl, al-Naẓẓām, and al-Ashʿari himself are but figures in the prologue to the main drama to be played out between Ibn Sīnā (d. A.D. 1037) and al-Ghazāli (d. A.D. 1111).

Neither the disenchantment of the Caliph al-Mutawakkil in A.D. 848 nor the defection of al-Ashʿari in A.D. 912 brought about the end of Muʿtazilitism. The forces of extreme orthodoxy, led by Aḥmad ibn Ḥanbal (d. A.D. 855) who had suffered so much during the brief Muʿtazilite ascendency, were in full cry, first against the Muʿtazilites, and later against the new species of "rationalists," the Ashʿarites, who, in Hanbalite eyes, had won the battle but had decisively lost the theological war.[47] The Hanbalite repression was as stern as it was unrelenting, and it continued even beyond the espousal of the Ashʿarite cause by the Seljuk vizier Niẓām al-Mulk (d. A.D. 1092) and his attempts to propagate the new positions.[48]

45. Al-Shahrastāni, *loc. cit.*, says that this was al-Muʿammar's motive and it should be recalled that the Manichaeans were among the chief foes of the Muʿtazilites.
46. All through its history Muʿtazilitism had its attractions for men who were not primarily theologians: the philosophers al-Kindi (d. *ca.* A.D. 873), al-Tawḥidi (d. A.D. 1010), and Abū al-Ḥusayn (d. A.D. 1044) were associated with the movement. Al-Jāḥiẓ (d. A.D. 872), the famous litterateur and natural scientist, was a student of al-Naẓẓām.
47. According to the later Hanbalite Ibn Taymīyah (d. A.D. 1328), who had the advantage of both historical perspective and first-rate intellectual equipment, the evil genius who left his mark on al-Ashʿari as well as on many of the subsequent Ashʿarites was the Muʿtazilite teacher of al-Ashʿari, al-Jubbā'i (d. A.D. 915/6); *Minhāj*, IV, 154; *Bughyat*, p. 107. On Ibn Taymīyah see pp. 200–203 below.
48. The travails of the "Hanbalite years" and the Hanbalites' later displacement to the Ayyubid domains of Syria and Egypt are narrated in I. Goldziher, "Zur Geschichte der hanbalitischen Bewegungen," *ZDMG*, LXII (1908), 1–28, and H. Laoust, "Le Hanbalisme sous le califat de Baghdad," *REI*, XXVII (1959), 67–128. An example of the hardships suffered by the Ashʿarites at the hands of the Hanbalites is the migrations forced upon a man like al-Khatib al-Baghdadi (see p. 271–272 below).

Though there were still Muʿtazilites to be found in Baghdad in the tenth and eleventh centuries,[49] the focus of their activity shifted to the East. ʿAbd al-Jabbār (d. A.D. 1025),[50] who was the head of the Muʿtazilites in Baghdad, was summoned, in A.D. 976, to a provincial court in Rayy where he filled a high municipal post. Among his pupils was Abū Rashīd al-Nisabūri (*fl. ca.* A.D. 1068), a former Ashʿarite who was "converted" to Muʿtazilitism.[51]

The move of ʿAbd al-Jabbār was not an isolated phenomenon. After the collapse of the liberal Buwayhid dynasty in A.D. 1055, the tempo of Muʿtazilite activity in the eastern provinces, and particularly in Khawarizm,[52] increases and continues well into the twelfth century. It is Khawarizm that produces the last great figures of Muʿtazilitism, Maḥmūd ibn Jarīr al-Ḍabbi (d. A.D. 1113) and his famous student al-Zamakhshari (d. A.D. 1144),[53] and later in the same century Fakhr al-Dīn al-Rāzi (d. A.D. 1209) journeyed to Khawarizm to hold discussions (*munāẓarāt*) with Muʿtazilites of the area.[54]

49. Prominently Abū al-Qāsim ʿAli al-Murtaḍā (d. A.D. 1044); see Ibn Khallikān (trans. de Slane), II, 156–60; *GAL*, I² 510–12, Suppl. I, pp. 704–706.

50. *GAL*, Suppl. I, pp. 343–44, to be completed by S. M. Sterne, art. "ʿAbd al-Djabbār b. Aḥmad," *EI²*, I, 59–60. None of his extant works on dogma has been edited. The lost *Ṭabaqāt al-muʿtazilah* formed the basis of the Muʿtazilite section in the *Sharh ʿuyūn al-masā'il* of Abū Saʿīd al Bayḥaqi (d. A.D. 1101) and the heresiography of Ibn al-Murtaḍā; see Ritter, "Häresiographen," p. 42.

51. *GAL*, Suppl. I, p. 344; his *Masā'il fi al-khilāf bayn al-baṣrīyin wa al-baghdādīyin* is a collection of points debated between the Muʿtazilite schools of Baghdad and Basrah. The section on atomism, *al-kalām fi al-jawāhir*, has been edited by A. Biram (Leyden, 1902), and given a running commentary by M. Horten, *Die Philosophie des Abu Rachid* ... (Bonn, 1910).

52. I. Goldziher, *Der Islam*, III (1912), 218–23; B. Spuler, *Iran in früh-islamischen Zeit* (Wiesbaden, 1952), pp. 155–56; there was a general cultural renaissance in the eastern provinces during this period affecting not only theology, but also philosophy, science, and *belles-lettres*; see B. Spuler, *op. cit.*, p. 262, n. 5 ,and G. Weit, *Soieries persanes* (Cairo, 1947), pp. 148–53.

53. Ibn Khallikān (trans. de Slane), III 321–26; Yāqūt, *Irshād*, VII, 147–51; *GAL*, I², 344–50, Suppl. I, pp. 507–13. His most celebrated work is the *Kashshāf ʿan ḥaqā'iq*, a commentary of the *Qur'ān* most recently printed in Cairo, 1953, and frequently commented, glossed, and abridged by later authors. From the origins of the Muʿtazilite movement the science of Qur'anic comment (*tafsir*) was one of the weapons employed against the extreme orthodox intent on a literal interpretation of the Scripture. The methodology used by the Muʿtazilites was that known as "allegorical," a methodology likewise in use, though with far less restraint, in the *bāṭinīyah* sects. Muʿtazilite *tafsir*, and particularly the work of al-Zamakhshari, is studied in I. Goldziher, *Die Richtungen der islamischen Koranauslegung* (Leyden, 1920), pp. 99–179.

54. Al-Subki, *Ṭabaqāt*, V, 35.

KALĀM

In the Muslim view of history, God raises up in each century a reformer of the religion of His people. Thus in the year A.H. 300 (A.D. 912/3) Abū al-Ḥasan ʿAli ibn Ismāʿīl al-Ashʿari, a student of the eminent Muʿtazilite al-Jubbāʾi ascended the pulpit of the mosque of Basrah and made a solemn declaration to the congregation: "Be ye witnesses that I have not been following the religion of Islam, and that I now embrace Islam and that I repent of the Muʿtazilite views which I held." Then he came down.[55]

The effect must have been somewhat less than electric, for the same source tells us that Muʿtazilitism prevailed until the time of al-Baqillāni (d. A.D. 1013) who routed the Muʿtazilites in Baghdad and spread the doctrine of al-Ashʿari to the East and to the West.[56] The passage concluded with the interesting comment: "Al-Baqillāni was on the most friendly terms with the Hanbalites and was buried in the cemetery of the Imām Aḥmad ibn Ḥanbal." A recent student of al-Baqillāni has added his own postscript to the career of the later theologian: "The main virtues of his works appear to be those proper to a careful and industrious compilation."[57]

What, then, happened in theology in the span covered by the careers of the three "centenary reformers," al-Ashʿari, al-Baqillāni, and al-Ghazāli, the period marking the birth and early growth of Muslim Scholastic theology, *kalām*?

55. The account is found in the chief source for the life of al-Ashʿari, the *Tabyīn kadhib al-muftari* of Ibn ʿAsākir (d. A.D. 1176); see p. 264 below (ed. Damascus, 1928), p. 40; the *Tabyīn* has been translated by R. McCarthy, *The Theology of al-Ashʿari* (Beyrouth, 1953), pp. 147–230, including, *ibid.*, pp. 211–30, a list of al-Ashʿari's works. Of these, the following have been edited: *al-Ibānah ʿan uṣūl al-diyānah* (Cairo, 1929); trans. W. Klein, *The Elucidation of Islam's Foundation* (New Haven, 1940); *al-Lumaʿ fī al-radd ʿalā ahl al-zaygh wa al-bidaʿ*, ed. R. McCarthy, *op. cit.*, pp. 1–73 of the Arabic text; trans. *ibid.*, pp. 5–116; *Maqālāt al-islāmīyīn*, ed. H. Ritter (Istanbul, 1929), see p. 257 below; *Istiḥsān al-khawd fī ʿilm al-kalām* (ed. Hyderabad, 1925); trans. R. McCarthy, *op. cit.*, pp. 119–34; see *GAL*, I², 207–208, Suppl. I, pp. 345–46; W. Watt, art. *s.v.*, *EI²*, I, 694–95; W. Thompson, "Al-Ashʿari and his al-Ibānah," "*Moslem World*, XXXII (1942), 242–60.
56. *Tabyīn* (trans. McCarthy), p. 202.
57. R. McCarthy, *EI²*, I, 959.

The first thing to be noted about this earliest stage in the development of *kalām* is that it was in no sense revolutionary. Rather, it represents the affirmation of the "middle position" in the dogmatic disputes of the preceding generation.[58] Viewed by the Muʿtazilites, this brand of Ashʿarism is a retreat in the direction of Hanbalite reaction, an impression deliberately cultivated by al-Ashʿari himself. But judged by the standards of the old orthodoxy, the Ashʿarite statement is a considerable concession to the Muʿtazilite intellectualism and the now-flourishing Hellenism in Baghdad (the public teaching of *falsafah* in Baghdad antedates al-Ashʿari's "conversion" by ten years).

The conciliatory nature of the Ashʿarite theses is apparent in their views on the divine attributes and on human responsibility. The Anthropomorphists had said that the Qurʾanic description of God's attributes must be accepted as literally true. The Muʿtazilites had replied by stripping (*taʿṭīl*) Him of His attributes only, it should be noted, to safeguard the divine unity. The Ashʿarite solution was to adopt the *via remotionis* (*tanzīh*): God has these qualities described in the *Qurʾān*, but there is no analogy between them and the *apparently* similar qualities in man.

Again, the strict determinists had denied man any responsibility for his acts. At least some of the Muʿtazilites held that man generated his own acts and for these he was held responsible. The Ashʿarites affirmed the traditional theses of God's immediate control over all of His creation and admitted that God created both the act of willing and the external act which followed ("habitually," the Ashʿarites would maintain); but with an obvious bow in the direction of the Muʿtazilites the Ashʿarites posited a third "moment" where by God created a further accident whereby the act may be imputed to the alleged agent.[59]

58. The Ashʿarite positions were clearly recognized as mediatory by al-Juwayni (d. A.D. 1085), the teacher of al-Ghazāli; see *Tabyīn* (trans. McCarthy), pp. 171–75. There is a synoptic view of these "middle" theses in Gardet-Anawati, *Théologie musulmane*, pp. 58–59. Ashʿari was by no means the first to occupy this middle ground. There were some who took up conciliatory positions as early as the days of Ibn Ḥanbal, notably Ibn Kullāb (d. A.D. 855); see J. van Ess, "Ibn Kullab und die Mihna," *Oriens*, XVIII–XIX (1967), 92–142.
59. The technical term "acquisition" (*kasb*) was probably first used in Muʿtazilite circles; see W. Watt, "The Origin of the Islamic Doctrine of Acquisition," *JRAS* (1943), pp. 234–47.

A second and more important development in the period begun by al-Ash'ari is the fact that certain individuals who generally passed as orthodox managed to disengage the methodology of *kalām*—and it is abundantly clear from al-Ash'ari's *Istiḥsān* that *kalām* is in the first instance a methodology—from its Mu'tazilite stigma and gradually to introduce it into the mainstream of orthodox Islam.

Al-Ash'ari's own views on *kalām* and on its legitimacy as a theological method appear to be somewhat ambivalent. In the *Ibānah* he takes as his theological *loci* the *Qur'ān*, tradition, and, significantly, the views of Ibn Ḥanbal, a position straight out of the old orthodoxy But in his other preserved works, he in fact leans heavily on rational arguments. Whether this be duplicity or the slow groping for new solutions, Al-Ash'ari had the wisdom to see that if one were going to differ with the Mu'tazilites, one could not refute them merely by quoting the *Qur'ān*. Theology has its own Gresham's Law and the arrival of dialectic and formal logic inevitably drives out the *argumentum ex Sacra Pagina*. With the appearance of the Mu'tazilites this inexorable process went into operation and the days of passive adherence (*taqlīd*) were numbered.[60]

The Hanbalites were not deceived by the pious protestations of the *Ibānah*. As Ibn 'Asākir implicitly admits, and as history clearly shows, the Ash'arite *via media* made little impression at first: in Hanbalite eyes the Mu'tazilite and the Ash'arite were equally reprehensible. Ibn 'Asākir dates the changed circumstances from the days of al-Baqillāni (d. A.D. 1013), but in this he appears precipitate.[61]

The evolution of Ash'arism must be sought principally in the areas of methodology and epistemology; individual dogmas held by al-Ash'ari are not much altered by later theologians; but in the

60. Al-Ash'ari explicitly concedes this in the opening paragraphs of the *Istiḥṣān*. According to Pines, *Atomenlehre*, p. 2, it was the virtue of Ash'arism that it preserved the omnipotence of the pre-Islamic Allah. In the context that Pines is discussing this, it is true; but it is equally true that al-Ash'ari, by ceding a foothold to *kalām*, effectively exposed the orthodox community to the not-to-be denied presence of the God of the Philosophers.

61. George Makdisi has recently pointed out, *BSOAS*, XXIV (1961), 46–48, that there is little ground for maintaining the traditional position that the change in the fortunes of Ash'arism date from the Niẓām al-Mulk's founding of a university, the Niẓāmīyah, in Baghdad to propagate the new doctrines. Not only is it a mistake to assert that Ash'arism was officially taught there, but there is every evidence that Hanbalism continued to thrive.

propaedeutic area known as the *asbāb al-ʿilm* and in the organization of theological treatises there is a perceptible if intermittent progress.[62]

The question of the *asbāb* had already been raised by the Muʿtazilites, both in its jurisprudential context where they finally accepted the Shafiʿite position of the inferiority of reason to tradition, and as part of the theological problematic where they continued to support the autonomy of reason.[63] Al-Ashʿari will not go quite that far. By *kalām* he seems to have understood the use of philosophical concepts in dealing with theological problems.[64] This he will admit without at the same time troubling himself with philosophical principles. Although he never faced the problem squarely, it is certain that he would not accept reason as a source of new and certain knowledge; it is, in fact, quite unthinkable in the light of his occasionalism.[65]

There were, however, bolder spirits who were discussing the problem of the *asbāb al-ʿilm* more knowingly than al–Ashʿari and more systematically than the Muʿtazilites. But before pursuing further the *asbāb* problem, some general positions must be traced.

According to the philosophers there are four general sources of knowledge: sense perception, intuition, speculation or discursive knowledge, and tradition.

On sense perception there was little dispute. Al-Baghdādi mentions the Sophists (*sūfistāʾīyah*) who call into doubt the testimony of the senses;[66] but by and large the Islamic community united in affirming the validity of sense perception.

Intuition (*ʿaql*=*nous* of *Anal. post.*, II, 19) presented a far more complicated problem. The philosophers, following Aristotle, allowed

62. The earliest form of theological *systema*-work, the creed (*ʿaqīdah*), is supplanted, except for catechetical purposes, by systematic treatises markedly similar to the Western *summa*. Al-Ashʿari still used both forms, but by the time of al-Baqillāni (*Tamhīd*) and al-Baghdādi (Usūl) the *summa* has won the day. The development in the organization of treatises is excellently illustrated in Gardet-Anawati, *Théologie musulmane*, pp. 136–86.

63. For a general treatment of the *asbāb* problem see A. Wensinck, *The Muslim Creed*, and Gardet-Anawati, *Théologie musulmane*, pp. 374–86; both works are directed toward the more purely theological aspects of the problem.

64. For example, in *Istiḥsān* (trans. McCarthy), pp. 120–21.

65. See p. 148 above.

66. *Uṣūl*, pp. 6–7.

an immediate perception of the first principles (*awwāliyāt*), usually exemplified by the axioms of geometry,[67] but frequently including moral conventions accepted by all peoples, a certain reflection of the Stoic *koinai ennoiai*. The philosophers debated the *awwāliyāt* on a metaphysical level, whether such concepts were innate or reached, as Aristotle seems to indicate, by a kind of "sifting" abstraction performed on the *sensata*. In *kalām*, however, the question of the moral conventions had direct theological implications. The Muʿtazilites affirmed a rational knowledge of the first principles of the moral law and, as we have seen, constructed out of it their theory of a natural religion (*fiṭrah*).[68] The *mutakallimūn* denied such a knowledge of moral conventions.

A knowledge of the *awwāliyāt* is grounded ultimately in intelligible forms united with matter. But there is another type of intuitive knowledge which knows the *intelligibilia* that are separated from matter. This type of intuition, generally known as *maʿrifah* (*gnosis*), opens into the problem of prophecy and sufism.

The third source of knowledge, speculation (*naẓar* or *fikr* = *dianoia*),[69] is the sticking point of the entire *falsafah-kalām* controversy. Is the reasoning process a source of new and necessary knowledge? The *falāsifah*, grounded in the Aristotelian doctrine of syllogistic *ananke*, maintained that it was; the *mutakellimūn*, starting from an affirmation of divine omnipotence, denied the causal principle implicit in *naẓar* and hence the autonomy of *naẓar*.[70]

The final channel, tradition (*khabar*), is not really a source at all, but is ultimately reducible to an intuitive revelation (thus falling into the domain of *maʿrifah*) and the validity of sense perception. The early dispute on this question centers in consensus (*ijmāʿ*) as a guarantee for the *tradita*. Al-Naẓẓām maintained that the community

67. E.g., Ibn Sīnā, *Najāt*, pp. 100–101.

68. Al-Shahrastāni, *Milal*, p. 84.

69. In this particular terminology the emphasis is on method; the *kind* of knowledge in question is otherwise called simply *ʿilm* (*episteme*).

70. It may have been that the early Ashʿarites were not entirely aware of the syllogistic *ananke*, but they at least knew the basic difference between the paratactical and non-necessitating reasoning involved in analogy, which they admitted, and the more ambitious claims of syllogistic reasoning.

could err in its consensus.[71] Al-Ash'ari wrote a refutation of this position,[72] and the orthodox community was unanimous in accepting the validating nature of *ijmā'*.

This epistemological *schema*, already fully elaborated in al-Fārābi,[73] does not appear in Muslim *kalām* until al-Baghdādi.[74] It does, however, occur in the work of a Jewish theologian of Baghdad who was contemporary with both al-Fārābi and al-Ash'ari.

Sa'adyā (the more common Hebrew transcription is Saadya) ibn Yūsuf al-Fayyūmi (d. A.D. 942), resident in Iraq since A.D. 915, was director (*gaon*) of the Talmudic academy of Sura from A.D. 928 and composed his *Book of Doctrines and Beliefs* in A.D. 933.[75] The *Amānāt* is, in fact, the earliest systematic work of *kalām* that we possess, and Sa'adyā's position vis à vis the Qaraites has its obvious analogies with that of al-Ash'ari toward the Mu'tazilites.[76]

71. Al-Shahrastāni, *Milal*, p. 64; al-Baghdādi, *Farq* (trans. Halkin), p. 177.

72. Listed on Ibn Fūrak's list in R. McCarthy, *op. cit.*, pp. 227, 387.

73. Most completely in the *Arā' ahl al-madīnah al-fāḍilah.*

74. *Uṣūl*, pp. 4–32; *Farq* (trans. Halkin), pp. 172–77.

75. The three full-length studies of Sa'adyā are: J. Guttmann, *Die Religionsphilosophie des Saadia* (Göttingen, 1892); H. Malter, *Saadia Gaon, His Life and Works* (Philadephia, 1921); M. Ventura, *La Philosophie de Saadia Gaon* (Paris, 1934), all of which contain elaborate bibliographical lists. For an excellent sketch of Sa'adyā's career in terms of his milieu see S. Baron, "Saadia's Communal Activity," *Saadia Anniversary Volume* (New York, 1943), pp. 9–74. The Arabic original of the *Kitāb al-amānāt wa al-i'tiqādāt* was edited by S. Landauer (Leyden, 1880), and the medieval Hebrew translation done by Jehudah ben Tibbon, ed. D. Slucki, (Leipzig, 1864). Both editions were used in the complete translation by S. Rosenblatt, *The Book of Beliefs and Opinions* (New Haven, 1948), and the abridged but richly annotated version by A. Altmann, *The Book of Doctrines and Beliefs* (Oxford, 1946).

The epistemology of the *Amānāt* and, incidentally, of Sa'adyā's other major theological work, his commentary on the *Sefer Yisirah* (see G. Vadja, *REJ*, CVI (1941–1945), 64–86), has been studied in some detail: I. Efros, "Saadia's Theory of Knowledge," *IQR*, n.s. XXXIII (1942–1943), 133–70; A. Heschel, "The Quest for Certainty in Saadi's Philosophy," *ibid.*, pp. 265–313; *idem*, "Reason and Revelation in Saadia's Philosophy," *JQR*, n.s. XXXIV (1943–1944), 391–408.

76. The Qaraites, a sect founded by Anan ben David (*fl. ca.* A.D. 750–775), rejected tradition and held that Scripture should be the subject of personal scrutiny, a position apparently influenced by the Muslim jurist Abū Ḥanīfah (d. A.D. 767) whom Anan knew personally.

The chief primary sources on the Qaratites include two written in Arabic: the heresiographical section of a legal work written by the Qaraite al-Qirqasāni, *Kitāb al-anwār wa al-marāqib*, ed. L. Nemoy (2 vols., New York, 1939–1940). Part I of Nemoy's edition is an heresiography, Part II a treatise on the *asbāb al-'ilm*, and Part III a refutation of the heretical opinions expressed in Part I. The other is a list of Qaraite doctors by the chronicler Ibn al-Hīti (*fl. ca.* A.D. 1430), ed., in Hebrew characters, and trans. G. Margoliouth, *JQR*, IX (1897), 429–33. On the Qaraite philosophers see: I. Markon and J. Heller, art. "Karäer," *Encyclopedia Judaica*, IX, cols. 923–51; S. Paznanski, *The Karaite Literary Opponents of Saadiah*

In Saʿadyā the discussion of the *asbāb al-ʿilm* is cast in the form of a prolegomenon, exactly as it is in the later *kalām* works of al-Baghdādi and al-Ghazāli. He acknowledges the three "philosophical" sources of sense perception, intuition, and knowledge which is inferred by logical necessity (*ʿilm mā dafaʿat al-ḍarūrah ilayhi*), to which he adds, as a member of the "community of monotheists," authentic tradition (*khabar ṣādiq*).[77]

Saʿadyā, like al-Ashʿari, had to face objections. Was the use of reason in theology valid?[78] Yes, answers Saʿadyā, for two reasons: to verify what we have learned from tradition and to refute our opponents.[79] The first reason, a genuine *fides quaerens intellectum*, was not to have a long life among the *mutakallimūm*; the second, *fides erigens propugnaculum*, was in the forefront of al-Ghazāli's thinking and was to dominate all post-Ghāzali *kalām* of the orthodox school.

A comparison between Saʿadyā and al-Ashʿari is not extremely flattering for the latter. The *Amānāt* is a sophisticated and sagacious piece of work. Saʿadyā is quite capable of dealing with the complicated question of the sources of doubt and error[80] and he attempted to fix in philosophical terms the distinction between faith and reason, the precise difference between the *amānāt* and *iʿtiqādāt* of the title of his work.

The first question raised in the body of the text is that of creation, and, after giving his own theory of creation *ex nihilo*, he proceeds to the statement and refutation of twelve other theories propounded by Plato, the Indians, Manichaeans, Hippocrates, Aristotle, the Atomists, and, finally, four species of sceptics.[81] The problem of scepticism, a commonplace in later dogmatic works like those of al-Baghdādi, Ibn Ḥazm, and Fakr al-Dīn al-Rāzi, is here treated for the first time, not, it will be noted, in the context of epistemology, but

Gaon (London, 1908). The second volume of J. Mann's *Texts and Studies in Jewish History and Literature* (Philadelphia, 1935), is devoted to Qaraite studies, and particularly pp. 3–283 on the Near Eastern Qaraites.

77. *Amānāt* (ed. Landauer), pp. 12–14, (trans. Rosenblatt), pp. 16–18.

78. Compare al-Ashʿari, *Istiḥsān* (trans. McCarthy), pp. 120 and ff.

79. *Amānāt* (trans. Rosenblatt), pp. 27–28.

80. See A. Heschel, *JQR*, n.s. XXXIII (1942–1943) 289–98.

81. For the identification of these theories see M. Ventura, *La Philosophie de Saadia Gaon*, pp. 113–71.

as part of the complex of proofs for creation.[82] Of such things al-Ash'ari knew very little and apparently cared even less.

Where did Sa'adyā acquire this relatively extensive knowledge of Greek philosophy? The elaborate creation arguments and elements in his treatment of the *asbāb al-'ilm* suggest that the answer may well be in the considerable Syriac and Arabic Philoponus literature.[83] Whatever its immediate sources, the *Amānāt* illustrates in both its organization and its problematic the degree to which Greek thinking in general and Aristotelianism in particular was transforming theology in the first half of the tenth century.

What is characteristic of this first flow of Hellenistic philosophy into *kalām* is that, to all appearances, the philosophical thinking had been previously "theologized" in a Christian environment, either in the Christian wing of the sixth-century Alexandrian school or in the Aramaic Monophysite and Nestorian centers of the Diocese of Antioch or the school of Nisibis. The second wave of al-Fārābi and Ibn Sīnā, first apparent in al-Ghazāli, was to be more philosophical, more secular, and hence more objectionable.

The period in the history of *kalām* between al-Ash'ari and al-Ghazāli is not very well known from a doctrinal point of view. Ibn 'Asākir has provided a list of the followers of al-Ash'ari;[84] many of them are merely names, but for others there exists some biographical material, manuscripts, and an occasional edited work.

Little is known about first-generation disciples of al-Ash'ari such as Abū al-Ḥusayn al-Bāhili;[85] but in the next generation there are

82. The creation proofs go back, via the Mu'tazilites and John Philoponus, to older Greek sources like Aristotle himself. At what stage the *adversarii*-paraphernalia was added it is impossible to say; see H. Wolfson, "The Kalām arguments for creation in Saadia, Maimonides, and Saint Thomas," *Saadia Anniversary Volume* (New York, 1943), pp. 197–245.

83. There is a marked resemblance between Sa'adyā's treatment of the *asbāb* and the opening section of Philoponus' commentary on the *Anal. post* (ed. Wallies), pp. 3–6. Guttmann, *Die Religionsphilosophie des Saadia*, p. 22, n. 5, had already pointed out the presence of a similar handling of the *asbāb* in the *Rasā'il* of the Sincere Brethren (ed. Cairo) II, 334 and III, 228. Later literature, following Guttmann, suggests that the *Rasā'il* were a source for Sa'adyā, but attempts at dating the *Rasā'il* give little ground for that contention; at best they were contemporary with Sa'adyā.

84. *Tabyīn* (trans. McCarthy), pp. 177–83; there is a more completely annotated translation of the *fihrist* in A. Mehren, *Exposé de la Reforme de l'Islamisme* (Leyden, 1878).

85. See Ibn Khallikān (trans. de Slane), II, 655.

important figures like al-Baqillāni (d. A.D. 1013),[86] Ibn Fūrak (d. A.D. 1015/6)[87] and, most important of all since he leads to al-Ghazāli, Abū Isḥāq al-Isfarā'ini (d. A.D. 1027/8).[88] Abū Isḥāq's most significant student was Abū Manṣūr ibn Tāhir al-Baghdādi (d. A.D. 1037)[89] who, like his master, spent most of his professional career in the East, at Nisabur and Isfara'in. Another pupil of Abū Isḥāq is the little-known Abū al-Qāsim al-Iskāf (d. A.D. 1062)[90] who was, in turn, the teacher of the celebrated al-Juwayni (d. A.D. 1085), surnamed Imām al-Ḥaramayn.[91]

Al-Juwayni stands at the turning point for Ash'arism. Driven from his home by the intensity of the anti-Ash'arite feeling, he spent the years A.D. 1058–1062 in Mecca and Medina. When he was summoned back to Nisabur by the new Seljuk regime, he resumed his teaching in a *madrasah* built expressly for this purpose by the orthodox (i.e., Ash'arite) and imaginative vizier Niẓām al-Mulk.[92]

86. Al-Khaṭib al-Baghdādi, *Ta'rikh*, V, 379–83 (including mention of a trip to the court of the Byzantine emperor); Ibn Khallikān (trans. de Slane), II, 671–72; *GAL*, I², 211; Suppl. I, p. 349; R. McCarthy, art. *s.v.*, *EI²*, I, 958–59; Gardet Anawati, *Théologie musulmane*, pp. 62–64. Father McCarthy has likewise prepared a new edition (Beyrouth, 1957) of the *Tamḥid*, al-Baqillāni's dogmatic work.

87. Ibn Khallikān (trans. de Slane), II, 673–74; *GAL*, Suppl. I, p. 277; his *Bayān mushkil al-aḥādith* has been edited by R. Köbert, *Analecta Orientalia*, XXII (Rome, 1941), who has also collected all the biographical information.

88. Surnamed *Rukn al-din*, "Pillar of Religion," the first of many scholars to be given such an honorific title; Ibn Khallikān (trans. de Slane), I, 8–9; al-Subki, *Ṭabaqāt*, III, 111–14 (including a note on a debate between al-Isfarā'ini and the Mu'tazilite 'Abd al-Jabbār; *GAL*, Suppl. I, p. 667. None of his genuine works has survived.

89. Ibn Khallikān (trans. de Slane), II, 149–50; al-Subki, *Ṭabaqāt*, III, 238–42; *GAL*, I², 482, Suppl. I, pp. 666–67; A. Tritton, art., *s.v.*, *EI²*, I, 909; Gardet-Anawati, *Théologie musulmane*, pp. 185–86. The dogmatic work *Uṣūl al-din* was edited in Istanbul, 1928, and its doctrine résuméd, in the form of a creed, in the *Farq* (trans. Halkin), pp. 171–229; for this latter heresiography, see p. 245 below.

90. Ibn Khallikān (trans. de Slane), II, 120; F. Wüstenfeld, *Der Imam el-Shafi'i und seine Abhänger* (Göttingen, 1890), p. 399.

91. Ibn Khallikān (trans. de Slane), II, 120–23; al-Subki, *Ṭabaqāt*, II, 70–71, and III, 170–204; *GAL*, I², 486–88, Suppl. I, pp. 671–73; M. Schreiner, *ZDMG*, III (1898), 491–502; Gardet-Anawati, *Théologie musulmane*, pp. 65–67; among his *dogmatica* the following have been published; *al-Irshād fi uṣūl al-i'tiqād*, ed. and trans. J. Luciani (Paris, 1938), and, more recently, the Arabic text alone (Cairo, 1950); *al-'Aqidah al-niẓāmiyah* (ed. Cairo, 1948), and trans. H. Klopfer, in *Das Dogma des Imam al-Haramain al-Djuwaini* (Cairo-Wiesbaden, 1958), pp. 27–109; a third *kalām* work, *al-Shāmil fi uṣūl al-din*, is still unedited; see Gardet-Anawati, *op. cit.*, pp. 181–85.

92. Al-Maqrizi, *Khiṭāt*, IV, 192; Ibn Khallikān (trans. de Slane), I, 8; says that a *madrasah* had previously been founded in that same city for Abū Isḥāq al-Isfarā'ini. A similar university was opened in Baghdad in A.D. 1067 for the jurist Abū Isḥāq al-Shirāzi: Ibn Khallikān (trans. de Slane), II, 164.

The new state support was decisive in the struggle of Ashʿarism against both the Muʿtazilites and Hanbalites. But somewhere between al-Baghdādi[93] and al-Juwayni's student, al-Ghazāli, there intervenes in the world of *kalām* the massive influence of Ibn Sīnā (d. A.D. 1037) and, through him, the entire impact of Greek philosophy in its secularist form.

According to his own account, al-Ghazāli (d. A.D. 1111) was the first to devote "thought and attention" to philosophy.[94] Insofar as this means direct contact with philosophical texts it is probably true. But even before al-Ghazāli, the incursion of an increasingly philosophical epistemology into *kalām* can be traced, particularly in al-Juwayni.[95] For a wider vision of philosophy, for an exact appreciation of its dangers, and a methodological refutation of its heretical theses, *kalām* is, however, clearly in the debt of al-Ghazāli.

But before discussing the collision of *falsafah* and *kalām* in the person of al-Ghazāli, it is necessary to return to the beginnings of the *falsafah* movement in Islam.

FALSAFAH

When a Muslim author uses the term *falsafah*, he may mean either of two things: in its earliest acceptation it refers to the Greek and Roman thinkers and the systems they erected.[96] After al-Ghazāli, however, use of the word has a marked polemical tone; *falsafah* refers to a rationalism which opposes the epistemological bases of *kalām*: it means, finally, Ibn Sīnā.[97]

93. Though the influence of the *falāsifah* is quite marginal in his extant works, they were perhaps treated more extensively in the lost *al-Milal wa al-niḥal*; see *Farq*, p. 254, and trans. Halkin, p. 92, n. 4.

94. *Munqidh* (trans. Watt), pp. 84–85.

95. This is the so-called *via moderna*; see Gardet-Anawati, *Théologie musulmane*, pp. 72–73, and p. 191 below.

96. E.g., al-Masʿūdi, *Tanbīh* (trans. de Vaux), pp. 163 ff.

97. E.g., al-Shahrastāni, *Milal* (trans. Haarbrucker), II, 213.

The emphasis on Ibn Sīnā and, to a lesser extent, al-Fārābi, was unfortunate in that it distorted the true picture of the development of *falsafah* in Islam. This is not to suggest that al-Ghazāli was jousting with a straw man. He had undoubtedly analyzed the situation correctly in directing his polemic against Ibn Sīnā who was not only an original and dynamic thinker but a propagandist as well. But al-Ghazāli, much like Aristotle himself, was a polemicist and not a historian of philosophy. He was not interested in the circumstances that created Ibn Sīnā: one looks in vain into the *Maqāṣid* and the *Tahāfut* for even the most jejune of sketches on the birth and growth of the philosophical tradition which was to provoke and, at the same, transfigure not only al-Ghazāli but also many another of his coreligionists.

Falsafah, being an exotic growth in Islam, depended for its birth and development on the translation mevement. There was no Arab Thales pondering the possibility of reducing all things to the principle of sand. Instead, we are confronted by al-Kindi, by all counts the very first Arab *faylasūf,* reading the *Metaphysica,* which had been translated for him by a certain Asṭāt.[98] Asṭāt, or Eustathius, is typical of the early translators. From *ca.* A.D. 750 to A.D. 850, the period of the *vetustiores,* a group of apparently unconnected and little-known individuals began translating Greek philosophical works into Arabic. The translations themselves were literal and studded with transcriptions where the technical resources of Arabic lexicography failed. They covered a wide range of material: logical and metaphysical treatises, Aristotle's *zoologica,* doxographies, *pinakes,* and histories of philosophy, and, despite all their imperfections and crudities, they were the spark to the intellectual tinder. The brilliant effects are to be seen in al-Jāḥiẓ, al-Masʿūdi, Muʿtazilite physics, and, above all, in the work of al-Kindi and his followers.

98. *Fihrist,* p. 251, l. 28.

THE SCHOOL OF AL-KINDI

To speak of the "school" of al-Kindi in a philosophical context is, strictly speaking, incorrect. A chain of teacher-pupil relationships beginning with al-Kindi and covering three generations of scholars can be established from the biographical sources, but of the individuals concerned, only three, al-Kindi himself, al-Sarakhsi, and al-ʿĀmiri, can properly be called philosophers. Nor are the implications of the laconic "was a student of" entirely clear; attention has already been drawn to the scarcity of information on the teaching of philosophy, particularly during this early period.[99]

Al-Kindi's (d. *ca.* A.D. 873) own philosophical origins are obscure.[100] What is certain is that he belonged to the circle at the court of the Caliphs al-Maʾmūn and al-Muʿtaṣim where the intellectual climate was dominated by Muʿtazilite thinkers like Abū al-Ḥudhayl and al-Naẓẓām. Al-Kindi was almost certainly himself a Muʿtazilite,[101] and during the reaction against the Muʿtazilites under al-Mutawakkil he suffered reprisals, including the confiscation of his library.[102]

A product of the translation movement, which had scarcely begun during his lifetime, al-Kindi is a somewhat curious figure. More of a theologian than the later Baghdad Peripatetics, most notably in

99. See pp. 72—75 above.

100. A catalog of al-Kindi's works is given in *Fihrist*, pp. 255–61, and al-Qifṭi, pp. 368–76; there is additional biographical information in Ibn Juljul, *Ṭabaqāt*, pp. 73–74 and al-Bayḥaqi, *Tatimmat*, # 21; for the MSS. see *GAL*, I², 230–31, Suppl. I., pp. 372–74; H. Ritter, "Schriften Jaʿqub ibn Ishaq al-Kindis in Stambuler Bibliotheken," *Archiv Orientàlni*, IV (1932), 313–72. A considerable number of his works have found their way into print, particularly in the series edited by H. Ritter, R. Walzer, and M. Guidi, *Studi su al-Kindi*, 3 vols., published in *Memorie Lincei* (Rome, 1938–1939), and the collection by M. Abu Ridah, *Rasāʾil al-Kindi* (Cairo, 1950, 1953). The Latin versions have been done by A. Nagy, *Die philosophischen Abhandlungen des al-Kindi* (*Beiträge*, II, [Münster, 1897]). Among the more recent studies see Cruz Hernandez, *Filosofia Musulmana*, I, 66–73, R. Walzer, "New Studies on al-Kindi," *Oriens*, X (1957), 203–32, and *idem*, *Oriens*, III (1950), 4–11; F. Rosenthal, "Al-Kindi als Literat," *Orientalia*, II (1942), 262–88; *idem*, "Al-Kindi and Ptolemy," *Studi Orientalistici in onore Giorgio Levi della Vida*, II (Rome, 1956), 436–56; P. Kraus, *Bulletin de l'Institut d'Egypte*, XXIII (1940–1941), 269, nn. 1–3.

101. See R. Walzer, *Oriens*, III (1950), 5.

102. Uṣ., I, 207.

his views on the relationship of philosophical truth and revelation, he was at the same time markedly more of a philosopher than his Muʿtazilite contemporaries, standing not on the logical fringes of the Aristotelian corpus but Aeschylus-like at its center. The metaphysical, physical, and psychological problems inherent in Aristotelianism would be further refined by later thinkers, but most of them are already present in the first of the *falāsifah*.[103]

Among the pupils of al-Kindi were the geographer Abū Zayd al-Balkhi (d. A.D. 934),[104] the traveler, historian, and philospher Aḥmad ibn al-Ṭayyib al-Sarakhsi (d. A.D. 899)[105] who, in connection with his work as an Aristotelian commentator, invented a forty-character alphabet which he used for the transcription of Persian, Syriac, and Greek words[106] and, finally, the astronomer and historian Abū Maʿshar al-Balki (d. A.D. 866).[107]

The "school" is represented in the next generation by two students of Abū Zayd: Abū al-Ḥasan al-ʿĀmiri (d. A.D. 922)[108] and the encyclopedist Ibn Farighūn (*fl. ca.* A.D. 950).[109]

Viewed as a group, the scholars flowing from al-Kindi are notable for their encyclopedic interests: logic, metaphysics, the natural sciences, history, and ethics. Both the number and breadth of al-Kindi's fields of interest as they are reflected in his bibliography are enormous. There was also a concern with the philosophical texts: al-Kindi, Abū Zayd, and al-Sarakhsi were commentators of the Aristotelian *corpus*, and though al-Kindi was not well known to the Baghdad Peripatetics,[110] the works of Abū Zayd and al-Sarakhsi were

103. On the difference between al-Kindi and the theological Muʿtazilites see L. Gardet, *Mélanges Étienne Gilson* (Toronto-Paris, 1959), pp. 269–70.

104. Al-Bayhaqi, *Tatimmat*, # 22; Yāqūt, *Irshād*, I, 141–52; *GAL*, I², 263, Suppl. I, p. 408; D. M. Dunlop, art. "Al-Balki," *EI²*, I, 1003.

105. *Fihrist*, pp. 261–62; *GAL*, I², 231–32, Suppl. I, p. 375; F. Rosenthal, *Aḥmad b. al-Ṭayyib Al-Sarakhsi* ([New Haven, 1943] life, work, fragments), later brought up to date in "New Fragments of al-Sarakhsi," *JOAS*, LXXI (1951), 135–42.

106. Rosenthal, *Technique*, pp. 25–26.

107. See p. 255 below.

108. See 256 below.

109. See p. 109–110 above.

110. Al-Nadīm, who was a part of the group around Yaḥyā ibn ʿAdi, has a list of al-Kindi's works (*Fihrist*, pp. 225–61), but very little information about his life.

known and used,[111] and al-ʿĀmiri was himself a member of the circle of Abū Sulaymān.[112]

Al-Kindi was an almost exact contemporary of Ḥunayn ibn Isḥāq, and it is probable that he knew the translator-physician personally from the court of al-Maʾmūn. We know, however, that in his own philosophical work al-Kindi used the older translations of Ibn Naʿimah and Eustathius, and that al-Sarakhsi, too, was still relying on the *veteres*.[113] But whatever the effect on al-Kindi and his students, Ḥunayn and his son Isḥāq translated or retranslated a great part of the Aristotelian writings, and this had an immediately perceptible influence on the newly born Peripatetic School of Baghdad.

THE PERIPATETICS OF BAGHDAD

The story of the continuity of the philosophical school at Alexandria into Muslim times and its ultimate transfer to Baghdad, told largely on the authority of al-Fārābi,[114] is by now well known.[115] Sometime about A.D. 900 the three Harran masters, al-Quwayri,[116] Yuḥannā ibn Ḥaylān,[117] and Abū Yaḥyā al-Marwazi,[118] came to Baghdad and began lecturing on philosophy. They are also credited in the bibliographical sources with Aristotelian commentaries,[119] but it is not known whether or not these were composed before or after the move to Baghdad.

A number of emphases that set off these early transplanted "Alexandrians" from al-Kindi and his followers are immediately ap-

111. Al-Tawḥidi, *Muqābasāt*, p. 148, and pp. 61 ff.
112. *Ibid.*, pp. 301–307.
113. *Fihrist*, p. 250, l. 3.
114. Preserved in Uṣ., II, 135.
115. See Meyerhof, "Alexandrian nach Baghdad," pp. 405–12, and p. 17 above.
116. *Fihrist*, p. 262.
117. Qifṭi, p. 277; Uṣ., II, 135.
118. *Fihrist*, p. 263.
119. *Fihrist*, pp. 249, 262, 263.

parent. First, they were purely and simply philosophers and not encyclopedists. Their philosophy was Aristotelian. Finally, they were professional teachers. These same elements persevered in the Baghdad philosophical movement as it developed from these modest beginnings. In the first generation of students under the Harran masters were al-Fārābi (d. A.D. 950)[120] and Abū Bishr Mattā (d. A.D. 940),[121] a Christian. With Abū Bishr, the work of translation was taken up by the school, and activity in the translation, editing, and commenting the Aristotelian texts is a characteristic of the Baghdad group down to A.D. 1050, the period of the *recentiores*.[122]

Central in the school was the Christian Yaḥyā ibn ʿAdi (d. A.D. 974),[123] a student of both al-Fārābi and Abū Bishr, and teacher or consultant for all the philosophical luminaries who flourished in Baghdad[124] at the turn of the eleventh century: al-Nadīm,[125] Abū Sulaymān al-Sijistāni,[126] al-Tawḥīdi,[127] Ibn al-Samḥ,[128] ʿIsā ibn ʿAli,[129] Ibn Zurʿah,[130]

120. Ṣāʿid, *Ṭabaqāt* (trans. Blachère), pp. 107–109; Bayḥaqi, *Tatimmat*, # 17; Qifṭi, pp. 277–78; Uṣ., II, 134–45; Ibn Khallikān (trans. de Slane), III, 307–11; *GAL*, I², 232–36, Suppl. I, pp. 375–77, 957–58; M. Steinschneider, *Al-Fārābi, des Arabischen Philosophen Leben und Schriften*, (inventory of works. [St. Petersburg, 1869]). The various works of al-Fārābi are treated in their proper context *passim*, hence only the more general studies will be mentioned here; Cruz Hernandez, *Filosofia Musulmana*, I, 73–104; R. Walzer, *Oriens*, III (1950), 11–19; I. Madkour, *La place d'al-Farabi dans l'école philosophique musulmane* (Paris, 1934); E. I. J. Rosenthal, *Political Thought in Medieval Islam* (Cambridge, 1962), pp. 122–42; Meyerhof, "Alexandrien nach Baghdad," pp. 416–17.
121. See p. 60, n. 18 above.
122. See pp. 60–61 above.
123. See p. 60, n. 20 above.
124. Not all the philosophers associated with the group spent their entire careers in Baghdad, a practice which would have been quite incompatible with the wanderlust of scholars in medieval Islam. Al-Fārābi, for instance, later went to the Hamdanid court at Aleppo (Qifṭi, p. 279), and Ibn Suwār was caught in the cultural corvée thrown out by Maḥmūd, Sultan of Ghazna, the same one that Ibn Sīnā managed to avoid: *Chahār maqālah* (trans. Browne), pp. 84–85).
125. See pp. 277–280 below.
126. See pp. 255–256 below.
127. See p. 131 above.
128. Tawḥīdi, *Muqābasāt*, pp. 139, 160; *idem*, *Imtāʿ*, I, 34; Qifṭi, pp. 411–12; S. M. Stern, "Ibn al-Samḥ," *JRAS* (1956), pp. 31–44.
129. ʿĪsā ibn ʿAli abū al-Qāsim, son of the vizier ʿAli ibn ʿĪsā (d. A.D. 946), and not the ʿĪsā ibn ʿAli who was one of the translators for Ḥunayn ibn Isḥāq (see Meyerhof, *Isis*, VIII [1926], 710); Tawḥīdi, *Imtāʿ*, I, 36–37; *GCAL*, II, 157; *GSL*, pp. 241–42; Meyerhof, "Alexandrien nach Baghdad," p. 421; for his lexicon see p. 40 above.
130. See p. 60 n. 22 above.

Ibn Suwār,[131] and Ibn abī Sa'īd.[132] Philosophically, Yaḥyā was a commentator, and theologically, he was an apologist; in neither case did he leave behind a systematic presentation of his views. What we know of his work on Aristotle is transmitted through his students, chiefly Ibn Suwār.

After the death of Yaḥyā the leadership of the Baghdad school probably passed to Abū Sulaymān. He had studied under Abū Bishr and Yaḥyā and was patronized by the Buwayhid master of Baghdad, 'Aḍud al-Dawlah (d. A.D. 983). Abū Sulaymān is an enigmatic figure in the school. He is frequently quoted in both ancient and modern works as a source on the history of *falsafah*, and he is the central figure in the philosophically oriented dialogues of al-Tawḥīdi. Yet al-Nadīm, who calls him "my professor,"[133] knows practically nothing of his works.[134] Al-Qifṭi says that he commented certain Aristotelian books,[135] but there is no recollection of them in the critical work done by later members of the school like Ibn Suwār and Ibn al-Samḥ. He had certainly studied the works of Aristotle,[136] yet it is by no means clear in what other sense he may be called an Aristotelian.

Apparently Abū Sulaymān marked a change in direction for at least part of the Baghdad school. The work of editing and commenting the *corpus*, the "textual branch," continues in the previously mentioned Ibn al-Samḥ, Ibn Suwār, and Ibn Zur'ah, and their students Abū al-Ḥusayn al-Baṣri (d. A.D. 1044),[137] and Abū al-Faraj

131. See p. 60 n. 23 above.

132. Ibn abī Sa'īd ibn 'Uthmān ibn Sa'īd al-Mawsili, a Jewish physician-philosopher of Mosul who addressed some of his difficulties on the current peripateticism to Yaḥyā. The correspondence is preserved in BM or. 8096, foll. 22a–26b and has recently been studied by S. Pines, "A Tenth Century Philosophical Correspondence," *PAAJR*, XXIV (1955), 103–36. According to Pines, *op.cit.*, p. 136, Ibn abī Sa'īd is the first known Jewish Aristotelian; but the sophistication of his thought gives little reason to suggest that he was in any sense a pioneer. In the course of the correspondence he cites the *Categoriae*, *De inter.*, *Physica*, *De coelo*, and the *Meta.*, as well as Themistius, Porphyry, and John Philoponus.

133. *Fihrist*, p. 241, l. 14.

134. *Ibid.*, p. 264.

135. P. 283.

136. Tawḥīdi, *Muqābasāt*, p. 246, explicitly says that he studied the *De anima* under Abū Sulaymān in A.D. 981.

137. A student of Ibn al-Samḥ who used his lecture notes on the *Physica* to prepare the edition preserved in MS Leyden Warner 583; Ibn Khallikān (trans. De Slane), II, 672–73; *GAL*, I², 600, Suppl. I, p. 829; S. M. Stern, *JRAS 1956, pp. 36–38.*

ibn al-Ṭayyib (d. A.D. 1043).[138] Abū Sulaymān, on the other hand, concerned himself with introducing philosophy into the wider circle of theologians, grammarians, lawyers, and littérateurs. Al-Tawḥīdi (d. A.D. 1018)[139] is the finest example of the "humanistic branch," but the same emphases may be seen in ʿIsā ibn ʿAli (d. A.D. 1001), Ibn Hindū (d. A.D. 1029),[140] and the famous historian-philospher Miskawayh (d. A.D. 1030).[141]

THE MEDICAL CIRCLE

The true afterlife of the Baghdad school is to be found in the circles of philosopher-physicians which are such a conspicuous feature of the intellectual life of medieval Islam. Ḥunayn was as eminent a physician as he was a translator, and his activity in this latter field was a result not of a consuming love for Aristotle but of an interest in the medical writings of Galen and Hippocrates. He was trained by a physician, Ibn Māsawayh (d. A.D. 857),[142] and patronized by the famous Bakhtīshūʿ family, personal physicians to the early Caliphs.[143] From the Bakhtīshūʿ family and the medical school at Jundeshapur which they dominated,[144] through Ibn Māsawayh and Ḥunayn into the translation movement, and hence into philosophy itself, flow the strong medical emphases which can be followed until *falsafah* at last loses its Hellenic coloration and becomes the preserve of the Muslim theologians of the thirteenth century.

Among the Baghdad Peripatetics the most eminent physicians were Ibn Zurʿah, Ibn Suwār, and his student Ibn al-Ṭayyib. The

138. See p. 61, n. 24 above.
139. See p. 131 above.
140. See p. 125, n. 91 above.
141. See p. 126 above.
142. Uṣ., I, 175–83; *GAL*, I², 266, Suppl. I, p. 416.
143. See *GCAL*, II, 109–12.
144. See pp. 44–45 above.

latter had as his disciple Ibn Buṭlān (d. A.D. 1063),[145] the philosopher and physician who engaged in the famous "great debate" with the Egyptian physician Ibn Riḍwān.[146] Among Ibn Zur'ah's students was the little-known philosopher Ibn al-Āmidi[147] who was in turn one of the professors of the physician and gnomonologist al-Mubashshir.[148]

The medical activity in Baghdad centered in its numerous hospitals, and their first general superintendent was Abū 'Uthmān al-Dimashqi, a translator of the school of Ḥunayn who did some of the extant versions of the *Organon*.[149] He was succeeded in that post by the Sabian convert to Islam, Sinān ibn Thābit (d. A.D. 942).[150] In A.D. 982 the Buwayhid 'Aḍud al-Dawlah, the patron of Abū Sulaymān, opened in Baghdad the hospital henceforward to bear his name. The most renowned of its directors was Ibn al-Tilmidh (d. A.D. 1165)[151] who had as his rival at the Caliphal court the philosopher-physician Abū al-Barakāt.[152]

The Baghdad tradition of the philosopher-physician was carried west to the Ayyubid realms in the person of one of Ibn al-Tilmidh's disciples, Ibn al-Maṭrān (d. A.D. 1191), the author of a history of philosophy.[153] Its fruits, nurtured in the hospitals of Cairo and Damascus, are to be seen in Maimonides (d. A.D. 1204), al-Dakhwār

145. Qifṭi, pp. 294–315; Uṣ., I, 241–43; *GAL*, I², 636, Suppl. I, p. 885; *GCAL*, II, 191–93; Schacht-Meyerhof, *Medico-Philosophical Controversy*, *passim*.

146. *GAL*, I², 637–38, Suppl. I, p. 886; the background and substance of the dispute is treated at length in Schacht-Meyerhof, *The Medico-Philosophical Controversy*.

147. Uṣ., I, 235.

148. Uṣ., II, 99; al-Mubashshir's other teachers were Ibn Riḍwān and the mathematician Ibn al-Ḥaytham; see pp. 126–128 above.

149. Uṣ., I, 234; for Islamic hospitals in general see D. M. Dunlop and G. S. Colin, art. "Bimaristān," *EI*², I, 1222–25, and Sarton, *Introduction*, II, 1, p. 248 and III, 2, p. 1249.

150. Uṣ., I, 220–24; *GAL*, I², 245, Suppl. I, p. 386; Chwolsohn, *Ssabier*, I, 569–77; Sinān was the son of the philosopher Thābit ibn Qurrah (see p. 60, n. 13 above) and the father of the historian Thābit ibn Sinān (see p. 289 below.

151. Qifṭi, p. 340; Uṣ., I, 259–76; al-Bayhaqi, *Tatimmat*, # 87; Yāqūt, *Irshād*, VII, 243–47, Barhebraeus, *Chron. Syr.* (trans. Budge), pp. 289–90; *GAL*, I², 642, Suppl. I, p. 891; M. Meyerhof, art. *s.v.*, *EI*, Suppl., pp. 95–96; Abū al-Faraj ibn al-Ṭayyib also lectured at the 'Aḍudi Hospital (Uṣ., I, 239).

152. See pp. 172–173 below.

153. See p. 270 below.

(d. A.D. 1230), al-Qifṭi (d. A.D. 1248),[154] Ibn abī Uṣaybiʿah (d. A.D. 1270),[155] and Ibn al-Nafīs (d. A.D. 1288).[156]

IBN SĪNĀ

Such was the background that produced Ibn Sīnā (d. A.D. 1037).[157] One of his teachers was the physician Abū Sahl al-Masīḥi (d. A.D. 1010)[158] who, according to al-Bayḥaqi, was trained in Bagh-

154. See pp. 280–281 below.
155. See pp. 262–264 below.
156. The intellectual, and particularly the philosophical, vitality of the Cairo medical circle has recently been testified to by a fragment retrieved from the Cairo Geniza. A list preserved in Cairo and edited by D. Baneth in *Tarbiz*, XXX (1960), 171–85 (Arabic text in Hebrew letters with Baneth's Hebrew translation and notes), records a sale of books from the library of a physician in A.D. 1190. The 103 books, all secular in content, are chiefly medical and philosophical, and include both translations from the Greek and original Arabic works. For the intellectual and historical background of these times seen against the work of Ibn al-Nafis see J. Schacht, "Ibn al-Nafis et son Theologus Autodidactus," *Homenaje a Millas-Vallicrosa*, II (Barcelona, 1956), 325–45.
157. Ibn Sīnā is the only figure in the *falsafah* tradition who has left us, in addition to an immense body of works, some idea of his own intellectual development. His autobiography, completed by his student al-Jawzajāni, has been preserved in al-Qifṭi, pp. 413–26, and in Uṣ., II, 2–20. It has been translated into English by A. J. Arberry, *Avicenna on Theology*, and into German, with an introduction and commentary, by P. Kraus, "Eine arabische Biographie Avicennas," *Klinische Wochenschrift* (1932), pp. 1880–84.
The bibliographers have credited Ibn Sīnā with nearly two hundred titles, and there have been some recent attempts at correlating these with the preserved MSS., notable in Turkish by O. Ergin (Istanbul, 1937), in Arabic by M. Anawati (Cairo, 1950); abridged in French in *Revue thomiste*, LI (1951), 407–40, and in Persian by Y. Mahdawi (Teheran, 1954). M. Plessner has tried to put some order in the chaos of the psychological opuscula in his "Beiträge zur islamischen Literaturgeschichte," *Ignace Goldziher Memorial Volume*, II (Jerusalem 1958), 71–82. There is additional MS. information in *GAL*, I², 589–99, Suppl. I, pp. 812–28, and M. Cruz Hernandez, *Filosofia Musulmana*, I, 105–10.
Where Ibn Sīnā's works have been treated in the appropriate context above, the various editions and studies pertaining to each have been described. Here some recent general studies may be cited: L. Gardet, *La pensée religieuse d'Ibn Sīnā* (Paris, 1951); *idem*, "L'Humanisme gréco-arabe: Avicenne," *Journal of World History*, II (1954–1955), 812–34; S. Afnan, *Avicenna. His Life and Works* (London, 1958); E. Troilo, "Lineamento e interpretazione del Sistema filosofico di Avicenna," *Memorie Lincei*, Ser. 8, Vol. VII (1956), 397–446; M. Cruz Hernandez, *op.cit.*, I, 111–52.
158. Qifṭi, pp. 408–409; Uṣ., I, 327–28; al-Bayḥaqi, *Tatimmat*, # 47; *GAL*, I², 273–74, Suppl. I, pp. 423–24; *GCAL*, II, 257–79; according to *GAL*, I², 274, de Jong's catalog of the library of the Royal Dutch Academy of Sciences notes a copy of Abū Sahl's *talkhīs* of the *De coelo*; I have not been able to verify this.

dad.[159] Another was the obscure ʿAbdallāh al-Nātili (*aliter* al-Tātili)[160] who, by Ibn Sīnā's own account, started his gifted student on the traditional Aristotelian *cursus* with the *Eisagoge*. Another specifically mentioned influence operating on him was the Ismāʿīli propaganda and theses he heard being discussed in his father's house.[161]

In his autobiography Ibn Sīnā describes himself as soon outstripping his teachers and continuing his philosophical education under his own power. His efforts bore prodigious fruit. Despite a career filled with the most varied intellectual and political activity, he assembled a huge, and by his own admission, uncritical (*bilā munāẓarah*[162]) compendium of the Aristotelian system, the *Kitāb al-shifā'*.[163] It is this *summa*, the first philosphical encyclopedia in Islam, which represented Ibn Sīnā's teaching for the West. Probably, though not certainly, it was also this work which al-Ghazāli had in his sights in the *Tahāfut*.[164] Posterity, at least in Islam, did not entirely agree with the importance attached to the *Shifā'*; it was the more dense and more mystical *Ishārāt* which provoked later investigation, commentaries, and conflicts.[165]

Neither the *Shifā'* nor the *Ishārāt*, however, represents Ibn Sīnā's final thoughts on Aristotle. Recent documents have served to illuminate the final states of Ibn Sīnā's philosophical career and particularly his relations with the Baghdad Peripatetics.

The first of these is the *Letter to al-Kiyā*[166] explaining the purpose of a work of his entitled *Kitāb al-inṣāf*. In the latter he had commented the entire Aristotelian *corpus*, this time in a critical fashion. The sole copy had been destroyed, but Ibn Sīnā proposed to redo it. Whether he managed to reconstitute the entire work is unknown, but

159. Al-Bayhaqi, *loc. cit.*
160. Al-Bayhaqi, *Tatimmat*, # 19.
161. Uṣ., II, 3.
162. Qifṭi, p. 420.
163. See pp. 105–107 above.
164. See pp. 187–190 below.
165. See p. 195 below.
166. Text printed in A. Badawi, *Arisṭū ʿind al-ʿarab* (Cairo, 1947), pp. 119–22; the pertinent section is translated by S. Pines, *AHDL*, XXVII (1952), 6–9.

parts of it are in fact extant and have been published.[167] Unlike the *Shifā'*, which is a continuous narrative, the *Inṣāf* is cast in the form of marginal glosses.

In the course of the *Letter to al-Kiyā*, Ibn Sīnā mentions that he has divided scholars into "Occidentals" and "Orientals" (*mashrīqīyīn*) and that the latter will criticize the former until the truth is reached and there is an arbitration (*inṣāf*).[168] Thus is raised once again the vexed question of the "Oriental Philosophy" (*al-ḥikmah al-mashriqīyah*) which seems to play such an important role in the thought of Ibn Sīnā.[169] Pines, in a recent study that he has devoted to these texts, identifies the "Occidentals" with the Peripatetics of Baghdad,[170] and on the basis of another still-unpublished text,[171] he makes a strong case that the exact opponent envisioned by Ibn Sīnā is Abū al-Faraj ibn al-Ṭayyib whose philosophy, as we know from other sources,[172] found little favor with Ibn Sīnā. The dialogue between Ibn al-Ṭayyib and Ibn Sīnā is now in the process of reconstruction.[173]

The *Letter to al-Kiyā* has cast a sharper light on the differences existing between Ibn Sīnā and the prevalent Peripatetic currents in Baghdad. The point at issue here was one apparently touching on

167. The extant sections are on the *De anima*, the *Theologia*, and Lambda of the *Metaphysica*, all published in Badawi, *op. cit.*, pp. 22–116; the section on the *Theologia* has been translated by G. Vadja in *Revue thomiste* (1951), pp. 346–406.

168. Badawi, *op. cit.*, p. 121.

169. *Al-ḥikmah al-mashriqīyah* is mentioned in the introduction to the *Shifā'* where it appears to be something in the non-Greek tradition. It appears again in the new fragments of the *Kitāb al-inṣāf*, particularly in the notes relating to the *De anima*; finally there is an extant treatise of Ibn Sīnā entitled *Manṭiq al-mashrīqīyin* and printed in Cairo, 1910. Who are the "Orientals" and what is "Oriental Philosophy"? The first impulse was to identify it with the illuminative philosophy (*ḥikmah ishrāqīyah*) of al-Suhrawārdi (d. A.D. 1191). This possibility was ruled out on philological grounds by A. Nallino, "Filosofia 'orientale' od 'illuminativa,'" *RSO*, X (1923–1925), 433–67. Further, Suhrawārdi himself had seen the Avicennan books that claimed to have embodied the "Oriental Philosophy" and said it was nothing more than the usual Peripateticism; see H. Corbin, *Les motifs zoroastriens dans la philosophie de Sohrawardi* (Teheran, 1946), p. 21. Current opinion is divided between seeing in the "Oriental Philosophy" an older Iranian or at least a non-Aristotelian tradition (Goichon, Gardet), or the thinly masked position of Ibn Sīnā himself (Pines). Exactly what this philosophy involves cannot be clearly determined in the present state of the texts.

170. "La 'philosophie orientale' d'Avicenne et sa polemique contre les Baghdadiens," *AHDL*, XXVII (1952), 6–37.

171. MS. Oxford Bodl. Hunt 534, foll. 13b–15b.

172. Uṣ., I, 239.

173. See the edition of Ibn al-Ṭayyib's *Maqālah fī al-quwwah al-ṭabī'iyah* and Ibn Sīnā's rejoinder edited by H. Ulken, *Ibn Sīnā Risaleleri*, I (Ankara, 1953), 57–71.

the survival of the soul.[174] There were, however, many other points where Ibn Sīnā departed from the Aristotelian theses in logic,[175] psychology,[176] physics,[177] and metaphysics,[178] and probably the distance widened between Ibn Sīnā and the *traditio* with the further evolution of the *ḥikmah mashriqīyah*. He was, however, universally reckoned as an Aristotelian, not only by his opponents among the *mutakallimūn*, but also by the adherents of another, different Greek philosophical strain which ran side by side with the Aristotelian tradition.

THE PLATONIC TRADITION

Platonism in Islam no more existed in a pure state than did Aristotelianism; the purity of both systems was considerably altered in the syncretistic tinkerings characteristic of Middle Platonism,[179] and the Muslim philosphers continued the process. They did, however,

174. Pines, *AHDL*, XXVII (1952), 12–20.

175. See A. M. Goichon, *Livre des Directives et Remarques* (Paris, 1951), pp. 46–66, for the influence of Galen and the Stoics.

176. E.g., the notorious doctrine of the separated agent intellect (*Shifā* [ed. Teheran], II, 618) and his valuable precisions on the *vis aestimativa* (see Bakoš' ed. of the *De anima* section of the *Shifā'*, pp. 45, 61–62); according to Ibn Rushd, *Tahāfut al-tahāfut* (ed. Bouyges), pp. 546–47, it was Ibn Sīnā who first posited this faculty; but the concept was already present in the thinking of al-Fārābi.

177. E.g., his distinction between *tempus* (*zamān*), *aevum* (*dahr*), and *aeternitas* (*sarmad*); see *'Uyūn al-ḥikmah* (ed. Badawi), p. 28, and Pines, *Atomenlehre*, p. 51, n. 3. In the evolution of the metaphysical notion of *quwwah* (*dynamis*) into the physical concept of *impetus* Ibn Sīnā was merely following the lead already given by Yaḥyā ibn 'Adi; see S. Pines, "Les précurseurs musulmans de la théorie de l'impetus," *Archeion*, XXI (1938).

178. E.g., his adoption of an emanation theory; see N. Carame, *Metaphysices Compendium* (Rome, 1926), pp. xxi-xxvi. The important distinction between essence and existence is frequently credited to al-Fārābi on the basis of a text in the *Fuṣūṣ fi al-ḥikmah*, e.g., E. Gilson, *History of Christian Philosophy in the Middle Ages* (New York, 1955), pp. 185–86, and p. 639, n. 9; but the credit must be restored to Ibn Sīnā: the text is apparently his; see P. Kraus, *Bulletin de l'Institut d'Egypte*, XXIII (1940–1941), 270, n. 3, and S. Pines, *REI* (1951), pp. 121–24.

179. See K. Praechter, *RE*, 2nd ser. VIII *Halbband* (1932), cols. 1171–75, for the metaphysical theories; on the alteration of the physical theses of Plato see W. Jaeger, *Nemesios von Emesa* (Berlin, 1914), pp. 68 ff.

recognize Platonism as an entity, and some of the Platonic theses had an important and interesting career among the *falāsifah*.[180]

Apparently the Platonic dialogues were translated into Arabic at the same time as the Aristotelian corpus,[181] but, unlike the Aristotelian versions, none of the Platonic translations has survived, and an investigation of the preserved Platonic quotations has led to a serious doubt that there ever was an integral, verbal translation of a Platonic work into Arabic.[182] What the Arabs certainly had were résumés, some, like Galen's paraphrase of the *Timaeus*,[183] the compendium of the *Leges* preserved by al-Fārābi,[184] and the same author's summary of Plato's philosophy[185] already created within the Greek tradition. From such material and from the apparently abundant doxographical and gnomological sources available to the Arabs,[186] a kind of Islamic Platonic tradition was constructed.

Platonic influences appear early among the *falāsifah*. Both al-Kindi[187] and Thābit ibn Qurrah (d. A.D. 901)[188] wrote treatises based on Platonic material. Platonism likewise found considerable favor among the professed Peripatetics. Al-Fārābi has already been mentioned and his student Yaḥyā ibn ʿAdi, too, busied himself with *Platonica*.[189] Abū Sulaymān made a collection of Platonic

180. For a general orientation on Islamic Platonism see: R. Klibansky, *The Continuity of the Platonic Tradition During the Middle Ages* (London, 1939), pp. 14–18; F. Rosenthal, "On the Knowledge of Plato's Philosophy in the Islamic World," *Islamic Culture*, XIV (1940), 387–422; R. Walzer, art. "Aflāṭūn," *EI²*, I, 234–36; *idem*, "Some Aspects of Platonism in Islamic Philosophy" in *Entretiens sur l'antiquité Classique* III *Recherches sur la Tradition platoncienne* (Geneva, 1955), pp. 203–26.

181. *Fihrist*, pp. 245–46.

182. F. Rosenthal, *Islamic Culture*, XIV (1940, 393.

183. Edited, in the translation of Ḥunayn (see Ḥunayn, *Risālah*, # 126), by P. Kraus and R. Walzer, *Galeni Compendium Timaei Platonis* (*Plato Arabus*, I), London 1951.

184. F. Gabrieli (ed.), *Alfarabius Compendium Legum Platonis* (*Plato Arabus*, III) [London, 1952]); see the important corrections by M. Mahdi, "The *Editio Princeps* of Farabi's Compendium Legum Platonis," *Journal of Near Eastern Studies*, XX (1961), 1–24, and L. Strauss, "How Farabi read Plato's *Laws*," *Mélanges Massignon*, III (Damascus, 1957), pp. 319–44.

185. F. Rosenthal and R. Walzer (ed.), *Alfarabius de Platonis Philosophia* (*Plato Arabus*, II) [London, 1943]).

186. See pp. 120–129 above.

187. *Al-Qawl fi al-nafs al-mukhtaṣar min kitāb Arisṭū wa Flāṭūn*, ed. M. Abu Ridah in *Risālah al-Kindi*, I (Cairo; 1950), 272–81.

188. Al-Masʿūdi, *Murūj*, I, 19; al-Masʿūdi himself wrote a Platonic work: *op. cit.*, II, 209.

189. *Fihrist*, p. 246; according to al-Masʿūdi, *Tanbīh* (trans. de Vaux), p. 171, Yaḥyā was a follower of the system of al-Rāzi; the precise import of this remark is unknown.

dicta[190] and is depicted by al-Tawḥīdi discussing various problems in Plato's philosophy.[191] Miskawayh, who was also connected with the Baghdad school,[192] made extensive use of the Platonic material[193] and the Platonic interest was still alive in the time of Ibn Rushd.[194]

From the time of al-Fārābi it was undoubtedly the Platonic ethic and political theory that made the deepest impression on Muslim thinkers. The metaphysics was largely overwhelmed by Neoplatonic emanationism. In the realm of Platonic physics, however, there is an interesting line of development leading directly into the controversies surrounding Ibn Sīnā and beyond.

The name most closely associated with Platonic physics is that of Abū Bakr Muḥammad ibn Zakarīyā al-Rāzi (d. A.D. 925), who was active both in Baghdad and in his native Rayy as a physician, philosopher, and alchemist.[195] The most markedly non-Aristotelian aspects of the physical theory advanced by al-Rāzi are the presence of the five eternal principles: Creator, soul, matter, time (or eternity, *dahr*), and space (or void, *khalā'*) and, hence, of absolute time independent of bodies. Further, the universe is not eternal, as it is in the Aristotelian system, but comes about in a determined moment of time by reason of the "fall" of the soul and its conjunction with another eternal principle, matter.[196]

190. In the *Ṣiwān al-ḥikmah* translated from the epitome in BM or. 9033 by F. Rosenthal, *Islamic Culture*, XIV (1940), 407–408.
191. *Muqābasāt*, pp. 259–60; *Imtā'*, II, 44–49.
192. Al-Tawḥīdi, *Imtā'*, I, 35.
193. E.g., Platonic ethics in the *Tahdḥib al-akhlāq* (See R. Walzer, "Some Aspects of Miskawaih's *Tahdhīb al-Akhlāq*," *Studi Orientalistici in onore di Giorgio Levi della Vida*, II [Rome, 1956], 603–21.) and Platonic proofs for the immortality of the soul in the *Fawz al-asghar*. (See F. Rosenthal, *Islamic Culture*, XIV [1940], 398–402).
194. His commentary on the *Respublica*, lost in Arabic, has been published from the Hebrew version by E. I. J. Rosenthal (Cambridge, 1956). Ibn Rushd was apparently still using the Galenic paraphrases mentioned by Ḥunayn in his *Risālah*, # 126.
195. Most of the philosophical works have been either edited or reconstructed from anti-Rāzi polemic by P. Kraus in *Razis opera philosophica* (Cairo, 1939). The best study of his physical system remains Pines, *Atomenlehre*, pp. 34–93, with additional notes in the same author's article on Abū al-Barakāt in *REJ*, CIII (1938), 4–64; CIV (1938), 1–33, and his *Nouvelles Études sur* ... *Abū al-Barakāt* (Paris, 1955), pp. 55–61. Al-Rāzi's connection with alchemy was in the best "Platonic" tradition; see Kraus, *Jābir*, II, 48–54.
196. These theses are put forward in the physical works pieced together by Kraus, particularly in the *al-'ilm al-ilāhi* (Kraus, *Razis opera philosophica*, pp. 170–90) and *al-qawl fī al-qudamā' al-khamsah* (*ibid.*, pp. 195–216); the doctrine of the fall of the soul is found in *al-qawl fī al-nafs wa al-kālam* (*ibid.*, pp. 282–90).

Al-Rāzi presents a peculiar problem in sources. He had access to the *Timaeus* as commented by Plutarch and Galen,[197] and for his theory of space and time he does give explicit credit to Plato.[198] In another of his works, *Maqālah fīmā ba'd al-ṭabī'ah,*[199] he shows an acquaintance with the Greek doxographical material and his Arab predecessors al-Kindi and Thābit ibn Qurrah. He was certainly a student of Aristotle and is known to have commented several of his works.[200] But what particularly struck al-Rāzi's contemporaries and successors was the doctrine of the five eternal principles; they were, however, uncertain about its origins. Al-Mas'ūdi[201] and Ṣā'id al-Andalusi[202] connect the eternal principles with Pythagorean doctrines. But in another place al-Mas'ūdi associates al-Rāzi with the Sabians of Harran,[203] and this becomes the accepted opinion of later authors.[204] Al-Rāzi himself occasionally attributed the doctrine to the pre-Socratics and particularly to Democritus,[205] while at other times he maintained that it was the doctrine of the Harranians.[206] This connection of Greek physical theory with the Harranians[207] is apparently an elaborate historical hoax promoted by writers of the school of al-Kindi (Abū Zayd, al-Sarakhsi, and al-Kindi himself) and presumably by al-Rāzi. As Kraus has pointed out,[208] the association of the Harranians with the pre-Socratics appears for the first time in al-

197. Al-Bīrūni, *Risalah,* # 58; *Fihrist,* p. 301, line 5; Pines, *Atomenlehre,* p. 73, n. 1.
198. Kraus, *op. cit.*, pp. 305, 307.
199. *Ibid.* pp. 116–34; it is not, despite its title, a work on Aristotelian metaphysics.
200. E.g. *Categoriae,* De *intera., Anal. pr., Physica*; see *Fihrist,* pp. 248, 249, 299.
201. *Tanbīh* (trans. de Vaux), p. 162.
202. *Ṭabaqāt* (trans. Blachère), pp. 74–75.
203. *Murūj,* IV, 67–68.
204. Al-Shahrastāni, Fakhr al-Dīn al-Rāzi, al-Ṭūsi, etc.; see Kraus, *op. cit.*, p. 191.
205. See E. Sachau, *Alberuni's India,* I (London, 1910), 319, and Ibn Taymīyah, *Minhāj,* I, 97.
206. Kraus, *op. cit.*, p. 187.
207. The branch of the sect known as the Sabians (*al-sābi'īyah* originating in the town of Harran (Carrhae) and to be distinguished from the Babylonian or Mandaean branch. In the Muslim mind the Harranians were chiefly associated with a pagan planet worship and brilliant scholarship in the mathematical and physical sciences; see al-Mas'ūdi, *Murūj,* IV, 61–69; al-Shahrastāni, *Milal,* pp. 203–40; D. Chwolsohn, *Die Ssabier und der Ssabismus* (2 vols.; St. Petersburg, 1856). For the Sabian mathematician and philosopher Thābit ibn Qurrah see p. 60, n. 13 above; the historian Thābit ibn Sinan is treated on p. 289 above.
208. *Op. cit.*, p. 192, following a suggestion of Massignon in *Oriental Studies* ... *E. G. Browne* (Cambridge, 1922), p. 333.

Rāzi and is repeated only by later writers using al-Rāzi as a source.[209]

The physical and metaphysical theories put forward by al-Rāzi did not meet with general acceptance among the *falāsifah.* He was attacked by Muʿtazilites (Abū al-Qāsim al-Balkhi), Ismāʿīlis (Nāṣir-i Khusraw) and orthodox Aristotelians (al-Fārābi, Maimonides) alike.[210] But he had at least one sympathetic listener: the Jewish convert to Islam, Abū al-Barakāt (d. A.D. 1165) who had received his training in the Baghdad medico-philosophical circle under Saʿīd ibn Hibāt Allāh (d. A.D. 1102).

Abū al-Barakāt is frequently linked with al-Rāzi as an exponent of the Platonic physics. The statement is true enough in the realm of theses on absolute time and space where the positions of the two philosophers are similar and clearly owe far more to Plato than to Aristotle or his followers.[211] But thanks to a series of perceptive Studies by Solomon Pines, Abū al-Barakāt has emerged as much more than a latter-day Rāzi or a critic of Ibn Sīnā.[212]

Like Ibn Sīnā, whom he frequently follows, Abū al-Barakāt stands both within and without the Aristotelian tradition. In the preface to his encyclopedic *Kitāb al-muʿtabar,* he announced his intention of following the outline of the Aristotelian system point by point. But within the same introduction a theme is announced that is the very antithesis of the Aristotelian approach to philosophy: the weighing of philosophical truths in the scale of intuitive a priori judgments.[213]

There is, of course, a place for intuitive knowledge (*nous*) in Aristotle, though not, it would seem, completely independent of sen-

209. If the Harranian philosophy is a myth, al-Rāzi's Greek material is authentic enough; for the possible doxographical connections see p. 124, n. 84 above.

210. For these anti-Rāzi polemics see Kraus, *op. cit.,* pp. 167–69.

211. Pines, *Atomenlehre,* pp. 82–83.

212. S. Pines, "Études sur Auhādazzamān abū al-Barakāt al-Baghdādi," *REJ,* CIII (1938), 4–64, and CIV (1938), 1–33; *idem, Nouvelles Études sur ... abū al-Barakāt* (Paris, 1955); *idem,* "La conception de la conscience de soi chez Avicenne et chez abū al-Barakāt al-Baghdādi," *AHDL,* XXIX (1954), 21–98; *idem,* "Studies in Abū al-Barakāt's Poetics and Metaphysics," *Scripta Hierosolymitana,* VI (1960), 120–98.

213. *Muʿtabar,* I, 4, and, more clearly, III, 35, 62.

sation.[214] The important point, however, is that the axioms thus intuited have an ontological necessity. In Abū al-Barakāt's intuitions (*shuʿūr*), the necessity is psychological: they carry with them a certitude that is invincible. There is another no less striking difference: for Abū al-Barakāt the primary intuition is not of existence but of *ipseitas* (*dhāt*).[215]

A clear example of the two radically different systems at work is in the question of the existence of the soul. The Aristotelian method of proof is inevitably a march backward from the *sensibilia* through operation and faculty to the principle; for Abū al-Barakāt there is no *processus*: the existence of the soul is proven by my immediate and unshakable intuition of my own existence.

The proof was not, in fact, original. It is identical with Ibn Sīnā's famous example of "l'homme volant" suspended in air so that none of his senses is operating but who is, nonetheless, aware of his own existence.[216] But for Ibn Sīnā it was merely a proof, valid only in this case. He did not, as has been pointed out, push it to its consequences even in this restricted area.[217] In the case of Abū al-Barakāt it was a method. The weapon of a priori knowledge (*maʿrifah awwalīyah*) is used against the whole structure of Peripatetic psychology, and it is through his application of the same criterion that Abū al-Barakāt arrives at Razian or, better, Platonic positions on absolute time and absolute space.

The result was not, as had been promised in the introduction of the *Muʿtabar*, a kind of *sanatio in radice* of the current Peripateticism; much of Ibn Sīnā is taken over verbatim.[218] But a confrontation of Abū al-Barakāt with his contemporaries reveals a bold and original posture in philosophy. There was no lack of thinkers who

214. *Anal. post.*, II, 19; see J. Le Blond, *Logique et Méthode chez Aristotle* (Paris, 1939), pp. 131–40.
215. Pines, *Studia Hierosolymitana*, VI (1960), 156.
216. Used in the *De anima* section of the *Shifāʾ* but as a proof for the spirituality of the soul; in *Ishārāt* (ed. Forget), p. 119, the proof is for the existence of the soul; for the further fortunes of "l'homme volant" in the history of philosophy see E. Gilson, *AHDL*, IV (1929), 40, n. 1.
217. S. Pines, *AHDL*, XXIX (1954), 92.
218. *Idem*, *Studia Hierosolymitana*, VI (1960), 125.

attacked the Aristotelian system. However, the others had the cover of an alternate tradition (the Platonism of al-Rāzi, for instance) or the impelling motive of the protection of the Faith (al-Ghazāli and the *mutakallimūn*); the critique of Abū al-Barakāt was apparently motivated by nothing other than a genuinely philosophical mind, a stand not without precedent: *amicus Avicenna*; *magis amicus veritas*.

BĀṬINĪYAH MOVEMENTS

Bāṭinīyah (esoteric) is the descriptive epithet given to a complex of movements which arose within the Shiʿite wing of the Islamic community toward the middle of the ninth century and some of which survive to the present. It is but one of a series of names used to describe what was at the same time a dynastic, theological, and popular effort to subvert the Sunnite *status quo*. In Egypt it was associated with the rise of the Shiʿite Fatimids, and, in the Persian Gulf principalities and Mesopotamia, with a series of popular uprisings instigated by the Qarmatians. Politically it had to do with the schism in the Shiʿite community connected with allegiance to one or the other of the two pretenders to the spiritual leadership of the group: Mūsā al-Kāẓim on the one hand and Ismāʿīl on the other; hence the designation of the latter group as the *Ismāʿīlīyah*.

At the death of the Fatimid Caliph al-Mustanṣir in A.D. 1094, another split of allegiance took place, this time within the Ismāʿīlis themselves, some following al-Nizār and others following his brother al-Mustaʿli. The Nizāri group, under the leadership of Ḥaṣan al-Sabbāḥ (d. A.D. 1124), took firm root in Persia both politically and intellectually. The crusaders who were in contact with the Syrian outposts of the Nizāris were sufficiently impressed by some of the more obvious political aspects of the system but knew nothing of the highly articulated theology of the fearsome "Assassins," who were finally destroyed by the Mongol capture of the Alamut fortress in A.D. 1256.[219]

The distinction, chiefly political, between Qarmatian, Fatimid, Ismāʿīli, and Nizāri need not detain us here. What is characteristic of the intellectual life of all the branches of this movement is the contrast instituted between *ẓāhir*, the external practices of religion, frequently indistinguishable from those of orthodox Sunnism, and *bāṭin*, the "interior" doctrine revealed, in degrees, to the initate.

The *bāṭin* embraced two areas: the exegesis of the *Qur'ān* and the law peculiar to the sect, and the system known as *ḥaqā'iq*, a cosmography of the physical and spiritual world elaborated from the Greek science and pseudo-science of the day, Neoplatonic emanation theories, and the undefinable but almost tangible gnosticism that had been in the air of the Fertile Crescent since at least the time of Simon Magus.

Apart from the numerous treatments devoted to them by their opponents in histories, heresiographies,[220] and polemics, there is extant a considerable *bāṭinīyah* literature from the pens of the sectaries themselves.

Connected with the earlier Qarmatian-Fatimid period is the encyclopedia known as the *Rasā'il* of the "Sincere Brethren" (*Ikhwān al-ṣafā'*).[221] From the Fatimid period proper, i.e., from A.D. 909 to the institution of the "New Call" by Ḥaṣan al-Sabbāḥ, are preserved the Arabic works of al-Nasafi, (d. A.D. 943)[222] Abū Ḥātim al-Rāzi (d. *ca.* A.D. 942),[223] Abū Yaʿqūb al-Sijistāni (*fl. ca.* A.D. 971)[224] Ḥamid al-Din al-Kirmāni (d. *ca.* A.D. 1020)[225] whose *Kitāb al-riyāḍ* mirrors a

219. The fate of the Syrian posts was sealed some fourteen years later by the Mamluk Baybars.

220. See p. 246 below.

221. See pp. 113–115 above; for the relationship between Fatimids and Qarmatians see W. Madelung, "Fatimiden und Bahrainqarmaten," *Der Islam*, XXXIV (1959), 34–88.

222. Ivanow, *Guide*, pp. 35–36; S. M. Stern, *BSOAS*, XXIII (1960), 78–80, who calls him the founder of Ismāʿīli philosophy.

223. Ivanow, *Guide*, pp. 32–33; *GAL*, Suppl. I, p. 323; Kraus, *Jābir*, II, 274–75; his most considerable extant work, the *Kitāb al-zinah*, a handbook of theological terminology, has rencently been edited by H. Hamdani (2 vols, to date; Cairo, 1957–1958).

224. Ivanow, *Guide*, pp. 33–35; S. M. Stern, art. "Abū Yaʿkub al-Sīdji," *EI²*, I, 160.

225. Ivanow, *Guide*, pp. 43–46; *GAL*, Suppl. I, p. 325; for his encyclopedia, the *Rahat al-ʿaql*, see p. 113 above.

controversy in Ismā'īli *ta'wīl* going back to al-Nasafi and involving both Abū Ḥātim al-Rāzi and al-Sijistāni.[226] The final figure in the Arabic series is al-Mu'ayyid fī al-Dīn al-Shirāzi (d. A.D. 1077).[227]

Part of the same tradition, though writing in Persian, is the traveler and philosopher Nāṣir-i Khusraw (d. *ca.* A.D. 1077)[228] the author of the Ismā'īli tract *Jami' al-ḥikmatayn*.[229]

There are a number of attractive points in the Ismā'īli system which its proponents used to good propaganda effect. Philosophically there are two points to be noted: it is precisely a *system* providing an integrated world view for Islam; and, it is rooted in an infallible source of knowledge.

The Mu'tazilites had begun to integrate some of the physical sciences of the Greeks into their theology; but the work was spotty and, as has been mentioned, the borrowings do not always concur with the theological positions they were intended to support. What the Ismā'īlis took from the Greek sources was far more complete: Aristotle's orderly treatment of the physical sciences and, as a bridge between Allah and this visible world, the hierarchical emanation theory of Plotinus as represented in the *Theologia*, wrongly thought to be Aristotle's.[230]

The Ismā'īlis were quick to exploit the systematic aspects of their material. Al-Baghdādi describes the methods they used to undermine the traditional faith of their prospective converts.[231] They proposed conundrums about the physical world which their listeners, trained in the purely Islamic sciences, were unable to answer. Al-Baghdādi had his own answer to this: the pious Muslim should point out to the Ismā'īli that there is nothing particularly arcane in this

226. A. Tamer (ed.), (Beyrouth, 1960); studied in W. Ivanow, *Studies in Early Persian Ismailism*² (Bombay, 1955), pp. 87–122.
227. Ivanow, *Guide*, pp. 47–49; *GAL*, Suppl. I, p. 326.
228. Ivanow, *Guide*, pp. 89–96; Browne, *Literary History*, II, 218–46; W. Ivanow, *Nasir-e Khosraw and Ismailism* (Bombay, 1948).
229. H. Corbin and M. Mo'in (ed.) (Teheran-Paris, 1953).
230. There were numerous adjustments. The Ismā'īli emanation runs in two series: the Plotinian, with new intermediaries to bring it more in line with the Ptolemaic vision of the universe, and a *bāṭin* series where the various emanations are hypostatized into members of the Ismā'īli chain of command.
231. *Farq*, p. 291 and ff.

Wissenschaft since Aristotle had set it all down long before the Ismā'ilis chanced upon the scholarly scene.

The Ismā'īli retort brings us back to the *Jami' al-ḥikmatayn* of Nāṣir-i Khusraw, which is essentially an exercise in *ta'wil* applied to selected positions of the *falāsifah*.[232] To know Aristotle is not enough, the Ismā'īli would answer; one must be adept at extracting the true, i.e., the hidden (*bāṭin*), meaning of what he and the other philosophers have said.

The *Jami'* is not directed against the philosophers but against a common enemy, the *ahl al-tafsīr* (the literalist exegetes of the *Qur'ān*) and the *ahl al-taqlīd* (those who accept articles of faith on authority alone). The Ismā'īlis were certainly using the expression *taqlīd* in their own private context. Their objection to the "passive believers" is that they accepted the orthodox tradition. The Ismā'īlis had their own brand of *taqlīd* founded on the infallibility of their *Imām* who was, however, hidden; the *Imām*'s "revelations" were passed on by the more Pythian of his exegetes (*ḥujjah*). Ash'arite *kalām* was in many ways far more committed to a position of *fides quaerens intellectum* than the Ismā'īlis with all their attacks on orthodox *taqlīd*.

The traditionalists (*ahl al-ḥadīth*) and the Ismā'īlis were really quarreling about the *content* of faith, and, ultimately, about the source of revelation. For the former the sole source of revelation was the Prophet; what he had revealed was the *Qur'ān* as authoritatively interpreted by responsible members of the orthodox community. For the Ismā'īlis the successive *Imāms* were also a source of revelation; what they revealed were more pregnant methods of contemplating the whole of creation, including the *Qur'ān*. It is precisely another tradition, no more and no less intellectualist than the tradition emanating from the Prophet.

The inclusion of various elements of Greek cosmology and psychology[233] is, in fact, a deceit; the Ismā'īli system did not suggest,

232. For an example of Qur'anic *ta'wil* see the Ismā'īli *Tafsīr* work published by R. Strothmann in *Abhandlungen Göttingen*, Ser. 3, # 31 (1944–1945).

233. The word "psychology" is not entirely apposite. The Ismā'īlis were far more interested in the celestial psychology of the world-soul than in the more prosaic study of its human counterpart. Nāṣir, for instance, gives a textual citation of the *De anima*, quoting with ap-

as did the Sufis and the Muʿtazilites, followed by many of the later Ashʿarites, that a knowledge of Allah could be gained by independent intellectual and contemplative activity as well as through revelation.

Al-Kirmāni is quite clear on this point in his discussion of the Greek philosophers.[234] The philosophers, particularly Aristotle, were eminent in their own time, but they relied solely on their own opinions and intellects (*arā' wa ʿaqūl*) and reached a point no higher than the well-meaning pagan of pre-Islamic times, the *ḥanīf*. Unfortunately they could not profit by (Ismāʿīli) revelation. This is the task Nāṣir set before himself in the *Jamiʿ*: to perform an exegesis (*ta'wīl*) on the positions reached by the philosphers and thus bring them into line with the wisdom vouchsafed by Ismāʿīli revelation (*ʿilm al-dīn*).

The revelation of the *Imām* is passed on to the succeeding generations of the faithful solely by authorized teaching (*taʿlīm*), and it is this peculiarly dogmatic aspect of the *bāṭinīyah* that al-Ghazāli fastens upon in *al-Qisṭās al-Mustaqīm*,[235] one of the several works he devoted to a refutation of the *bāṭinīyah* movement.[236] The *Qisṭās* is a curious solution to the dilemma of the dogmatism of Ismāʿīli *taʿlīm* and the rank anarchy of every-man-his-own exegete. According to al-Ghazāli it is nonsense to say that everything we need to know for salvation is handed down by an *Imām*; there must also be a place for working out positions on rational grounds. But—and here al-Ghazāli applies the safeguard—there are definite rules for the application of such things as syllogisms, rules that are contained in the *Qur'ān*. The rest

proval Aristotle's definition of the soul (*Jamiʿ*, ed. Corbin, p. 113 of the text), but the intricacies of *ta'wīl* soon lead him back to the *coelestia*; "l'anthropologie ismaélienne s'achève en une angélologie" (*ibid.*, Introduction, p. 120). The *locus classicus* for this "celestial psychology" is the *Kitāb al-riyāḍ* of al-Kirmāni.

234. See H. Corbin in his edition of the *Jamiʿ* of Nāṣir, Introduction, p. 59, n. 130.

235. V. Chelhot (ed.) (Beyrouth, 1959), trans. *idem*, "*Al-Qisṭas al-Mustaqīm* et la connaissance rationelle chez Ghazali," *BIFEO*, XV (1955–1957), 8–98.

236. Al-Ghazāli reviews his work against the *bāṭinīyah* in *Munqidh* (ed. Damascus), p. 54. Among the other published authors who have contributed to the anti-Ismāʿīli polemic: al-Ḥammādi (12th cent.?), *Kashf asrār al-bāṭinīyah* (Cairo, 1939); al-Daylami (*fl.* A.D. 1308), *Bayān madhab al-bāṭinīyah*, ed. R. Strothmann (*Bibl. Islamica*, XI [Istanbul, 1939]); what may be the most important treatise of all, the *Kashf al-asrār al-bāṭinīyah* of the tenth-century Muʿtazilite Abū al-Qāsim al-Busti, is still unedited in a unique Milan MS.; see S. M. Stern, *BSOAS*, XXIII (1960), 70.

of the treatise, cast in the form of a talk with an Ismāʿīli, follows from this: Certain verses in the *Qur'ān* are shown to be rules (*mawāzin*) for the use of the categorical (three figures), hypothetical, and disjunctive syllogism, certainly as astonishing a piece of exegesis as anything in the Ismāʿīli arsenal.

In his other polemical works against the *bāṭinīyah*, al-Ghazali refutes some of the more flagrantly unorthodox of the Ismāʿīli theses: their metaphysics,[237] their prophetology, their imamology, their views on the future life of the soul; but it was their dogmatism which, to the end, impressed him as the most serious threat to the traditional faith of Islam.[238]

BIBLIOGRAPHICAL NOTES

1. MUʿTAZILITES

As is customary, most of our knowledge comes from the heresiographers. There are, however, a few original Muʿtazilite documents; these will be noted in the text following. For the heresiographers see pp. 342–44 below.

The section on the Muʿtazilites in the *Fihrist* of al-Nadīm was badly mutilated in the MSS. that Flügel used in preparing his edition. Far better texts have since come to light:

J. Fück, "Neue Materialen zum Fihrist," *ZDMG*, XC (1936), 298–321.

Idem, "Some Hitherto Unpublished Texts on the Muʿtazilite Movement . . .," *Professor Muhammad Shafi Presentation Volume* (Lahore, 1955), pp. 51–74.

A. J. Arberry, "New Material on the *Kitāb al-Fihrist* of Ibn al-Nadīm," *Islamic Research Association Miscellany*, I (Oxford, 1949), 19–45. The crucial dates for the secondary material on the Muʿtazilite movement are 1925 and

237. I. Goldziher, *Streitschrift des Ghazali gegen die Batinijja-Secte* (Leyden, 1916); pp. 43–49 (this work contains a partial edition of al-Ghazāli's *al-Mustaẓhiri*); al-Ghazāli, like al-Baghdādi (*Farq*, p. 269 and ff.), connects the *bāṭinīyah* with the dualists and the Magians.

238. F. Jabre, *La Notion de Certitude selon Ghazali* (Paris, 1958), pp. 294–368, and *idem*, *MIDEO*, I (1954), 102; ". . . nous avons essayé de reconstituer les faits qui ont influencé l'oeuvre de Ghazali. A partir de 486 H./1093 celle-ci n'eut qu'un seul but: remplacer dans les croyances de ses contemporains l'infaillibilité de l'imam batinite par celle du Prophète, seul intermediaire entre Dieu et l'humanité."

1929, marking the publication of the first Mu'tazilite source of the early period (al-Khayyāt), and of the earliest heresiography to treat of them (al-Ash'ari). Among the earlier studies which could not profit by these publications:

H. Steiner, *Die Mu'taziliten oder die Freidenker im Islam* (Leipzig, 1865).

T. Houtsma, *De Strijd over het Dogma in den Islem tot op al-Ash'ari* (Leyden, 1875).

H. Galland, *Essai sur les Mu'tazilites* (Geneva, 1906).

The important precisions that must be must be made on the basis of the new material are resumed in:

H. Nyberg, art. "al-Mu'tazila," *Shorter EI*, pp. 421–27.

A. Nader, *Le Système philosophique des Mu'tazila* (Beyrouth, 1956).

A. Amin, *Duhā al-islām*, III (Cairo, 1949), 21–207.

The study by Nader, despite its wealth of material, illustrates a deficiency in the work to date on this important sect: very little attention has been given to its internal development. There is a tendency to describe general Mu'tazilite theses and omit their evolution. Again, little has been done in describing the course of later, i.e., post-Ash'ari, Mu'tazilitism; the best preliminary sketch is by I. Goldziher, "Aus der Theologie des Fachr al-Din al-Razi," *Der Islam*, III (1912), 213–47, espec. pp. 213–23.

2. ATOMISM

This crucial area, which embraces the problems of both primary and secondary causality, predestination, and the divine attributes, has been studied rather more thoroughly than the other aspects of Mu'tazilite dogma. Attention was long ago focused on it by the attacks of the *falāsifah*, especially in the now-classic text in Maimonides' (d. A.D. 1204) *Dalīl*, I, Chap. 73 (trans. Friedländer), 120-33, most recently studied by D. B. MacDonald, "Continuous creation and atomic time in Muslim scholastic theology," *Isis*, IX (1927), 326–44, and M. Fakhry, *Islamic Occasionalism* (London, 1958) pp. 25–32. Now however, a much earlier account of Mu'tazilite atomism is at hand in al-Ash'ari's *Maqālāt* (ed. Ritter), pp. 301 ff. The texts in Ash'ari have, in turn, served as the point of departure for the two standard studies of atomism:

O. Pretzl, "Die frühislamische Atomlehre," *Der Islam*, XIX (1931), 117–30

S. Pines, *Beiträge zur islamischen Atomenlehre* (Berlin, 1936).

3. KALĀM

Gardet-Anawati, *Théologie musulmane*, pp. 23–93.

I. Goldziher, *Vorlesungen über den Islam*[2] (Heidelberg, 1925), pp. 117–32.

M. Horten, *Die philosophischen Probleme der spekulativen Theologie im Islam* (*Renaissance und Philosophie*, Heft 3 [Bonn, 1910]).

D. B. MacDonald, *The Development of Muslim Theology, Jurisprudence and Constitutional Theory* (New York, 1903), pp. 186–242.

Idem, art. "Kalām," *Shorter EI*, pp. 210–14.

M. Schreiner, "Beiträge zur Geschichte der theologischen Bewegungen im Islam," *ZDMG*, LII (1898), 463–510, espec. pp. 486–510 on the period between al-Ash'ari and Ibn Taymiyah.

W. Watt, *Islamic Philosophy*, pp. 82ff.

A. J. Wensinck, *The Muslim Creed* (Cambridge, 1932).

Ibn Khaldūn, *Muqaddimah* (trans. Rosenthal), III, 49–52.

In addition to these general studies of *kalām* there is an extensive literature on one or another of the points of the problematic of the *mutakallimūn*. The best introduction to this problematic and its literature are Father Anawati's bibliographical additions to an important article by S. de Beaurecueil, "Une preuve de l'existence de Dieu chez Ghazzali et S. Thomas," reprinted in *MIDEO*, III (1956), 207–58.

4. FALSAFAH

The bibliography on *falsafah*, at first sight embarrassingly abundant, is quickly reduced to more modest proportions. Numerous philosophical texts have been edited and many individual thinkers and problems studied; these will be noted as they occur in the text. There have been, on the contrary, but few attempts to write the *history* of *falsafah*. Indeed, it may be persuasively argued that at present it is neither possible nor desirable to attempt such a synthesis. The few who have attempted it have, quite naturally, concentrated their attention on the peaks: al-Kindi, al-Fārābi, Ibn Sīnā, Maimonides, Ibn Rushd; quite unnaturally, the lesser slopes have been almost completely neglected.

Falsafah first attracted the attention of historians of philosophy in connection with its influence on medieval Western thought. The credit for this belongs chiefly to Renan's classic *Averroès et l'averroisme* (first ed.; Paris, 1852). At about the same time Munk began approaching the *falāsifah* from the direction of the Jewish *mutakallimūn* (*Mélanges de philosophie juive et arabe* [first ed.; Paris, 1859]).

From the time of Renan, Western interest in Muslim philosophy and theology has continued unabated. Identification and cataloging of the MSS of the Arabo-Latin translations of both Aristotle and the *falāsifah* themselves are proceeding at a good pace, though many of the most important Latin texts are still unedited (e.g., the Latin translation of the *Shifā'*). The Latin Averroism described by Renan has been more carefully defined and an entirely new strain of Latin Avicennism uncovered. The results have been incorporated into almost every survey of medieval philosophy, but reference need be made only to the latest and the best: E. Gilson, *History of Christian Philosophy in the Middle Ages* (New York, 1955), pp. 181–231: "Arabian and Jewish Philosophy": and, from a slightly different point of view but with the same emphasis on the western afterlife: G. Quadri, *La philosophie arabe dans l'Europe médiévale des origines a Averroès* (Paris, 1947).

The orientalist suffers from a more critical lack of basic work on the MSS. The work on *falsafah* necessarily waits upon a systematic study of the translation literature, especially in its linguistic aspects, an area that has hardly been entered.

The first attempt to give an overall view of *falsafah* was that of T. de Boer, *Geschichte der Philosophie im Islam* (Stuttgart, 1901 [English translation, London, 1903]), a work almost entirely lacking in documentation (a deficiency which is somewhat remedied in the Arabic translation by M. Abu Ridah) and betraying a Western medieval point of view by its total neglect of the post-Averroan philosophical movements. Max Horten, on the other hand, has, in the course of his numerous studies, investigated almost every aspect of *falsafah*, including the later, generally neglected figures like Mollā Sadrā (d. A.D. 1640). Many of Horten's articles will be cited on the following pages but reference must be made here to three attempts at a synthesis, each written from a somewhat different point of view:

"Die syrische und arabische Philosophie" in Überweg-Geyer, pp. 287–325.

Art. "Falsafah," *EI*, II, 48–52.

Die Philosophie des Islam in ihren Beziehungen westliches Orientes (Munich 1924).

Where once Horten was almost alone in the field, *falsafah* has, in the last thirty years, profited by the labors of more than a score of gifted scholars to whom each line of the present study is indebted, and to no one more than to Richard Walzer. Trained as both a classicist and an orientalist, Walzer has concentrated on drawing the Greek and Arabic material together. Some of the more general results can be seen in his "Islamic Philosophy" in *The History of Philosophy Eastern and Western*, II (London, 1953), 120–48, and *Greek into Arabic. Essays on Islamic Philosophy* (Cambridge, Mass., 1962).

The most comprehensive and, in many ways, the best treatment of *falsafah* by a contemporary scholar is M. Cruz Hernandez, *Historia de la Filosofia Española: Filosofia Hispano-Musulmano* (2 vols.; Madrid, 1957), whose scope is wider than the title suggests. Even here, however, the later Eastern *falāsifah* are neglected. A much briefer treatment, but integrated with the parallel developments in *kalām*, is W. Montgomery Watt, *Islamic Philosophy and Theology* (Edinburgh, 1962), pp. 41–49, 93–98, 132–45.

To insure more systematic results the study of *falsafah* is currently being organized along cooperative lines under the general direction of Father Anawati of the Institut Dominicain d'Études Orientales, Cairo; see G. Anawati, "Philosophie médiévale en Terre d'Islam," *MIDEO*, V (1958–1959), 175–236. Finally two recent bibliographical studies should be mentioned: J. Menasce, *Arabische Philosophie* (*Bibliographische Einführung in das Studium des philosophie*, #6 [Bern, 1948]), and G. Vadja, *Jüdische Philosophie* (*Bibliographische Einführung* ... # 19 [Bern, 1950]).

VII

THE TRIUMPH OF KALĀM

Theology, the philosophical predator of the myth-maker's imaginative ideas about the nature and existence of God, grew from the modest position it held in the speculations of Plato and Aristotle into one of the consuming passions of later Greek philosophy. Debates on the existence and providence of God, provoked by the Epicureans and eagerly pursued by the Stoics, dominate the philosophical discourse for half a millennium after Aristotle; it was the Greeks themselves who reduced philosophy to its status of "handmaiden of theology."

Purely religious sentiments played only a marginal role in those debates. Consideration was given from time to time to the culture's investment in the Homeric vision of the supernatural life or to the social and political values of the traditional Roman religion, but the unfolding of a theology, transcendent on the Platonic model or immanent in the Stoic fashion, generally proceeded on traditional philosophical lines.

Late antiquity possessed no great intellectual or institutional counterweight to check this development. The priesthoods were moribund, and the mystery cults parochial and fragmented. Apollo had ceased speaking from his great shrines. The interest of the politicians was pragmatic, while the great masses of the people pursued their own private religious visions. In his own sphere the God of the philosophers went undenied. Christianity, however, had both the integrity and, eventually, the strength to resist, with effects on the philosophical tradition that have already been described.

The new "sacred theology" of the Christian Church took as its guideline the divinely inspired revelation of its Scriptures, and the church's cautious progress into philosophical discourse was constantly attended by a concern that this Scriptural testimony be neither ignored nor distorted. Associated with the hierarchy in their jealous protection of orthodoxy was the secular arm of the newly Christianized state. From the fourth century onward, theology was the joint concern of bishop, philosopher, and politician. Outside participants were not welcomed, and the last, sixth-century descendents of the secular tradition deriving from Plato and Aristotle had to be most circumspect in their work, to the point, perhaps, where the Christian John Philoponus was used as a "front" by his unbaptized and suspect masters at Alexandria.

In the Greek tradition Christianity was a latecomer; *falsafah*, on the other hand, was born into the already swelling bosom of an Islam dominated by a political "Commander of the Faithful" and supervised by an alert and pious rabbinate of lawyers and saints. The only secular masters to whom the Muslim *falāsifah* could appeal belonged to another, vanished culture. The clash between a *falsafah* derived from this secular Hellenic tradition and the forces of a Scriptural Islam was inevitable.

The first threat to Islamic orthodoxy at the hands of Hellenic *falsafah* was met, successfully in the eyes of later Muslim partisans of *kalām*, by al-Ashʿari. The threat was serious chiefly because it was novel and unexpected, but the philosophical and theological naivete of the Muʿtazilites gave way to the far more sophisticated and systematic presentation of the philosophical position by Ibn Sīnā. This second, far more ominous challenge was met by an equally systematic, equally sophisticated theologian, Abū Ḥāmid ibn Muḥammad al-Ghazāli (d. A.D. 1111).[1]

1. *GAL*, I², 535–46. Suppl. I, pp. 744–56. The bibliography on the manifold aspects of al-Ghazāli's creative activity is immense. Only the most important and most recent studies, particularly those referring to his connection with *falsafah*, will be mentioned here.

When al-Ghazāli took up, in the name of Islamic orthodoxy, the challenge posed by *falsafah* in general and Ibn Sīnā in particular it seemed that the issue between revelational based faith and unaided reason was irrevocably joined. But Ghazāli was as little likely to slay *falsafah* as Basil of Caesarea to eradicate Hellenism. When the polemic finally abated Islam found that the experience of al-Ashʿari had been repreated: *falsafah* as such was further weakened, but in its place stood the scholastic *kalām*, faithful in principle to the revelation of the *Qur'ān*, but unmistakably the product, in shape and procedure, of the Hellenic tradition in philosophy, orthodox and at the same time Aristotelian.

Life and works: the most complete sketch of his biography by D. B. Macdonald has been brought up to date and reprinted in *Shorter EI*, pp. 111–14; the basic sources for the biography have been restudied by F. Jabre, "La Biographie et l'Oeuvre de Ghazali reconsiderées à la lumière des *Ṭabaqāt* de Sobki," *MIDEO*, I (1954), 73–102, with new emphasis on the *bātinīyah* movements. On the important question of the chronology and authenticity of the Ghazāli-*corpus* see W. M. Watt, "The Authenticity of the Works Attributed to Al-Ghazāli," *JRAS* (1952), pp. 24–45; G. Hourani, "The Chronology of Ghazāli's Writings," *JAOS*, LXXIX (1959), 225–33; and A. van Leeuwen, "Essai de bibliographie d'al-Ghazzāli," *Ibla*, LXXIX (1958), 221–27.

The basic document for the intellectual development of al-Ghazāli is the autobiographical *Munqidh min al-dalāl* (ed. Damascus, 1939; Cairo, 1955) trans. W. M. Watt, *The Faith and Practice of Al-Ghazali* (London, 1953).

The great systematic work, the *Iḥyā' ʿulūm al-din*, (4 vols.; ed. Cairo, 1927–1933), is not a work of either speculative theology or philosophy but deals with sound religious practices. There is, however, a preliminary section (I, 5–79) on the rational premises of religion.

Of the works devoted to philosophy, the two most important are the *Maqāṣid al-falāsifah* (ed. Cairo, 1936), a statement of the philosophical system of Ibn Sīnā intended as a kind of propaedeutic to the *Tahāfut al-falāsifah*, ed. M. Bouyges (*Bibl. Arab. Schol.*, II [Beyrouth, 1927]), and trans. S. Kamali (typescript Montreal, 1955). Other works are devoted to logic and the refutation of the *bāṭiniyah*.

Al-Ghazāli's classic statement of the Ashʿarite *kalám* is the *Iqtiṣād fi al-iʿtiqād* (ed. Cairo, n.d.); there is a paraphrastic translation by M. Asin Palacios, *El justo medio en la creencia* (Madrid, 1929).

Finally, there are a series of works on mysticism, notably the *Mishkāt al-anwār* (ed. Cairo, 1934), trans. W. Gairdner (London, 1924).

The most recent assessments of al-Ghazāli's thought, with abundant critical comments on the older studies by Macdonald, Obermann, Wensinck, Asin Palacios, *et al.* are:

F. Jabre, *La Notion de Certitude selon Ghazāli* (Paris, 1958).

Idem, *La Notion de la "Maʿrifah" chez Ghazāli* (Beyrouth, 1958).

M. Abu Ridah, *Al-Ghazāli und seine Widerlegung der griechischen Philosophie* (Madrid, 1952).

M. Cruz Hernendez, *Filosofia Musulmana*, I, 153–83.

AL-GHAZĀLI AND *FALSAFAH*

Al-Ghazāli's view of *falsafah* is twofold. He is unequivocably opposed to those of its theses that are in open contradiction to revelation or to tradition. This is the work of the *Tahāfut*: to extract from their works the heretical theses maintained by the *falāsifah* and to refute them not *qua* heretical but as bad philosophy. The motive and the method of the *Tahāfut* are two very different things.

On the subject of philosophy as a methodology he is not quite so forthright. Al-Ghazāli was above all a historical realist. To reject discursive reasoning as a source of knowledge in theology was manifestly impossible; the days of Ibn Hanbal had passed and al-Ghazāli had neither the inclination nor the ability to turn back the clock. What he did set out to do, and the sequel suggests that he was not entirely successful, was to regulate the position of speculation vis à vis the other "channels of knowledge," i.e., revelation and tradition.

The question as posed by the Muʿtazilites and answered by al-Ashʿari had to do with the allegorical interpretation (*taʾwīl*) of the *Qurʾān*. Al-Ghazāli treats it in the same context:

a) If reason can demonstrate that the literal interpretation of the *Qurʾān plane repugnat*, the passage in question is to be interpreted allegorically since revelation and reason are not mutually contradictory.[2]
b) If the demonstration is directed to showing the absurdity of dogmas fundamental to the faith, e.g., the resurrection of the body and the divine knowledge of singulars, the demonstration is to be rejected and the demonstrator is an infidel (*kafīr*).[3]

The problem is also studied by al-Ghazāli as it had been posed by Saʿadyā:

2. *Iqtiṣād* (ed. Cairo), p. 95; trans. Asin, p. 319.
3. *Faysal* (ed. Cairo), pp. 56–62; trans. Asin, pp. 517–22.

> *Inasmuch as all matters of religious belief, as imparted to us by our Master, can be attained by means of research and correct speculation, what was the reason that prompted wisdom to transmit them to us by way of prophecy and support them by means of visible proofs and miracles rather than intellectual demonstration?*[4]

Al-Ghazāli would not have been entirely happy with the wording of the question: "all matters of religious belief" cannot be demonstrated by reason alone. Nor does reason pronounce on the morality of truths. Hence there is a clear moral necessity for revelation.[5] If the question be asked in another way: what, then, is the necessity for *kalām* since revelation suffices for salvation? Al-Ghazāli would point out that there are two classes of men: the simple believers and the "intellectuals," and that for these latter there is not sufficient conviction in revelation alone.[6]

These are the positions adopted by al-Ghazāli speaking as a *mutakallim*, in what might be called his "Ashʿarite stance." But when he draws back from the subject and takes a more general view of the terrain, the perspectives are somewhat different. In the *Munqidh* he examines the courses open to an intellectual Muslim: the way of *kalām*, the way of *falsafah*, and the mystic gnosis (*maʿrifah*). *Kalām* is indeed legitimate, but it is primarily defensive; it is an instrument fashioned for the defense of the Sunni credo.[7] Its value is relative bacause it is based on postulates that are essentially foreign to revelation,[8] notions like necessary and contingent being, substance and accidents.[9] Al-Ghazāli realizes that *kalām* is in its essence philosophical and differs from *falsafah* only in that it will not blindly follow reason into areas where revelation and tradition have spoken. And this is his quarrel with the *falāsifah*: he wants them to retreat

4. *Amānāt* (ed. Landauer), p. 24; trans. Rosentblatt, p. 31.
5. *Iqtiṣād* (ed. Cairo), p. 95; trans. Asin, p. 317. The same distinction is made by al-Juwayni, *Irshād* (trans. Luciani), p. 305.
6. *Qisṭās* (ed. Chelhot), p. 85.
7. *Munqidh* (trans. Watt), p. 81.
8. *Ibid.*, pp. 81–82.
9. *Muṣṭasfa* (ed. Cairo, 1937), p. 4.

from the infidel theses: 1) there is no resurrection of the body; 2) God knows the universals but not the singulars; and 3) the universe is eternal *a parte ante* and *a parte post*. In all else the *falāsifah* are no worse than the Muʿtazilites: temerarious innovators but still orthodox.[10]

Nowhere does al-Ghazāli appear as a fideist. Though he protects the convictions of the "simple believer" and recognizes its advantages, he realizes equally well that it is not always enough. What he wishes to do is to reestablish the hierarchy of knowledge. All truth is from on high; the simple adherence to it on human authority is a position open to doubts and hesitations; it is not dangerous, but it is weak. On the other hand, the rational search for truth falls short of a complete realization of its goal; it is dangerous in that it leads a man to think that he is sufficient unto himself.

A third change of perspective leads to more fundamental questions pertaining to the *asbāb al-ʿilm* themselves. There is a passage in the *Iḥyā'* where al-Ghazāli addresses himself to the *asbāb*:[11] in addition to the necessary knowledge (*ʿilm durūri*) which is innate in man and which is nourished by the *Qur'ān*, man attains knowledge either by a laborious process of acquisition (*iktisāb*) based on the deductive method (*istidlāl*), or by direct inspiration which may be either a personal enlightenment (*ilhām*) or the revelation vouchsafed to the prophets (*wahy*). Acquired science and inspiration differ neither in regard to their place of operation nor to their cause, but only in their mode (*ḥāl*).

When it comes to an explanation of how the rational process works, al-Ghazāli is less certain of himself. There comes into play a view of causality inherited from the earlier Ashʿarites and diametrically opposed to the Aristotelian *ananke* which al-Ghazāli has apparently embraced. Question XVII of the *Tahāfut* is dedicated to the destruction of secondary causality with no less vigor than that of the

10. *Munqidh* (trans. Watt), pp. 96–97.
11. *Iḥyā'* (ed. Cairo, 1933), III, 16–17. This important passage has been translated and commented by L. Gardet, *Revue thomiste*, XLIV (1938), 569–78.

Ash'arites.[12] Yet in the *Mi'yār*, and by implication in the other logical works, there is an equal insistence that necessary and true premises lead, by demonstration, to necessary and true conclusions.[13]

Both the *falāsifah* and the Mu'tazilites had adopted the Aristotelian view of knowledge: the former by accepting the principle of causality (*'illah*) pure and simple; the latter, speaking in a more theological context, by invoking their peculiar doctrine of "generation (*tawallud*).[14] Al-Ash'ari denied any causal link between demonstration and knowledge and posited instead the notion of "customary sequence (*'ādah*), a principle obviously incapable of grounding certitude.

Al-Ash'ari, behaving as all occasionalists necessarily must, proceeded to erect a rational superstructure on this irrational foundation. But the epistemological difficulty did not escape later, more perceptive writers. Al-Ghazāli's teacher, al-Juwayni, takes up the problem in the opening pages of his *Irshād*.[15] He is very certain what the nexus between *naẓar* and *'ilm* is *not*: it is not the *tawallud* of the Mu'tazilites nor the *'illah* of the *falāsifah*; nor is it, at least by implication, the Ash'arite occasionalist *'ādah*. All al-Juwayni is willing to say is that *naẓar* "includes" the conclusion.

The operative, or rather, the nonoperative word here is "necessary" (*wājib*). Neither al-Juwayni nor al-Ghazāli would utter it. Fakhr al-Dīn al-Rāzi (d. A.D. 1209) finally does so, but only after making it clear that the necessity is rational (*'aqli*) and not ontological.[16] Nowhere is the fundamental difference between *falsafah* and *kalām* clearer. The *mutakallimūn* wish to play the game; indeed, at this stage in their development they *must* play the game. But such has been the impact of the Ash'arite denial of secondary causality

12. Ibn Rushd recognizes the epistemological consequences of such a denial: "Denial of cause implies the denial of knowledge, and the denial of knowledge implies that nothing in this world can be really known, and that what is supposed to be known is nothing but opinion, that neither proof nor definition exist, and that the essential attributes which compose definitions are void." *Tahāfut al-tahāfut*, ed, Bouyges, p. 522; (trans. Van der Bergh), p. 319.

13. *Mi'yār*, p. 159.

14. See p. 144 above.

15. Luciani (trans.), pp. 14–16.

16. The various positions on the relationship between *naẓar* and *'ilm* are resumed by al-Jurjāni in his commentary on the *Mawāqif* of al-Īji (ed. Cairo, 1907), pp. 241–48; on these authors see pp. 203–204 below.

that even the direct influence of philosophy on *kalām* did not succeed in restoring it to a system which is, in fact, based on the premise that such causality actually does exist. Al-Rāzi's theory of the "rational bond" enabled the *mutakallimūn* to proceed philosophically; but henceforward they had to be content with the empty Scotist game of essences.

Al-Ghazāli's "destruction" must be considered as only a qualified success. The theses singled out as heretical in the *Tahāfut* were thoroughly discredited, as they already had been in orthodox circles. In his attacks on both the *falāsifah* and the *bāṭinīyah* sects he was aided by the changing political climate. The liberally inclined Buwayhid masters of the Abbasid Caliphate had given way, after a brief Muʿtazilite interlude under Tughril Beg, to the stricter orthodoxy of the Seljuk Alp Arslān. To this general movement toward Ashʿarite orthodoxy, al-Ghazāli brought the moral authority of a respected teacher and a sincerely devout Muslim.

If, however, he truly purposed to restrict philosophizing to the modest area allowed it in the *Iqtiṣād*, his intention was not realized. The *Shīfaʾ* which al-Ghazāli attacked directly was neglected; but the thirteenth century turned instead to the *Ishārāt* which had a long series of commentators, not from among the *falāsifah*, but from the Ashʿarite *mutakallimūn*.

After A.D. 1050 the fortunes of *falsafah* in the East go into decline. The eminence of Ibn Sīnā's pupils barely reaches through one generation: Bahmanyār (*ca.* A.D. 1038–1060),[17] Ibn Zaylah (d. A.D. 1048),[18] and al-Masʿūmi (d. A.D. 1038)[19] are lost in the shadow of

---

17. Al-Bayḥaqi, *Tatimmat*; *Chahār maqālah* (trans. Browne), p. 92; *GAL*, I², 599–600, Suppl. I, p. 828; Bahmanyār, a Zoroastrian, was one of Ibn Sīnā's students whose discussions with the master are recorded in the *Mabāḥithāt* (see p. 91 above). Among his works al-Bayḥaqi mentions ethical, logical, and musical treatises. Two of his metaphysical tracts, *Risālah fi al-mawjūdāt* and *Risālah fi mawḍūʿ alʿilm al-maʿrūf bimā baʿd al-ṭabiʿah*, have been edited (Leipzig, 1851).
18. Abu Manṣūr al-Ḥusayn ibn Ṭāhir: al-Bayḥaqi, *Tatimmat*, # 50; *Chahār maqālah* (trans. Browne), p. 92; also said to be a Zoroastrian, though al-Bayḥaqi doubts this. His commentary on the *Ḥayy ibn Yaqẓān* is extant, and, according to al-Bayḥaqi, he also wrote an abridgement of the *physica* of the *Shīfaʾ*.
19. Abū ʿAbdallāh al-Masʿūmi: al-Bayḥaqi, *Tatimmat*, # 52; *GAL*, I², 599, Suppl. I, p. 828; according to his teacher's own testimony, he played Aristotle to Ibn Sīnā's Plato.

their teacher, and al-Jawzajāni is best known as Ibn Sīnā's biographer.[20] If Abū al-Barakāt (d. A.D. 1165) be excepted, and appreciative but hasty recognition given the minor philosophical talents of the physicians spreading from the Baghdad hospitals to Ayyubid Egypt and Syria, the true *falāsifah* must be sought, after the death of Ibn Sīnā, in western Islam: in North Africa and *al-Andalus*.[21]

The thirteenth century was, nonetheless, filled with philosophical activity. From Fakhr al-Dīn al-Rāzi at its beginning, to the students of al-Ṭūsi at its end, the *mutakallimūn* of the *via moderna* explored the Avicennan synthesis of the Aristotelian tradition.

THE CENTURY OF RĀZI AND ṬŪSI

Typical of the later theologians who tried to hew to the Ghazālian line was the *mutakallim* and heresiographer al-Shahrastāni (d. A.D. 1153)[22] a pupil of Abū al-Qāsim al-Anṣāri (d. A.D. 1118), one of the students of al-Juwayni,[23] and a teacher at the Baghdad Niẓāmīyah (A.D. 1116–1119). Al-Shahrastāni continues the attack against Ibn Sīnā in more or less the same terms as the *Tahāfut* of al-Ghazāli. But the latter man had neither the pious reputation nor the mystic appeal of al-Ghazāli, and, in the eyes of the orthodox, must have appeared to be propagating a different *falsafah*, but a *falsafah* nonetheless. He was accused of being a Shiʿite and an Ismāʿīli.[24] Maḥmūd al-Khawārizmi, who attended al-Shahrastāni's discussions in Khawarizm in the years before the Baghdad professorship, reports that the lectures were carried out on a purely

20. Al-Bayhaqi, *Tatimmat*, # 51; *Chahār maqālah* (trans. Browne), pp. 92, 157–58; the biography of Ibn Sīnā, actually a continuation of his autobiography, is preserved in al-Qifṭi and Ibn abī Uṣaybiʿah; on al-Jawzajāni's redaction of the *Shifā'* see pp. 89–91 above.
21. See pp. 215–220 below.
22. For the biographical data see pp. 285–287 below. His dogmatic work was edited with a partial translation by A. Guillaume, *Nihāyat al-iqdām fī ʿilm al-kalām* (Oxford, 1934).
23. Ibn Khallikān (trans. de Slane), II, 675.
24. Guillaume, *op. cit.*, p. xi.

naturalistic level; philosophical theses were rejected or defended, but never was there an invocation of the proof from revelation.[25]

As the twelfth century turns to the thirteenth, the naturalism that Maḥmūd found reprehensible in al-Shahrastāni becomes the order of the day in theology. Later *mutakallimūn* looked right through al-Ghazāli back to Ibn Sīnā. This in no sense implies a rejection of al-Ghazāli but an interest in the problematic as posed by Ibn Sīnā rather than in the solution à la Ghazāli. Ibn Khaldūn (d. A.D. 1406), looking back across a century, describes the resultant confusion:

> *Recent speculative theologians, then, confused the problems of theology with those of philosophy, because the investigations of theology and philosophy go in the same direction, and the subject and problems of theology are similar to the subject and problems of metaphysics. Theology and metaphysics, thus, in a way come to one and the same discipline. The recent theologians, then, change the order in which the philosophers had treated the problems of physics and metaphysics. They merged the two sciences in one and the same discipline. Now, in that discipline, they first discussed general matters. This was followed successively by the discussions of the corporeal things and the matters that belong to them, and so on to the end of the discipline. The imām Ibn al-Khaṭīb, for instance, proceeded in this manner in the Mabāḥith al-mashriqīyah, and so did all later theologians. The science of speculative theology thus merged with the problems of philosophy, and theological works were filled with the latter.*[26]

The *imām* Ibn al-Khaṭīb mentioned by Ibn Khaldūn is Fakhr al-Dīn Muḥammad ibn ʿUmar al-Rāzi (d. A.D. 1209), the scholar most singly responsible for undoing the work of al-Ghazāli.[27]

25. Yāqūt, *Muʿjam* (ed. Wüstenfeld), III, 343–44.

26. *Muqaddimah* (trans. Rosenthal), III, 152, and compare *ibid.*, III, 52–55, as well as Ḥājji Khalifah II, p. 100, where the blame is put on al-Ṭūsi; this analysis of later *kalām* was certainly not original with Ibn Khaldūn; al-Taftazāni (d. A.D. 1390) whom Ibn Khaldūn had certainly read (*Muq.*, III, 117) gives a similar judgment in his commentary on the *ʿAqʾāid* of al Nasafi (pp. 14–15; trans. Elder, pp. 9–10).

27. Qifṭi, pp. 190–92; Uṣ., II, 23–30; al-Subki, *Ṭabaqāt*, V, 33–40; Ibn Khallikān (trans. de Slane), II, 652–56; Barhebraeus, *Chron. Syr.*, p. 425 (trans. Budge, p. 366); *idem, Taʾrīkh*, p. 418; *GAL*, I², 666–69, Suppl. I, pp. 920–24; J. H. Kramers, art. "al-Rāzi," *Shorter EI*,

Al-Rāzi, though he spent his entire life in the eastern domains of the Ghorids and the Khawarizmshahs, was a product of the *kalām* of Baghdad through teachers reaching back to al-Ghazāli and al-Juwayni.[28] Unlike al-Shahrastāni, his knowledge of *falsafah* does not come from a mere conning of the *Maqāṣid*, the *Tahāfut*, and the standard heresiographies, but from a study of the philosophers themselves, especially Abū al-Barakāt, whose physical theories loom large in the *Mabāḥith*. He was, in fact, decried as an Aristotelian and a heretic[29], and, though he admits to having studied Aristotle, he claims that he is not an adherent of that brand of philosophy.[30]

Ibn Khaldūn was correct: al-Rāzi was a philosopher-theologian, joining together what al-Ghazāli had gone to such great pains to separate. Though he repudiated the one and criticized the other, al-Rāzi was both an Aristotelian and an Avicennan; although he spoke severely of both al-Ghazāli and al-Shahrastāni,[31] he was a confirmed Ash'arite and was unrelenting in his attacks on the Mu'tazilites.

It was al-Rāzi who brought Ibn Sīnā's *Ishārāt* back into prominence by his critique of this work, and his *Lubāb al-ishārāt* begins a series of pro- and anti-Avicennan commentaries.[32] The *Muḥaṣṣal*

pp. 470–71; Sarton, *Introduction*, II, 1, p. 364. Of his truly encyclopedic literary production, the most important of the published dogmatic and "Hellenizing" works are: the early work on physiognomy *Kitāb al-firāsah*, ed. and trans. Y. Mourad, *La physiognomie arabe et le Kitāb al-Firāsa de Fakhr al-Dīn al-Rāzi* (Paris, 1939); the *dogmatica*: *Asās al-taqdīs* (ed. Cairo, 1910); *Kitāb al-arba'īn fī uṣūl al-dīn* (ed. Hyderabad, 1934); *Muḥassal afkār al-mutaqaddimūn wa al-muta'akhkhirūn* (ed. Cairo, 1903 and 1905), and an analytical translation by M. Horten, *Die philosophischen Ansichten von Razi und Tusi*; *idem*, *Die spekulative und positive Theologie des Islam nach Razi und ihre Kritik durch Tusi* (Leipzig, 1912); the *philosophica*: *al-Mabāḥith al-mashriqīyah* (2 vols.; ed. Hyderabad, 1924); *al-Munāẓarāt* (ed. Hyderabad, 1936), and analyzed by P. Kraus, *Islamic Culture*, XII (1938), 131–53; his commentary on the *Ishārāt* of Ibn Sīnā, *Lubab al-ishārāt* (ed. Cairo, 1908); for al-Rāzi's important commentary on the *Kashshāf* of al-Zamakhshari see I. Goldziher, "Aus der Theologie des Fachr al-Din al-Razi," *Der Islam*, III (1912), 213–47; for the heresiography see p. 245 n. 16 below.

28. Ibn Khallikān (trans. de Slane), II, 655.

29. Barhebraeus, *Chron. Syr.*, p. 425.

30. *I'taqidāt*, pp. 91–92.

31. *Munāẓarāt*, pp. 25–26; al-Shahrastāni's *Milal* was, according to al-Rāzi, nothing more than a reworking of al-Baghdadi's *Farq* and the *Ṣiwān al-ḥikmah* of Abū Sulaymān.

32. Against al-Rāzi and in defense of Ibn Sīnā are the *Kashf al-tamwihāt* of al-Amidi and the *Ḥall mushkilāt al-ishārāt* of al-Ṭūsi (included in the Cairo, 1957, ed. of the *Ishārāt*); of the two reconciliatory works, the *Muḥākamah* of al-Tustari (d. *ca.* A.D. 1306) and the *Muḥākamāt* of Quṭb al-Dīn al-Taḥtāni (d. A.D. 1364; see pp. 289–290 below), it was the latter, together with the glosses of Quṭb al-Dīn al-Shirāzi and al-Dawwāni (d. *ca.* A.D. 1506; see pp. 199–200, 211–212 below. which became the *textus* for Sunni Islam.

is the first theological work to devote a true section to philosophical questions instead of the somewhat hasty prolegomena of the earlier Ashʿarites.[33] The *Mabāḥith* is one of the earliest of the philosophical encyclopedias by a theologian.[34]

When the works of al-Rāzi began circulating farther west, they found an outstanding exegete in Kamāl al-Dīn ibn Yūnus (d. A.D. 1242),[35] the scientific and philosophic polymath of Mosul who had studied in the Niẓāmīyah in Baghdad before taking up a teaching post in Mosul. Nothing of his philosophical works is extant, but by him were formed three important scholars who, with al-Rāzi's students, dominate the philosophical activity of the mid-thirteenth century.

Contemporary with Ibn Yūnus and the best philosopher-theologian of the Ayyubid kingdoms was Sayf al-Dīn al-Āmidi (d. A.D. 1233),[36] who was trained in Baghdad, apparently under Christian and Jewish teachers in philosophy,[37] and taught in *madrasahs* in Damascus and Cairo. In addition to his important *kalām* work *Abkār al-afkār*,[38] he composed a philosophical encyclopedia, the *Daqā'iq al-ḥaqā'iq*,[39] a work on methodology, *al-Iḥkām fī uṣūl al-aḥkām*,[40] and in his commentary on the *Ishārāt* took up the defense of Ibn Sīnā against Fakhr al-Dīn al-Rāzi.[41] Al-Āmidi's philosophizing led to a charge of heresy, but after a self-imposed retirement he managed to clear himself and resume his work.

Among al-Rāzi's students were the logicians al-Khūnaji (d. A.D. 1249),[42] and al-Urmawi (d. A.D. 1283),[43] and the encyclopedist

33. Gardet-Anawati, *Théologie musulmane*, pp. 162–64.
34. Only the *Talwiḥāt* of al-Suhrawārdi (d. A.D. 1191) is earlier. The *Muʿtabar* of Abū al-Barakāt is the work of a *faylasūf*.
35. Ibn Khallikān (trans. de Slane), III, 466–74; Uṣ., I, 306–308; al-Subki, *Ṭabaqāt*, V, 158–62; *GAL*, Suppl. I, p. 859; Sarton, *Introduction*, II, 2, p. 600.
36. Qifṭi, pp. 240–41; Uṣ., II, 174–75; Ibn Khallikān (trans. de Slane), II, 235–37; al-Subki, *Ṭabaqāt*, V, 129; *GAL*, I², 494, Suppl. I, p. 678.
37. Qifṭi, p. 241.
38. Still unpublished; see Ahlwardt, *Arabischen Handschriften Berlin*, # 1741; according to Ritter, *Der Islam*, XVIII (1928), 53, the *Abkār* was an important source for the *Mawāqif* of al-Īji (see pp. 204–205 below.
39. The apparently unique—and incomplete—MS is the Princeton-Garrett # 828.
40. Ed. Cairo, 1914.
41. *Kashf al-tamwihāt*; unedited (see *GAL*, Suppl. I, p. 816).
42. Qadi in Cairo; see *GAL*, I², 607, Suppl. I, p. 838.
43. Later in his career professor in Konia; see pp. 205 and 207, n. 101 below.

al-Abhari (d. A.D. 1265),[44] who had also studied under Ibn Yūnus at Mosul. Al-Abhari was the author of two of the most popular philosophical works of later Islam: a handbook of logic, the *Īsāghūji*,[45] and the philosophical encyclopedia *Hidāyat al-ḥikmah*, frequently glossed by later commentators.[46] The *Hidāyat* follows the usual division into logic, physics, and metaphysics,[47] and the treatment is philosophical throughout. This *summa* of philosophy, together with al-Kātibi's *Ḥikmat al-ʿayn*, remained in constant and wide circulation in the East and were still standard philosophical textbooks at the al-Azhar *madrasah* in Cairo at the beginning of the nineteenth century.[48]

The other eminent disciples of Ibn Yūnus were Severus (*aliter* Yaʿqūb) bar Shakko (d. A.D. 1241), the Syriac encyclopedist,[49] and Nāṣir al-Dīn al-Ṭūsi (d. A.D. 1274).[50]

The career of Ṭūsi illustrates the vitality of the Greek learning in what were, to say the least, unpromising times. A member of the Shiʿite sect, though educated by a Sunni teacher, al-Ṭūsi was "kidnapped" by the Ismāʿīlis and sent to Alamut where he remained until its capture by the Mongols in A.D. 1256.[51] He somehow managed to

44. Athīr al-Dīn Mufaḍḍal ibn ʿUmar: Ibn Khallikān (trans. de Slane), III, 468–69; Barhebraeus, *Taʾrikh*, p. 445; *GAL*, I², 608–11, Suppl. I, pp. 839–44; Sarton, *Introduction*, II, 2, p. 867.
45. See p. 78 above.
46. Including Ibn Mubārakshāh, the teacher of al-Jurjāni and al-Fanāri (see p. 208, n. 106 below); in particularly frequent use were the superglosses of al-Dawwāni's student al-Maybudi (d. A.D. 1498); see Ahlwardt, *op. cit.*, # 5065 and p. 213 below.
47. Al-Maybudi's glosses omit the logic.
48. See p. 78 above.
49. Barhebraeus, *Chron. Eccles.*, II, 409–12; *GSL*, pp. 311–12; Sarton, *Introduction*, II, 2, p. 603; his theological encyclopedia, the *Book of Treasures*, has been analysed by F. Nau, "Notice sur le Livre des Trésors de Jacques de Bartela ...," *JA*, Sér. 9, Vol. VII (1896), 286–331; see pp. 107–108 and 132–133 above.
50. Al-Ṣafadi, *Wāfi* (ed. Ritter), I, 179–83; Barhebraeus, *Chron. Syr.*, p. 529 (trans. Budge, pp. 451–52); *GAL*, I², 670–76, Suppl. I, pp. 924–33; Browne, *Literary History*, II, 484–86; Sarton, *Introduction*, II, 2, pp. 1001–1113; R. Strothmann, *Die Zwolfer-Schiʿa. Zwei religionsgeschichtliche Characterbilder aus der Mongolzeit* (Leipzig, 1926), pp. 16–87. His most important *philosophica* and *dogmatica* are: the logical treatise in Persian, *Aṣās al-iqtibās* (ed. Teheran, 1947); the unpublished *divisio* work *Aqsām al-ḥikmah* (see Berlin, # 5076); the brief philosophical work *al-Fuṣūl* (ed. Teheran, 1956), in the Persian original and the Arabic. trans by al-Astarabadhi (d. A.D. 1618); his commentary on the *Ishārāt*, printed in the Cairo, 1957, ed. of the *Ishārāt*; his critical commentary on the *Muḥassal* of al-Rāzi; the *kalām* treatises *Tajrīd al-ʿaqāʾid* and *Qawāʾid al-ʿaqāʾid*; and the Persian ethical treatise *Akhlāq-i Nāṣiri* (ed. Teheran, 1933).
51. The true relationship between al-Ṭūsi and the Ismāʿilis is unclear. Ivanow goes further than most in associating him with the group; see *Taṣawwarāt* (Leyden, 1950), pp. xxiv–xxvi.

disassociate himself from his Ismāʿīli taint and entered the service of the new Mongol lords of the Abbasid Caliphate. He served Hulagu as vizier and was appointed (A.D. 1259) chief of the famous observatory and library at Maraghah in Adharbayjan, where he stayed until shortly before his death in A.D. 1274.

Caught in the crumbling of the old order and the fashioning of the new, al-Ṭūsi was able to construct a *corpus* of scientific, philosophical, and theological work of impressive proportions.[52] His scientific output, chiefly in the field of astronomy, was almost entirely Greek-derived, and his approach to the problems of theology was along the Hellenizing lines already set down by al-Rāzi, though not always in accordance with the solutions suggested by al-Rāzi. In both his commentary on the *Muḥaṣṣal* and that on the *Ishārāt*, al-Ṭūsi casts himself in the role of the defender of Ibn Sīnā against the attacks of al-Rāzi.

Of wider vogue than these two polemically oriented works was al-Ṭūsi's *systema*-work of *kalām*, *Tajrīd al-ʿaqāʾid*, with its three standard commentaries by Ibn al-Muṭahhar al-Ḥilli (d. A.D. 1326),[53] al-Iṣfahāni (d. A.D. 1348),[54] and al-Qushji (d. A.D. 1474).[55] The *Tajrīd*, especially as seen through the eyes of al-Ḥilli, was the first elaboration of a genuine *kalām* treatise for Shiʿite theology, a move which, in effect, opened the way for *falsafah* into the Persian theological tradition of the succeeding centuries. This was not, to be sure, the Shiʿites' first taste of Hellenic ideas. For some time the extremist wing of the sect (*qhulāt*) had been incorporating gnostic and Neoplatonic concepts into a system of hypostatized emanations.[56] The *qhulāt* were attacked by Sunnis and Shiʿites alike, but it was not until the Shiʿites adopted the by-now conservative Aristotelian-Avicennan *kalām* that they had an effective dogmatic weapon against the extremists.[57]

52. Fifty-seven items in *GAL*; sixty-four in Sarton.
53. A student of al-Ṭūsi; see nn. 58–59 below.
54. See p. 203, n. 81 below.
55. See p. 210 below.
56. See I. Goldziher, "Neuplatonische und gnostiche Elemente im *Hadith*," *ZA*, XXII (1908), 317–44.
57. The chief methodological difference between Ashʿarite *kalām* and post-Ṭūsi Shiʿite theology

Al-Ṭūsi's student and Shi'ite propagandist Ibn al-Muṭahhar al-Ḥilli (d. A.D. 1326)[58] did not share his teacher's wide philosophical and scientific interests. His field was law and theology and in this latter domain he built on the *kalām* foundations of al-Ṭūsi, chiefly by commenting the *logica, metaphysica,* and *dogmatica* of the older man.[59]

Both al-Kātibi (d. A.D. 1276) and Quṭb al-Dīn al-Shirāzi (d. A.D. 1311) were more faithful reflections of their teacher. Al-Kātibi[60] worked with al-Ṭūsi at the Mongol observatory at Maraghah, and there is in manuscript a record of a dispute between the two men on metaphysics;[61] but the bulk of al-Kātibi's work is cast in the form of the handbook and the encyclopedia, especially the widely read *Ḥikmat al-'ayn*[62] developed out of an earlier work, the *'Ayn al-qawā'id fī al-manṭiq wa al-ḥikmah.*[63] Al-Kātibi also followed al-Ṭūsi's lead as a commentator of al-Rāzi; still to be determined is the relation between al-Kātibi's commentary on the *Muḥaṣṣal* of al-Rāzi (entitled *al-Mufaṣṣal*) and al-Ṭūsi's criticism of the same work, composed in A.D. 1270, shortly before his death.

Quṭb al-Dīn al-Shirāzi[64] was a more catholic and a more original scholar than al-Kātibi. Trained by his father and others in medicine

is the relatively greater emphasis given to the crucial Shi'ite theses on prophetology and the imamate.

58. Al-Tunakābuni, *Qiṣāṣ al-'ulamā'*, # 88 (ed. Teheran, 1935), pp. 355–64; *GAL*, II², 211–12, Suppl. II, pp. 206–209.

59. His commentary on al-Ṭūsi's important *kalām* work, *Tajrīd al-'aqā'id*, has recently been published (Qumm, 1953).

60. 'Ali ibn 'Umar al-Qazwīni al-Kātibi: al-Kutubi, *Fawat*, # 301 (ed. Cairo, 1951), p. 134; Mustawfi Qazwini, *Ta'rikh-i Guzida* (ed. Browne), I, 844–55; *GAL*; I², 612–14, Suppl. I, pp. 845–48; Sarton, *Introduction*, II, 2, p. 868.

61. See *GAL*, I², 672, # 7, Suppl. I, p. 848.

62. The contents, excluding the logic, are résuméd in Ahlwardt, *Arabischen Handschriften Berlin*, # 5080; the received version of the *Ḥikmat al-'ayn* included the commentary of Ibn Mubārakshāh (see p. 208, n. 106 below) and the glosses of al-Jurjāni (see p. 206 below) and, among the Ottoman *mutakallimūn*, the superglosses of Khaṭibzādah (d. AD. 1495) see Tashköprüzādah, *Shaqā'iq* (trans. Rescher), pp. 93–96, and *GAL*, II², 296, Suppl. II, p. 320.

63. A third encyclopedia, *Jami' al-daqā'iq fī kashf al-ḥaqā'iq*, is extant in a few MSS.

64. Maḥmūd ibn Mas'ūd (to be distinguished from the theologian of the next generation, Quṭb al-Dīn Muḥammad ibn Muḥammad al-Rāzi al-Taḥtāni): al-Subki, *Ṭabaqāt*, VI, 248; al-Shawkāni, *al-Badr al-tāli'*, II, 299–300; and a valuable autobiographical-type document prefaced to his commentary on the first part of Ibn Sīnā's *Qanūn*. This has been reproduced in the 1939 Teheran edition of the author's *Durrat al-tāj*, pp. 9–13 of the Introduction; *GAL*, II², 274–75, Suppl. II, pp. 296–97; Sarton, *Introduction*, II, 2, pp. 1017–20.

and by al-Ṭūsi in astronomy and metaphysics, he taught and published in all these fields, as well as serving on diplomatic missions for the Mongol Khans. His philosophical productions are somewhat overshadowed by the scientific, but there is a marked interest in Ibn Sīnā. He taught the *Shifā'* in Damascus[65] and, in addition to his own unpublished commentary on the *Ishārāt*, it was he who urged al-Taḥtāni to write the work reconciling the views of al-Rāzi and al-Ṭūsi vis à vis Ibn Sīnā.[66] Like so many others of his thirteenth-century contemporaries, al-Shirāzi put together a philosophical encyclopedia, *Durrat al-tāj*, divided into *logica, metaphysica, physica, mathematica,* and *theologica* and prefaced with an essay on the division of the sciences.[67] Finally, he was the author of one of the earliest commentaries on al-Suhrawārdi's work on mystical theology, *Ḥikmat al-ishrāq*.

IBN TAYMĪYAH

In the intellectual history of Islam, Ibn Taymīyah (d. A.D. 1328) is classified as a reactionary.[68] To his predominantly Shafi'ite contemporaries in Mamluk Cairo and Damascus, his teaching was redolent of the old, discarded fundamentalism; in the eyes of his political

65. Al-Shawkāni, *op. cit.*, p. 399.
66. So Ḥājji Khalīfah, *Kashf*, # 743; al-Shirāzi himself glossed the *Muḥākamāt* of al-Taḥtāni.
67. Persian text edited, without the *mathematica* (5 vols.; Teheran, 1939–1942).
68. Taqi al-Dīn abū al 'Abbās ibn Taymīyah: his major biographies have been edited: al-Karmi, *al-Kawāqib al-durrīyah* (Cairo, 1911), and Ibn 'Abd al-Hādi, *al-'Uqud al-durrīyah* (Cairo, 1938); al-Kutubi, *Fawāt*, I, 34–45; al-Shawkāni, *al-Badr*, I, 63–74; *GAL*, II², 125–27, Suppl. II, pp. 119–26; H. Laoust, *Essai sur les doctrines sociales et politiques de ... ibn Taymiyah* (Cairo, 1939); *idem*, *Contribution à une étude de la methodologie canonique d'ibn Taymiyah* (Cairo, 1939); M. Schreiner, *ZDMG*, LII (1898), 540–63, LIII (1899), 51–66; M. al-Bitar, "al-'Aql wa al-naql 'ind al-imām ibn Taymīyah," *RAAD*, XXXIII (1958), 56–79. Ibn Qayyim's bibliography of the works of his teacher has been edited by S. Munajjid, *Asmā' mu'allafāt ibn Taymīyah* (Damascus, 1953). The chief works directed toward theology and philosophy are: *Minhāj al-sunnah al-nabawīyah fī naqd kalām al-shī'ah wa al-qadarīyah* (4 vols.; ed. Cairo, 1903–1904); *Buqhyat al-murtād fī al-radd 'alā al-mutafalsifah wa al-qarāmīyah wa al-bāṭinīyah* (ed. Cairo, 1911); *al-radd 'ala falsafat ibn Rushd* (Cairo, n.d.), pp. 128–40; *al-Qiyās fī al-Shar' al-islāmi* (ed. Cairo, 1927), trans. H. Laoust, *Contribution* ... pp. 113–216.

masters he was simply intractable; this unhappy combination of attitudes resulted in long periods of his career being spent in prison. The Ibn Taymīyah of modern scholarship is, predictably, a somewhat more sympathetic figure.

Although first and foremost a jurist, there was very little in the theological development of Islam up to his own day that escaped Ibn Taymīyah's highly developed historical sense. It is interesting to see the growth of *falsafah* and *kalām* through his eyes, for he had the advantage of a perspective of two centuries on the work of al-Ghazāli, as well as an awareness of what had happened in the interval. Since the last decades of the eleventh century, the theology of Islam had seen philosophy return to the attack in the person of the Spanish Peripatetics Ibn Bājjah, Ibn Ṭufayl, and Ibn Rushd, a revived Shiʿism propagandized by Ibn al-Muṭahhar al-Ḥilli and supported politically by the Mongol Khans, the shaping of the "new" *kalām* in the hands of al-Rāzi and al-Ṭūsi, and, finally, the powerful impetus given to the theology of Sufism by Ibn al-ʿArabi (d. A.D. 1240).

Ibn Taymīyah's view of *kalām* is considerably dimmer than even al-Ghazāli's. It is unlikely, he says, that God did not reveal the truth until the time of the *falāsifah*.[69] There is a tendency throughout to identify the *falāsifah* and the *mutakallimūn*. It was the Muʿtazilites who fashioned *kalām*,[70] and both they and the *falāsifah* had drunk from the same polluted springs, notably the doctrine of the Sabians of Harran.[71]

Just as al-Ashʿari emerges from the pages of Ibn Taymīyah as a latter-day Muʿtazilite, so, too, does al-Ghazāli since he was formed, and thus corrupted, by the philosophical doctrine of the Sincere Brethren, al-Tawḥīdi, and—final irony—Ibn Sīnā.[72] Ibn Taymīyah is particularly severe with Fakhr al-Dīn al-Rāzi, who was more re-

69. See the text of the *al-ʿAqīdah al-ḥamawīyah* quoted by Schreiner, *ZDMG*, LII (1898), 542, n. 2.

70. *Minhāj*, IV, 144–45.

71. *ZDMG*, LIII (1899), 72, where the text specifically mentions al-Fārābi; on the Sabians of Harran see p. 171, n. 207 above.

72. H. Laoust, *Essai*, pp. 82–83, where attention is called to the large debt which Ibn Taymīyah nonetheless owed to al-Ghazāli for his logic, ethics, and mystical doctrine.

prehensibly Mu'tazilite than any of his predecessors,[73] and al-Ṭūsi who, together with his pupil al-Ḥilli, plays an important part in the anti-Shi'ite tenor of the *Minhāj*.[74]

Such are Ibn Taymīyah's general views on kalām and *falsafah*, based on a not inconsiderable acquaintance with his adversaries, both theological and philosophical.[75] But it is only one side of the coin. Ibn Taymīyah was neither a Qur'ānic fundamentalist nor a Muslim Peter Damian intent on tearing the syllogistic wiring out of the walls of the House of Theology. He was, on the contrary, more Aristotelian than the *mutakallimūn* whom he criticized.

In cosmology, physics, and metaphysics there is an attempt to hold the line against the "Rūmis, Greeks, Persians, and Indians," but Ibn Taymīyah is taken neatly on the flank by the Aristotelian logic.

The works on methodology have, as one of their principle aims, the restoration of the *Qur'ān* and tradition to the head of the hierarchy of the *uṣūl al-fiqh*, this in the face of a growing tendency on the part of the predominant Shafi'ite jurists to exalt a consensus of the jurisprudents (*ijmā'*) above all the other *uṣūl*. Ibn Taymīyah's counterstroke is to show that the *Qur'ān* and tradition are themselves usable through the intermediacy of a judicious use of analogy (*qiyās*), and that this method of procedure is more faithful to the data of revelation than recourse to *ijmā'*.

Qiyās is the cornerstone of Ibn Taymīyah's attack on the Shafi'ite *ijmā'*, and his concern for its proper application carries him into the problems of logic. His defense of *qiyās* is both knowing and spirited and, it should be noted, extremely Aristotelian.[76] The *Qiyās fī al-shar' al-islāmi* opens with an insistence that true judicial analogy is based on the syllogism which searches out not superficial resemblances between

73. *Buqhyat*, pp. 107–108.
74. See espec. pp. 99–100.
75. H. Laoust, *Essai*, p. 86, has adduced evidence for a knowledge of *al-Madīnah al-fāḍilah* of al-Fārābi, the *Ishārāt* of Ibn Sīnā, the *Ḥayy ibn Yaqẓān* of Ibn Tufayl, and the *Faṣl Kashf 'an manāhīj*, and *Tahāfut al-tahāfut* of Ibn Rushd. Another important source was the heresiographies of al-Ash'ari, Ibn Ḥazm, and al-Shahrastāni; *ibid.*, pp. 93–94.
76. H. Laoust, *op. cit.*, pp. 87–88, 243–44.

terms, but the cause (*ʿillah*).[77] In describing the rational syllogistic process, Ibn Taymīyah proceeds serenely without any of al-Ghazāli's hesitations on the subject of secondary causality,[78] and though he is severe in his criticism of al-Rāzi's methodology, his Aristotelian view of the syllogism and his insistence on the role of *qiyās* is in perfect harmony with post-Rāzian epistemology.

The efforts of Ibn Taymīyah mark the last serious attempt to purify *kalām* of at least some of its Hellenic aspects. As such it was a failure. Whatever may be said of the effects of his work in jurisprudence and his attacks on Sufism, and it must be confessed that these were his chief interests, the Greek lineaments of *kalām* were by now too deeply etched ever to be erased without destroying theology itself.

AL-ĪJI, GLOSSATORS, AND SUPERGLOSSATORS

The two premier *kalām* texts of Sunni Islam are the work of a pair of Persian savants from the district of Shiraz: al-Bayḍāwi (d. *ca.* A.D. 1286) and al-Īji (d. A.D. 1355).

Not much is known about the formation of al-Bayḍāwi,[79] a scholar whose reputation as a theologian has been somewhat overshadowed by the place he holds in the history of Qur'ānic exegesis.[80] But from his *Ṭawāliʿ al-anwār min maṭāliʿ al-anẓār* it is clear that he has gone to the school of al-Rāzi.[81] The work has an introduction and three parts (*possibilia,* the essence and attributes of God, prophetol-

77. Pp. 5–7.
78. I.e., on an epistemological level; Ibn Taymīyah, like al-Ghazāli, held no strong belief for the physical atomism current in the Ashʿarite school; see H. Laoust, *op. cit.*, p. 175.
79. Abū Saʿīd ʿAbdallāh ibn ʿUmar Nāṣir al-Dīn al-Bayḍawi: al-Subki, *Ṭabaqāt*, V, 59; Tashköprüzādah, *Miftāḥ*, I, 436; *GAL*, I², 530–34, Suppl. I, pp. 738–43; Sarton, *Introduction*, II, 2, pp. 870–71; J. Robson, art. *s.v.*, *EI²*, 1, p. 1129.
80. For his *Anwār al-tanzīl*, largely an expurgation of the Muʿtazilite *Kashshāf* of al-Zamakhshari, see T. Nöldeke and F. Schwally, *Geschichte des Qorans²*, II, 176, and J. Robson, *art. cit.*
81. Ed. Cairo, 1905, with the commentary of al-Iṣfahāni (d. A.D. 1348); see Ahlwardt, *Arabischen Handschriften Berlin* # 1772, and Gardet-Anawati, *Théologie musulmane*, pp. 164–65.

ogy), with the bulk of the treatment given over to the metaphysics of the *possibilia*.

Al-Īji,[82] a "second-generation" student of al-Bayḍāwi, is the seal of the *via moderna* in *kalām* and the opening of the truly scholastic phase of Muslim theology. As a text, the *Mawāqif fī ʿilm al-kalām*[83] holds a position in *kalām* analogous to that of the *Libri quattuor sententiarum* of Peter Lombard; it is the *textus* par excellence. But unlike the *Sententiae,* it was not a point of departure; in its function as the final position of unquestioned orthodoxy it is more redolent of the *Summa theologica.*

The *Mawāqif* is divided into six parts, of which the first is a treatment of the *asbāb al-ʿilm.*[84] The second, third, and fourth treatises deal with the questions of general metaphysics and physics (being, necessary and possible beings, substance, accidents, etc.). The fifth treatise is on natural theology (essence of God, His unity, attributes, and operations), and, finally, the sixth treatise is devoted to the "traditional questions" of prophetology, eschatology, faith, and the imamate, with a final, brief appendix on sects.

If the *Mawāqif* is compared to a work of "middle" *kalām* like the *Iqtiṣād* of al-Ghazāli or the *Irshād* of al-Juwayni, and then with a relatively primitive document like the *Ibānah* of al-Ashʿari, the immense distance traversed in the course of those five centuries is immediately apparent. Al-Ashʿari's work is a thinly disguised *credo* developing in the direction of the Muʿtazilite problematic. In al-Juwayni and al-Ghazāli there are still creedal affinities and the *adversarii* are still principally the Muʿtazilites. But the hand of Ibn Sīnā is visible in the new sections devoted to epistemological and metaphysical problems. The *Mawāqif* is unabashedly a work of metaphysics and natural theology constructed on a Rāzian (i.e., an Avicennan) framework. In al-Īji the triumph of *falsafah* is almost complete. A small corner is still devoted to the "traditional questions," but taken in its entirety the

82. Al-Subki, *Ṭabaqāt,* VI, 108; Tashköprüzādah, *Miftāḥ,* I, 169–70; al-Shawkāni, *al-Badr,* I, 326; *GAL,* II² 267–71, Suppl. II, pp. 287–93; Sarton, *Introduction,* III, 1, pp. 628–29.

83. Text alone edited Cairo, 1938; see Gardet-Anawati, *Théologie musulmane,* pp. 165–69, 370–72.

84. Including a résumé (ed. Cairo, 1938), pp. 9–10, of the earlier polemics on the subject.

Mawāqif is more of a tribute to Aristotle than to al-Ash'ari. This is, essentially, the final position of medieval Sunni Islam. What follows is only the unbroken chain of glossators of Īji, of commentators of Abhari, and of "reconcilers" of Rāzi and Ṭūsi.

The first of the "reconcilers" has already been mentioned in passing: Quṭb al-Dīn al-Rāzi al-Taḥtāni (d. A.D. 1365),[85] who divided his professional career between the eastern provinces and Damascus where he taught the biographer and jurist Tāj al-Dīn al-Subki.[86] In addition to his *Muḥākamāt*,[87] al-Taḥtāni's work reflects both his own interest in logic and the usual pattern of the philosopher-theologians of the period: commentaries on the *Maṭāli'* of al-Urmawi and the *Shamsīyah* of al-Kātibi, a commentary on the philosophical *tafsīr*-work of al-Zamakhshari; his chief original work was the *al-Tasawwarāt wa al-taṣdiqāt*.[88]

The classic commentator of the *Mawāqif* of al-Īji, indeed, his commentary has almost become part of the text of the *Mawāqif*, is the Persian theologian al-Jurjāni (d. A.D. 1413).[89] A native of Astarabadh, al-Jurjāni intended beginning his logical studies with al-Taḥtāni at Herat. But that scholar was by then far too ancient to oblige him; he advised him to go instead to Cairo. This he did and, together with the Turk al-Fanāri, studied logic and the *Mawāqif* of al-Īji under Ibn Mubārakshāh[90] and Akmal al-Dīn al-Bābarti.[91] After a stay in the Ottoman domains, al-Jurjāni returned to the East and took up a teaching post in Shiraz. When Timur took Shiraz in A.D. 1387, al-Jurjāni was absorbed into his court and was taken to Samarqand where he served as a kind of court theologian. After

85. Al-Subki, *Ṭabaqāt*, VI, 31; Ibn al- 'Imād, *Shadharāt*, VI, 207; *GAL*, II², 271, Suppl. II, pp. 393–94; Sarton, *Introduction*, III, 1, pp. 629–30.
86. See p. 248, n. 24 below.
87. See p. 195, n. 32 above.
88. Ed., with the commentary of Mīr Zāhid al-Harawi (d. A.D. 1687) and numerous glosses (Cawnpore, 1870).
89. 'Ali ibn Muḥammad al-Sayyid al-Sharīf: Tashköprüzādah, *Shaqā'iq* (trans. Rescher), pp. 96–97; al-Sakhāwi, *Daw'*, V, 328–30; al-Shawkāni, *al-Badr*, I, 488–90; *GAL*, II², 280–81, Suppl. II, pp. 305–306; Sarton, *Introduction*, III, 2, p. 1461.
90. See p. 208, n. 106 below.
91. *GAL*, II², 97, Suppl. II, pp. 89–90.

Timur's death in A.D. 1405, al-Jurjāni returned to Shiraz where he died.

The main line of al-Jurjāni's work was focused on logic and theological comment. A considerable amount of attention is given to definition literature,[92] and to the classification of the sciences;[93] but his most famous and widely studied work was undoubtedly his commentary on the *Mawāqif*.[94] The comment, like the text itself, is completely in the spirit of al-Rāzi, and it was largely through this combination of Īji-Jurjāni that the philosophized *kalām* of the preceding century became the standard fare in the Sunni schools.[95]

The other eminent *mutakallim* at the court of Timur was al-Taftāzāni (d. A.D. 1390),[96] a student of al-Īji and Quṭb al-Dīn al-Taḥtāni. He spent his entire professional life in the various cities of the East and was the rival of al-Jurjāni for the theological affections of Timur. The two theologians engaged in a series of debates in the presence of the Sultan, from which encounters al-Jurjāni apparently emerged victorious.

In theology al-Taftāzāni was a Maturidite and it was in his commentary on the creed of the earlier Maturidite theologian Abū Ḥafṣ al-Nasafi (d. A.D. 1142)[97] that his theological ideas found their greatest dissemination.[98] He commented most of the other theological logical, and legal classics as well. His one original contribution to

92. E.g., the *Ta'rīfāt*, ed. G. Flügel (Leipzig, 1845; Cairo, 1903); the definitions in al-Taftazāni are quite similar to those in the *Ta'rīfāt*: see E. Elder, *A Commentary on the Creed of Islam* (New York, 1950), p. xxi.

93. *Maqālīd al-'ulūm fi al-ḥudūd wa al-rusūm*; unpublished, see *GAL*, II², 280, # 4.

94. Text and commentary, together with the glosses of Hasan Čelebi al-Faḥnāri (see p. 208 below and al-Siyālkūti (d. A.D. 1657); see *GAL*, II², 550, Suppl. II, pp. 613–14, 8 vols.; (Cairo, 1907).

95. There is a list of no less than thirty-five different sets of glosses to Īji-Jurjāni in Ahlwardt, *Arabischen Handschriften Berlin*, # 1812.

96. Sa'd al-Dīn Maḥmūd ibn 'Umr: Ibn al-'Imād, *Shadharāt*, VI, 319–22; al-Shawkāni, *al-Badr*, II, 303–305; *GAL*, II², 278–80, Suppl. II, pp. 301–304; Sarton, *Introduction*, III, 2, pp. 1462–64; C. A. Storey, art. *s.v. EI*, IV, 604–607.

97. See *GAL*, I², 548–50, Suppl. I, pp. 758–62.

98. *Sharḥ 'aqā'id al-Nasafi* (ed. Cairo, 1916), and trans. E. Elder, *A Commentary on the Creed of Islam* (New York, 1950); for the distinction of Ash'arite and Maturidite in theology see Elder, *op. cit.*, pp. xxiii–xxxi, and Gardet-Anawati, *Theologie musulmane*, pp. 60–61; the glossator-history of al-Taftāzāni's commentary can be seen in *GAL*, Suppl. I, pp. 758–60.

kalām literature, the *Masqāsid al-ṭalibīn,* is a short *aporia-lysis* work directed mainly against the Muʿtazilite positions.[99]

The transplantation of *kalām,* now shot through with logical, physical, and metaphysical elements from *falsafah,* from the old Islamic centers to the new territories conquered by the Turks in Anatolia, is described in the opening pages of Tashköprüzādah's *Shaqāʾiq.*[100] Starting from the earlier Seljuk settlements at Konia and Qaraman,[101] the Islamic learning followed the Ottoman armies to their new capitals; the first *madrasah* was established at Izniq (Nicaea) under Urkhan,[102] and others followed at Brussa, Adrianople, and, after its fall in A.D. 1453, at what was formerly Constantinople.

When the "Persianizing" Fatimids were dislodged from Egypt, the country was "Turkified" by the succeeding Ayyubids and Mamluks; but when the Turks themselves came to Anatolia, it was a Persian Islam that they brought with them.[103] The *Shaqāʾiq* with its lists of teachers who received their education in the East under Timurid and Safavid auspices confirms this Persian influence; but it also mentions other equally eminent scholars who went to Syria and Egypt to study there.

One of the earliest of the Cairo-trained savants was Shams al-Dīn Muḥammad al-Fanāri (d. A.D. 1431),[104] who began his studies under Jamāl al-Dīn al-Aqsarāʾi in the *madrasah* of Qaraman[105]

99. Ed. Istanbul, n.d.; the *Maqāsid* in an abridged version forms the second part of the author's *Tahdhīb al-manṭiq wa al-kalām* and though this latter work was widely read, it was only the first part on logic which was copied; the *kalām* section fell into disuse.

100. For this author and his work see pp. 287–288 below.

101. Most of the "first generation" of scholars under the Sultan Urkhan were from Qaraman; an important figure in the intellectual life of Konia was Sirāj al-Dīn al-Urmawi, a student of Fakhr al-Dīn al-Rāzi and the author of a widely used treatise on logic, *Maṭaliʿ al-anwār fī al-manṭiq*: see Barhebraeus, *Taʾrīkh,* p. 445. Al-Urmawi was the teacher of Tāj al-Dīn al-Kurdi, the second head of the Izniq *madrasah* (*Shaqāʾiq* [trans. Rescher], p. 3).

102. *Shaqāʾiq* (trans. Rescher), p. 2.

103. C. H. Becker, *Islamstudien,* I (Leipzig, 1924), 156–57; the "Persian stage" in the life of the early Anatolian Turks has been described by J. H. Kraemers, "Islam in Asia Minor," *Analecta Orientalia,* I (Leyden, 1954), 22–32, to which may be added the case of Khidhrbeg ibn Jalāl al-Dīn (d. A.D. 1459), who apparently never studied outside Anatolia but who composed poetry in Arabic, Turkish, and Persian: *Shaqāʿiq* (trans. Rescher), p. 55.

104. *Shaqāʾiq* (trans. Rescher), pp. 11–15; *GAL,* II², 303–304, Suppl. II, pp. 328–29; Sarton, *Introduction,* III, 2, pp. 1465–66.

105. Al-Aqsarāʾi called his youngest students "Peripatetics" because they received their instruction walking along beside him en route to his lectures; his middle students were "Stoics"

and with his father Ḥamzah al-Fanāri, a student of Saḍr al-Dīn al-Qonawi (d. A.D. 1273) who, in turn, had been the pupil of the mystic Ibn al-ʿArabi during the latters's residence in Anatolia. At the death of al-Aqsarāʾi, al-Fanāri accompanied the recently arrived al-Jurjāni to Cairo where they studied under the Afghan *shaykh* Shams al-Dīn ibn Mubārakshāh.[106]

Al-Fanāri was the founder of a family of Turkish scholars who stretch across the length of the fifteenth century. It is tempting to call this period the "golden age" of Turkish *kalām*, and, in contrast with the following years, it was. But the last real theologian in Islam was, until quite modern times, al-Īji, and al-Jurjāni was his Cardinal Cajetan: the "golden age" was in reality nothing more than a series of glosses to al-Jurjāni's commentary of the *Mawāqif*, to Jurjāni on Isfahāni on Bayḍāwi, and to Jurjāni on Taḥtāni on Urmawi, a dreary enough prospect for even the most ardent lover of the Turks and/or *kalām*.[107]

From a strictly theological point of view, the most important member of the Fanāri family was Ḥasan Čelebi ibn Muḥammad-shāh al-Fanāri (d. A.D. 1481),[108] professor at Adrianople, Izniq, and Istanbul. His chief dogmatic work consisted of glosses on Jurjāni's commentary on the *Mawāqif*,[109] and his other literary activity was typical of the work of this textbook age: glosses on al-Bayḍāwi's commentary on the *Qurʾān*; in law glosses on al-Taftazāni's commentary on the *Tanqīh al-uṣūl* of Saḍr al-Sharīʿah al-Thāni (d. A.D. 1346/1347); and in rhetoric glosses on al-Taḥtāni's commentary on Jamāl al-Dīn al-Qazwīni's (d. A.D. 1338) abridgement of the *Miftāḥ al-ʿulūm* of al-Sakkāki (d. A.D. 1229).[110]

because they were taught in one of the outer porches of the *madrasah*. Al-Faḥnāri was one of the "Stoics"; see *Shaqāʾiq* (trans. Rescher), p. 9, and *GAL*, Suppl. II, p. 328.

106. Chiefly known for his scientific work, but sought out by al-Jurjāni because of his proficiency in logic, especially his mastery of al-Taḥtāni's commentary on the *Matali*ʿ of al-Urmawi; see *GAL*, II², 614 and the charming anecdote in *Shaqāʾiq* (trans. Rescher), pp. 96–97.

107. Or of Arabic and/or science which were the credentials of George Sarton who found nonetheless, little to love in the outer darknesses of the fifteenth century; see *Homenaje a Millas-Vallicrosa*, II (Barcelona, 1956), 303–24.

108. *Shaqāʾiq* (trans. Rescher), pp. 120–22; *GAL*, II², 297, Suppl. II, pp. 321–22.

109. Frequently printed; see *GAL*, Suppl. II, p. 290.

110. A standard medieval authority on rhetoric; see *EI*, IV, 80–81.

An anecdote in the *Shaqā'iq* suggests that perhaps the world of the fifteenth-century *mutakallimūn* was not limited to the narrow horizons of al-Taftāzāni and al-Jurjāni.[111] The Sultan Muḥammad II (A.D. 1451–1481) summoned two of Ḥasan Čelebi's contemporaries, Khājazādah (d. A.D. 1488)[112] and 'Alā' al-Dīn al-Ṭūsi (d. A.D. 1482),[113] to write a critique of al-Ghazāli's *Tahāfut* and Ibn Rushd's *Tahāfut al-tahāfut*. Khājazādah's work was ready in four months,[114] al-Ṭūsi's in six.[115] The Sultan judged Khājazādah's the better treatise, and the discouraged Ṭūsi returned to his native Persia.

There is little point in following Ottoman *kalām* further along its increasingly scholastic path except to note some aspects of the educational system in which theology had become enshrined. Pedagogically, the culture was "textual," i.e., the *kalām* classics of Jurjāni and Taftāzāni were glossed by the professor. The *madrasahs* were built and subsidized by the Sultans, who in this early stage of Ottoman *kalām* hired and fired the professors and otherwise took an active interest in theological questions. The daily stipend for a professor of theology or of law was from fifty to eighty dirhams a day.[116] Arabic, the "ecclesiastical language" of Islam, was used throughout in the composition of dogmatic works.

Arabic was likewise the language for the Turkish scholars whose primary interests were in the natural sciences, but who also tried their

111. P. 59 of Rescher's translation.

112. *Shaqā'iq* (trans. Rescher), pp. 76–87; *GAL*, II², 297–98, Suppl. II, p. 279; professor in the *madrasah* at Brussa and the author of glosses on Jurjāni's commentary on the *Mawāqif*, which he knew by heart.

113. *Shaqā'iq* (trans. Rescher), pp. 58–60; *GAL*, II², 261–62, Suppl. II, p. 279; educated in Persia and professor at Brussa and then, after the fall of Constantinople, in the new *madrasah* in that city.

114. Entitled *Tahāfut al-falsifah* (Cairo, 1885); studied by M. Turker, *Üṣ tehāfüt bakimindan felsefe ve din munasebeti* (Ankara, 1956); see *idem, Études Méditerranéennes*, II (1957), 7–22.

115. *Al-Dhakhīrah fī al-muḥākamah* (Hyderabad, 1911). The Greek positions are still cited, e.g., on the origins of the human soul: Plato (p. 248) for preexistence, and Aristotle (p. 251) for generation, perhaps by way of al-Rāzi's commentary on the *Ishārāt* (*ibid.*, p. 227).

116. For purposes of comparison: Zayrek, a professor in Istanbul, found that he could live on twenty dirhams a day and he sent the balance of the fifty to a Sufi order (*Shaqā'iq* [trans. Rescher], p. 74). Two copies of al-Jurjāni's commentary on the *Mawāqif* (obviously not an exceedingly rare item!) made by Mollā Khusraw sold for six thousand dirhams after his death (*ibid.*, p. 71).

hand at either *kalām* treatises or encyclopedias.[117] The first of such, Qāḍīzādah al-Rūmi (d. *ca.* A.D. 1436–1446),[118] was an Anatolian Turk by birth, but pursued his career at the court of the amirs of Samarqand where he directed the royal observatory. Despite his essentially astronomical background, he studied in the more general field of the non-Islamic sciences with al-Jurjāni and glossed Mawlānāzādah's commentary on the philosophical encyclopedia of al-Abhari, the *Ḥidāyat al-ḥikmah.*[119] His student, ʿAlāʾ al-Dīnʾ al-Qushji (d. A.D. 1474),[120] reversed the process. After succeeding Qāḍīzādah as head of the Samarqand observatory, he emigrated to the Ottoman domains and ended his career as a professor in Istanbul. Celebrated as a mathematician and astronomer, he holds, nonetheless, a place in the history of *kalām*: it was his commentary on the *Tajrīd al-ʿaqāʾid* of al-Ṭūsi that become the standard treatment of the work and so formed the base for numerous Shiʿite superglosses.[121]

The line is continued in Luṭfi (d. A.D. 1494),[122] a student of the astronomer Sinān Pashā (d. A.D. 1481)[123] and, after his arrival in Istanbul, of al-Qushji. Both a mathematician and a theologian,[124] it was his work in this latter area that led to his downfall. After a brilliant career as librarian in Istanbul and as a professor there, in Brussa, and in Adrianople, he was accused, largely at the instigation of the *mutakallim* Khaṭībzādah,[125] of heresy and impiety and was decapitated in the Byzantine hippodrome of Istanbul.

The final figure among the Ottoman philosopher-theologians is a student of Luṭfi. Ibn Kamāl Pashā (*aliter* Kemālpashāzādah; (d.

117. This aspect of Ottoman intellectual life is treated in A. Adnan, *La Science chez les Turcs Ottomans* (Paris, 1939).

118. *Shaqāʾiq* (trans. Rescher), pp. 7–8.

119. *GAL*, I², 608.

120. *Shaqāʾiq* (trans. Rescher), pp. 102–104; al-Shawkāni, al-Badr, I, 495–96; *GAL*, II², 305, Suppl. II, pp. 329–30.

121. *GAL*, I², 671, Suppl. I, p. 926.

122. *Shaqāʾiq* (trans. Rescher), pp. 182–85; Ibn al-ʿImād, *Shadharat*, VIII, 23; *GAL*, II², 305–306, Suppl. II, p. 330.

123. *Shaq–ʾiq* (trans. Rescher), pp. 112–14.

124. His works include a classificatory list treatise on the Islamic sciences, tracts on general metaphysics, and commentaries on the *Mawāqif* of al-Īji and the *Maṭāliʿ* of al-Urmawi.

125. *Shaqāʾiq* (trans. Rescher), pp. 93–96; *GAL*, II², 296. Suppl. II, p. 320.

A.D. 1533)[126] was by first inclination a soldier; but seeing that the scholar was held in higher regard than the soldier, he began preparing for an academic career under Luṭfi in Adrianople. Success came swiftly: professor in law, civil magistrate in Adrianople, and military magistrate of Anatolia. It was in this latter function that he accompanied the Ottoman invasion of Egypt in A.D. 1516. On his return he resumed his professorship, teaching in Adrianople until his death.

The literary activity of Ibn Kamāl ranged over many fields: translation (Ibn Taghrībirdi's history into Turkish), poetry, history, *ṭabaqāt*, lexicography, rhetoric, *ḥadīth* and Qur'anic criticism, *kalām*, and philosophy. In these latter two areas, he continued in the tradition of comment (on al-Ghazāli's *Tahāfut* and the theological sections of al-Īji's *Mawāqif*), as well as composing some short, original treatises on metaphysics,[127] a doxographical *kalām* collection,[128] a study of the *zindīq*,[129] and questions on psychology,[130] all still unpublished.

The final pages in the history of *falsafah-kalām* are those written in Safavid Persia of the sixteenth and seventeenth centuries. The link between these Safavid theologians and the somewhat earlier tradition of philosophy in the eastern provinces, as represented by the school of Rāzi-Ṭūsi-Īji-Jurjāni, *et al.*, was the encyclopedist-theologian Jalāl al-Dīn al-Dawwāni (d. *ca.* A.D. 1500–1510),[131] whom the sources give as a student of al-Jurjāni. The connection, though chronologically unsound (al-Jurjāni died in A.D. 1413), is true enough in the sense of intellectual influence. Al-Dawwāni was one of the many glossators of al-Jurjāni's commentary on the *Mawāqif*,[132] but his writings reflect an interest that goes beyond the traditional problems

126. *Shaqā'iq* (trans. Rescher), pp. 243–45; Ibn al-ʿImād, *Shadharat*, VIII, 238; *GAL*, II², 597–612, Suppl. II, pp. 668–73; F. Babinger, *Die Geschichtsschreiber der Osmanen und ihre Werke* (Leipzig, 1927), pp. 61–63.

127. See Ahlwardt, *Arabischen Handschriften Berlin*, # 2338 and # 2339.

128. *Ibid.*, # 2763.

129. *Ibid.*, # 2792.

130. *Ibid.*, # 5364.

131. Al-Shawkāni, *al-Badr*, II, 130; Ibn al-ʿImād, *Shadharāt*, VII, 133; *GAL*, II², 281–84, Suppl. II, pp. 306–309.

132. *GAL*, II², 269.

of *kalām*. He was encyclopedist,[133] a logician (commentaries on al-Urmawi, al-Kātibi, and al-Samarqāndi), an ethician,[134] a metaphysician,[135] and the commentator of al-Suhrawārdi (d. A.D. 1191),[136] whose mystical philosophy was exercising an ever-growing influence on the East during this period.

Mystical tendencies are likewise discernible in two of the immediate students of al-Dawwāni.[137] Al-Farani (d. *ca.* A.D. 1485), who is known only from his commentary on the *Fuṣūṣ fī al-ḥikmah*, once attributed to al-Fārābi but now thought to be the work of Ibn Sīnā,[138] focuses on the new emphases of metaphysics and cosmology: the pantheistic implications of the emanation theory (matter is non-being) and its corollaries, the microcosm-macrocosm relationship in creation and the theme of the return of the soul to its

133. E.g., his unpublished *Unmūdhaj al-'ulūm*; the chief Eastern encyclopedists in the interval between Qutb al-Dīn al-Shirāzi (see pp. 199–200 above) and al-Dawwāni were: al-Muḥbūbi, called Saḍr al-Sharī 'ah al-Thāni (d. A.D. 1347; see *GAL*, II², 277–78, Suppl. II, pp. 300–301; Sarton, *Introduction*, III, 1, p. 628) whose *Ta'dīl al-'ulūm* is unpublished; see Ahlwardt, *Arabischen Handschriften Berlin*, # 5096; al-'Āmili (d. *ca.* A.D. 1352) a Shi'ite opponent of al-Ījī and the author of a Persian encyclopedia of the Hellenic and Islamic sciences, *Nafā'is al-funūn fī arā' al-'uyūn*, (2 vols., ed. Teheran, 1898–1899); see Sarton, *Introduction*, III, I, p. 632, and Plessner, *Bryson*, pp. 119–23; and the otherwise unknown Abū al-Ḥasan ibn Abīwardi, who was the author of the *Rawd al-janan*, preserved in BM Suppl. 728 and Berlin # 5110–11, and who probably was contemporary with or slightly later than al-Dawwāni. The lack of information on his *floruit* adds a note of irony to the epithet applied to Ibn Abīwardi in the Berlin MS.: "the Aristotle of his time and the Plato of his age."

134. He composed, on the model of an earlier work by al-Ṭūsi (see p. 197, n. 50 above), a Persian treatise on ethics entitled *Akhlāq-i Jalāli* (ed. Calcutta, 1911), and trans. W. Thompson, *The Practical Philosophy of the Mohammedan People* (London, 1839); see Browne, *Literary History*, III, 442–44, and Plessner, *Bryson*, pp. 104–13.

135. Two of his most widely read and commented works were the *Ithbāt al-wājib al-qadīmah* and the *Ithbāt al-wujūd al-jadīdah*; see Ahlwardt, *Arabischen Handschriften Berlin*, # 2328 and # 2335.

136. In addition to commenting the *Hayākil al-nūr* of Suhrawārdi, al-Dawwāni composed other independent works on mysticism, chiefly the *Risālat al-zawrā'* and the *Bustān al-qulūb*.

137. Mention should be made of a curious academic vendetta directed at al-Dawwāni by Ghiyāth al-Dīn al-Shirāzi (d. A.D. 1542), a somewhat later professor in the *madrasah* of Shiraz. His father, Mīr Saḍr al-Dīn al-Shirāzi (d. A.D. 1497; see *GAL*, II², 262, 544, Suppl. II, p. 279), was himself a competitor and commentator of al-Dawwāni, but in his opposition to al-Dawwāni he was outstripped by his son who directed a long series of attacks on every conceivable aspect of the work of al-Dawwāni; see al-Khawānsari, *Rawdāt al-jannān*, p. 640; *GAL*, II², 545, Suppl. II, p. 593; Zirikli, *al-A'lam*, VIII, 245–46. The most famous student of Ghiyāth al-Dīn was the *mutakallim* al-Lari (d. A.D. 1571) who spent most of his career in Aleppo; see Ibn al-'Imād, *Shadharāt*, VIII, 250; *GAL*, II², 553–54, Suppl. II, pp. 620–21; Zirikli, *op. cit.*, VII, 39.

138. See p. 246, n. 178 above.

Creator.[139] Al-Maybudi (d. *ca.* A.D. 1498)[140] composed a standard commentary on the *Ḥidāyat al-ḥikmah* of al-Abhari[141] and what is apparently a type of doxographical collection of Arab philosophers.[142] His mystical philosophy he reserved to a Persian commentary on the spurious *Diwān* of ʿAli ibn abī Ṭālib.[143]

A third student of al-Dawwāni, a certain ʿAbdallāh of Yazd, known only as the author of glosses on al-Jurjāni's commentary on a logical work by al-Kātibi,[144] leads directly into the circle of Shiʿite theologians under the Safavids: Bahāʾ al-Dīn al-ʿĀmili, Mīr Damad, Mollā Saḍrā, Muḥsin al-Fayḍ al-Kāshi, and ʿAbd al-Razzāq al-Lāhiji.

Al-ʿĀmili, a student of ʿAbdallāh al-Yazdi and a native of Syria, belongs to the scientific wing of the Hellenic tradition.[145] Like Quṭb al-Dīn al-Shirāzi, his chief interest was in astronomy and mathematics. Mīr Damad (d. A.D. 1631),[146] a contemporary of al-ʿĀmili and a fellow luminary in the circle of the Safavid Shah ʿAbbās (A.D. 1587–1629), is more purely the theologian, though not, to be sure, of the traditional *mutakallim* type. The Shiʿite community of the East displays the same spectrum of theology as Sunni Islam: from the Ibn Taymīyah-Ibn Ḥanbal type of anti-*falsafah*, anti-Sufism, e.g., al-Majlisi (d. A.D. 1700),[147] through the Hellenizing *mutakallim* of the Rāzi school, e.g., al-Ṭūsi, to the "illuminationist" *faylasūf*-theologian like Mīr Damad himself, and it is this latter group, the cultivators of what Corbin has called "L'avicennisme

139. See M. Horten, *Das Buch der Ringsteine Farabis mit dem Kommentare des ... El-Farani* (*Beiträge*, V, 3), Münster, 1906, pp. 5–6, 313–479.

140. *GAL*, II², 272, Suppl. II, p. 294; Browne, *Literary History*, IV, 57.

141. See M. Horten, *AGP*, XXII (1909), 418–21.

142. See Rieu, *Catalogue of the Persian Manuscripts in the British Museum*, II, 812.

143. Rieu, *op. cit.*, I, 19.

144. *GAL*, Suppl. I, p. 846; *ibid.*, p. 831.

145. Al-Muḥibbi, *Khulāṣat al-athār*, III, 440–55; al-Tunakābuni, *Qiṣāṣ al-ʿulamā*, # 37 (ed. Teheran, 1935), pp. 334–35; *GAL*, II², 546–47, Suppl. II, pp. 595–97; Browne, *Literary History*, IV, 427–28; Zirikli, *al-Aʿlam*, VI, 334–35; *EI*², I, 436.

146. Muḥammad Bāqir ibn Muḥammad Mīr Damad: al-Muḥibbi, *Khulāṣat al-athār*, IV, 301–302; al-Khawānsāri, *Rawḍāt al-jannāt*, pp. 114–16; al-Tunakābuni, *Qiṣās al-ʿulamā*, # 77 (ed. Teheran, 1935), pp. 333–35; *GAL*, Suppl. II, pp. 579–80; Browne, *Literary History*, IV. 428–29; H. Corbin, "Confessions extatiques de Mir Damad," *Mélanges Massignon*, I (Damascus 1956), 331–78.

147. *GAL*, Suppl. II, pp. 573–74.

sohrawardien," who from al-Dawwāni on are the true heirs of the Greek philosophical tradition in eastern Islam.

The two chief figures in this "School of Isfahan"[148] are Mīr Damad and his student Mollā Sadrā (d. A.D. 1640).[149] Both men are concerned with Islamic orthodoxy and are at some pains to point out and correct the differences between a purely philosophical position and the demands of Muslim revelation. The *Qabasāt* of Mīr Damad and the *Shawāhid al-rabūbīyah* of Mollā Ṣadrā are directed to this end. They are at the same time within the Hellenizing tradition. Mollā Ṣadrā commented the *Ḥidāyat al-ḥikmah* of al-Abhari,[150] the theological sections of Ibn Sīnā's *Shifā'*,[151] and composed his own theological *summa, al-Afsār al-ʿarbaʿa fī al-ḥikmah* which, externally at least, is a faithful reproduction of the Avicennan *genre*.[152]

Internally, however, the Aristotelian landscape has been considerably altered and the traditional philosophical emphases of Ibn Sīnā have been replaced by the researches of the "other" Ibn Sīnā of the *Ḥayy ibn Yaqẓān* and the final sections of the *Ishārāt*. Mollā Ṣadrā frequently cites Aristotle in the *Afsār*, but it is the Neoplatonic Aristotle of the *Theologia*. The usual Avicennan emanationism is complemented by an ontological monism reminiscent of Ibn al-ʿArabi and the ever more important stress on the return of the soul to God and its reabsorption into the bosom of the Necessary Being. It is, in short, a philosophical world dominated by the "illumination" (*ishrāq*) of al-Suhrawārdi.

The new synthesis of the School of Isfahan is the final statement of the Aristotelian tradition in the *kalām* of the East. It is, when compared with the long-since-arrested growth of that same tradition

148. Some of the lesser-known members are passed in review by H. Corbin, *Mélanges Massignon*, I, 344–48.

149. Muḥammad ibn Ibrāhīm Ṣadr al-Dīn: al-Khawānsāri, *Rawdāt al-jannāt*, pp. 331–32; *GAL*, II², 544, Suppl. II, pp. 588–89; Browne, *Literary History*, IV, 429–32; A. Zanjani, *RAAD* IX (1929), 661–80, 723–41, and X (1930), 29–43.

150. Teheran, 1895; see M. Horten, *AGP*, XXII (1909), 387–406.

151. For the commentary on the *Shifā'* by al-ʿAlawi (d. *ca.* A.D. 1644–1650), a student of Mīr Damad, see H. Corbin, *Mélanges Massignon*, I, 345–46.

152. 4 vols., Teheran, 1865); there is an analysis and a partial translation by M. Horten, *Die Gottesbeweise bei Schirazi* (Bonn, 1912, and) *Das philosophische Systeme von Schirazi* (Straßburg), 1913).

in the Mamluk and Ottoman lands of the West,[153] a thing of vitality and imagination and by no means unworthy of the eleventh-and twelfth-century thinkers who inspired it, nor of the Hellenic world view which, no matter how overgrown with Indian and Iranian *exotica,* is at its base.[154]

It is, nonetheless, a long way from the *Metaphysica* to Mollā Ṣadrā. The *corpus* had long since fallen from view, and the concern of the later *mutakallimūn* was not directly with Aristotelianism, but with the philosophical problems posed by Ibn Sīnā as they were relevant in a theological context. Of all this the medieval West knew nothing: the *loquentes in lege Maurorum* were not Rāzi, Ṭūsi, Īji, and Jurjāni, but rather the earlier generation of *mutakallimūn* as seen through the eyes of the last of the pure *falāsifah,* the Peripatetics of Spain.

IBN RUSHD

The Christian Visigothic culture absorbed by the Arabs in Spain stands in sharp contrast to the fruitful encounters with the Syrian Christians in the East. That there was some meaningful contact in the West is clear enough from Ibn Juljul's use of both Orosius and Isidore of Seville,[155] but another event reported by that historian is even more revealing in the philosophical context. When the Greek text of Dioscorides was sent to Spain by Constantine VII Porphyrogenitus in A.D. 948, there was no one there to read the Greek.[156] The Visigoths stood helpless as transmitters of the Greek philosophical

153. The prime *kalām* texts at the Azhar university in Cairo are, for this last period: al-Taftāzāni on the *'Aqīdah* of Abū Ḥafs al-Nasafi and the same author's *Maqāsid al-ṭalibīn* (see pp. 206–207 above); al-Īji's *Mawāqif* (see pp. 203–205 above) and the introductory text of al-Sanusi (d. A.D. 1486), *Umm al-barāḥīn* (numerous editions; it has been translated by M. Horten, *Die Katechismen des Fudali und des Sanusi* [Bonn, 1916], pp. 45–53); see Heyworth-Dunne, *Introduction to the History of Education in Modern Egypt,* pp. 55–56.

154. See the remarks of A. Bausani quoted in *RNSP,* LVII (1959), 664.

155. See p. 268 below.

156 Uṣ (ed. Jahier and Noureddine), pp. 36–40.

heritage. The consequence of this intellectual poverty was that *falsafah* came to Spain from the East, and even then through a variety of secondhand influences, chiefly through Mu'tazilite sources[157] and a conglomeration of Gnostic and Neoplatonic material.[158] Nor did the severity of Spanish orthodoxy allow it that brief period of grace that led to the flowering of Peripatetic studies in ninth- and tenth-century Baghdad. Almost from the beginning *falsafah* was an object of suspicion in Spain.

The first direct contact with the main stream of Peripateticism comes with the *faylasūf* Ibn Abdūn who resided in Baghdad in A.D. 956–971, and studied with Abū Sulaymān and Thābit ibn Sinān.[159] With Ibn Abdūn begins the growth of Aristotelianism in Spain; on his return he taught al-Kattani (d. *ca.* A.D. 1029) who was, in turn, the professor of Ibn Ḥazm (d. A.D. 1064).[160]

But Ibn Ḥazm is not an Aristotelian in any proper sense of the word. He may adapt facets of the Aristotelian system, but it is for ends that lie outside the domain of philosophy. A slightly younger contemporary, Abū al-Ṣalt Umayyah (d. A.D. 1134),[161] who spent the years A.D. 1096–1111 in Egypt, is closer to the tradition, and his *Taqwīm al-dhihn*[162] is a fairly straightforward reworking of the Aristotelian logic. But here, too, it is still a question of secondary, derivative Aristotelianism. The texts themselves are nowhere in sight.

The situation does not change until the time of Ibn Bājjah (d. A.D. 1138), the first great Spanish Peripatetic.[163] The bibliographers

157. See Cruz Hernandez, *Filosofia Musulmana*, I, 211–14.

158. *Ibid.*, I, 221–25.

159. Ṣā'id (trans. Blachère), p. 71.

160. For Ibn Ḥazm's encyclopedia see p. 112, n. 52 above. The best guide to this difficult period before Ibn Bājjah is the article by D. M. Dunlop, "Philosophical Predecessors and Contemporaries of Ibn Bājjah," *Islamic Quarterly*, II (1955), 100–16.

161. Uṣ (ed. Jahier and Noureddine), pp. 54–80; *GAL*, I², 641, Suppl. I, p. 889; J. M. Millas, art. *s.v. EI²*, I, 149.

162. A. Gonzalez Palencia (ed. and trans.) (Madrid, 1915).

163. Uṣ. (ed. Jahier and Noureddine), pp. 80–87; Qifṭi, p. 406; Ibn Khallikān (trans. de Slane), pp. 130–33; *GAL*, I², 601, Suppl. I, p. 830; Cruz Hernandez, *Filosofia Musulmana*, I, 337–68; D. M. Dunlop, "Remarks on the Life and Works of Ibn Bājjah," *Proceedings of the 22nd International Congress of Orientalists* (Leyden, 1957), pp. 188–95. One of the basic Ibn Bājjah MSS, Berlin Ahlwardt, # 5060 (Wetzstein I, 87), disappeared "toward the East" at the end of World War II; see the remarks of Prof. Kahle in *RAAD*, XXXIII (1958), 97.

credit him with a series of commentaries on Aristotle and, equally significant, glosses on al-Fārabi's commentaries.[164] Ibn Bājjah not only had the text of Aristotle at hand, but he was also working directly in the tradition of al-Fārabi and Ibn Sīnā, who came into Spain with the same wave of influences which, in the half-century A.D. 1050–1100, introduced both the *Rasā'il* of the Sincere Brethren, and the works of al-Ghazāli. It is ironic that the full strength of the *falsafah* tradition begins emerging in Spain at the time when it has run its course in the East and is being absorbed into *kalām*.But such is exactly the case with Ibn Bājjah; his published works place him in direct affiliation with Baghdad Peripateticism, and particularly with al-Fārabi.[165]

The work of Ibn Rushd (d. A.D. 1198),[166] to an even more marked degree than that of his predecessor, indicates a reversal in the course of *falsafah*. The *falsafah* tradition had been moving, chiefly under the influence of Ibn Sīnā, away from the texts themselves in the direction of general works of synthesis. Indeed, in eastern Islam the *corpus* finally disappeared from sight, and with it the whole tradition of scholarly Aristotelianism pursued with such care and fidelity in the school of Baghdad. For the later *mutakallimūn* Aristotle was an *auctoritas*, usually mediated through Ibn Sīnā.

With Ibn Rushd there is a return to the text. In A.D. 1168 he had been introduced in the court of the Almohad "philosopher-king" Abū Ya'qūb Yūsuf (d. A.D. 1184) by his mentor Ibn Ṭufayl.[167] Ibn

164. Uṣ. (ed. Jahier and Noureddine), pp. 84–85. Many of these are still extant though unfortunately none has been published.

165. *Tadbīr al-mutawaḥḥid*, ed. and trans. M. Asin Palacios, *El Regimen del Solitario* (Madrid, 1946); *Risālah al-widā'*, ed. and trans. *idem*, "La Carta de Adios de Avempace," *Al-Andalus*, VIII (1943), 1–87; *Risālah al-ittiṣāl*, ed. and trans. *idem*, "Tratado de Avempace sobre la union del intellecto con el hombre," *Al-Andalus*, VII (1942), 1–47, and text alone in A. Ahwani, *Ibn Rushd. Talkhīṣ kitāb al-nafs* (Cairo, 1950), pp. 102–18; *Risālah fī al-nafs*, ed. M. Al-Mas'umi (Damascus, 1960); see *idem*, *RAAD*, XXXIII (1958), 96–111.

166. Complete bibliography in *GAL*, I², 604–606, Suppl. I, pp. 833–36, and Cruz Hernandez, *Filosofia Musulmana*, II, 27–30, to which should be added: R. Arnaldez, "La pensée religieuse d'Averroes," *Studia Islamica*, VII (1957), 99–114, VIII (1957), 15–28, X (1959), 23–41; M. Fakhry, *Islamic Occasionalism and its Critique by Averroes and Aquinas* (London, 1958), pp. 83–138; E. I. J. Rosenthal, *Political Thought in Medieval Islam* (Cambridge, 1958), pp. 175–209.

167. Ibn Rushd himself calls him a "philosopher-king" in his commentary on Plato's *Republica*.

Rushd was then forty-two years of age, the well-known author of a medical encyclopedia, the *Kullīyāt*, whose work on Aristotle by then consisted of a series of minor paraphrases (the *jawāmiʿah*) on the *Organon*. Al-Marrākushi describes what followed:

> *Abū Bakr ibn Ṭufayl summoned me (Ibn Rushd) one day and told me, "Today I heard the Prince of Believers complain of the difficulty of expression of Aristotle and his translators, and mention the obscurity of his aims, saying, 'If someone would tackle those books, summarize them (yulakhkhiṣuhā) and expound their aims, after understanding them thoroughly, it would be easier for people to grasp them.' So if you have in you abundant strength for the task, perform it. I expect you will be equal to it, from what I know of the excellence of your mind, the purity of your nature, and the intensity of your application to science. I myself am only prevented from this undertaking by my age, as you see, my occupation with government service, and the devotion of my attention to matters which I hold more important." Abū al-Walīd (Ibn Rushd) said: "This is what led me to summarize (talkhīṣ) the books of the philosopher Aristotle.*[168]

Thus began the series of major Aristotelian commentaries which extended over the rest of his life to within three years of his death in A.D. 1198.[169]

The series opens with the type implicitly demanded by Yūsuf, expanded paraphrases of the type known as *talkhīs*,[170] which differ only in scale from the earlier *jawāmiʿah*. There is an interruption in the period A.D. 1179–1180 when Ibn Rushd turns toward pressing questions of theology. These are the three opuscula on the relationship of *falsafah* and revealed religion, the *Faṣl al-maqāl*, *Damīmah*, and

II, iii, 1–2, and XVII, 3; on his career, see the sketch in Hourani's work cited in note 168 below.

168. *Muʿjib*, pp. 174–75; trans. by G. Hourani, *Averroes on the Harmony of Religion and Philosophy* (London, 1961), p. 13.

169. For the *Aristotelica* see Uṣ (ed. Jahier and Noureddine), pp. 136–39; Alonso, *Teologia*, pp. 51–98; Cruz Hernandez, *Filosofia Musulmana*, II, 47–64; H. Wolfson, *Speculum*, VI (1931), 412–27.

170. See p. 97 above.

al-Kashf ʿan manāhij al-adillah,[171] followed in A.D. 1180 by his answer to al-Ghazāli's *Tahāfut*, the *Tahāfut al-tahāfut*.[172] The Aristotelian commentaries are then résuméd, but in a completely new form. For the next ten years Ibn Rushd devoted himself to expounding parts of the *corpus* through the *tafsīrāt*,[173] the large and elaborate commentaries *per modum commenti* on the *Analytica posteriora* (1180), *Physica* (1186), *De coelo* (1188), *De anima* (1190), and *Metaphysica* (1190). Done in the Greek tradition of Alexander of Aphrodisias, they represent, with their massive learning and control of both the text and the previous literature of comment, the apogee of Aristotelianism in Islam.

In one sense these commentaries are the continuation and culmination of the *falsafah* tradition; Ibn Rushd draws continuously from his Arab predecessors: al-Fārabi, Ibn al-Ṭayyib, Ibn Sīnā, Ibn Bājjah. But from another point of view they are a rejection of that tradition, and particularly of the Avicennan version of that compound of Aristotelian and Neoplatonic thought which had begun to be assembled in late Antiquity and which was so much a part of *falsafah*. Not only does Ibn Rushd disassociate himself from these Neoplatonic positions,[174] but it is notable that he did not, with the dubious exception of the *De plantis*, comment a single one of the *pseudepigraphica*. Indeed, this disassociation from the Neoplatonic synthesis forms the basis of a good deal of the argumentation in the *Tahāfut al-tahāfut*. Ibn Rushd will answer al-Ghazāli as a philosopher, not, however, as an Avicennan, but as an Aristotelian.[175]

The approach in the *opuscula* is quite different. Here Ibn Rushd borrows a Ghazālian technique and meets the theologians' objections

171. M. J. Muller (ed.), *Philosophie und Theologie von Averroes* (Leyden, 1859); trans. *idem* (Munich, 1875); ed. G. Hourani ([Leyden, 1959] extracts only from Kashf), and trans. *idem*, *Averroes on the Harmony of Religion and Philosophy* (London, 1961).

172. M. Bouyges (ed.), (Beyrouth, 1930); (trans.) S. Van den Bergh (2 vols.; London, 1954).

173. See pp. 93–94 above.

174. See for example, *Tahāfut* (ed. Bouyges), p. 184 (trans. Van den Bergh), p. 111, where he rejects emanationism, as well as the series of texts cited in Cruz Hernandez, *Filosofia Musulmana*, II, 71–75.

175. A freedom from Ibn Sīnā does not, of course, imply an entirely radical Aristotelianism; Ibn Rushd never freed himself from the Greek commentators, particularly Alexander of Aphrodisias.

to *falsafah* on their own grounds. The forces of Ash'arism were strong in the Peninsula, and during most of his career, Ibn Rushd, despite the protection of an enlightened prince, had to contend with the orthodox *fuqahā'* and their popular supporters, an opposition which in A.D. 1195 gained the ear of Yūsuf's successor and took the form of a violent persecution of the *falāsifah*.[176] The *Faṣl* and its related treatises were written before those unhappy days, but they reflect some of the atmosphere of hostility which must have been present long before that last virulent outburst.

The events of A.D. 1195 that led to the banishment of Ibn Rushd are not important in themselves. They are only another intermittent symbol of Islamic orthodoxy's inability to accept the *falsafah* tradition and especially in the case of a thinker as bold and as outspoken as Ibn Rushd. Assimilation there was—the entire history of *kalām* shows it—but when confronted with radical *falsafah*, Islamic orthodoxy reacted with determination and frequently with violence.

They all perished together, Spanish Islam, Arabian Aristotelianism, and Ibn Rushd. But there were heirs; within a century all three had come to life again at the University of Paris.

176. Marrākushi, *Mu'jib*, pp. 223–25.

EPILOGUE: THE EASTERN AND THE WESTERN ARISTOTLE

N. A. Daniel has recently retold the story of the misunderstandings and the distortions in the medieval West's attitude toward Islam.[1] It is an unhappy tale, but it has, fortunately, a brighter counterpart: while the Christian could not and would not look upon the Muslim as a slightly misled believer in the One True Deity, the medieval scholar recognized and acknowledged the community of interest and heritage that linked him to Cordova and Baghdad, as well as to contemporary Paris and ancient Athens. Beginning about A.D. 1100 for the sciences and some fifty years later for philosophy, the intellectual life of Western Christendom and Eastern Islam joined and held contact in Spain[2] and Sicily.[3]

For philosophy these contacts resulted in the new translations of Aristotle done in Latin, though frequently by way of a vernacular intermediary prepared by an Arab or Jewish collaborator,[4] from the

1. *Islam and the West* (Edinburgh, 1958).

2. At Toledo, chiefly by scholars like Dominic Gundisalvo and Ibn Dāwūd who were connected with the court of the Archbishop Raymond of Toledo (A.D. 1126–1151), and by Herman the German (d. A.D. 1187), and Alfred of Sareshel (*fl. ca.* A.D. 1187), all of whom either were trained or worked in Spain; see pp. 224–225 below.

3. The only Aristotelian translator working in Sicily at this time was Henry Aristippus who held a high position at the court of William I of Sicily (d. A.D. 1166); see p. 225, n. 10 below.

4. None of these intermediary vernacular translations has survived. There are, of course, Hispanicisms visible in the Latin translations prepared in Spain just as there are Syriacisms in the Arabic translations, but for a study of the techniques employed in the Western vernacular versions, recourse must be had to more popular works like the Alexander Romance and *Kalīlah wa Dimnah* for which Castilian translations have been preserved; see, for example,

Arabic. Viewed in terms of their effect on Western thought, these new translations of the *corpus* were of only secondary import; from about the same time, *ca.* A.D. 1150, the West's narrow Boethian base of Greco-Latin translations was being widened by new versions also done from the Greek and completely independent of what was going on in Spain and Sicily. Of far greater impact, however, was a related aspect of Islamic Aristotelianism, the translation of the Muslim and Jewish scholastics, al-Kindi (Alkindius) al-Fārābi (Alpharabius), Ibn Sīnā (Avicenna), al-Ghazāli (Algazel), Ibn Bājjah (Avempace), Ibn Jabīrol (Avencebrol), Ibn Maymūm (Maimonides), and Ibn Rushd (Averroes), all of whom came to the Latins as fully accredited interpreters of Aristotle.

The effect of this new material was immediate and electric. Shortly after A.D. 1200 the influence of Ibn Sīnā began manifesting itself in the Arts Faculty of Oxford and Paris, followed some thirty years later by the first suggestions of Averroism. The outcry mounted and in A.D. 1277, the church began to purge itself of the more obviously heretical theses of the *falsafah* tradition. Even then, the influence of Ibn Rushd was be no means dead; repulsed by the theological faculties, this particular brand of Aristotelianism found a refuge in the Italian universities, where it continued to thrive as a philosophical movement until well into the seventeenth century.

Thus, for about one hundred and fifty years, the books of the Arab philosophers were studied in Christian Europe without prejudice to the reader's orthodoxy,[5] and though scholars like Albert the Great or Thomas Aquinas might be harsh in their judgments on Islam, they approached a text of Ibn Sīnā or Ibn Rushd with a quite different frame of mind.

Modern historians of philosophy have not been unmindful of this rather interesting and romantic chapter in the history of Western thought, but by reason of the many scholarly and temperamental

J. Alemany, *La antiqua version castellana del Calila y Dimna cotejado con al original arabe de la misma* (Madrid, 1915), and A. Hottinger, *Kalila und Dimna. Ein Versuch zur Darstellung der arabisch-altspanischen Übersetzungskunst* (Bern, 1956).

5. The Arab scientific books were read for a considerably longer period; see G. Sarton, "Scientific Literature transmitted through the Incunabula," *Osiris*, V (1948), 41–245.

problems involved, they have tended to treat the Arab philosophers in terms of their Latin translations,[6] even though many of these, most notably Ibn Sīnā's, are still unedited and represent but a fraction of the work of these men and only a part of the overall vision of *falsafah*.

It is clear, then, that even though Aristotelianism represents an unbroken tradition that stretches across eighteen or nineteen centuries from the philosopher's death, it is still possible to distinguish various stages in its progress. Some attention has already been paid to what might be called its ancient stage, when both the substance and methodology of Aristotelianism was being formulated and organized.[7] What follows, the medieval phase, is essentially one of transmission, even though the system continues to grow through the inevitable syncretism, usually effected through the *pseudepigraphica*, as well as the contributions of individual thinkers whose own insights flow into the literature of comment and thus into the system itself.

The medieval, transmission phase of Aristotelianism has two separate moments. This book has been concerned with one of them: the progress of Aristotelianism into the oriental world of Islam. The other Aristotelianism, the passage of Aristotle into Western Christianity, took place under quite different linguistic and cultural circumstances, Yet the two show a remarkable series of parallels.

The first parallel is both obvious and fundamental to the rest: in both Latin and Arab Peripateticism, Aristotle is represented by a translation literature extending over rather long periods. In the West it began *ca.* A.D. 355 with the Latin version of the *Categoriae* of Marius Victorinus and, more importantly, with the work of Boethius who, *ca.* A.D. 507, set himself to translating the entire *Organon*. Only the *Categoriae* and the *De interpretatione* are preserved,[8] but he

6. The same criticism applies to the editors of philosophical texts, both in Greek and in Arabic, who do not consult the parallel *testimonia*. Editors of Aristotle have, save for Minio-Paluello, generally neglected the Oriental versions, nor have the editors of *Aristoteles arabus* shown any interest in the manuscript material on the Arabo-Latin translations.

7. See Chap. I, above.

8. Though he cites elsewhere what are apparently his versions of the *Analytica priora* and *Topica*; see *De differentiis topicis* in *PL*, LXIV, 1173C, 1184D, 1216D.

provided the only direct textual contact with Aristotle for a philosophical and theological culture that was primarily oriented toward Plato and the Neoplatonists.

From *ca.* A.D. 1150, there began appearing in the West new translations from Greek and Arabic reworking the Logic and covering the rest of the *corpus* as well. The versions from Arabic were completed about the middle of the thirteenth century but were soon supplanted by a new wave of translations from the Greek. The final series, again from the Greek, were produced in Italy in the fifteenth century by men like Theodore of Gaza (d. *ca.* A.D. 1473), George of Trebizond (d. A.D. 1485/1486), and John Argyropolis (d. A.D. 1486), names that ring of Byzantium and the Renaissance.

The oriental translations begin at about the same time as the Latin *veteres*. The earliest known examples are those of Probha (*fl. ca.* A.D. 450), not, however, into Arabic, but into Syriac. In Islam as in the West there existed a bilingual intermediary group: the Muslims and Jews of Spain for the Western Scholastic, and the Syrian Christians for the Muslim. The climax of this early translation literature was in the work of Sergius (d. A.D. 536) and the translators trained by Severus Sebokht (d. A.D. 667).

In neither the post-Boethius West nor the post-Probha East was it simply a question of a purely philosophical tradition. Before Aristotelianism came East or West in its Syro-Arab or Latin garb, it had been met by another powerful tradition, Christianity, and both had come away from the encounter transformed. The Patristic synthesis of Aristotle and Revelation was only part of a much larger pattern which emerging Christianity had worked out as a *modus vivendi* with its pagan heritage. Both the Syriac and Latin *veteres* occur in this context: they were restricted to the parts of the Logic that were of immediate use to the study of theology.

What disturbed the equilibrium of this first Christian synthesis of Aristotle was a fresh outburst of translation activity in the centers of mixed culture: Syro-Arab Baghdad, Muslim-Christian Toledo, and Greek-Arab-Norman Palermo flashed with the striking of old flint into new tinder. In Baghdad between *ca.* A.D. 770 and A.D. 1000, alsmost the entire *corpus* and a great number of Greek commentators as well were translated into Arabic. Similarly in the West, James of Venice (*fl. ca.* A.D. 1150–1180),[9] Henry Aristippus (d. A.D. 1162),[10] and Gerard of Cremona (d. A.D. 1187)[11] introduced the "new Aristotle" of the latter sections of the *Organon*, the *naturalia*, the *psychologica*, and the *metaphysica*,[12] while in Toledo, Dominic Gundisalvo (d. A.D. 1181)[13] and Ibn Dāwūd (Avendeath), who flourished in the middle of the same century,[14] made available in Latin translation the comment or near-comment of a number of eminent *falāsifah*.

Something has already been said of the effect of these translations in the Islamic milieu. They opened the world of the Hellenes to the medieval Arab and transformed his view of history and of the sciences. More pertinent to "professional" Aristotelianism was the foundation of a philosophical school in Baghdad *ca.* A.D. 900 and the beginnings of the *falsafah* tradition. Within a generation this small group of scholars was turning its attention to the editing and commenting of the newly arrived corpus, an interlude of perhaps a century (A.D. 920–1020), which bears comparison with anything done earlier in Alexandria or later in Paris.

The analogous philosophical movement in the West provoked by the "new Aristotle" is less well known. Gundisalvo and Ibn Dāwūd, already mentioned as translators, were also philosophers.[15] But Spain was merely the port of entry for the *Aristotelica*. Scholars trained there returned to the northern universities where they took up

9. See L. Minio-Paluello, "Jacobus Veneticus Graecus, Canonist and Translator of Aristotle," *Traditio*, VIII (1952), 265–304.

10. See the *Praefationes* to the editions of his translation of the *Meno* (*Plato Latinus*, I [London, 1940]) and the *Phaedo* (*Plato Latinus*, II [London, 1950]).

11. See B. Boncompagni, "Della vita e delle opere di Gherardo Cremonae," *Atti Lincei*, Ser. 1, Vol. IV (1851), 387–449.

12. For the history of these translations see M. Grabmann, "Aristoteles im 12. Jahrhundert," *Mittelalterliches Geistesleben*, III (Munich, 1956), 64–124.

13. See M. Alonso, "Las traducciones del arcediano Domingo Gundisalvo," *al-Andalus*, XII (1947), 295–338; on the date of his death *ibid.*, VIII (1943), 155–88.

14. See M. Alonso, "Traducciones del arabe al latin por Juan Hispano (Ibn Dāwūd)," *al-Andalus*, XVII (1952), 129–51; M.-T. d'Alverny, "Avendauth?" *Homenaje a Millas-Vallicrosa*, I (Barcelona, 1954), 19–43.

15. See M. Alonso, "Ibn Sīnā y sus primeras influencias en el Mundo Latino," *Revista del Instituto Egipcio de Estudios Islamicos*, I (1953), 36–57.

careers of teaching and writing. Roger of Hereford, Alexander Neckham, and Alfred Sareshel, all connected in one way or other with Spain or Sicily, wrote on the new Aristotle in England *ca.* A.D. 1200; lectures on the *libri naturales* were begun at Oxford in the first decade of the thirteenth century by John Blund.[16]

We can only surmise that the same thing was happening in Paris at about the same time, since in A.D. 1210 and 1215 there appeared the famous ecclesiastical bans against the study and reading, *publice vel secreto*, of the *libri naturales* of Aristotle[17] and, significantly, his commentators and abbreviators, probably a reference to the *falāsifah*, and primarily to Ibn Sīnā's *Kitāb al-shifā'*.[18]

What was the significance of the Paris ban? The current opinion is that it was promoted by the Theology Faculty in an effort to block what was considered dangerous philosophical proclivities in the Faculty of Arts, a group traditionally associated with the study of grammar, rhetoric, and logic.[19]

Indeed, this was the reason behind the prohibitions of A.D. 1210–1215, the concern of conservative theologians over the strong new current of Aristotelianism and its effects on the theogical synthesis finds its parallel in a strikingly similar reaction on the part of the orthodox in Islam against the growth in authority of the Aristotelian *falāsifah* in their midst. We have seen that almost from the beginning of the translation movement the problematic and material of Greek philosophy was being adopted for the solution of theological problems. The Mu'tazilite philosopher-theologians mingled in the philosophical circles at the Caliphal court and were accused by their opponents of having derived their godless ideas from the Greeks. Indeed, the subversion of traditional ideas was even

16. On the early English Aristotelians see D. A. Callus, *Introduction of Aristotelian Learning to Oxford* (*Proceedings of the British Academy* XXIX [London, 1943]).
17. H. Denifle, *Chartularium Universitatis Parisiensis*, I, # 11 and # 20.
18. See R. de Vaux, *Notes et Textes sur l'Avicennisme Latin* (*Bibliothèque thomiste*, XX [Paris, 1934]), pp. 45–54.
19. See M. Grabmann, *I divieti ecclesiastici di Aristotele sotto Innocenzo III e Gregorio IX* (Rome, 1941), pp. 57–69. The entire question of Aristotle in the Paris of the thirteenth century has been treated by F. Van Steenberghen in his excellent *Aristotle in the West. The Origins of Latin Aristotelianism*, trans. by L. Johnson (Louvain, 1955).

more radical than in the West which already had a Greek-model theology with which to confront the new Islamic version of Aristotle. The traditionalists in Islam had no such weapon at this stage. The reaction, born of rage and frustration, was not long in coming.

It is one of the myths of Muslim theological historiography that al-Ash'ari deserted the Mu'tazilites in A.D. 912 and forged the instrument of *kalām*, that peculiar blend of traditional material and Greek methodology, against their impieties, and *kalām* thus carried the day and became the official stance of Islam. The reality was quite otherwise. The Ash'arite brand of *kalām* was not very different from the kind of thing that had been evolving in Mu'tazilite circles, and when the extreme orthodox Hanbalites, who had suffered during the earlier Mu'tazilite ascendency (A.D. 833–848), rose up against their tormentors, they made no distinction between Ash'arite and Mu'tazilite: both had tampered with the Qur'anic legacy.[20]

The Hanbalites did not have the ecclesiastical apparatus of the Theology Faculty at Paris, but they possessed the connivance of the civil arm, and for over a century Baghdad rang with the terror of a Hanbalite witch hunt. An exactly parallel reaction took place in Spain where the vizier of Hāshim II, al-Manṣūr (d. A.D. 1002), burned the philosophical texts in the library of Cordova at the instigation of the orthodox *fuqahā'*.

In the West, theology had gone too far down the Hellenic path to be confronted with a simple choice of Hanbalism or *kalām*. A Hanbalite attitude had perhaps been possible for a Peter Damian (d. A.D. 1072), but it was no longer feasible in the first half of the thirteenth century. Bonaventure apart, the citadel fell quietly and swiftly: while the Parisian Arts Faculty observed the ban on the *libri naturales* in the decades after A.D. 1215 and contented itself with logical and ethical studies, Aristotelianism, lightly wearing its Arab garb, passed in among the theologians. From the time of William of Auvergne, writing *ca.* A.D. 1225, there is an almost

20. See the remarks of Ibn Taymīyah on al-Ash'ari in his *Minhāj*, IV, 154, and the *Bugyat*, p. 105; according to Ibn Taymīyah, al-Ash'ari and his successors still bore the Mu'tazilite stigma of his teachers.

tangible Avicennan Aristotelianism present in the thinking of the Parisian *magistri regentes*.[21]

Within a very short time, *ca.* A.D. 1230–1240, a new force began exerting itself in theological studies. The Latin translations of Ibn Rushd, done by Michael Scotus in Spain and in Sicily,[22] made their appearance in Paris at about this time and initiated a new orientation—and reaction—to Aristotle. But the description of Latin Averroism must be postponed for a closer look at the synthesis of philosophy and *kalām*.

In both Paris and Baghdad, theology learned to live with the new Aristotle. In the West, the synthesis is chiefly associated with the names of Albert the Great (d. A.D. 1280) and Thomas Aquinas (d. A.D. 1274); in the East, it was effected by what are at first glance two very unlikely candidates: Ibn Sīnā (d. A.D. 1037), a philosopher who ostensibly rejected theology, and al-Ghazāli (d. A.D. 1111), author of *The Destruction of Philosophy*.

The situation in Paris about the middle of the thirteenth century was similar to that in Baghdad in A.D. 950. Al-Fārābi had just died, but his work was carried forward by Yaḥyā ibn ʿAdi and his students. Al-Nadīm, a friend of Yaḥyā, writing in A.D. 987, has left a bibliography of work done in the school, a catalog that manages to catch some of the excitement generated by the "new learning." But the Peripatetic school, apparently untouched by the Hanbalite

21. The description and analysis of this phase of Aristotelianism has generated a bibliography of imposing proportions. Beginning with the now-classic studies by Etienne Gilson, "Pourquoi Saint Thomas a critiqué Saint Augustin," *AHDL*, I (1926–1927), 5–128, and "Les sources greco-arabes de l'Augustinisme avicennisant," *ibid.*, IV (1929), 5–149, the role of Ibn Sīnā in the theological speculation of the early thirteenth century has been traced in increasingly elaborate detail; see the résumé of the discussions in F. van Steenberghen, *The Philosophical Movement in the Thirteenth Century* (London, 1955), pp. 3–18. The influence of Ibn Sīnā did not cease with the ascendency of the Averroean point of view; it is pervasive in St. Thomas as can be seen in the textual analysis of C.Vansteenkiste, "Avicenna-Citaten bij S. Thomas," *Tijdschrift voor Philosophie*, XV (1953), 457–507, and in the more metaphysical study by A. Forest, *La Structure metaphysique du concret selon Saint Thomas d'Aquin* (Paris, 1931).

22. Michael was in Spain before A.D. 1224 when he joined the Papal Curia; the period *ca.* A.D. 1228–1236 was spent at the court of Frederick II in Sicily; see C. H. Haskins, "Michael Scot in Spain," *Estudios Eruditos in memoriam Adolfo Bonilla y San Martin*, II (Madrid, 1930), 129–34; *idem*, "Michael Scot and Frederick II," *Isis*, IV (1921–1922), 250–75, and M. Grabmann, "Kaisar Frederich II und sein Verhältnis zur aristotelischen und arabischen Philosophie," *Mittelalterliches Geistesleben*, II (Munich, 1936), 103–37.

difficulties, suddenly disappears from view after the death of Abū al-Faraj ibn al-Ṭayyib in A.D. 1043.

In Paris the ban against Aristotle began being disregarded on the Arts Faculty sometime *ca.* 1240, when the Englishmen Roger Bacon and Robert Kilwardby were lecturing there on the *libri naturales*. In A.D. 1255, the situation had so changed that the entire *corpus* was officially restored to the syllabus of the Faculty of Arts.[23] It was in this atmosphere that Albert began his encyclopedic paraphrase that would "render Aristotle intelligible to the Latins,"[24] an open embrace of the Greek philosopher by an esteemed member of the theological side of the House.

Ibn Sīnā is an even more obvious product of the tenth-century Peripatetic renaissance in Baghdad. Though he did not belong formally to the school and was not on the best of terms with its current leader, Ibn al-Ṭayyib, he was an open and enthusiastic admirer of al-Fārābi, whom he considered quite the best of the Aristotelian commentators. His own interest in Aristotle was acute but not slavish, and when he turned to commenting the *corpus*, he used the same paraphrastic approach later favored by Albert.

It is immediately evident that Ibn Sīnā and Albert had quite different views on philosophy and theology. Albert was a professional theologian who nonetheless held Aristotle in high esteem. Ibn Sīnā was a penetrating and justly celebrated philosopher who could not have been much impressed by the primitive state of contemporary *kalām*. The *Shifā'* is a work of philosophy pure and simple; so, too, are Albert's paraphrases, and the two projects accomplished the same end: by reason of the reputation of their authors and the stature of the works themselves, Aristotle could no longer be ignored by the theologians.

The task of responding fell to two theologians with excellent credentials: Thomas Aquinas and al-Ghazāli. Thomas' was by far the easier charge, for what Albert had posed was not a challenge but a lead, and the Italian's effective synthesis of Aristotelianism with the

23. See H. Denifle, *op. cit.*, I, 277–79.
24. See p. 105, n. 31 above.

older Augustinian tradition was the logical conclusion of a process already begun by his German professor. It was accomplished by adaptation: distinguishing Aristotle from his commentators,[25] accepting what could be accepted and made sense, and practicing a judicious *ta'wīl* on the rest.

Ghazāli's *Tahāfut* is, needless to say, no *Summa theologica*; there is no adaptation here. Nor is it, again, exactly what it describes itself to be. A destruction of philosophy would presumably involve a destruction of the philosophical method. What we find instead are twenty propositions, three of which are heretical, while the rest are what a Western theologian might term temerarious. Al-Ghazāli proceeds to the attack not as a theologian but as a philosopher *inter pares*; the propositions are shown to be bad philosophy. Whatever al-Ghazāli may have intended, the implication of the *Tahāfut* is clear for all to see: by meeting the philosophers, principally Ibn Sīnā, on their own terms, the battle was shifted to a ground where the opponents of philosophy could not hope to win, and post-Ghazāli *kalām* is, in fact, nothing more than philosophy's progressive occupation of territory already tacitly ceded by al-Ghazāli, a Saint Thomas *malgré lui*.[26]

It was a dearly-bought victory for both sides. *Kalām* was progressively more *falsafah*-ridden both in form and in substance, but *falsafah* itself no longer had an independent existence in the Islamic East. Ibn Sīnā's disciples descend, within a generation, into a faceless mediocrity; the school of Baghdad ends with the death of Ibn al-Ṭayyib in A.D. 1043. Both Abū al-Barakāt (d. A.D. 1165) and 'Abd al-Laṭīf al-Baghdādi (d. A.D. 1231) are still worthy of the name of

25. In the West the commentators never replaced the texts as they did in the East after Ibn Sīnā. In the middle of the thirteenth century, William of Moerbeke, a Flemish Dominican, began a new series of translations from the Greek (see M. Grabmann, *Guglielmo di Moerbeke, O.P.* [Rome, 1946]) which effectively freed the Paris theologians from their Arab bondage. His translation of Proclus' *Elementatio theologica*, for example, was completed in A.D. 1268, and shortly thereafter, Thomas, in commenting the *De causis*, could identify this latter as a pseudepigraph derived from Proclus, a piece of intelligence never vouchsafed to the Arabs who considered the *De causis* as Aristotle's to the end.

26. This was precisely the judgment rendered on him when, *ca.* A.D. 1106, his works were introduced into Spain and shortly thereafter committed to the flames by the orthodox *fuqahā'* of Cordova; see al-Marrākushi, *Mu'jib*, p. 64.

faylasuf, but the rest, if it is not silence, is not much more than a whisper.[27]

The philosophical tradition in Spain, which had early and direct contact with the Baghdad Peripatetics, managed to survive. The glories of Spanish Peripateticism, Ibn Bājjah (d. A.D. 1138) and Ibn Rushd (d. A.D. 1198), postdate the influence of al-Ghazāli, whose works came to the peninsula *ca.* A.D. 1106, but the work of Ibn Rushd, pregnant with the possibilities of a renewal of scholarly Aristotelianism in Islam, found no successor. In July, A.D. 1212, Spanish Islam received its death blow at Las Navas de Tolosa.

Averroism, however, was far from dead. Ibn Rushd's commentaries, translated into Latin by Michael Scotus, made their appearance in Paris *ca.* A.D. 1230–1240. The repercussions were manifold. First, they promoted the growth of Aristotelian scholarship, a return to the texts and the exegetical commentary from the cruder *quaestiones* of Roger Bacon and paraphrases of Albert. Secondly, Ibn Rushd himself presented a threat to Crhistian theology, particularly in his peculiar doctrine of the unity of the possible intellect.[28] Finally, there is the vexed question of Latin Averroism.

In A.D. 1277, Stephan Tempier, Bishop of Paris, published a list of 219 condemned propositons.[29] From *ca.* A.D. 1266, what were the personal positions of Ibn Rushd had developed into a movement

27. The reasons for this are as complex as the reasons for the more general cultural decline which settled over Islam at about this time. *Falsafah's* failure to infiltrate the school system has been touched upon on pp. 74–75 above, and in a symposium held in Bordeaux in 1957 to discuss the general *anakylosis* in Islam, Arnaldez made reference to one of the decay germs lodged in the entrails of *falsafah* itself: "La raison philosophique de cette ankylose . . . semble être celle que nous signalions au début: une sorte de cécité intellectuelle en face des problèmes véritablement philosophiques . . . elle s'est attachée à des points de détail ou à des questions secondaires . . . sans jamais définir un problème d'ampleur vraiement philosophique . . . Les causes historiques d'ordre général, une ambiance fermée d'orthodoxie réligieuse ont pû favoriser et accélerer ce mouvement de décadence; elles ne suffisaient à la déterminer et a l'expliquer." See R. Brunschvig and G. von Grunebaum, *Classicisme et déclin culturel dans l'histoire de l'Islam* (Paris, 1957), p. 259; compare Cruz Hernandez, *Filosofia Musulmana*, II, 8–9.

28. The reaction to this position was somewhat slow in building up; the first refutation was apparently Albert's *De unitate intellectus contra Averroem* (*ca.* A.D. 1256); on Albert and Ibn Rushd see D. Salman, "Albert le Grand et l'averroisme latin," *Revue des sciences philosophiques et théologiques*, XXIV (1935), 38–64, and R. Miller, "An Aspect of Averroes' Influence on Saint Albert," *Mediaeval Studies*, XXVI (1954), 57–71.

29. H. Denifle, *Chartularium*, I, 543–88.

within the Parisian Arts Faculty,[30] and it was against this movement that the decree was primarily aimed. The propositions include, as a matter of fact, far more than Averroean heterodox theses, and in its larger context the condemnation was directed against Aristotle's vision of the world and its workings, and against the Arabs' reckless pursuit of philosophical rationalism.[31] It was, in short, Christian theology's *Tahāfut* directed not now against the still somewhat conciliatory positions of al-Kindi, al-Fārābi, and Ibn Sīnā, but against the more intransigent rationalism of Ibn Rushd.[32]

The decree of A.D. 1277 was no more successful than al-Ghazāli's *Tahāfut*. The latter may have contributed to the decline of *falsafah* in eastern Islam, but it did not forestall Ibn Rushd at the other end of the Islamic world in Spain. Similarly, radical Aristotelianism, openly embracing Ibn Rushd as its patron, flourished in the universities of northern Italy after its rejection in Paris.[33] And while there was no aftermath to Ibn Rushd in Islam,[34] the tradition of a purely secular Aristotelianism runs well into the seventeenth century in the

30. The movement, variously called "Latin Averroism" and "heterodox Aristotelianism," is primarily associated with the name of Siger of Brabant (d. A.D. 1281). Siger's exact relationship to Ibn Rushd is still the subject of warm debate; see F. van Steenberghen, *The Philosophical Movement in the Thirteenth Century* (London, 1955), pp. 75–93.

31. On the wider implications of the prohibition, see E. Gilson, *History of Christian Philosophy in the Middle Ages* (London, 1955), pp. 406–10. In a curious postscript to the decree, M.-T. d'Alverny has described a Paris MS (BN *lat. 6286*), a *majmū'* whose Arab-derived sections had been mutilated in the wake of Stephan Tempier's proscription; see *AHDL*, XVII (1949), 223–48. The other side of the coin may be seen in the works of John of Gagow (d. A.D. 1507), who was for forty years professor in the Faculty of Arts at the University of Cracow. His five most frequently cited authorities are Ibn Sīnā (80 times), Albert (97 times), Thomas (128 times), Giles of Rome (161 times), and Ibn Rushd (213 times); see S. Swiezawski, *Mélanges E. Gilson* (Toronto-Paris, 1959), pp. 613–50.

32. The West did not know the treatises in which Ibn Rushd refined his position on the relationship of philosophy and the *sharī'ah*; the *Tahāfut al-tahāfut, Faṣl al-maqāl*, and *Kashq'an manāhij* were never translated into Latin.

33. On this phase of Averroism see E. Renan, *Averroes et l'Averroisme*[2] (Paris, 1861), pp. 322–424, and M. Grabmann, "Das Aristotelesstudium in Italien zur Zeit Dantes," *Mittelalterliches Geistesleben*, III (Munich, 1956), 197–212.

34. Was there ever a radical, damn-the-theological-consequences philosophical tradition in Islam? Al-Rāzi (d. A.D. 923)—who was not an Aristotelian—comes to mind (see pp. 170–172 above), but recently H. S. Nyberg has made the interesting suggestion that the notorious al-Rawāndi (see p. 139 n. 8 above) was just such a "radical Aristotelian," and that his persecution by Mu'tazilite and orthodox alike was due to his uncompromising embrace of the Aristotelian—and heretical—position on the eternity of the universe; see R.Brunschwig and G. von Grunebaum, *Classicisme et déclin culturel dans l'histoire d'Islam* (Paris, 1957), p. 133.

West, a tradition which was, in Gilson's words, "a repetitious and obdurate Aristotelianism. It forgot nothing; it learned nothing."

In reality, there were two such secular Aristotelianisms, and Gilson's remarks were addressed to the first of these. This was the Italian tradition which, in its final stages, saw the authority of Ibn Rushd, *che'l gran comento feo*, challenged by that of Alexander of Aphrodisias. The latter's patron was Pietro Pomponazzi (d. A.D. 1254) the dominant figure in Renaissance Averroism. Once again, the church reacted, and both positions, the Averroean and the Alexandran, on the immortality of the individual soul, were condemned in the Bull *Apostolici Regiminis*, issued in the eighth session (December 19, 1513) of the Fifth Lateran Council.

The second renaissance of Aristotelianism was that which grew not from a disenchanted Scholasticism, but from a more fruitful contact with the scholarly traditions of the Byzantine Empire. Mention has already been made of the new translations done from the Greek in the fifteenth century by men who had come from Constantinople to Italy in the train of the Council of Florence (A.D. 1438–1445). Though a Latin-minded theologian like Bessarion had on obvious interest in Scholasticism, the work of most of these Byzantine savants in Italy was oriented toward more peculiarly Renaissance interests; its context was not the University of Paris but the Mistra of George Gemistos Plethon and the Platonic Academy of Florence.[35]

It is idle to speculate what might have happened if fifteenth-century Islam had received an intellectual stimulant of the magnitude of the Greek impact on Europe. Such was not to be; Byzantium, India, and China, all potential sources of an Islamic *cinquecento*, never struck the spark, and nothing more was to be heard of the Aristotelian *corpus* in the East.

35. On Plethon and his circle see F. Masai, *Plethon et la platonisme de Mithra* (Paris, 1956); for Bessarion and his circle, L. Mohler, *Kardinal Bessarion als Theologe, Humanist, und Staatsmann* (3 vols.; Paderborn, 1923–1942); H.-G. Beck, *Kirche und theologische Literatur im byzantinischen Reich* (Munich, 1959), pp. 767–70, and G. Cammelli, *I dotti bizantini e l'origine dell'umanismo II Giovanni Argiropulo* (Florence, 1941).

There were, however, other developments in the tradition. We have already seen how, shortly after the introduction via translation of the "new Aristotle," a synthesis was worked out between theology and Aristotelianism. In the West, this took place in the middle decades of the thirteenth century. In the East, where theology was in a more primitive state at the beginning of the process, the synthesizing operation took the better part of three centuries (*ca.* A.D. 800–1100).

In neither case did the synthesis pass serenely to the next generation. From *ca.* A.D. 1270, the Thomistic "solution" was subjected to a series of attacks from the adherents of the older Augustinian approach to theology.[36] This so-called "controversy of the *correctoria*" was directed against a few isolated points in Thomas; it was succeeded by something far more portentous, a full-scale dismantling of the Thomistic synthesis. From Duns Scotus (d. A.D. 1308) through Durand of St. Porcain (d. A.D. 1334) to William of Ockham (d. *ca.* A.D. 1350) runs the course of a new tradition. Though these men differed among themselves on various points—William was the professed opponent of much that had been said by Scotus — they were in agreement on the relationship of theology and philosophy: the two elements so laboriously joined by Thomas were separate and distinct disciplines.[37] Thus began the *via moderna* in Western theology; radically empiricist and hence at base anti-rationalistic in its approach to theology, it was the school that dominated in the universities of England, France, and Germany dur-

36. See F. Ehrle, "Der Kampf um die Lehre des hl. Thomas in den ersten fünfzig Jahren nach seinem Tode," *Zeitschrift für katholische Theologie*, XXXVII (1913), 266–318; *idem*, "L'agostinismo e l'aristotelismo nella Scolastica del secolo XIII," *Xenia thomistica*, III (Rome, 1925), 14–21, 38–76, 517–88, and P. Glorieux, *Les premières polémiques thomistes I Le "Correctorium Corruptorri Quare"* (*Bibliothèque thomiste*, IX [Kain, 1927]).

37. The best introduction to this central movement of the fourteenth century is the series of studies done by C. Michalski which originally appeared in the *Bulletin de l'Academie polonaise des sciences et des lettres, Classe d'Histoire et de Philosophie* and which are here listed by the date of their Cracow offprints: "Les courants philosophiques a Oxford et a Paris pendant le XIVe siècle" (1921); "Les sources du criticisme et du scepticisme dans la philosophie du XIVe siècle" (1924); "Le criticisme et le scepticisme dans la philosophie du XIVe siècle" (1926); "Les courants critiques et sceptiques dans la philosophie du XIVe siècle" (1927); "La physique nouvelle et les différents courants philosophiques au XIVe siècle" (1928).

ing the fourteenth and fifteenth centuries, and was still being taught at Erfurt during Luther's student days there.[38]

The *correctoria* controversy finds its echoes in Islam; the period between Fakhr al-Dīn al-Rāzi (d. A.D. 1209) and al-Ṭūsi (d. A.D. 1274) witnessed the debate on the *Ishārāt*, a controversy not, it will be noted, about al-Ghazāli, but about his adversary, Ibn Sīnā. The struggle goes on as if al-Ghazāli had never written, and though Rāzi and Ṭūsi may differ on points of detail, they are both Avicennans and Hellenizers at heart.[39]

One looks in vain, however, for an attack on synthetic *kalām* of the magnitude of Latin Nominalism. Indeed, it is quite the contrary which is true. Ibn Khaldūn's analysis of post-Ghazali *kalām* has already been quoted,[40] and while his own sentiments are worthy of an Ockham, it is not they but the situation he is describing that is of interest here. The analysis is an accurate one and provides an interesting yardstick against which to measure the work of al-Ghazāli. Yet Ibn Khaldūn's view is not quite all-encompassing. Perhaps he passed over Ibn Taymīyah (d. A.D. 1328) because he considered him a *faqīh* rather than a theologian; but it is a perilous omission: the Hanbalite jurist represents the last serious attack on philosophizing *kalām* until modern times.

38. The most influential of the later scholastics in the Erfurt milieu were John of Wesel (d. A.D. 1480) and Gabriel Biel (d. A.D. 1495). The former was, on Luther's own testimony, still a force at the university: "Zu Erfurt die hohe Schule mit seinem Buchern regiert [hat), aus welchen ich daselbs auch bin Magister worden," i.e., *Magister artium* for which Luther pursued the course between A.D. 1501–1505 when he probably read some of John's commentaries on the *corpus*; see G. Ritter, "Studien zur Spatscholastik III Neue Quellenstücke zur Theologie des Johann von Wesel," *SBAWHeidelberg* (1926–1927), Heft 5. Luther's marginal notes on Biel's commentary on the *Sentences* have been preserved (ed. H. Degering [Weimar, 1933]). How much Luther was shaped in the school of Ockham apparently depends on what one thinks of Luther and/or Ockham. Catholic scholars (e.g., Denifle, Grisar), who care for neither, see Luther as a more deviant member of an already deviant tradition; Protestants, on the other hand, are not anxious to have their *Heldentheolog* reduced to the stature of a Gabriel Biel and hence tend to draw Luther away from the *via moderna*; see K. A. Meissinger, *Der katholische Luther* (Bern, 1952), pp. 104–106, and O. Scheel, *Martin Luther Vom Katholizimus zur Reformation*, II³ (Tübingen, 1930), 422–61.

39. See, for example, al-Rāzi's philosophical encyclopedia, *al-Mabāḥith al-mashriqīyah* (ed. Hyderabad, 1924), the discussions in the *Munāẓarāt* (analyzed by P. Kraus, *Islamic Culture*, XII [1938], 131–53, and al-Ṭūsi's logical treatise, *Asās al-iqtibās* [ed. Teheran, 1947]).

40. See p. 194 above.

There are obvious parallels that can be drawn between Ibn Taymīyah and Luther *vis à vis* the synthesis, but perhaps it is more instructive to dwell on the differences. There is, above all, a great difference in degree. What Luther did he did wholeheartedly. He was as immersed in *kalām* as the Muslim, but he managed to fight his way clear. Ibn Taymīyah was methodologically a *mutakallim* to the end.[41] Perhaps this was as much a question of history as of temperament. Luther was in a situation where the synthesis was disintegrating; if not he in his generation, then almost certainly another such man in the next would have arisen to deliver the blow. In the time of Ibn Taymīyah, *kalām* was petrifying; the Hanbalite was a theological sport.[42] It is also symptomatic of the differing circumstances that Luther could and did turn to an attack on Aristotle himself.[43] Ibn Taymīyah, true to the tradition of the times, could no longer see Aristotle clearly through his Muslim antagonists.

Almost contemporary with Ibn Taymīyah was al-Īji (d. A.D. 1355) and a line of commentators who, like Muslim Penelopes, do and undo the warp and woof of the now-classic texts of *kalām*. Much the same judgment has been passed on the Scholasticism of the fifteenth–seventeenth centuries in the West. From the restoration of Thomism by John Capreolus (d. A.D. 1444) down to Descartes' contemporary, John of St. Thomas (d. A.D. 1644), it is the age of the commentator. Without attempting a detailed comparison with something as little studied as postĪji *kalām*,[44] there are some important differences that spring to the eye, and at least one of these is germane in the present context. Later Islamic *kalām* had forgotten all but the name

41. See, for example, his *Qiyās fi al-shar' al-islāmi* where the analysis of *qiyās* is as Aristotelian as anything written by Ibn Sīnā.

42. Ibn Taymīyah the man and not the general Hanbalite attitude toward *falsafah* which is a fundamental strain running through almost the whole of Muslim history; see I. Goldziher, "Stellung der alten islamischen Orthodixie zu den antiken Wissenschaften," *Abh.AWBerlin* (1915), Heft 8.

43. See P. Petersen, *Geschichte der aristotelischen Philosophie im protestantischen Deutschland* (Leipzig, 1921), pp. 33–37. Like the pre-Fārābi Syrians, Luther had no objection to the logic as a propaedeutic; his quarrel was with the intrusion of it into theology.

44. Or, rather, post-Ghazali *kalām*; after A.D. 1111, orientalists appear to lose interest in the *mutakallimūn*; the only monuments to these men are some very bad Hyderabad lithographs of their works.

of Aristotle; the doctrine was still there buried beneath layers of Neoplatonism and Iranian exotica, but the texts themselves had disappeared, save, perhaps, for an occasional not-very-convincing citation, usually by way of Ibn Sīnā.

In the West, however, the tradition of scholarly Aristotelianism continued uninterrupted within the framework of Christian *kalām*. One example must suffice. With Francisco de Vittoria (d. A.D. 1546), the intellectual center of later Thomism had shifted from Italy and France to Spain and Portugal. It was in the theological faculty of the University of Coimbra that the Portuguese Jesuits began publishing the *Commentarii collegii coimbricensis Societatis Jesu* that covered the *corpus* in eight volumes,[45] a series not entirely unworthy of being set beside the other earlier monuments of a now-dying tradition, the works of Ibn Rushd and the *Commentaria in Aristotelem graeca.*

45. I. Emanuel de Goes (d. A.D. 1957), *In octo libros physicorum* (Coimbra, 1591); II. *Idem, In quattuor libros de coelo* (Coimbra, 1592); III. *Idem, In libros meteorum* (Coimbra, 1592); IV. *Idem, In libros qui parva naturalia appellantur* (Coimbra, 1592); V. *Idem, In libros ethicorum ad Nichomachum* (Coimbra, 1595); VI *Idem, In duos libros de generatione et corruptione* (Coimbra, 1595); VII. *Idem, In tres libros de anima*, ed. Cosmos Maggalliano: Balthazar Alvarez (d. A.D. 1630), *Tractatus de anima separata*; Cosmos Maggalliano (d. A.D. 1624), *Tractatio aliquot problematum ad quinque sensus sectantium* (Coimbra, 1595); VIII. Pedro da Fonseca (d. A.D. 1597), *In universam dialecticam Aristotelis*, ed. Sebastiao do Couto (Venice, 1606). Da Fonseca had previously commented the *Metaphysica* (Rome, 1577), but it did not form part of this collection.

APPENDIX: SOURCES FOR THE HISTORY OF THE ARISTOTELIAN TRADITION IN ISLAM

What the Arabs knew about the Greeks they knew from the Greeks; there is little evidence to suggest that the Muslim historian or philosopher attempted to puzzle out, on the basis of the available texts, the relationship of Plato, let us say, and Pythagoras. They had almost nothing to say on the subject of Neoplatonism, though they were themselves suffused with it, for the precise reason that their Greek sources apparently deserted them somewhere in the general vicinity of Middle Platonism.

The chief vehicles used by the Greeks to transmit material pertaining to the history of philosophy, the *bioi*, *diadoche*, and *peri haireseon* of the Hellenistic tradition, found rather unequal use among the Arabs. A fourth type, the doxographies or collections of "theses" grouped according to subject matter, does not strictly pertain to historical sources, but is, of course, an important instrument for the transmission of philosophical doctrine and has been treated in this context.[1]

The Arabic philosophical *vitae* — the genre is chiefly represented by Abū Sulaymān and al-Mubashshir — betray the strong ethical

1. Pp. 120–124 above.

bias present in the biographical tradition of Peripatetics, Stoics, and Pythagoreans alike; the bulk of the material is gnomonological, and even where a Muslim author is no longer treating the material in the same context, as in the heresiography of al-Shahrastani, the gnomonolgical flavor still comes through.[2]

There is no evidence that the Arabs possessed a *diadoche*-type history of philosophy. They knew of the succession Socrates-Plato-Aristotle, but this was a commonplace of the Aristotelian *vita* which they inherited. Excluding this, the Arabic treatises showing a sense of development in Greek philosophy take as their point of departure a chronological rather than a succession principle, and the philosophers after Theophrastus, a period for which the Alexandrians had orderly lists of Scholarchs, tend to trail off into a welter of names.

Although the succession principle is not very marked in the progression of philosophers, there is more evidence that the Arabs had access to Greek medical histories of the *diadoche*-type. Such is clearly the case for the sources of Ibn abī Uṣaybiʿah. A much earlier example is the *History of Physicians* of Iṣḥāq ibn Ḥunayn where there is an explicit attempt to correlate the chronology of the philosophers with that of the physicians. The conclusion, then, of the medical *diadoche* at Galen may explain the confusion of the relative chronology of the later philosophers.

The works *peri haireseon*, like the *bioi*, were incorporated in the Neoplatonic schools into the opening lectures preliminary to the comment on the individual works of a philosopher. The Aristotle *vita* was of this type, and a reading of the *vita* was followed by a discussion of the Aristotelian philsophy under ten headings, the first of which was "On the Names of the Philosophical Schools";[3] discussions of the Greek schools, like those in al-Masʿūdi and Ṣāʿid, go back to such abbreviated treatments and not to the full-blown *peri haireseon* of Hellenistic times.

As in the case of the doxographical material, the exact historical sources used by the Arabs are difficult to ascertain. Anonymous

2. On the Arabic gnomonological literature see pp. 124–128 above.

3. See pp. 80–81, 86 above.

collections of ethical *sententiae* culled from both poetical and philosophical sources, the chief ingredient of the Arab *vitae*, multiply in late antiquity and early Byzantine times; the school handbooks are equally nameless. But for at least two Greek authors the ground is somewhat firmer. Porphyry's *Philosophos historia* was extant in both a Syriac and an Arabic version, the latter probably by Ibn Suwār, and served as a source for al-Nadīm, al-Mubashshir, and al-Shahrastāni.[4] Porphyry's work, however, did not progress beyond Plato. The pseudepigraphic *History of Physicians*, attributed to John Philoponus, is less well known.[5] It is cited in the Arab tradition, and we get our clearest idea of it from the work of Isḥāq of the same name, which was based on an abbreviated version of the pseudo-Philoponus.

Though the Greek historical material translated into Arabic was meager and ill-identified, there exists in Arabic, Syriac, and Persian a rich historical literature, a great part of which is devoted to the intellectual life of Islam in general and to the "Greek sciences," the lives and bibliography of the *falāsifah* and *mutakallimūn*, and to the vagaries of the Aristotelian *corpus* in particular.

SECULAR, ECCLESIASTICAL, AND CULTURAL HISTORIES

Muslim secular chronicles do not generally begin *ab origine mundi* in the Christian and Jewish fashion and hence are not concerned with the era of the historical Aristotle or his Greek successors. Their value, then, is limited to the development of Aristotelian studies among the Muslims themselves.

4. *GGL*, II 854–55; *Fihrist*, p. 245; F. Altheim and R. Stiehl, *Porphyrios und Empedokles* (Tübingen, 1954), pp. 7–26; F. Rosenthal, *Orientalia*, VI (1937), 59.
5. *Fihrist*, p. 286; M. Meyerhof, "Joannes Grammatikos ... und die arabische Medizin," *Mitteilungen des Deutschen Instituts für ägyptische Altertumskunde*, II (1932), 1–21; Steinschneider, *Al-Farabi*, p. 174; F. Rosenthal, *Oriens*, VII (1954), 56–57.

What will be found in such sources varies according to the background, education, and emphases of the individual author. Contrast, for instance, the annals of al-Ṭabari (d. A.D. 923) with those of one of his continuators, Thābit ibn Sinān (*q. v.*). The former is the product of a purely Islamic background, trained in the traditional sciences and chiefly interested in political events. Thābit, on the other hand, is a member of a family with a long tradition of work in philosophy and the other Hellenic sciences. The annals of Thābit become an important source for later cultural historians, biographers, and bibliographers interested in the non-Islamic tradition, while al-Ṭabari, for all his immense importance for the political history of the period, has almost nothing to add to the cultural history of later Hellenism.

In the Thābit tradition belong many of the Christian chroniclers of the Muslim period: Eutychius, Michael the Syrian, Barhebraeus (*qq.v.*), all products of the lingering twilight of Hellenic humanism and hence interested in the by-products of such a humanism.

The interest and value of the Islamic political history for later Aristotelianism increases as the pure chronicle shades off into other historical genres. The political histories of Ibn al-Jawzi, al-Dhahabi, and of the Spanish historian al-Maqqari (*qq. v.*), for instance, are as much biography as they are history. The historian of Egypt, al-Maqrīzi, is not only interested in political events but devotes large sections of his work to topography, archaeology, and, most important for our purposes here, cultural history.

Oriental ecclesiastical histories are, despite their professed limitations, of more germane interest to the historian of philosophy than the purely secular history. In the Syrian milieu which they describe, philosophy was studied in the theological schools and was the concern of clerics alone. The ebb and flow of this church-grounded philosophy and the lives of its eminent practitioners are described on the pages of the Syriac ecclesiastical writers; the anonymous of Séert, and the church chronicles of Barhebraeus (*qq.v.*).

The term "cultural history" is used here in the broadest possible sense and is meant to cover the historical works that have to do with the development of ideas, sciences, and "schools" related to the Hellenic tradition.

Works of this type bear the closest of all affiliations to Greek prototypes. As has been remarked, the parentage is not always clear. The *History of Physicians* of Isḥāq ibn Ḥunayn (*q.v.*) can be traced back to pseudo-Philoponus, and Ammonius was probably the source for al-Āmiri's (*q.v.*) *History of Greek Philosophy*. Nothing, however, is known of the Greek model for the *History of Physicians* of Ibn al-Dayā (*q.v.*).

More common than the mere adaptation of a Greek model is the assimilation of the Hellenic material into a larger context where the Arab material appears as a continuation and expansion of categories originally postulated of a non-Islamic milieu. The most complete work of this type is the *Classes of Nations* of Ṣā'id al-Andalusi (*q.v.*), but it is a system likewise apparent in the *History* of al-Ya'qūbi (*q.v.*) and the *Various Types of Knowledge* preserved in the *Tanbīh* of al-Mas'ūdi (*q.v.*).

The concept of the continuity of culture is cardinal in the writings of the Arab "Hellenists." It is, for example, a commonplace in the biographical dictionary of al-Qifṭi (*q.v.*), in the *ṭabaqāt* works of Ibn Juljul and Ibn abī Uṣabi'ah (*qq.v.*), and in the bibliography of al-Nadīm (*q.v.*) which, though cast in other historical forms, are in reality cultural histories.

One of the earliest propagators of the "we are but Hellenes" theme in the area of philosophy was al-Fārābi. An explicit statement of the unbroken link between later Greek philosophy and early Arab *falsafah* is found in Ibn abī Uṣaybi'ah;[6] but this is merely a quotation; his source is the lost work of al-Fārābi entitled *The Appearance of Philosophy*.[7] A similar passage occurs in the *Tanbīh* of al-Mas'ūdi where it is given without source but has obviously derived from the same material.[8]

6. II, p. 135.
7. For this historical work of al-Fārābi see, in addition to the two cited passages, Qifṭi, p. 280, line 4; Steinschneider, *Al-Farabi*, pp. 85–86, and especially Meyerhof, "Alexandrien nach Baghdad," pp. 394 and 405–406.
8. *Tanbīh*, pp. 121–22.

HERESIOGRAPHIES

According to one of the traditional utterances attributed to the Prophet, Islam was to be rent by no less than seventy-three different sects. From this fertile suggestion grew the flourishing literature of Islamic heresiography dedicated to describing and cataloging these prophetically foreseen dissidents.

As in Christianity, the literature produced within many of the sects has almost entirely disappeared, and the reconstruction of the history and doctrines of the unorthodox groups must be done from the heresiographies and the polemics of their opponents.[9]

The point of departure in Islamic dissidence was almost certainly political and grew out of the power struggles that marked the establishment and passing of the Umayyad dynasty (A.D. 661–750). But the introduction of the "new learning" in the early ninth century provided fresh material for the elaboration of truly systematic heresy. Thus, two of the most important and influential of the dissident groups, the Muʿtazilites and the *bāṭinīyah* sects, were in full and vigorous contact with Greek thought, and the polemical and systematic use to which they put this material was another, and important, aspect of the pervasiveness of Aristotle in the East, a fact which by no means escaped the attention of the orthodox heresiographers.

Generally, the heresiographers came to their subject from a doctrinal rather than an historical direction. This is the approach of al-Ashʿari (*q.v.*), and his *Maqālāt* is as much a treatise on *kalām* as it is a heresiography.[10]

9. There is no treatment of heresiography as a genre, though the extensive material for such a study has been surveyed in I. Goldziher's review of the 1910 Cairo edition of the *Farq* of al-Baghdādi in *ZDMG*, LXV (1911), 349–63, and again, more elaborately and with indications on the MSS, by H. Ritter, "Mohammedanische Häresiographen," *Der Islam*, XVIII (1929), 34–55. The remarks and analyses in Gardet-Anawati, *Théologie musulmane*, pp. 145–152, are largely doctrinal.

10. The close relationship between heresiography and both *kalām* and *fiqh* is illustrated in the *al-Baḥr al-zakhkhār* of Ibn al-Murtaḍā (d. A.D. 1437), an immense collection of philosophical and theological *Wissenschaft* cast in vaguely historical lines. The introduction includes, among other things, a heresiography (*Kitāb al-milal wa al-niḥal*), a treatise on Muʿtazilite dogma, and a collection of philosophical definitions useful to the student of *kalām* (*Kitāb*

The whole file of classical Islamic heresiography proceeds in the same manner: al-Malaṭi (d. A.D. 987),[11] al-Baghdādi (d. A.D. 1040),[12] al-Isfarā'ini (d. A.D. 1078),[13] and Ibn Ḥazm (d. A.D. 1064).[17] In all these works, history is subordinated to dogma; of Aristotelianism, concealed in one way or another under the guise of heretical theses, there is much; for the texts and commentaries, for the *falāsifah*, they are of little direct importance.

There were, of course, exceptions. The heresiography entitled *Sects of the Shiʿah*, formerly attributed to al-Nawbakhti but now ascribed to a Saʿd Allāh al-Ashʿari al-Qummi (*fl. ca.* A.D. 960),[15] shows an awareness of purely philosophical problems. But the genuine watershed for the heresiographers' attitude toward *falsafah* was the publication and diffusion of the works of Ibn Sīnā (d. A.D. 1037). The distinction of erecting *falsafah* into a full-blown Islamic heresy belongs to Ibn Sīnā, and the credit for calling this development to the attention of the Muslim community must go to al-Ghazāli (d. A.D. 1111). Al-Shahrastāni (*q.v.*) is the type of post-Avicennan heresiographer with his attacks on Greek philosophy, including, of course, Ibn Sīnā himself. Two notable later heresiographers in the same vein, though from quite different points of view, were Ibn al-Jawzi (*q.v.*) and Fakhr al-Dīn al-Rāzi (d. A.D. 1209).[16]

riyāḍah al-afhām fī laṭīf al-kalām); all this by way of introduction to a work which is primarily concerned with law; see Ahlwardt, *Arabischen Handschriften Berlin*, # 4894. The section on the Muʿtazilites has been published by T. W. Arnold (Leipzig, 1902).

11. *Al-Tanbīh wa al-radd ʿalā ahl al-ahwāʾ wa al-bidāʾ*, ed. S. Dedering (*Bibliotheca Islamica*, 9 [Leipzig, 1936]); *GAL*, Suppl. I, p. 348; Ritter, "Häresiographen," p. 41.

12. *Kitāb al-farq bayn al-firaq* (ed. Cairo, 1910); Part I trans. K. Seelye (New York, 1920), and Part II by A. Halkin (Tel Aviv, 1936); *GAL*, I², 482, Suppl. II, pp. 666–67; Ritter, "Häresiographen," pp. 42–43.

13. *Kitāb al-tabsīr fī al-dīn* (ed. Cairo, 1955); Ahlwardt, *Arabischen Handschriften Berlin*, # 2801; *GAL*, I², 484, Suppl. I, p. 669; Ritter "Häresiographen," p. 44.

14. *Al-Faṣl fī al-milal* (5 vols.; ed. Cairo, 1928–1929); there is an extended translation and study by M. Asin Palacios *Abenhazem de Cordoba y su historia de las ideas religiosas*, (5 vols.; Madrid, 1927–1932). Ibn Ḥazm's purpose is a religious critique and the various sects, Islamic, Christian, and Jewish, are reviewed from that point of view. Like so many other Muslims of even the most stringent orthodoxy—al-Ghazāli and Ibn Taymīyah come immediately to mind Ibn Ḥazm is a species of Aristotelian *malgré lui*; see R. Arnaldez, *Grammaire et théologie chez Ibn Ḥazm de Cordoue* (Paris, 1956), pp. 206–13.

15. *Firaq al-shiʿah*, ed. H. Ritter (*Bibliotheca Islamica*, 4 [Istanbul, 1931]); for the new ascription see *Oriens*, VII (1954), 204.

16. *Iʿtiqādāt al-muslimin wa al-mushrikin* (ed. Cairo, 1938). In Chaps. 1–9, al-Rāzi treats the

The Ismāʿilis present a peculiar problem in heresiography.[17] There is extant a fairly extensive literature originating from within the sect as well as polemical tracts by their opponents. But, in addition to this, there are notices on the Ismāʿīlis and their doctrines inserted in Persian historical works. The *Siyāsat-nāmah*[18] of the eminent Seljuk vizier Niẓām al-Mulk (d. A.D. 1092 at the hands of an Ismāʿīli assassin) is not a history pure and simple but a treatise on government illustrated from contemporary history and in which Chapters 44–47 constitute a species of heresiography devoted to both the Zoroastrians and the Ismāʿīlis. Similarly, there are passages on the Ismāʿīlis and their tenets (here, specifically, the Nizāri branch) in the *Collection of Histories* of Rashīd al-Dīn Faḍl Allāh (d. A.D. 1318)[19] and the *History of the World Conqueror* of ʿAtā-Malik al-Juwayni (d. A.D. 1283).[20]

The Syrian inclination toward heresiography usually found its release in the form of polemic, but note will be taken of the Jacobite Dionysius bar Salibi and the Nestorian Theodore bar Koni (*qq.v.*).

ṬABAQĀT AND BIOGRAPHIES

The usual translation of *ṭabaqāt* as "classes" is an accurate enough description of the final stage of development of this genre of historical writing. The works entitled *ṭabaqāt* take the form of

Islamic sects and then, in Chap. 10, begins a discussion of the non-Islamic groups; Jews, Christians (including an interesting collection known as the "Followers of Porphyry"), Magi, Dualists (Manichaeans, Dayṣanīyah, Marcionites, Mazdakites), Sabians (see p. 171, n. 206 above), and, finally, the Philosophers; for al-Rāzi as a philosopher-theologian see pp. 194–196 above.

17. See pp. 174–179 above.

18. Ed. C. Shefer (Paris, 1891); trans. *idem* (Paris, 1893).

19. *Jamiʿ al-tawārīkh*; the pertinent section has been edited by R. Levy, *JRAS* (1930), pp. 509–36; see S. M. Sterne, *BSOAS*, XXIII (1960), 85–89.

20. *Ta'rīkh-i Jahan-Gusha*, ed. M. Qazwini ("Gibb Memorial Series," XVI, 1–3 [London, 1912, 1916, 1937]); trans. J. Boyle, *The History of the World Conqueror* (2 vols.; Manchester, 1958). Juwayni mentions (trans. Boyle, II, 666) that he had access to the library at Alamut and inspected the Ismāʿili documents there.

biographies of the individuals within some specialized, usually scholarly, class; as, for example, lawyers, physicians, *Qur'ān* readers, etc.[21]

Originally, however, *ṭabaqāt* had a somewhat different connotation, more akin to "layers" and analogous to the Greek *diadoche* works. Important for the criticism of the chains of authorities by which traditions concerning the Prophet were transmitted was an exact determination of the relative chronology of the transmitters and, to a lesser extent, their place of residence. The earliest *ṭabaqāt* works attempted to facilitate this criticism by arranging the transmitters in successive generations beginning with those in a position to take *viva voce* traditions from the Prophet himself. They served the function later taken over by the *ijāzah* or "certificat de lecture" appended to manuscripts.

Though the criticism of transmission chains may have been the original purpose of the *ṭabaqāt,* the genre soon surpassed these modest limits; in the context in which it is used here, it means simply biographies of a given class of men.[22]

As far as concerns Aristotle and Aristotelians, the two most important types of *ṭabaqāt* are those devoted to "learned men" (*ʿulamāʾ*) and the local *Gelehrtengeschichte.*

What were originally treatises devoted to the "layers" of tradition (*ḥadīth*) transmitters—the *Ṭabaqāt* of Ibn Saʿd (d. A.D. 845) is an obvious example—were quickly extended to the other "sciences." There is an impressive literature in Arabic devoted to men learned in the Islamic sciences;[23] but works on poets, philolo-

21. F. Loth, "Ursprung und Bedeutung der Ṭabaqāt," *ZDMG,* XXIII (1869), 593–614; T. de Boer, art. "Ṭabaḳāt," *EI,* Suppl., 214–215; Rosenthal, *Historiography,* pp. 82–84, 88–94; *Idem,* "Die arabische Autobiographie," *Analecta Orientalia* XIV, (1937), 1–40.

22. Some idea of the wide range of types and classes that was encompassed by the Arab *ṭābaqāt* works may be gained from an examination of the pages devoted to this genre by some of the bibliographers: al-Dhahabi (reproduced by al-Sahawi and translated in Rosenthal, *Historiography,* pp. 316–19), al-Ṣafadi (trans. E. Aman in *JA,* Ser. 10, Vol. XIX [1912], 277–95), and Ḥājji Khalīfah (ed. Flügel, IV, # 7879–7933).

23. The Muslims customarily divided the fields of knowledge or the sciences (*ʿulūm*) into "Arab" or "traditional" (*naqlīyah*), or Islamic on the one hand, and "Greek" or "foreign" or "rational" (*ʿaqlīyah*) on the other; likewise, the *ʿālim* (pl. *ʿulamāʾ*) was one skilled in the Arab sciences, while the *ḥākim* (pl. *ḥukamāʾ*) has about him a definite association with the Greek

gists, traditionalists, and jurists are only peripheral to our subject.[24] Far more germane are the *ṭabaqāt* collections given over to devotees of the "Greek sciences."

The original work in this domain appears to be the *Classes of Physicians and Sages* of the Spaniard Ibn Juljul (*q.v.*). Both Ibn Juljul and his learned imitator Ibn abī Uṣaybiʿah (*q.v.*) extend the "classes" back into Greek and Roman times, an indication that the *diadoche* principle was at least as operative here as that of *ṭabaqāt* and that Ibn Juljul may have been continuing some Greek model.

Though superficially resembling the *ṭabaqāt*, the *Ṣiwān al-ḥikmah* of Abū Sulaymān al-Sijistāni (*q.v.*) and its continuation by al-Bayḥaqi (*q.v.*) are likewise imitative, in this instance, of the *Philosophos historia* of Porphyry, and their chief interest is not biography but *sententiae*.

While the *ṭabaqāt* works frequently specialized in one or other of the "professions," there was also a distinct movement back in the direction of a purely chronological arrangement. These later collections, probably influenced by Ibn al-Jawzi and al-Dhahabi's introduction of necrologies into the annalistic framework of secular history, are not merely concerned with traditionalists. Their embrace covers the *ʿulamāʾ*, the men learned in the sciences of Islam. There is a series of such works covering, by century, the period between A.D. 1300 and A.D. 1788: Ibn Hajar al-ʿAsqalāni (d. A.D. 1449),[25] al-Sakhāwi (d. A.D. 1497),[26] al-Khafāji (d. A.D. 1659),[27] al-Muḥibbi (d. A.D. 1699),[28] al-Murādi (d. A.D. 1791).[29] The first thousand years

sciences. The noun from the latter root, *ḥikmah*, is frequently used as a nontechnical synonym for *falsafah* or for the Greek learning in general.

24. Of all the specialized collections, the most important for the purposes of the present study are: *Ṭabaqāt al-naḥwiyīn* of Jalāl al-Dīn al-Suyūti (d. A.D. 1505), usually employed in its abbreviated form under the title *Bughyat al-wuʿāt* (Cairo, 1909); al-Dhababi's (d. A.D. 1348) *Tadhkirat al-ḥuffāẓ* (4 vols.; Hyderabad, 1897), abridged and continued in al-Suyūti's *Ṭabaqāt al-ḥuffāẓ*, ed. F. Wüstenfeld (Göttingen, 1833); Tāj al-Dīn al-Subki's (d. A.D. 1370) *Ṭabaqāt al-shafiʿīyah* (6 vols.; Cairo, 1905–1906).

25. *Al-Durar al-kāminah* (4 vols.; Hyderabad, 1929–1931); GAL, II², 80–84, Suppl. II pp. 72–76.

26. *Al-Ḍawʾ al-lāmiʿ* (12 vols.; Cairo, 1934–1936); *GAL*, II², 43–44, Suppl. II, pp. 31–33.

27. *Rayḥānat al-alibbāʾ* (Cairo, 1888); *GAL*, II², 368–69, Suppl. II, 396.

28. *Khalāsat al-athār* (4 vols.; Cairo, 1868); *GAL*, II², 377–79, Suppl. II, pp. 403–404.

29. *Silk al-durar* (4 vols.; Cairo, 1874–1883); *GAL*, II², 379, Suppl. II, pp. 155–56.

of Islam (to A.D. 1591) are covered in the biographical chronicle of Ibn al-ʿImād (d. A.D. 1679).[30] Finally, scholarship in the detached areas of the Islamic community is treated in three separate *ṭabaqāt* collections. Ottoman *savants* of the period A.D. 1299–1560 are dealt with in the *Anemones of Learned Osmanlis* of Tashköprüzādah (*q.v.*), while the lines of eminent Shiʿite scholars of Persia can be found in the works of al-Tunakābuni (d. *ca.* A.D. 1890)[31] and al-Khawānsāri (d. A.D. 1895).[32]

The tradition of geographical distinctions in *ṭabaqāt* works is already present in Ibn Saʿd, and by the middle of the tenth century, there was a tendency to group *ḥadīth* scholars according to localities, as in the works on *The Learned Men of Africa* by Ibn Tamīm (d. A.D. 945) and al-Khushāni (d. A.D. 981). It was in Spain, however, that the local *Gelehrtengeschichte* reached its apogee in scholars like Ibn al-Faraḍi, his continuators Ibn Bashkuwāl and Ibn alʿAbbār, and al-Ḍabbi (*qq.v.*). These Spanish historians not only broadened the base of their biographical material, but Ibn al-Faraḍi introduced the method of alphabetical arrangement, thus destroying the very concept of *ṭabaqāt*.

While *al-Andalus* was a strong socio-geographical concept in the minds of the western Arabs, loyalties in the older, more central sections of the Islamic world tend to focus more on the urban centers, and it is these that become the measure of "history." Two of the most famous, the *History of Baghdad* by al-Khaṭīb al-Baghdādi (*q.v.*) and the *History of Damascus* by Ibn ʿAsākir (*q.v.*), are not really histories at all but are, apart from an historical and topographical introduction, collections of biographies that take as their unifying element a relationship, however brief and superficial, of the subject to the city in question.

The final extension of the biographical collections beyond the categories of time and place implicit in both the *ṭabaqāt* and the

30. *Shadharāt al-dhahab fī akhbār man dhahab* (8 vols.; Cairo, 1931–1932); *GAL*, Suppl. II, p. 403.

31. *Qiṣāṣ al-ʿulamāʾ* (Teheran, 1953); Browne, *Literary History*, IV, 354–56.

32. *Rawḍāt al-jannāt* (Teheran, 1948); Browne, *Literary History*, IV 356–57; *GAL*, Suppl. II, p. 828.

Gelehrtengeschichte is the biographical dictionaries. The alphabetically arranged *History of Learned Men* of al-Qifṭi (*q.v.*) is still at least partially within the *ṭabaqāt* tradition in that it limits its scope to the devotees of *ḥikmah* (here, the non-Islamic sciences), a limitation, obviously, to the very things that interest us the most. The true biographical dictionary is the work of Yāqūt, Ibn Khallikān,[33] and al-Ṣafadi (*qq.v.*).

All these works on the lives of the *ʿulamāʾ* have, with the exception of the more Hellenic oriented collections of Ibn Juljul, Ibn abī Uṣaybiʿah, and al-Qifṭi, nothing to do with Aristotle as such, nor even with the *falāsifah*; they are Islamic in their outlook and their horizons are the horizons of *fiqh*, of *ḥadīth*, and of *kalām*. Their pertinence for the Aristotelian tradition lies in a development in the intellectual life of Islam: in the mid-twelfth century, the line of pure *falsafah* dies out in the East; thenceforward, the tradition is borne by the theologians of the *via moderna*.[34] It is their lives that fill the pages of the later *ṭabaqāt* and biographical dictionaries.

BIBLIOGRAPHIES

An important parahistorical genre cultivated by the Arabs was the collection of bibliographical material.[35] And, though two of the collections that follow are by Christians, the motives prompting Christian and Muslim in the direction of bibliography were quite different.

The two Christian works, lists of authors and their works, by the Nestorian ʿAbdishūʿ and the Copt Abū al-Barakāt ibn Kabr

33. Continued by al-Kutabi (d. A.D. 1363), *Fawāt al-wafayāt* (2 vols,; Cairo, 1951), and by Ibn al-Qādi (d. A.D. 1616), *Durrat al-hijāl*, ed. D. Allouche (2 vols.; Rabat, 1934–1936).

34. See pp. 193ff. above.

35. Ahlwardt, *Arabischen Handschriften Berlin*, I, 54–55; G. Vadja, *Les certificats de lecture et de transmission dans les manuscrits arabes de la Bibliothèque Nationale* (Paris, 1957); S. Munajjid, "Ijāzāt al-samāʿi fi al-makhṭūṭāt," *RIMA*, I (1955), 232–51; A. Ahwani, "Kutub barnamaj al-ʿulamāʾ fī al-andalus." *RIMA*, I (1955), 91–125.

(*qq.v.*), are clearly canonical in their intent, i.e., they provided a list of the "received" authors of their respective groups. The collection of Abū al-Barakāt is more catholic in its scope, including author lists (clearly labeled) for the heretical sects, as well as syllaby of condemned propositions. Both collections have a roughly chronological framework.

The two representative Muslim authors, al-Nadīm and Tashköprüzādah (*qq.v.*), find their inspiration elsewhere. Both the *Fihrist* and the *Miftāḥ al-saʿādah* are arranged according to a principle ultimately deriving from a division of the sciences, similar to the arrangements found in the encyclopedia of al-Khawārizmi and the division works of al-Fārābi and Ibn Sīnā.[36] Within each of the divisions, e.g., logic, physiognomy, medicine, etc., the authors are set down in chronological order and to each author is devoted: (1) a *vita*, and (2) a bibliography of his works.[37]

The later Turkish author, Ḥājji Khalīfah (*q.v.*), did away with the classificatory division of al-Nadīm and Tashköprüzādah and substituted a somewhat more practical alphabetical organization.

The bibliography of al-Nadīm was compiled from manuscripts and library lists, but by the time of the two later Ottoman authors, there were additional *Hilfmittel* for the bibliographer: the *ijāzah* and the *barnamaj* or *thabt*. Both documents are essentially attempts to put on a sound basis the all-important science of tradition (*ḥadīth*). The *ijāzah* was a certification given by Shaykh A to Shaykh B attesting that Shaykh B had heard, or had otherwise received, a specified work (in its original context a work including traditions), and, therefore, was a legitimate link in a chain of transmitters going back to the Prophet. The best *ijāzāt* are always quite specific, frequently listing such details the condition of the text transmitted, as well as its name, place and circumstances of the transmission, names of witnesses, etc. The worst are cast in the form of "I give Shaykh B license to transmit anything he heard from me,"

36. See pp. 84–85 above.

37. In Tashköprüzādah, the list of the author's works is often followed by a list of their respective commentaries.

or, *O tempora, o mores*, "I license Town X and their offspring to transmit all my *ḥadīth.*"

The *barnamaj* is an individual bibliography of the books read, or heard read, by a scholar and the professors with whom he had studied. In essence, it is a collection of individual *ijāzāt*. Its pertinence to philosophy lies, like the *ṭabaqāt*, in the ambivalent nature of the later philosopher-theologians, men whose interests included both *kalām* and the *falsafah* which it had incorporated.

THE PRIMARY SOURCES: CLASSIFICATION BY AUTHOR

The bio-bibliographical material that follows cannot pretend to be all inclusive; the winnowing out of *Aristotelica* from the riches of the Muslim and Eastern Christian historical tradition is a continuing work. The intent here is merely to signal the chief sources from which our knowledge of the oriental Aristotle and his followers is derived, to indicate the background of the historians who concerned themselves with this matter and their mutual affiliations. Most of them are represented by extant works; others have been absorbed into more encyclopedic collections like Ibn abī Uṣaybiʿah's.

With one really major exception, the "Ptolemy" source for the list of Aristotle's writings that is found only in the Arabic tradition (al-Qifṭi and Ibn abi Uṣaybiʿah), what the Syrians and the Arabs have to tell us about Aristotle adds but little to what we know from the Greek sources. But what they have to say of that startling cultural cross-fertilization, oriental Aristotelianism, is considerable. It is a subject which seems to have fascinated the Arabs quite as much as it does us who look back upon it from such a far remove.

Some of the men treated here were themselves philosophers, and their interest in things Aristotelian was natural and comprehensible. Many were physicians, and their interest was equally natural since they were in the van of the new Hellenism. But others were Islamic lawyers, judges, theologians, monks, secretaries, officials in chancelleries, and, most informative of all, a tenth-century Baghdad bookseller. The happy combination of the very learned and the merely curious from Spain to Afghanistan has served Aristotelianism well.

THE PRIMARY SOURCES

Steinschneider, *Arabischen Übersetzungen*, pp. 8–32. Apart from Steinschneider, the chief Western effort in dealing with the following authors *qua* sources for Aristotelianism has been in connection with the *vita* and *pinax*. Thus:

A. Baumstark, "Syrisch-arabische Biographieen des Aristoteles," *Aristoteles bei den Syrern* (Leipzig, 1900), pp. 1–130.

J. Kippert, "Quellenforschungen zu den arabischen Aristoteles Biographieen," in *Studien auf dem Gebiete der griechisch-arabischen Übersetzungsliteratur* (Berlin, 1894), pp. 3–38.

A. Müller, "Das arabische Verzeichniss der Aristotelischen Schriften," *Morgenländische Forschungen* (Leipzig, 1875), pp. 1–32.

M. Steinschneider, *Al-Farabi*, pp. 191–98, and, incorporating the results of these earlier researches, I. Düring, *Aristotle in the Ancient Biographical Tradition* (Göteborg, 1957).

F. Rosenthal has gone over the sources handled by Baumstark, *et al.*, as well as material still in MS., on behalf of some of the other Greek philosophers, and these studies, though not dealing directly with Aristotle, are models for the meticulous treatment of texts pertinent to the history of philosophy *apud Arabes*: "Arabische Nachrichten über Zenon der Eleaten," *Orientalia*, VI (1937), 21 ff.

"On the Knowledge of Plato's Philosophy in the Islamic World," *Islamic Culture*, XIV (1940), 387–422.

"Some Pythagorean Documents Transmitted in Arabic," *Orientalia*, X (1941), 104 ff., 383 ff.

ABDISHŪ

ʿAbdishūʿ bar Barīka

Metropolitan of Nisibis from A.D. 1291 until his death in A.D. 1313; biblical commentator, canonist, theologian, poet, and historian. His activity in the field of history extended, as we know from his own catalog, into heresiography, but the only work that has been preserved is the bibliographical catalog. Mentioned, but unpreserved, are other writings on Greek philosophy which, judging from their title and subject matter, betray an interest more Hermetic than Aristotelian.

BIBLIOGRAPHICAL NOTE

Jugie, *Theologia*, V, 38, and index *s.v.*; *GSL*, pp. 323–324.

The catalog has been edited in Assemani, *Bibliotheca orientalis*, III, 1, pp. 326–61, and translated in G. B. Badger, *The Nestorians and their Rituals*, II, 361–79; see J. Vosté, *Muséon*, LX (1947), 172.

ABŪ AL-BARAKĀT IBN KABAR

Shams al-Riʾāsah abū al-Barakāt ibn Kabar (*aliter* Kubr, Kibr, Kabr)

Priest of the Coptic Church in Cairo and secretary of the Mamluk *amīr* Baybars al-Manṣūri (d. A.D. 1325); with whom he collaborated on an Islamic history. His own work was in the field of lexicography, homiletic, and, principally, in the composition of the massive theological encyclopedia, *The Lamp of Darkness*, embracing dogma, early Christian history, canon law, Scripture, liturgy, and, in Chapter VII, a catalog of Christian authors who wrote in Arabic with a bibliography for each. Abū al-Barakāt died in A.D. 1324.

BIBLIOGRAPHICAL NOTE

E. Tisserant, L. Villecourt, and G. Wiet, "Recherches sur la personalité et la vie d'Abū l-Barakāt Ibn Kubr," *Revue de l'Orient chrétien*, XXII (1921–1922), 373–94; E. Tisserant, art. "Kabar (Shams al-Riʾāsah abū al-Barakāt ibn Kabar)," *DTC*, VIII, 2, cols. 2293–96; *GCAL*, II, 438–45; an edition that covered only Chaps. I and II was begun by Tisserant, Villecourt, and Wiet in *PO*, XX (1929), 579–734. The catalog has been edited apart by W. Riedel, "Der Katalog der christlichen Schriften in arabische Sprache von Abū al-Barakāt," *Nachrichten von der königl. Gesell. der Wissen. Göttingen*, phil.-hist. Kl., V (1902), 635–706. For the history by Baybars al-Manṣūri see *GAL*, II², 54, Suppl. II, p. 43.

ABŪ MA'SHAR AL-BALKHI

Abū Ma'shar Ja'far b. Muḥ. b. 'Umar al-Balkhi

Although primarily an astronomer, the citations from some of his cited works indicate that his interests went beyond this field. His *Kitab al-ulūf* was used by both Ibn Juljul and Ṣā'id (*qq.v.*) as a source on Hermes, by Ibn abī Uṣaybi'ah (*q.v.*) on Asclepius and Indian astronomy. From other scattered references, it appears that the *Kitāb al-ulūf* was a history of the temples of the world by millennia. More enigmatic is the *Kitab al-madhākarāt*, cited by both Ṣā'id and al-Qifṭi (*q.v.*), in both instances on the translation literature. Abu Ma'shar died in A.D. 886.

BIBLIOGRAPHICAL NOTE

Fihrist, p. 277; Qifṭi, p. 152; al-Mas'ūdi, *Murūj*, IV, 91; *GAL*, I², 250–51, Suppl. I, pp. 394–95 (nn. 1 and 15); J. M. Millas, art; *s.v.*, *EI²* I, 139–40; J. Lippert, "Abu Ma'shar's *Kitab al-ulūf*," *WZKM*, IX (1895), 351–58.

ABŪ SULAYMĀN

Abū Sulaymān al-Sijistāni al-Manṭiqi

One of the students of Yaḥyā ibn 'Adi and, in turn, the leader of the Baghdad philosophical school, Abū Sulaymān composed a *Ṣiwān al-ḥikmah*, what originally appeared to be a history of Greek philosophy. In addition to Abū Sulaymān's own personal influence, primarily to be seen in al-Tawḥīdi's *Muqābasāt*, the *Ṣiwān* was widely used as a source by contemporary (al-Nadīm) and later authors (Ibn al-Maṭrān, Ibn abī Uṣaybi'ah, al-Shahrastāni). The work itself has not yet been found, but epitomes are extant, though unedited, and from the material in these, it is becoming increasingly clear that the *Ṣiwān* was essentially gnomonological, much like its continuation into Islamic times by al-Bayḥaqi (*q.v.*). Another of Abū Sulaymān's compositions, the *Ta'alīq ḥikmīyah*, is quoted by Ibn abī Uṣaybi'ah on Asclepius (I, p. 15), Aristotle (I, p. 57), and John Philoponus (I, p. 105), and also by Ibn al-Maṭrān in his *Bustān*.

BIBLIOGRAPHICAL NOTE

Steinschneider, *Arab. Übers.*, pp. 22–23; Meyerhof, "Alexandrien nach Baghdad," p. 420; the Turkish MSS of the epitome are described by M. Plessner, *Islamica*, IV (1931), 534–38. There is a description of the contents of BM *or.* 9033 in D. M. Dunlop's "Biographical Material from the Ṣiwān al-Ḥikmah," *JRAS* (1956), 82–89. For Abū Sulaymān as the source of al-Shahrastāni's material on the "Shaykh al-Yūnāni" (Plotinus) see Henry-Schwyzer, *Plotini Opera*, II (Paris-Brüssels, 1959), xxxiii. Abū Sulaymān is treated in his philosophical context pp. 162–163 above.

AL-ʿĀMIRI

Abū al-Ḥasan Muḥ. b. Yūsuf al-ʿĀmiri

This philosopher and disciple of al-Kindi's student Abū Zayd al-Balkhi[38] composed a history of Greek philosophy wihch was complete in Bukhara in A.D. 985. It is cited by Abū Sulaymān (*q.v.*) in the preface to his *Ṣiwān al-ḥikmah*. The manuscript has recently been discovered in an Istanbul library.

BIBLIOGRAPHICAL NOTE

M. Minovi, *Université de Teheran. Revue de la Faculté des Lettres*, IV, 3 (1957), p. 70, # 10: *al-Amad ʿalā al-abad*. The *Deftir-l kutubkhane-i medrese-i Servili* (Istanbul, 1893), does not identify the various parts of MS # 179 to which the *Amad* belongs.

ANON.

Anon. Chronicle of Séert

A secular-ecclesiastical history by an unknown Nestorian author *ca.* A.D. 1036.

BIBLIOGRAPHICAL NOTE

Edited and translated by A. Scher, *PO*, IV, 215–312; V, 217–344; VII, 95–203; XIII, 437–639; *GCAL*, II, 195–96; *GSL*, p. 5; C. F. Seybold, *ZDMG*, LXVI (1912), 742–46.

38. See p. 159 above.

AL-ASHʿARI

Abū al-Ḥasan ʿAli b. Ismāʿīl

Al-Ashʿari is a man whose reputation and works have overshadowed his life. Apart from his birth in Basrah (*ca.* A.D. 873/4) and his death in Baghdad in A.D. 935, tradition has preserved two salient events in his career: he was a pupil of the renowned Muʿtazilite of Basrah, al-Jubbāʾi, and in A.D. 912 he experienced a conversion from the Hellenism-inclined Muʿtazilites to the more severe orthodoxy of the type represented by Aḥmad ibn Ḥanbal.

The *Dogmas of the Islamic Theologians* represents al-Ashʿari's attack on the Muʿtazilites drawn up on the form of an heresiography, to which is added a creed and a discussion of the different opinions on *kalām*. The approach of al-Ashʿari is doctrinal rather than historical, and hence the use of the *Dogmas* as source for the development of either Muʿtazilitism or *falsafah* is limited to one of influence. What is clearly manifest is the degree to which the philosophical approach to theology in use among the Muʿtazilites had touched even their opponents. The entire third part of the *Dogmas* is, for instance, devoted to a discussion of such concepts as substance, accident, motion, and rest.

BIBLIOGRAPHICAL NOTE

Ibn Khallikān (trans. de Slane), II, 227–28; *Maqālāt al-islāmīyīn*, ed. H. Ritter (2 vols.; Istanbul, 1929); Ritter, "Häresiographen," pp. 39–40; R. Strothmann, "Islamische Konfessionskunde und das Sectenbuch des Ashʿari," *Der Islam*, XIX (1930–1931), 193–242; for al-Ashʿari as a theologian see pp. 147–152 above.

BARHEBRAEUS

Gregorius Abū al-Faraj Barhebraeus (*arabice* Ibn al-ʿIbri)

Son of a Jewish physician of Melitene where he was born in A.D. 1225/6. The family was driven from their home in A.D. 1243 by the Mongol incursions and settled in the vicinity of Antioch. Barhebraeus received his education in logic and medicine from a Nestorian monk, but he was himself a member of the Jacobite Church. In A.D. 1246 he was consecrated bishop and governed various dioceses until A.D. 1264, when he was appointed Maphrian, i. e., Patriarchal vicar for the eastern dioceses, a post he held until his death in A.D. 1286.

There is no questioning the preeminence of Barhebraeus in his church and in his culture. He was at the same time its greatest and its last luminary. As a scholar, his learning was derivative, but massive nonetheless. As a historian, he has the virtue of an awareness of not only his own Syriac culture but the all-engulfing Islamic milieu as well. The histories, like Barhebraeus himself, move between both worlds.

The so-called *Syriac Chronicle* is a world history composed in Syriac and covering the period from Creation to A.D. 1286, and continued by the author's brother, Barsauma, down to A.D. 1288. The *Ecclesiastical Chronicle,* likewise in Syriac, is a church history from Old Testament times to the author's day and includes Nestorians as well as Jacobites. Both rely heavily on Michael the Syrian (*q.v.*). Barhebraeus himself was responsible for the Arabic recension of the *Syriac Chronicle* entitled *An Abridged History of the Dynasties.*

BIBLIOGRAPHICAL NOTE

The most important biographical source is the notes from the hand of the author himself and his brother, Barsauma, in *Chron. Eccles.*, II, 431–85; T. Nöldeke, *Orientalische Skizzen* (Berlin, 1892), pp. 250–74; *GSL*, pp. 312–20; Jugie, *Theologia*, I, 474–78, and Index *s.v.*; *GCAL*, II, 272–81.

Secular history: P. Bruns and G. Kirsch (ed. and trans.), *Bar Hebraei Chronicon syriacum* (2 vols.; Leipzig, 1789); P. Bedjan (ed.), *Chronicon Syriacum* (Paris, 1890); E. A. W. Budge (trans.), *The Chronography of Bar Hebraeus* (2 vols.; Oxford, 1932).

Arabic recension: P. Salhani (ed.), *Ta'rīkh mukhtaṣar al-duwal* (Beyrouth, 1890 [see *GAL*, I^2, 428, Suppl. I, p. 591]).

Ecclesiastical history: J. B. Abeloos and T. Lamy (ed. and trans.), *Chronicon Ecclesiasticum* (2 vols.; Louvain, 1872–1877).

AL-BAYḤAQI

Ẓahīr al-Dīn ʿAli ibn Zayd abū al-Ḥasan al-Bayḥaqi

Ẓahīr al-Dīn al-Bayḥaqi, to be distinguished from the historian Sharf al-Dīn al-Bayḥaqi, was, according to his autobiography, born in the district of Bayhaq in A.D. 1106. His studies were long and elaborate: the traditional Arab subjects occupied him until the age of twenty-six, and then, after a four-month interim as a magistrate in Bayhaq, he began advanced work on the Hellenic sciences in A.D. 1132. In A.D. 1136, he went to Sarakhs and there, under Muḥammad ibn abī Tāhir of Merv, known as Quṭb al-Zamān (biography: *Tatimmat*, #70), he began the study of philosophy. After Ibn abī Tāhir's death in A.D. 1142, he went to Nisabur and remained in that area until his own death in A.D. 1170.

The autobiography preserved by Yāqūt has a catalog of seventy-three of his works on Persian and Arabic on a wide variety of subjects, of which but three have been preserved: a work on astronomy, a history of his native city in Persian (*Ta'rīkh-i Bayḥaq*, completed in A.D. 1168; Sharf al-Dīn al-Bayḥaqi has an identically named work), and the *Continuation of the Ṣiwān al-ḥikmah*, a work originally composed in Arabic. The *Continuation* is a collection of one hundred and eleven biographies (the Persian version has five additional entries) of Persian and Arab scholars, mostly from the eastern provinces. It differs from the *Ṣiwān* of Abū Sulaymān (*q.v.*), of which it is the continuation, in that, with one exception (#20, John Philoponus), it deals with Islamic scholars, while the *Ṣiwān* devoted articles to the Greeks as well. But like the *Ṣiwān*, the treatment is principally gnomonological; the actual historical material, precious as it is for eastern scholarship, is overshadowed by the aphorisms.

BIBLIOGRAPHICAL NOTE

Yāqūt, *Irshād*, V, 208–18 (including the autobiography); see the analysis in M. Shafi, "The Author of the Oldest Biographical notice of ʿUmar Khayyām ..., *Islamic Culture*, VI (1932), 586–623; *GAL*, I², 395–96, Suppl. I, pp. 557–58; the *Tatimmat ṣiwān al-ḥikmah* have been edited in both the Arabic and Persian version by M. Shafi

(Lahore, 1935), and the Arabic alone by M. Kurd ʿAli under the title *Taʾrīkh ḥukamāʾ al-islām* (Cairo, 1946). There is an extensive analysis of the contents of the *Tatimmat* by M. Meyerhof, "ʿAli al-Bayḥaqi's Tatimmat ṣiwān al-ḥikma. A biographical work on the learned men of Islam," *Osiris*, VIII (1948), 122–217.

Dionysius (*aliter* Jacobus) bar Salibi

Jacobite philosopher, theologian, and canonist who died in A.D. 1171. According to the catalog of his works put together by Michael the Syrian (*Chronicle*, ed. Chabot, p. 699), he is the author of a *Refutation of All the Heresies*. The parts which are extant and which may or may not represent the entirety of the original are in the form of polemical treatises directed against Islam, the Jews, Nestorians, Melkites, Armenians, and idolaters.

BIBLIOGRAPHICAL NOTE

The tracts against Islam and the idolaters are still unedited (see *GSL*, p. 297, n. 1 and n. 6); on the Jews: J. de Zwann, *Dionysius bar Salibi's Treatise against the Jews* (Leyden, 1906); on the Nestorians: an analysis of the whole and a partial translation by F. Nau in *Revue de l'Orient chrétien*, XIV, 298–320; on the Melkites: A. Mingana, "Barsalibi's Treatise against the Melchites," *Woodbrooke Studies*, I (1927), 17–95; on the Armenians: *idem*, "The Work of Dionysius Barsalibi against the Armenians," *Bulletin of the John Rylands Library*, XV (1931), 489–599.

Elias bar Shinaya

Born A.D. 975, he was consecrated in A.D. 1008 as Nestorian Metropolitan of Nisibis; he died some time after A.D. 1049. Elias wrote in both Syriac and Arabic on an almost incredible range of subjects: grammar, canon law, apologetics, liturgy, and, what primarily concerns us here, history. His *Chronographia* is extant in both Syriac and Arabic: Part I is a world chronicle on the Eusebian model reaching to A.D. 1018; Part II is a collection of chronological tables.

BIBLIOGRAPHICAL NOTE

GSL, pp. 287–88; *GCAL*, II, 177–91; Jugie, *Theologia*, V, 35–36, and index *s.v.*; *Chronographia*, ed. E. W. Brooks, *CSCO script. syri.*, Ser. 3, Vols. VII–VIII (Louvain, 1907–1910). Of some interest are the "conversations" held with the vizier Abū al-Qāsim Ḥusayn ibn ʿAli al-Maghribi in A.D. 1026 on a variety of subjects including the preeminence of the Christians in grammar, lexicography, and rhetoric; see E. K. Delly, *La théologie de Elias bar Shinaja. Etude et traduction de ses Entretiens* (Rome, 1957).

ḤĀJJI KHALĪFAH

Muṣṭafā ibn ʿAbdallāh Kātib Čelebi

The work of the Turkish bibliographer Ḥājji Khalīfah, the *Revelation of Opinions of the Names of Books and Doctrines*, is the culmination of the attempts of medieval Islam to give an account of its literary output. The author was born *ca.* A.D. 1601/2 in Istanbul and spent most of his life as comptroller in the field offices of the Ottoman army, pursuing during the interim his higher studies in Istanbul, especially in the period A.D. 1636–1648 when he was made second assistant (*khalīfah*) in the Comptroller's Office in the capital, a post he held until his death in A.D. 1658.

Ḥājji Khalīfah is the very type of the Islamic polymath, a familiar but still incredible phenomenon. His literary activity ranged over the fields of law, astronomy, translation (Latin-Turkish), biography, history, and geography. The *Revelation*, written in Arabic, is itself the fruit of twenty years of preparatory labor in the libraries of Istanbul and Aleppo. The work is arranged, after a rather lengthy introduction on the meaning and division of the sciences, on an alphabetical basis, according to the name of the discipline, e. g., *ṭibb* (#7873), *manṭiq* (#13179). Within these articles there are historical surveys of the field, e. g., a brief history of philosophy under *ḥikmah* (#4382), and a list of books written on the subject.

BIBLIOGRAPHICAL NOTE

Steinschneider, *Arab. Übers.*, pp. 12–13; J. H. Mordtmann, art. *s.v.* *EI*, I, 204–206; A. Nallino, *Raccolta di Scritti*, V (Rome, 1944), 144–47;

F. Babinger, *Die Geschichtsschreiber der Osmanen und ihre Werke* (Leipzig, 1927), pp. 195–203; *GAL*, II², 563–65, Suppl. II, pp. 635–37. *Kashf al-ẓanūn*, ed. and trans. G. Flügel (7 vols.; Leipzig, 1835–1858 [Vol. VII contains an index of authors]).

IBN AL-ʿABBĀR

Abū ʿAbdallāh Muḥ. b. ʿAbdallāh b. al-ʿAbbār al-Quḍāʾi

Born in Valencia A.D. 1199, Ibn al-ʿAbbār filled the post of secretary to the governors of Valencia. In the face of the rising Aragonese tide of reconquest, he escaped with his family in A.D. 1238 to the court of the Hafsid Sultan of Tunis where he served as secretary until he fell from the Sultan's favor. In A.D. 1260 he was tortured and executed at the command of the Sultan al-Mustānṣir.

The *Complement to the Continuation*, i. e., a continuation of the biographical dictionary of Ibn Bashkuwāl (*q.v.*) was begun at the request of the traditionist Abū al-Rabīʿ ibn Salīm and the first redaction was completed in A.D. 1233, although the final touches were not added until A.D. 1249. Unlike the earlier works by Ibn al-Faraḍi and Ibn Bashkuwāl, the *Complement* attempts to give (in the Preface) an exact setting forth of sources. These are, in the main, Spanish traditionists.

BIBLIOGRAPHICAL NOTE

Pons-Boigues, *Historiadores*, # 253; *GAL*, I², 416, Suppl. I, pp. 580–81; *Takmilat al-silah*, ed. F. Codera (2 vols.; Madrid, 1887–1889), and additions (including the preface) from another MS by A. Bel and M. Ben Cheneb (Algiers, 1920).

IBN ABĪ UṢAYBIʿAH

Muwaqqaf al-Dīn abū al-ʿAbbās Aḥmad ibn al-Qāsim

Ibn abī Uṣaybiʿah was born into a notable medical family. His grandfather, Khalīfah ibn Yūnus, was in the medical service of Salāḥ al-Dīn in Cairo and his father, Shadīd al-Dīn al-Qāsim (A.D. 1180–1251), studied opthalmology in Cairo and later was on the staff of the famous hospital founded by Nūr al-Dīn ibn Zangi (A.D. 1146–1174) in Damascus where Ibn abī Uṣaybiʿ ah was born some time after A.D. 1194. He was educated in Damascus in both the Arab and the Greek sciences (philosophy under Rafīʿ al-Dīn al-Jīli, d. A.D. 1244).[39] He began his medical practice in Cairo in A.D. 1233/4, and after a year there and in the Nūri Hospital in Damascus, he was employed by the *amīr* ʿIzz al-Dīn Aybak at Sarkhad near Damascus. He died there in A.D. 1270.

His *Sources of Information on the Classes of Physicians* appeared in a first edition in A.D. 1242/3 and in an expanded second edition in A.D. 1268/9. It is a *ṭabaqāt* work clearly inspired by the arrangements to be found in Ibn Juljul and Ṣāʿid (*qq.v.*), both of whom were used as sources. Parts I–VIII are chronological, tracing the development of medical science from its invention (I and II) down through the Greeks (III–V), the Alexandrians (VI), early Islamic (VII) and early Abbasid physicians (VIII). Then follow short notices on the translators (IX). At this point, the chronological progression is dropped, and the remaining long chapters are devoted to the physicians of Iraq (X), Persia (XI), India (XII), Morocco and Spain (XIII), Egypt (XIV), and, finally, the author's own Syria (XV). Within all these sections the approach is strictly biographical: *vita*, catalog, sayings, poetry.

The *Sources* is rich in material on all the Arab Aristotelians from the beginning of Islam down to the thirteenth century. Ibn abī Uṣaybīʿah interprets the term "physician" in the widest possible sense, and there are very few of the *falāsifah* who did not have some connection with medicine. The section devoted to Aristotle is a curious mélange of information from both western (the enigmatic "Ptolemy Chennus") and oriental sources (al-Masʿūdi, al-Fārābi, Ibn Juljul, Ḥunayn, Abū Sulaymān, Ṣāʿid, and al-Mubashshir), chiefly interesting by reason of the elaborate catalog of Aristotle's works reproduced from the Ptolemy-source (Uṣ. I, 66–69).

BIBLIOGRAPHICAL NOTE

GAL, I², 397–98, Suppl. I, p. 560; Steinschneider, *Arab. Übers.*, pp. 11–12; A. Nallino, *Raccolta di Scritti*, V (Rome, 1944), 137–44. ʿ*Uyūn*

39. See Uṣ., II, 171–73.

al-anbā' fī ṭabaqāt al-aṭibbā', ed. A. Müller (2 vols; Königsberg-Cairo, 1884). Chaps. I and II trans. B. R. Sanguinetti, *JA*, Ser. 5, Vol. III (1854), 241–291; IV (1854), 178–213. The same translator published a version of Chaps. VII and VIII, *ibid.*, Vol. V (1885), 403–69, VI (1885), 131–90; the section in Chap. IV on Aristotle has been analyzed and studied by I. Düring, *Aristotle in the Ancient Biographical Tradition* (Göteborg, 1957), pp. 213–41 where the older literature is cited. There is a new edition and translation of Chap. XIII: H. Jahier and A. Noureddine, *Sources d'Informations sur les Classes des Medicins*: *XIIIe Chapitre*: *Medicins de l'Occident Musulman* (Algiers, 1958).

IBN 'ASĀKIR

Abū al-Qāsim 'Ali ibn al-Ḥasan Thiqat al-Dīn ibn 'Asākir

Born in A.D. 1106 and educated in the science of traditions to which he later devoted his career. In A.D. 1126 and the following years, he was in Baghdad and the eastern provinces on those journeys in pursuit of authentic traditions which were the hallmark of the true Islamic scholar. After his return to Damascus, he taught in the Nūri *madrasah*. He died in Damascus in A.D. 1176.

His *History of the City of Damascus* is an unashamed imitation of the work on Baghdad by al-Khaṭib al-Baghdādi (*q.v.*). There is the same historical sketch of the city followed by the biographies of illustrious Damascenes arranged in alphabetical order.

BIBLIOGRAPHICAL NOTE

Ibn Khallikān (trans. de Slane), II, 252–54; Yāqūt, *Irshād*, V, 139–46; *GAL*, I², 403–404, Suppl. I, pp. 566–67; Rosenthal, *Historiography*, p. 147. The *Ta'rīkh madīnat Dimashq* has not been edited in its entirety. The sumptuous edition which began appearing in 1951 in Damascus has not progressed beyond the Introduction. Even the abbreviated edition (7 vols.; Damascus, 1911–1932), is incomplete. For the *Tabyīn kadhib al-muftari*, Ibn 'Asākir's defensive biography of al-Ash'ari, see p. 210, n. I above.

IBN BASHKUWĀL

Abū al-Qāsim Khalaf ibn 'Abd al-Malik ibn Bashkuwāl al-Qurtubi

Born in Cordova in A.D. 1101 and educated in Seville where Ibn Rushd was one of his professors, he served both as magistrate in Seville and as a notary in Cordova, where he died in A.D. 1183.

His biographical dictionary, the *Continuation*, took up where a similar work by Ibn al-Faraḍi (*q.v.*) ended and carried the biographies down to A.D. 1139, when the work was completed. There are continuations of the *Continuation* by Ibn al-Zubayr al-Gharnati[40] and by Ibn al-ʿAbbār (*q.v.*).

BIBLIOGRAPHICAL NOTE

Ibn Khallikān (trans. de Slane), I, 491–92; Pons-Boigues, *Historiadores*, #200; *GAL*, I², 413, Suppl. I, p. 580; *al-Ṣilah fi akhbār aʿimmat al-andalus*, ed. F. Codera (2 vols.; Madrid, 1883); new edition (Cairo, 1955).

IBN AL-DAYĀ

Yūsuf ibn Ibrāhīm abū al-Ḥasan ibn al-Dayā and his son Abū Jaʿfar Aḥmad ibn Yūsuf ibn al-Dayā

The father, Yūsuf ibn Ibrāhīm, was a client of Ibrāhīm ibn al-Mahdi (pretender to the Caliphal throne, A.D. 817–819) and a member of the court circle surrounding the Caliph, al-Amīn (A.D. 802–813). At the death of his patron, Ibrāhīm, in A.D. 839, Yūsuf and his son, Abū Jaʿfar, migrated first to Damascus, then to Egypt where he was employed, and his son after him, as secretary to the governor, Aḥmad ibn Tulūn (A.D. 868–884). Yūsuf ibn Ibrāhīm died in A.D. 878, and his son in A.D. 951.

Both father and son are credited with a *History of Physicians*, now, unfortunately, lost. It did, however, serve to provide Ibn abī Uṣaybiʿah with material on Galen (Uṣ., I, 77–79, from Yūsuf) and Ḥunayn (*ibid.*, I, 190). Possibly the son continued his father's work into the Islamic period. Abū Jaʿfar also wrote a work on logic.

BIBLIOGRAPHICAL NOTE

Yūsuf ibn Ibrāhīm: Yāqūt, *Irshād*, pp. 157–60; Zirikli, *al-Aʿlam*, IX, 280–81.

40. Pons-Boigues, *Historiadores*, # 268; *GAL*, I², 415.

Abū Ja'far: al-Ṣafadi, *Wafi*, I, 54; *GAL*, I², 155, Suppl. I, 229; al-Zirikli, *Al-A'lam*, I, 258; Zaki Mubarak, *La prose arabe au IVe siècle de l'Hegire*, pp. 241–49.

IBN AL-FARAḌI

Abū al-Walīd 'Abdallāh ibn Muḥammad ibn al-Faraḍi

Born in A.D. 962 and educated in Cordova as a lawyer and a traditionist, although his studies extended into literature and history as well. In A.D. 992, he made the pilgrimage to Mecca and took the opportunity to study in some of the eastern centers: Qayrawan, Cairo, Mecca, and Medina. On his return to Cordova, he taught and then served as a magistrate in Valencia. He was slain in the Berber sack of Cordova in A.D. 1013.

His *History of the Learned Men of Spain* is a biographical dictionary, the first of its type for the West, which, with its continuation by Ibn Bashkuwāl and Ibn al-'Abbār (*qq.v.*), covers the field of Spanish biography from the Muslim conquest to the middle of the thirteenth century.

BIBLIOGRAPHICAL NOTE

Ibn Bashkuwāl, *Ṣilah*, # 567; Ibn Khallikān (trans. de Slane), II, 68–69; Pons-Boigues, *Historiadores*, # 71; *GAL*, I², 412, Suppl. I, pp. 577–78; Rosenthal, *Historiography*, p. 146; *Ta'rīkh 'ulamā' al-andalus*, ed. F. Codera, (2 vols.; Madrid, 1891–1892); new edition (Cairo, 1954).

IBN AL-JAWZI

Jamāl al-Dīn abū al-Faraj 'Abd al-Rahmān ibn al-Jawzi

Born in Baghdad A.D. 1116, he began his studies in the science of tradition at the age of seven, and for the rest of his career he dovoted himself to the study and propagation of the legal and theological system of Aḥmad ibn Ḥanbal. By temperament and training, Ibn al-Jawzi had little sympathy for the Hellenizing currents of the time. His main preoccupation was with Islam and its sciences, but the pursuit of these sciences led to the related fields of history and historiography, and to the disturbing elements that were troubling the orthodox conscience. It was the same motive that drove another, later Hanbalite, Ibn Taymīyah, to turn his attention to the problem of *falsafah*.[41]

The *Book of Rightly Ordered Things ... in the History of Kings and Nations* which Rosenthal characterizes as "the lowest level to which Muslim historiography, in its main representatives, ever sank," is neither pure chronicle nor pure biographical dictionary, but a combination of the two. It progresses chronologically, year by year, and each year is divided into two sections: one devoted to the political events of the year, and the second to the necrologies of scholars who died during that same period. The necrologies were, and this is the point of Rosenthal's crticism, "to serve the purpose of theological personality criticism," and they gradually force the purely political events into the background. The necrologies, many of them taken from Al-Khaṭīb al-Baghdādi (*q.v.*), are, however, important for the prosopography of the scholars of the time.

Ibn al-Jawzi's heresiography, the *Devil's Delusion*, written sometime before A.D. 1180, concerns itself more directly with philosophical material, especially in Chapter IV: "How he deludes in articles of religion and matters of piety" where the author investigates heresy among the "Sophists," "Physicists," dualists, and philosophers. The two main cited authorities in this regard are a doxographical collection of al-Nawbakhti[42] and an unnamed work by a certain Yaḥyā ibn Bishr ibn ʿUmayr al-Nihawāndi who, according to a remark in the text (p. 47), lived *ca.* A.D. 950, and a copy of whose work Ibn al-Jawzi found in the library of the Niẓamīyah *madrasah*. Al-Nihawāndi was apparently the authority on the dualists and astrologers, and his reported quote of Aristotle (p. 45) is in an astronomical context.

BIBLIOGRAPHICAL NOTE

Ibn Khallikān (trans. de Slane), II, 96–98; *GAL*, I², 659–66, Suppl. I, pp. 914–20; *Kitāb al-muntaẓam*, (10 vols.; ed. Hyderabad, 1938–1940); Rosenthal, *Historiography*, pp. 124–25; J. de Semogyi,

41. See pp. 200–203 above.
42. H. Ritter, *Der Islam*, XVIII (1929), 38, # 11.

"The Kitāb al-muntaẓm of Ibn al-Jawzi," *JRAS* (1932), pp. 49–76; *Talbīs iblīs* (ed. Cairo, 1948); there is a slightly abridged translation of the pertinent sections by D. S. Margoliouth in *Islamic Culture*, IX (1935), and X (1936).

IBN JULJUL

Abū Dā'ūd Sulaymān ibn Ḥassān ibn Juljul

Ibn Juljul was court physician to the Cordovan Caliph Hishām II (A.D. 976–1009) when he composed in, A.D. 987, his *Ṭabaqāt al-aṭibbā' wa al-'ulamā'*, a bio-bibliographical history of physicians and sages arranged in both historical and geographical order. The work is divided into nine chapters which deal with (1) the origins of wisdom and medicine, the three Hermes, Asclepius, Apollo; (2) Greeks and Romans (Hippocrates, Dioscorides, Plato, Aristotle, Socrates); (3) Greeks who flourished in the post-Persian era (Ptolemy, Cato, Euclid) (4) sages of the empire of the Caesars (Galen); (5) Alexandrians; (6) various pre-Islamic physicians and sages; (7) Islamic philosophers and physicians (i.e., those of the East from Bakhtīshū' to al-Rāzi'; (8) Maghribi sages; and (9) Andalusian sages.

Ibn Juljul names his own sources (pp. 2–3) as Abu Ma'shar's *Kitāb al-ulūf*, Orosius, St. Jerome's *Chronicle*, and Isidore of Seville (cited p. 41), a strong indication of the ties of the Western Caliphate with the Latin and Visigothic traditions. The work of Orosius figures in the celebrated anecdote transmitted through Ibn Abī Uṣaybi'ah[43] on the receipt in Cordova of a gift from the Byzantine Emperor Romanus (actually Constantine VII Porphyrogenitus; Romanus I Lecapenus abdicated in A.D. 944) in A.D. 948: a copy of Dioscorides and Orosius. The translation of Orosius presented no problem since "you have Latins in your country who can read it," and when the Greek of Dioscorides proved difficult, a translator was sent out from Constantinople.

In addition to these specifically cited sources, the *Classes* offers evidence of the arrival in Spain of translations done in the Baghdad circle. There are textual quotes from the pseudo-Aristotelian *Secreta*

43. Jahier-Noureddine (ed.), pp. 36–40.

secretorum (p. 67) translated by Ibn al-Biṭrīq (*fl. ca.* A.D. 835), the Hippocratic oath (pp. 11, 12, 17), Plato's *Leges* (p. 12), and Galen (pp. 17, 42, 43).

The *Classes*, later used by Ṣā'id al-Andalusi and Ibn abī Uṣaybi'ah (through Ṣā'id ?), represents an early biographical source independent of al-Nadīm's *Fihrist* with which it is exactly contemporary. The article on Aristotle (pp. 25–27) includes almost biographical detail but a list of works embracing the *naturalia* (the *De anima* is omitted), logica, and the "theology," an anecdote of the relationship between Alexander and Aristotle, and a quote from the *Secreta*.

BIBLIOGRAPHICAL NOTE

Uṣ. II, 46–48 (ed. Jahier-Noureddine, pp. 36–41), Sa'id *Ṭabaqāt*, pp. 80–81; Qifṭi, p. 190; *GAL*, I², 272, Suppl. I, p. 422; Steinschneider, *Arab. Übers.*, p. 23. The *Ṭabaqāt* now appears in a critical edition by F. Sayyid (Cairo, 1955). On the Arabic translation of Orosius see G. Levi della Vida, "La traduzione araba delle Storie di Orosio," *Al-Andalus*, XIX (1954), 257–93.

IBN KHALLIKĀN

Shams al-Dīn abū al-'Abbās Aḥmad ibn Muṣammad

Ibn Khallikān was born in A.D. 1211 and pursued his studies in Aleppo and Damascus. Beginning in A.D. 1238, most of his adult life was spent as a magistrate, then as chief magistrate in Cairo and Damascus, and as a professor of jurisprudence in various Cairene *madrasahs*. He died in A.D. 1282 in Damascus.

His chief work, the *Obituaries of Eminent Men*, was begun in Cairo in A.D. 1256, and completed, after numerous interruptions, in A.D. 1274. In his preface, Ibn Khallikān explicitly rejects the *ṭabaqāt* principle: the work is to be restricted to no particular class, though Companions of the Prophet and the vizier class are excluded, and is to proceed on a strictly alphabetical basis.

BIBLIOGRAPHICAL NOTE

Al-Subki, *Ṭabaqāt*, V, 14; Ibn al-'Imād, *Shadharāt*, V, 371–72; *GAL*, I², 398–400, Suppl. I, p. 561; *Kitāb wafayāt al-a'yān wa anbā' abnā' al-zamān,* ed. F. Wüstenfeld (2 vols.; Göttingen, 1835–1843); trans. with notes M. de Slane, *Ibn Khallikan's Biographical Dictionary* (4 vols.; Paris, 1843–1871).

IBN AL-MAṬRĀN

Muwaffiq al-Dīn As'ad ibn abī al-Fath Ilyās ibn al-Maṭrān

Ibn al-Maṭrān was born and reared in Damascus as a Christian. After travels in Byzantine territory and a period in Baghdad as a student of the dean of the 'Aḍudi Hospital, Ibn al-Tilmīdh, he returned to Damascus where he was converted to Islam in the time of Salāḥ al-Dīn whom he served as personal physician. He died in Damascus in A.D. 1191.

A work attributed to Ibn al-Maṭrān, the *Garden of Physicians,* has been partially recovered. It was apparently both gnomonological and doxographical in nature (Uṣ., II, 181). As sources, he used the gnomonology of Ḥunayn,[44] the biographical collection of Abū Sulaymān (*q.v.*), and the history of Thābit bin Sinān (*q.v.*); but he quotes philosophical texts as well: Aristotle's *De sensu,* Nicholas of Damascus' introduction to the *Ethica,* Abū Bishr's commentaries on the *Eisagoge, Categoriae,* and *De interpretatione,* al-Fārābi on the *Eisagoge,* and the marginal notes of Ibn Suwār on the enigmatic "Alinus."

BIBLIOGRAPHICAL NOTE

Uṣ., II, 175–81; Barhebraeus, *Chron. Syr.,* p. 380 (trans. Budge, p. 329); *GAL,* Suppl. I, p. 892; M. Shabibi, *RAAD,* III (1923), 2–8; Kraus, *Jābir,* I, lxiii–lxiv.

ISḤĀQ

Isḥāq ibn Ḥunayn

Isḥāq (d. A.D. 910), the translator of sections of the Aristotelian *corpus,* was, like his father, also concerned with the historical development of the history of medicine.

A work of his on this subject, the *History of Physicians,* usually associated with a similar work by John Philoponus, has recently been

44. See p. 125 above.

recovered and published. It is quite brief and, by Isḥāq's own admission, is modeled after Philoponus whose work he did alter somewhat: "Yaḥyā al-Naḥwi restricted himself to a chronology of physicians. I inserted [into his discussion] the philosophers who lived in the time of each one of the physicians, for the sake of greater completeness and perfection."[45] For the history of Aristotelianism it has been a disappointing find since it is concerned chiefly, with the Greek physicians and derived from late Greek sources.

BIBLIOGRAPHICAL NOTE

Fihrist, p. 285; Qifṭi, p. 80; Uṣ., I, 201. *Ta'rīkh al-aṭibbā*, ed. and trans. F. Rosenthal, *Oriens*, VII (1954), 61–80.

ʿISHODENAH

ʿIshodenah of Basrah

The otherwise unknown author from whose hands we have a bio-bibliographical collection known as the *Book of Chastity*, dealing with the major figures of eastern asceticism, i.e., in Iraq and Iran, and probably composed *ca.* A.D. 850. In addition, there is a catalog of his works in ʿAbdīshū (# 128) which indicates at least a partial interest in philosphy. Later authors also cite an *Ecclesiastical History* by ʿIshodenah.

BIBLIOGRAPHICAL NOTE

GSL, p. 234; the *Book of Chastity* has been edited, with a French translation, by J. B. Chabot in *Mélanges d'archeologie et d'histoire*, XVI (1896), 225–91, and the Syriac text alone by P. Bedjan, *Liber superiorum* (Paris, 1901), pp. 437–517.

AL-KHAṬĪB AL-BAGHDĀDI

Abū Bakr Aḥmad ibn ʿAli ibn Thābit al-Khaṭīb al-Baghdādi

Born in the vicinity of Baghdad in A.D. 1002, his career was entirely devoted to the collection, transmission, and critism of tradi-

45. Rosenthal (trans.), p. 75.

tions, a field in which he gained great renown. This enthusiasm was not shared by all, however, and because of the opposition of the Hanbalite faction in Baghdad, he had to take refuge in Syria where the Fatimid governor was with difficulty persuaded to spare his life. The arrival of the Seljuk Turks in Baghdad made the climate once more tolerable, and al-Khaṭīb returned there in A.D. 1069, and died in the city so closely associated with his name in A.D. 1071.

The *History of Baghdad* is not, despite its title, a history, but an alphabetically arranged dictionary of Baghdad notables with introductory chapters on the history and topography of the city and notices on the Companions of the Prophet. The Cairo edition included 7,831 entries.

BIBLIOGRAPHICAL NOTE

Ibn Khallikān (trans. de Slane), I, 75–76; Yāqūt, *Irshād*, I, 246–60; *GAL*, I², 401, Suppl. I, p. 563; *Rosenthal, Historiography*, pp. 146–47. *Ta'rīkh Baghdād*, (14 vols.; ed. Cairo, 1931). Part of the Introduction has been edited and translated by G. Salmon, *L'Introduction Topographique à l'Histoire de Baghdad* (Paris, 1904).

AL-MAQQARI

Abū al-ʿAbbās Aḥmad ibn Muḥammad Shihāb al-Dīn al-Maqqari

Born of a scholarly family at Tlemcen *ca.* A.D. 1591/2, al-Maqqari was trained principally in jurisprudence and the science of traditions. He was appointed *imām* and *mufti* in Marrakesh and then given a similar position in the Qarawiyin mosque in Fez in A.D. 1613. In A.D. 1617, he traveled to the East where he remained, chiefly in Cairo, Jerusalem, and Damascus. He died in Cairo in A.D. 1632.

The *Sweet Exhalation*, compiled in Morocco but written in the East, is actually two books: historical and literary studies of Spain, and a biographical treatment of the philologist-lexicographer Lisān al-Dīn al-Khaṭīb. In the historical section, Book V (Dozy, *et al.* [ed.], I, 463–943) and Book VI (*ibid.*, II, 2–103), is a biographical study devoted to the lives of scholars who had made the journey from the East to Spain, and vice versa.

BIBLIOGRAPHICAL NOTE

Wüstenfeld, *Geschichtsschreiber*, pp. 265–67; Pons-Boigues, *Historiadores*, pp. 417–19; *GAL*, II², 381–83, Suppl. II, pp. 407–408; first section of the *Nafḥ al-ṭīb*, ed. R. Dozy, G. Dugat, L. Krehl, W. Wright, *Analectes sur l'histoire et la litterature des Arabes d'Espagne* (2 vols.; Leyden, 1855–1861).

Mari ibn Sulayman

The *Book of the Tower* of this otherwise unknown Nestorian author of the twelfth century is an Arabic ecclesiastical encyclopedia for the Nestorian Church. What directly concerns us here is the historical section (V, 5) dealing with the Nestorian Catholici, a part that was abbreviated and prolonged into their own days by the two fourteenth-century authors ʿAmr ibn Mattā and Ṣalība ibn Yūḥannā.

BIBLIOGRAPHICAL NOTE

GCAL, II, 200–202, 216–18; H. Gismondi, (ed. and trans.) *Maris Amri et Slibae de patriarchis Nestorianorum commentaria* (4 parts; Rome, 1896–1899).

Abū al-Ḥasan ʿAli ibn al-Ḥusayn al-Masʿūdi

Nothing is known of the life of this scholar except a long list of travels which took him to Persia, India, Ceylon, the China Sea, Syria, and Egypt, where he died in A.D. 956.

Al-Masʿūdi's literary activity was extensive in the field of history and geography. Only two of his later works are preserved intact: the *Golden Meadows* (completed A.D. 947, revised the year of his death) and the *Notice*. Fortunately, both are in the nature of résumés which preserve the heart of the material from his earlier, more voluminous works. The *Notice* particularly preserves abstracts from a longer work devoted to intellectual history, the *Various Types of Knowledge*, which, even in abridgement, indicates that al-Masʿūdi was working from excellent source material on the history of philosophy, quite possibly the *Appearance of Philosophy* of al-Fārābi.

In a life filled with travels throughout the Islamic world and encounters with the great scholars of the time, it is difficult to be precise about the sources of the considerable philosophical baggage acquired by al-Masʿūdi. There is a strong hint, however. His sympathetic and well-informed statements on the group he calls "the people of investigation and insight," and his emphatic use of authorities like al-Kindi, al-Sarakhsi, and al-Jāḥiẓ on questions of natural philosophy suggest that al-Masʿūdi, like his philosophical authorities, may have belonged to the fringes of the Muʿtazilite movement which was then flourishing and which took at least part of its inspiration from Greek philosophical and scientific literature.[46] Thus, like al-Jāḥiẓ, he knows the *naturalia* of Aristotle and, like al-Kindi, he attempts to suffuse his Greek learning with a religious cast that is peculiarly Islamic. To this Muʿtazilite background add the culture of a man who had met everyone and seen everything between Egypt and the China Sea. The result is a man alert to all the crosscurrents of the intellectual life of the tenth-century islamic community and a particularly fine example of the enlightening and broadening effects of the Greek learning on the man of general culture in Islam.

BIBLIOGRAPHICAL NOTE

Fihrist, p. 154; Yāqūt, *Irshād*, V 147–49; *GAL*, I², 150–52, Suppl. I, pp. 220–21; I. Krachkovski, *Izbrannie Sochinenia*, IV (Moscow-Leningrad, 1957), 170–82; S. M. Ahmad, "Al-Masʿūdi's Contribution to Medieval Arab Geography," *Islamic Culture*, XXVIII (1954), 275–86; *Murūj al-dhahab*, ed. and trans. C. Barbier de Maynard and A. Pavet de Courteille (9 vols.; Paris, 1861–1877); *Tanbīh*, ed. M. de Goeje (*Bibliotheca Geographorum Arabicorum*, VIII [Leyden, 1894]); Carra de Vaux (trans.), *Le Livre de l'Avertissement et de la Révision* (Paris, 1897).

46. See. pp. 140–144 above.

ANNEX: TANBĪH[47]

I. The Kings of Greece

A. Philip

B. Alexander

C. Ptolemy Euergetes

D. Ptolemy Alexander

digression on the Bible: Arabic version by Hunayn; Jewish translations into Arabic

E. Ptolemy Lagos ... to 16. Cleopatra

II. A Summary of his book: *Various Types of Knowledge*

A. Genealogy of the Greeks

B. Roman Conquest

C. Biographies of the Greek Kings and particularly of Alexander: his life and expeditions, kings whom he met, citties he built, marvels he saw; his relationship with Aristotle (derivation of the name Aristotle); identification of Alexander with Dhū al-Qarnayn; history of the Diodochi

D. Histories of the Philosophers

which treated of God and which treated of nature; which were put to death; the break of Socrates, Plato, and Aristotle with the old tradition of Pythagoras, Thales, Sabians of Egypt (today the Sabians of Harran) as expressed in Aristotle's *De animalibus*; the views of Socrates and others on the emanation of the universe from the First Being; the philosophy of the soul, its properties and functions; the members of the body; intelligence, sleep, and the various sorts of dreams and their interpretation; political philosophy: types of social groups and the organization of the perfect city; the question of whether the king is one of the parts of the city or is alien, indicating the different solutions of Plato (in his book devoted to the description of the king of the ideal city, the true philosopher) and Aristotle (in his work on the government of the city, its parts, natural prototypes, the secondary authorities, non-ideal cities, their authorities and ends); the happiness after death obtained by members of the ideal city, and the ills attendant upon those who lived in non-ideal cities; what must be known and done to gain this hap-

47. Pp. 111–22 (trans. de Vaux, pp. 158–71); for an outline of the entire work see p. 117–118 above.

piness; criteria for distinguishing citizens of the model city; how they must live in other cities; the evil principles which dominate in non-ideal cities. View of philosophers on the principles of all existent tings:

1. First principle which has the plenitude of being and from which all things proceed.
2. Secondary principles (arranged in the same order as the heavenly bodies)
3. Agent intellect
4. Soul
5. Form
6. Matter
7. *Corporalia*
    a. heavenly bodies
    b. rational animals
    c. non-rational animals
    d. plants
    e. minerals and metals
    f. four elements

E. Views of Philosophers on Primary and Secondary Intelligence and Soul
    1. Intelligence: intermediary cause between God and creatures
    2. Souls
        a. definition of the rational soul
        b. end of the rational soul
        c. how the rational soul descends into the world of sense
    3. Man the microcosm

F. Teachings of Aristotle on the eternity of cause and effect (as put forth in *Physica* I, *De coelo*, *Metaphysica*), and the views of various philosophers on the eternity of the world and metempsychosis

G. Divisions of the Philosophical Schools[48]

H. History of Philosophy
    1. To Socrates
    2. Socrates to Eudemus
    3. Transfer of the seat of learning from Athens to Alexandria, thence to Antioch under ʿUmar ibn ʿAbd al-Azīz (A.D. 717–720), and finally to Harran under al-Mutawakkil (A.D. 847–861)
    4. From Quwayri to Yaḥyā ibn ʿAdi

48. See p. 86 above.

Michael the Syrian

Jacobite Patriarch of Antioch from A.D. 1166 until his death, aged seventy-three, in A.D. 1199. Michael's *Chronicle*, reaching as far as A.D. 1194/5, was in no sense the work of a cloistered scribe; Michael was himself part of the historical fabric of which he wrote. Apart from serious internal difficulties with his vicar for the Eastern Dioceses, Michael had to guide the Jacobite Church through the labyrinthine struggle going on in Syria between Byzantine, Armenian, Crusader, and Seljuk. It was in A.D. 1172, in comnection with a visit of the Sultan Qilij Arslan II (Sultan of Konia A.D. 1156–1192), that Michael had his discussions with the Muslim philospher Kamāl al-Dīn ibn Yūnus, then a young man but later to be the famous exegete of Fakhr al-Dīn al-Rāzi and the teacher of both Serverus bar Shakko and Naṣīr al-Dīn al-Ṭūsi.

BIBLIOGRAPHICAL NOTE

The best source for the life of Michael is his own *Chronicle*, ed. and trans. J. B. Chabot (3 vols.; Paris, 1900–1910); *GSL*, pp. 298–300; Jugie, *Theologia*, V, 473, and index *s.v.*; H. Gelzer, *Sextus Julius Africanus*, II, 1 (Leipzig, 1885), 402ff.

Abū al-Faraj Muḥammad ibn abī Ya'qūb (ibn) al-Nadīm al-Warrāq

Born the son of a Baghdad book dealer (*warrāq*), *ca.* A.D. 936, al-Nadīm has provided, in his celebrated *Catalogue*, the single most important document on philosophy among the Arabs. Most of what is known of his life must be pieced together from the *Catalogue*. Like his father, he was a Baghdadi and a book seller, circumstances which placed him in the very center of the Muslim and Christian intellectual life of the tenth-century East. His wide circle of friends included the most famous philosophers of the day, men involved in the Aristotelian movement at its height and whom al-Nadīm specifically mentions as sources of his information on the history of philosophy: Yaḥyā ibn 'Adi (p. 264, l. 8), Ibn Suwār (p. 245, l. 12), 'Īsā ibn 'Ali

(p. 244, ll. 6–7), and Abū Sulaymān al-Sijistāni whom he calls "my teacher" (p. 241, l. 14).

The *Catalogue* falls into two main parts. After an introduction on the art of writing, the *divisio* is announced: Sections 1–6 deal with the Islamic sciences: (1) *Qur'ān*: (2) Grammar; (3) History, Genealogy, Epistolographers, etc.; (4) Poetry; (5) *Kalām* (including a heresiography); (6) Law; the remaining four sections are given over to the non-Islamic sciences; (7) Philosophy and the "ancient" sciences; (8) Fiction, (9) History of the non-Islamic religions; (10) Alchemy.

The method of development is threefold: historical (history of philosophy, development of medicine, etc.), relying on both written and oral sources, biographical (usually quite brief), and purely bibliographical.

The date of the completion of the *Catalogue* (A.D. 987; the *Ṭabaqāt* of Ibn Juljul was written in the same year) falls in the final stages of the translation movement. The work of Ḥunayn and his school was completed and Yaḥyā ibn 'Adi had died over ten years before. Al-Nadīm is, then, a contemporary source for this movement; he was, in addition, a careful, intelligent observer, and the long and detailed passages devoted to the translation history of the various parts of the Aristotelian *corpus* are models of both clarity and historical prudence.

BIBLIOGRAPHICAL NOTE

J. Füch, "Eine arabische Literaturgeschichte aus dem 10. Jahrhundert nach Christus," *ZDMG*, LXXXIV (1930), 111–24, substantially résuméd in the same author's art., "al-Nadīm," *EI*, III, 808–809, but the statement that the author had visited Byzantine territory (based on *Fihrist*, p. 394, 14) is corrected in the later study: the Dār al-Rūm was a quarter of Baghdad; *GAL* I², 153–54. Suppl. I, pp. 226–27; Meyerhof, "Alexandrien nach Baghdad," p. 420; A. Nallino, Raccolta di Scritti, V (Rome, 1944), pp. 123–126; *Kitāb al-fihrist*, ed. G. Flügel, J. Roediger, and A. Müller (2 vols.; Leipzig, 1871–1872). A part of the section on philosophy (245–255) has been translated by A. Müller, *Die griechischen Philosophen in der arabischen Überlieferung* (Halle, 1872). Section Ten on Alchemy has likewise been translated by J. Fück, "The Arabic literature on Alchemy according to al-Nadīm," *Ambix*, IV (1951), pp. 81–144.

ANNEX: FIHRIST, VII, PART I[49].

Section Seven: On Philosophers and the Ancient Sciences and Books on these Subjects

Part One: Narratives concerning the natural philosophers and the logicians, their books, their translations and commentaries which are extant or mentioned or which were once extant but are so no longer.

I.
- A. Narratives on the origin of this book according to the opinions of scholars
- B. Another narrative
- C. Another narrative
- D. Another narrative

II. The reason why books on philosophy and the other sciences have multiplied in this land

III. (The translators)
- A. From Greek into Arabic
- B. From Persian into Arabic
- C. From Hindi and Nabataean

IV. (History of Greek Philosophy)
- A. The first philosophers
- B. Plato
- C. Aristotle
  - 1. *vita*
  - 2. *testamentum*
  - 3. the *corpus*
    - a. *Categoriae*
    - b. *De interpretatione*
    - c. *Analytica priora*
    - d. *Apodeictica, Anal. posteriora*
    - e. *Topica*
    - f. *Sophistica*
    - g. *Rhetorica*
    - h. *Poetica*
    - i. *Auscultatio physica*
    - j. *De coelo et mundo*
    - k. *De generatione et corruptione*
    - l. *De meteorologicis*
    - m. *De anima*

49. Pp. 238–65.

n. *De sensu et sensato*
o. *De animalibus*
p. *Theologia*
q. *Ethica*

D. Theophrastus
E. Diadochus Proclus
F. Alexander of Aphrodisias
G. Porphyry
H. Ammonius
I. Themistius
J. Nicholas
K. Plutarch
L. Olympiodorus
M. "Diafartis"
N. "Athaphroditus"
O. Plutarch *alter*
P. John the Grammarian
Q. Names of the philosophers whose dates and position in the series are unknown.

V. (History of Islamic Philosophy)

A. Al-Kindi
B. Al-Sarakhsi
C. Quwayri
D. Ibn Karnib
E. Al-Fārābi
F. Abū Yaḥyā al-Marwazi
G. Abu Yaḥyā al-Marwazi *alter*
H. Abū Bishr Mattā
I. Yaḥyā ibn ʿAdi
J. Abū Sulaymān al-Sijistāni
K. Ibn Zurʿah
L. Ibn Suwār ibn al-Khammār

AL-QIFṬI

Jamāl al-Dīn abū al-Ḥasan ʿAli ibn Yūsuf (ibn) al-Qifṭi

Born in A.D. 1172 into an Upper Egyptian family that traditionally supplied the local magistrate, he accompanied his father to Cairo where he received his education in the Arab sciences: *Qurʾān*, tradition, belles-lettres. In A.D. 1187, the family moved to Jerusalem, where the author's father was a magistrate in the chancellery of Salāḥ al-Dīn. In about A.D. 1201, al-Qifṭi went to Aleppo, where he completed his education and labored in the local *diwān*. Finally, in A.D. 1230, he retired and for six years lived in solitude, until A.D. 1236, when he accepted the post of vizier to the lord of the last Ayyubid stronghold of Aleppo. He died there in A.D. 1248.

The *History of Learned Men*, which we now possess, is not the work as composed by al-Qifṭi, but an abridgement completed shortly after the author's death by a certain al-Zawzani. As it stands, the work is a biographical dictionary embracing Christian, Muslim, Arab, Greek, Persian, and Indian scholars. The article devoted to Aristotle (pp. 27–53) employs a combination of methods. Mixed together is the *vita* and *pinax* from the Ptolemy source and the various kinds of information available in the Arab tradition: sayings from al-Mubashshir (on a lesser scale then in Ibn abī Uṣaybiʿah), a division of the *corpus* based on the classificatory lists of al-Nadīm, Ṣāʿid and al-Fārābi, and within this framework, bibliographical material on the translations, mostly from al-Nadīm, but with al-Qifṭi's own valuable additions on the later translation history, and some notes on the arrival and influence of Aristotelianism in Islam from al-Nadīm, Abū Sulaymān, and al-Fārābi.

BIBLIOGRAPHICAL NOTE

Yāqūt, *Irshād*, V, 477–94; al-Kutabi, *Fawāt*, II, 96; *GAL*, I², 396–97, Suppl. I, pp. 559–60; Steinschneider, *Arab. Übers.*, pp. 10–11; A. Nallino, *Raccolta di Scritti*, V (Rome, 1944), 126–37, and the introduction to Lippert's edition; *Ta'rīkh al-ḥuqamā'*, ed. J. Lippert (Leipzig, 1903). For the section on Aristotle, see I. Düring, *Aristotle in the Ancient Biographical Tradition* (Göteborg, 1957), and the literature cited there.

AL-ṢAFADI

Salāḥ al-Dīn Khalīl ibn Aybak al-Ṣafadi.

Born *ca.* A.D. 1296/7 in Ṣafad in Palestine. His profession was that of secretary, and he served as such in Syria and Egypt until appointed chief of the treasury in Damascus, a post he held until his death in A.D. 1363.

The *Complete Necrologies* is an enormous collection of about fourteen thousand biographies arranged, after the intrusion of the "Muḥammad" entries at the head of the list, in alphabetical order and embracing, according to Flügel's delightful rendering of the entry in Ḥājji Khalīfah (# 14155):

> socios prophetae, horum asseclas, principes, Emiros, judices, praefectos, Corani lectores, traditionarios, jurisconsultos, Sheikhos, viros pietate et sanctitate conspicuos, grammaticos, philologos, poetas, medicos, philosophos, disciplinarum philosopharum asseclas, rerum novarum studios, rationalistas et omnino viros quovis genere eruditionis claros praetermisit qui nominis celebritate inclaruerant aut doctriman firmiter callebant.

In his introduction (I, pp. 1–55), al-Ṣafadi sets out his sources for such a prodigious work, and they provide an interesting commentary on the range of historical material available to the fourteenth-century scholar. Al-Ṣafadi divides the purely historical works into local history (histories of towns and regions, Egypt, al-Andalus, Yemen, the Hejaz), world history (Ibn Khallikān finds his place here and al-Ṣafadi puts particular emphasis on the *History of Islam* of his personal friend, al-Dhahabi [A.D. 1348]), biographies of Sultans and viziers, *ṭabaqāt*-works on magistrates, *Qur'ān* readers, jurisconsults, poets, and finally a mixed collection including *ṭabaqāt* on Sufis, preachers, physicians (Ibn abī Uṣaybi'ah, Ṣā'id, Abū Ja'far ibn al-Dayā), grammarians, theologians, al-Nadīm's *Fihrist*, and Yāqūt's *Irshād.*

BIBLIOGRAPHICAL NOTE

F. Krenkow, art. *s.v. EI*, IV, 52–54; *GAL*, II², 39–41, Suppl. II, pp. 27–29. The *Wāfi bi al-wafayāt* is in the course of publication in the *Bibliotheca Islamica*, VI: H. Ritter (Istanbul, 1931); S. Dedering (Istanbul, 1949), *idem* (Damascus, 1953 and 1959 [as far as Muḥammad ibn Maḥmud]). The introduction had been ed. and trans. by E. Aman in *JA*, Sér. 10, Vol. XVII (1911), 251–308, XVIII (1911), 5–48, XIX (1912), 243–97. An index to the entire work was begun by G. Gabrieli and parts appeared in *Rendiconti Lincei*, Vols. XXII–XXV.

Abū al-Qāsim Ṣāʿid Al-Andalusi

Born in Almeria in Spain, he studied under the celebrated Ibn Ḥazm (d. A.D. 1064) and, after A.D. 1046, in the Toledo of the Berber chieftain, Yaḥyā al-Ma'mūn (A.D. 1037–1074), he pursued higher studies in mathematics and astronomy under Al-Waqqashi (d. A.D. 1063) and Al-Tujībi (d. A.D.1062). He refers in the *Ṭabaqāt* to his own publication in astronomy as well as to another on the history of religions, probably in the manner of Ibn Hazm's *Al-Faṣl fī al milal*.

The *Ṭabaqāt al-umam*, known under a variety of slightly differing titles, was composed in A.D. 1068, according to the author's own testimony.[50] It studies the development of "science" (in Ṣāʿid's context, philosophy, mathematics, the natural sciences) as practiced by seven "primitive" peoples (Persians, Chaldeans, Greeks, Romans and other Europeans, Copts, Turks, Indians, and Chinese)[51] and by his contemporaries. He first dismisses with a brief note those people who did not cultivate the sciences: the Turks, Chinese, Galicians, and Berbers. The heart of the *Ṭabaqāt* is a bio-bibliographical study of the scientific culture of the Indians, Persians, Chaldeans, Greeks, Romans, Egyptians, Arabs, and Jews.

The section on the Greeks will serve to illustrate his method. The section opens with a historical sketch that is chiefly concerned with Alexander, the Ptolemies, and the Roman conquest. Following is a geographical delimitation of the Greek lands and a few lines on the language. The individual Greeks are then taken up under the headings of Philosophy, Natural Science, and Mathematics. Finally, there is an *eisagoge*-type derivation and division of the Greek schools.

In the part on Roman science, Ṣāʿid evidences the usual confusion between Roman, Byzantine, and Christian. The historical sketch covers both Roman and Byzantine history, but all the sages cited here are Christians and Sabaeans (the Romans were, according

50. *Ṭabaqāt*, p. 63.
51. There is a similar list in Al-Masʿudi's *Tanbih*; p. 127 above.

to the author, Sabaeans before their conversion to Christianity) living under the Abbasids (Bakhtīshū', Ibn Masawayh, Ḥunayn, Thābit, etc.).

Ṣā'id's treatment of the Arabs is chronological up to the time of Al-Ma'mūn (d. A.D. 833), paying particular attention to the development of science under Al-Manṣūr and Al-Ma'mūn. The subject is then redivided, as in Ibn Juljul, along geographical lines and the Eastern and Andalusian Arabs are treated separately.

Among the authors cited in the *Ṭabaqat* are Al-Mas'ūdi's *Tanbih*,[52] Ḥunayn and Al-Fārābi on the origin of the Greek schools, the *Fihrist* on Ḥunayn, Ibn Qutaybah's *Kitāb al-ma'arif* on Christianity among the Arabs, Abū Ma'shar Ja'far Al-Balkhi's *Kitāb al-madhākarāt* on astronomy and the translators, and Al-Kindi on Apollonius of Perge. Uncited but clearly used is Ibn Juljul.

The section on Aristotle (*Ṭabaqāt*, pp. 24–27) passes almost directly to a bibliography of the Aristotelian *corpus*, distributed along the framework of a Hellenistic school *diairesis* and ending with the usual anecdotes illustrating the relationship between Aristotle and Alexander.

BIBLIOGRAPHICAL NOTE

The chief biographical source for Ṣā'id al-Andalusi is Ibn Bushkuwāl (*q.v.*), *Kitāb al-sīlah*, ed. Codera, # 535; *GAL*, I², 419, Suppl. I, p. 586. The text of the *Ṭabaqāt al-umam* has been edited by L. Cheikho (Beyrouth, 1912), and translated by R. Blachère, *Livre des Catégories des Nations* (Paris, 1935).

Annex: Ṭabaqāt

Part I

A. The Seven Primitive Nations
B. The Diversity of Nations; classification according to their aptitudes for the sciences
C. Nations which have not cultivated the sciences
D. Nations which have cultivated the sciences

52. *Inter alia: Ṭabaqāt*, p. 24, on the derivation of the name of Aristotle.

Part II

- A. Science in India
- B. Science among the Persians
- C. Science among the Chaldeans
- D. Science among the Greeks
  1. Historical Sketch
  2. Limits of the Greek lands
  3. Language
  4. Philosophers:

     Empedocles, Pythagoras, Socrates, Plato, Aristotle, post-Aristotelians, modern Hellenistic philosophers (i.e., Qusṭā ibn Lāqā)
  5. Physicians:

     Hippocrates, Galen, Asclepius, Erasistratus, Lycus, Paul
  6. Mathematicians:

     Apollonius of Perge, Euclid, Archimedes, and others including Simplicius and Poseidonius
  7. The Greek Schools:

     Pythagoreans, Stoics, Cynics, Sceptics, Epicureans, Peripatetics, a modern Pythagorean; Al-Rāzi
- E. Roman Science

  Historical sketch: Bakhtīshū', Ibn Masawayh, Ḥunayn, etc.
- F. Science among the Egyptians

  Hermes II, Proclus, Theon, Zosimus, etc.
  1. In General
     - a. General pre-Islamic
     - b. Time of the Prophet
     - c. Umayyads
     - d. Abbasids to Al-Ma'mūn
  2. Eastern Arabs

     (among the philosophers: Al-Kindi, Al-Sarakhsi, Al-Rāzi, Al-Fārābi)
  3. Andalusian Arabs
  4. Science among the Jews

AL-SHAHRASTĀNI

Abū al-Fatḥ Muḥammad ibn 'Abd al-Karīm al-Shahrastāni

Born in Khorasan, probably in A.D. 1076, he was educated as a jurist and a theologian and studied the latter science under Abū al-

Qāsim al-Anṣāri (d. A.D. 1118), a student of al-Juwayni. The entirety of his life, except for a three-year residence in Baghdad when he taught at the Niẓāmīyah *madrasah* (A.D. 1116–1119), was spent in the eastern provinces, where he died in his native Shahrastan in A.D. 1153.

The *Religious and Philosophical Sects* marks a great extension of the ground covered in the heresiographies of al-Ashʿari and al-Baghdādi (*qq.v.*). Not only are the Muslim sects treated but also those of the "people of the Book": Christians, Jews, and Persians. In Part II, which is concerned with philosophical rather than strictly theological positions, al-Shahrastāni embarks upon a discussion of the chief philosophical schools of paganism: the Sabaeans, Greeks, and Indians. Within Part II, the section devoted to Greek philosophy (ed. Cureton, pp. 251–429) falls into three parts: a division of the sciences (pp. 251–53), a treatment of the older philosophers (pp. 253–311) beginning with the Seven Sages and coming down to the Stoics, and, finally, the later philosophers (pp. 311–429) beginning with Aristotle (pp. 311–28) and ending with a long discussion of the positions of Ibn Sīnā (pp. 348–429), with but a few lines on the Islamic philosophers standing between the last Greek (Porphyry) and Ibn Sīnā.

Most of the material on the Greeks is gnomonological and stems immediately from al-Mubashshir and ultimately from Abū Sulaymān and the *De placitis philosophorum*.

A *History of Learned Men* is likewise attributed to al-Shahrastāni.

BIBLIOGRAPHICAL NOTE

Ibn Khallikān (trans. de Slane), II, 675–76; al-Bayhaqi, *Tatimmat*, # 86; *GAL*, I², 550–51, Suppl. I, pp. 762–63; Ritter, "Häresiographen," pp. 48–50. *Al-Milal wa al-niḥal*, ed. W. Cureton (London, 1846), and trans. T. Haarbrucker, *Religionspartien und Philosophischen Schulen* (Halle, 1850–1851). For Fakhr al-Dīn al-Rāzi's criticism of the *Milal* as derivative from al-Baghādi and Abū Sulaymān see P. Kraus, *Islamic Culture*, XII (1938), 146; on the use of Porphyry's *Philosophos historia* see F. Altheim and R. Stiehl, *Porphyrios und Empedokles* (Tübingen, 1954), pp. 8–19. The Plotinus excerpts transmitted by al-Shahrastāni under the name of "the Greek Sage" have been studied by F. Rosenthal, "Ash-Shaykh al-Yūnāni and the Arabic Plotinus Source," *Orientalia*, XXI (1952), 461–92, XXII (1953), 370–400, XXIV (1954), 42–66. *A Ta'rīkh al-ḥukamā'* is attributed to al-Shahrastāni in Ḥājji Khalīfah, # 2204 and Cureton (p. ii) apparently saw a MS. of the work.

Aḥmad ibn Muṣliḥ al-Dīn Tashköprüzādah

Born A.D. 1495 in Brussa the son of an eminent judge and sometime tutor to the Ottoman Sultan Selim I, he spent his entire life teaching in the *madrasahs* of Istanbul, Adrianople, and Brussa and as a magistrate in both Brussa and Istanbul. He died, after six years of blindness, in A.D. 1560.

In an important *ṭabaqāt*-work covering the years A.D. 1299–1560 entitled *Anemones on Learned Osmanlis*, Tashköprüzādah includes his own autobiography, a valuable document for tracing the course of a philosophical education. The list of books which he studied and on which he lectured is almost identical with a similar list of the texts used in the al-Azhar in Cairo in the late eighteenth century preserved in the historian al-Jabarti.[53]

After studies in Arabic lexicography and grammar, he began his study of logic with the commentary of Ḥusām al-Dīn al-Kāti (d. A.D. 1359) to the *Īsāghūji* of al-Abhari (d. A.D. 1264),[54] the commentaries of Quṭb al-Dīn al-Taḥtāni (d. A.D. 1364),[55] and al-Jurjāni (d. A.D. 1413),[56] to the *Shamsīyah* of al-Kātibi (d. A.D. 1276),[57] Then he took up the *Hidāyat al-ḥikmah* of al-Abhari, the *Mīzān al-quṣṭās* of al-Samarqāndi (*fl. ca.* A.D. 1291),[58] and the *Maṭāli' al-anwār* of al-Urmawi (d. A.D. 1283).[59] In theology the prime texts were the *Tajrīd* of al-Ṭūsi (d. A.D. 1274),[60] the *Tawāli' al-*

53. See p. 78 above.
54. See p. 197 above.
55. See p. 205 above.
56. See p. 205 above.
57. See p. 199 above.
58. *GAL*, I², 615–17, Suppl. I, pp. 849–50.
59. See p. 207, n. 101 above.
60. See p. 199 above.

anwār of al-Bayḍāwi (d. A.D. 1286),[61] and the *Mawāqif* of al-Īji (d. A.D. 1355).[62]

The fruit of these many years of study and teaching is the encyclopedia *The Key of Happiness*, composed in Arabic, which served as a kind of ecclesiastical language for both the Turkish and Persian speaking members of the Islamic community. It was later translated into Turkish by the author's son.

The *Key* is constructed according to an elaborate division of the sciences which Ḥājji Khalīfah has reproduced in the introduction of his *Kashf* (I, 32–41). Despite the articulation of the overall structure, the material within the various subgroups is disappointing in its scope and organization. The section on logic (I, 243–50) includes a definition of the science (Ḥājji Khalīfah has also borrowed these definitions) and an enumeration of the worthwhile books on the subject beginning with the logic from Ibn Sīnā's *Shifā'* and progressing through the thirteenth- and fourteenth-century textbooks that the author had read as part of his own logical education.

The section on metaphysics (*al-ʿilm al-ilāhi*: I, 255–63) is similarly organized except that it includes brief "historical" sketches of "Idris" (an apocryphal figure modeled on the prophet Enoch), Plato, Aristotle (pp. 258–59), al-Fārābi, al-Ṭūsi, and Suhrawārdi, an eclectic, if not a comprehensive, selection.

BIBLIOGRAPHICAL NOTE

F. Wüstenfeld, *Geschichtsschreiber*, pp. 241–46 (based on the autobiography); F. Babinger, *Die Geschichtsschreiber der Osmanen und ihre Werke* (Leipzig, 1927), pp. 84–87; *GAL*, II², 559–62, Suppl. II, pp. 633–34; *al-Shaqā'iq al-nuʿmanīyah fi ʿulamā' al-dawlah al-ʿuthmanīyah* (ed. Bulaq, 1881 [on the margins of Ibn Khallikān's *Wafayāt*]); O. Rescher (trans.) (Constantinople-Galata, 1927); *Miftāḥ al-saʿādah* (3 vols., ed. Hyderabad, 1910–1937). O. Rescher has translated the introduction to the *Miftāḥ* in his *Tasköprüzāde's miftāḥ as-saʿāde. Islamische Ethik und Wissenschaftlehre des 10. Jahrhundert* (Stuttgart, 1934).

61. See p. 203 above.
62. See p. 204 above.

THĀBIT IBN SINĀN

Abū al-Ḥasan Thābit ibn Sinān ibn Thābit ibn Qurrah

A member of the illustrious family of Sabians[63] originally from Harran, which produced a long line of eminent scholars in ninth- and tenth-century Baghdad. As in the case of the Christian Manṣūri family of Damascus, the clearly non-Islamic antecedents of the Qurrahs were apparently no obstacle to advancement into high government circles. Thābit ibn Sinān, like his grandfather the mathematician-translator-philosopher, Thābit ibn Qurrah,[64] was employed in the Caliphal *diwān*, and his father, Sinān ibn Thābit (m. A.D. 942), was director of the Baghdad hospital system.

Thābit ibn Sinān was likewise a physician but is best known for his *History*,[65] an account of the events from A.D. 902 down to the author's death in A.D. 973. According to the account in al-Qifṭi, Thābit used the materials available to him in the *diwān* in compiling the *History*. We cannot judge its actual merits since the *History* itself has not been found, although various continuations are extant. What focuses attention on the work is the philosophical background of the family and the use of the *History* by later writers working in the context of philosophical history and biography: Ibn al-Maṭrān, al-Qifṭi, and Yāqūt (*qq.v.*).

BIBLIOGRAPHICAL NOTE

Fihrist, p. 302; Ṣā'id, *Ṭabaqāt*, p. 81; al-Qifṭi, pp. 109–11; Uṣ., I, 224–26; Ibn Khallikān (trans. de Slane), I, 289 (the source quoted in n. 7 is, of course, al-Qifṭi and not his epitomator, al-Qawzani); Yāqūt, *Irshād*, II, 397–98; Chwolson, *Ssabier*, I, 578–81; for Yāqūt's use of Thābit see *Zeitschrift für Semitistik*, II (1924), 203, and *ZDMG*, LXV (1911), 802; for his use by Ibn al-Maṭrān: *RAAD*, III (1923), 7.

63. See p. 171, n. 207 above.
64. See pp. 59–60 above.
65. According to al-Mas'ūdi, *Murūj*, I, 19–20, his father also wrote a history that had a "philosophical introduction."

Theodore bar Koni (*aliter* Kewani)

The Nestorian author of a *Book of Scholia*, completed *ca.* A.D. 791–792 and divided into eleven parts (*memrē*). The first eight *memrē* are the scholia on the Old and New Testaments from which the work takes its name. *Memrē*, IX, consists of two polemical treatises against the Monophysites and the Arians. *Memrē*, X, is an exposition of the Christian faith, perhaps as an apologetic against Islam, in the form of a catechism. The final *memrē* is the heresiography including not only Christian sects but Greek and Persian paganism as well.

BIBLIOGRAPHICAL NOTE

ʿAbdīshū, # 133; *GSL*, pp. 218–19; A. Baumstark, *Oriens Christianus*, I (1901), 173–78; B. Vanderhoff, *ZDMG*, LXX (1916), 126–32. The *Book of Scholia*, ed. A. Scher, *CSCO*, script. syri., Ser. 2, Vols. LXV–LXVI (Louvain, 1910–1912); on *Memrē*, XI, see T. Nöldecke, "Bar Chone über Homer, Hesiod und Orpheus," *ZDMG*, LIII (1899); C. Clermont-Ganneau, "Empedocle, les Manichéens, et les Cathares," *JA*, Sér. 9, Vol. XV (1900), 179–86; F. Cumont, *La cosmogonie manichéenne d'après Theodore bar Koni* (Brussels, 1908); A. Baumstark, "Griechische Philosophen und ihre Lehren in syrische Überlieferung," *Oriens Christianus*, V (1905), 1–25; G. Furlani, "La filosofia nel Libro degli Scoli di Teodoro bar Kewanay," *Giornale della Societa asiatica italiana*, I (1926), 250–96; E. Beneviste, "Le témoignage de Théodore bar Koni sur le Zoroastrianisme," *Le Monde Orientale*, XXI (1932), 170–215.

Thomas of Marga

Brother of the Catholicus Theodosius, monk of Beth ʿAbe, then secretary to the Catholicus Abraham and finally. *ca.* A.D. 850, Metropolitan of the diocese of Beth Garmai. It was just before his elevation to this latter post that Thomas composed his *Book of Governors* (i.e., monastic superiors), ostensibly a history of the monastery of Beth ʿAbe but actually extending back to the very origins of Nestorian monasticism in the days of Abraham of Kashkar (d. A.D. 588).

BIBLIOGRAPHICAL NOTE

GSL, 233–34; *The Book of Governors*, ed. and trans. E. A. W. Budge (2 vols.; London, 1893). On Thomas himself see Budge's "Introduction," I, xvii–xli.

Aḥmad ibn abī Yaʿqūb al-Kātib al-ʿAbbāsi al-Yaʿqūbi

Though son of a governor of Egypt, al-Yaʿqūbi passed most of his life in Armenia and at the court of the Ṭahirids in Khorasan, where the *History* was most probably composed. After the fall of the Ṭahirids, he returned to Egypt where he died in A.D. 877.

The *History* treats of both "ancient" and Islamic history, continuing the latter down to A.D. 872 (Ḥunyan ibn Isḥāq, it will be recalled, died about five years after this). The pre-Islamic history ranges widely from China to the African Berbers. There are particularly lenghty sections on Patriarchal and Old Testament history (I, 1–73), on Jesus Christ (I, 73–88), and on the Kings of India (I, 92–106, with digressions on the climates and a creation myth). But for our purposes here, it is the space devoted to the Greeks and Romans (I, 106–78) that is most interesting, and the bulk of it (I, 106–61) is given over to the lives and works of Greek scholars, particularly Hippocrates (I, 106–107), Galen (I, 130–34), Nicomachus of Gerasa (I, 139–42), often confused with the father of Aristotle, Ptolemy (I, 150–61), and Aristotle (I, 144–50).

Much of the material in these collections is doxographical, but in other instances—and this is so in the case of Aristotle—al-Yaʿqūbi had available classificatory *pinakes*.[66] A comparison with the *Tanbīh* of al-Masʿūdi (*q.v.*) shows that al-Yaʿqūbi was less well informed than the later historian on Aristotle and on Greek philosophy in general. What al-Yaʿqūbi does have appears to come directly from a translation source, and, thouhg some of it bears the stamp of the Ḥunayn circle (the material on Hippocrates, including a rather complete list of his writings), other elements suggest a connection with the *veteres*:

66. See p. 83 above.

the philosophical vocabulary is markedly archaic and Syriacized. Words like *kiyān* (*physis*), for instance, and *rukn* (*stoicheion*), and *ʿunṣar* (*hyle*) were all replaced in the translations of Ḥunayn and in the *recentiores*.

BIBLIOGRAPHICAL NOTE

Yāqūt, *Irshād*, II, 156–57; M. de Goeje, "Über die Geschichte der Abbasiden von al-Jaʿqubi," *Travaux de la troisieme session du Congress Internationale des Orientalistes*, II (St. Petersburg-Leyden, 1879) 153–66; *GAL*, I², 258–60. Suppl. I, p. 405; Rosenthal, *Historiography*, pp. 114–16. *Taʾrīkh*, ed. M. Houtsma, *Ibn Wadih qui dicitur al-Jaʿqūbi Historiae* (2 vols.; Leyden, 1883); Nöldecke's review of this edition in *ZDMG*, XXXVIII (1884), 153–60 where some of the Syriac possibilities are indicated; the sections on the Greek scholars have been analyzed and partially translated by M. Klamroth, "Über die Auszüge aus griechischen Schriftstellern bei al-Jaʿqūbi," *ZDMG*, XL (1886), 189–233 (Hippocrates), 612–38 (Galen and other physicians), and *ibid.*, XLI (1887), 415–42 (the philosophers, chiefly Aristotle).

YĀQŪT

Shihāb al-Dīn Yāqūt (*aliter* Yaʿqūb) ibn ʿAbdallāh al-Ḥamawi al-Rūmi

Yāqūt, the Greek slave living by his wits, would have been at home in Roman times, but he also managed to make do in twelfth-century Islam. Born somewhere in Byzantine territory in A.D. 1179, he was captured and sold as a slave in Baghdad. His purchaser was an illiterate merchant who employed his talented Greek in commercial journeys to the Persian Guld and Syria. He was manumitted in A.D. 1199 and supported himself as a copyist, though still to some extent dependent on his former master. At the latter's death, Yāqūt helped himself to some of the estate and took up a life of travel, journeying east and west to Khorasan, Merv, Damascus, and Cairo, and, in the course of his wanderings, collecting material for his biographical dictionary, which he completed sometime before A.D. 1218, when he was in Khawarizm. The advent of the Mongols made a long stay there inadvisable, and in A.D. 1220 he was in Mosul; in

A.D. 1222 he began a two-year stay in Aleppo, courtesy of the father of his fellow biographer, al-Qifṭi (*q.v.*). In A.D. 1224 he was back in Mosul, finishing his geographical dictionary. After four years in Cairo, he died in Aleppo in A.D. 1229.

The *Guide to the Intelligent* is a biographical dictionary of learned men, more extensive than works limited to the learned of certain cities or localities, but at the same time narrower in scope than the later biographical dictionaries of Ibn Khallikān and al-Ṣafadi (*qq.v.*).

The investigation of Yāqūt's sources indicates that they were on a scale almost comparable to those of al-Ṣafadi. Particularly heavy use was made of al-Nadīm (*q.v.*). The other sources break down into the usual types: *ṭabaqāt*-works (traditionists, grammarians, poets, etc.), universal chronicles (including Thābit ibn Sinān [*q.v.*]), local histories (both Ibn ʿAsākir and al-Khaṭīb al-Baghdādi; he also knew the western literature: Ibn al-Faraḍi, Ibn Bashkuwāl), and anthologies. Most important, however, was the intervention, between Yāqūt and al-Ṣafadi, of the learned treatment of the translation literature by al-Qifṭi and Ibn abi Uṣaybiʿah.

Yāqūt had, nonetheless, one marked advantage over a biographer like al-Ṣafadi. He was a geographer, which was still very much a "Hellenic science," and as such had at least one direct contact with the Greek tradition, a connection far more apparent in the geographical work than in the biographical dictionary.

BIBLIOGRAPHICAL NOTE

Ibn Khallikān (trans. de Slane), pp. 9–22; F. Wüstenfeld, "Jacut's Reisen aus seinem geographischen Wörterbuch beschreiben," *ZDMG*, XVIII (1864), 397–493; *GAL*, I², 630–32, Suppl. I, p. 880. *Irshīd al-arīb ilā maʿrifat al-adīb*, ed. D. S. Margoliouth (7 vols.; Leyden-London, 1907–1926). The sources of the *Irshīd* were first investigated by G. Bergsträsser in his review of the first three volumes of Margoliouth's edition in *ZDMG*, LXV (1911), 797–811, and then more systematically by the same author in "Die Quellen von Yaqut's *Irshād*," *Zeitschrift für Semitistik*, II (1924), 184–215, and K. Rahman, "The Sources of Yaqut's *Irshād*," *ibid*, X (1935), 216–29.

INDEX

ABOUT THE AUTHOR

F. E. PETERS is Chairman of the Department of Classics at New York University. His A.B. and M.A. are from St. Louis University and his Ph.D. is from Princeton, in Islamic studies. His previous books are *Greek Philosophical Terms* and *Aristoteles Orientalis,* a study of the Eastern translation history of the individual works in the Aristotelian corpus. He is well-known for his Sunrise Semester course on television, "The Near East from Alexander to Muhammad."